THE
PHILIPPINES

About the Author

EVELYN SEBASTIAN PEPLOW was born in the Philippines but continued her education in the United States, passing her Masters in Journalism at Northwestern University in Evanston, Illinois. She has written features and books on travel. Her titles to date include *Hong Kong From A–Z*, and *Pollution: Our Common Enemy*. She has also edited various books including *China's Imperial Way*, *Twelve Hong Kong Walks*, *100 Acclaimed Tagalog Movies*, and *One of the Lucky Ones*—the autobiography of Lucy Ching.

About the Photographer

ALAIN EVRARD is a Belgian-born freelance photographer who has travelled extensively throughout Europe and Asia. His work has appeared in such magazines as *Newsweek*, *Time* and *National Geographic*, as well as in numerous guidebooks.

Acknowledgments

My special thanks to Director Edwin Trompeta—DOT Region VI and the other Regional Directors of the Department of Tourism; Information Director Abraham Dingle; Shirley Peralta and Bamba Ramos—DOT; Belen King, Natie Lim, Annie Rañoa, Pilar Vazquez, Celine Khalid, Beth Florentino, Jonalyn Nagnot and Marites Peñol for their help with this edition.

(front cover) One of the many coves on the island of Mindoro, a scuba diving paradise
(back cover) The head man of a Muslim village on the Zamboanga Peninsula, Mindanao

THE
PHILIPPINES

Evelyn Peplow

Photography by Alain Evrard

© 1999, 1997, 1991 Odyssey Publications Ltd
Maps © 1999, 1997, 1991 Odyssey Publications Ltd

Odyssey Publications Ltd, 1004 Kowloon Centre,
29–43 Ashley Road, Tsim Sha Tsui, Kowloon, Hong Kong
Tel. (852) 2856 3896; Fax. (852) 2565 8004; E-mail: odyssey@asiaonline.net

Distribution in the United Kingdom, Ireland and Europe by
Hi Marketing Ltd, 38 Carver Road, London SE24 9LT, UK

Distribution in the United States of America by
W.W. Norton & Company, Inc., New York

Library of Congress Catalog Card Number has been requested.

ISBN: 962-217-614-3

Grateful acknowledgment is made to the following authors and publishers:

Harper Collins Publishers and William Morris Agency for *The Marcos Dynasty* © Sterling Seagrave 1988

Alfred A Knopf and Bloomsbury Publishing Ltd for *Video Night in Kathmandu* © Pico Iyer 1988

Pete Fraser and Dunlop Group Ltd for *The Snap Revolution* by James Fenton, originally published in Granta Magazine, issue No 18

Solidaridad Publishing House for *Viajero* © F Sionil José 1993

Editor: Adam Nebbs
Series Co-ordinator: Jane Finden-Crofts
Design: Tom Le Bas and Stefan Hammond
Maps: Tom Le Bas
Cover Concept: Margaret Lee

Front and back cover photography: Keith Macregor
Photography by Alain Evrard
Additional photography/illustrations courtesy of Patrick Lucero 85, 147, 198, 238, 239, 294, 299, 306; Kevin Hamdorf 5, 141, 162–163; George Tapan 64; Veronica Garbutt 29, 214; Terry Duckham 20, 21, 60, 182; Michael A Jones 73, 290; Juny Binamira 290, 291; Magnus Bartlett 199; Keith Macregor 271; Dodie/Asiapix 39, 42, 83, 97, 126, 195, 281; Wattis Fine Art 16, 230

Production by Twin Age Ltd, Hong Kong
Printed in Hong Kong

*Mt Mayon, the country's most active volcano,
on the plains of Albay in the Bicol region*

Contents

A Moriones mask carved out of soft dapdap wood,
painted and decorated with feathers and palm leaves

Introduction

Tropical islands in faraway places have always appealed to the imagination of the romantic at heart. When they think of such islands, they picture palm trees fringing warm blue seas, pale moonlight shining on soft white sands, the chorus of birds at dawn and the chirping of crickets at night, brilliant flowers, smiling faces and festivals filled with laughter and song. The Philippines fits the picture. In this archipelago of 7,107 islands and islets, it is still possible to experience the tropical paradise of your dreams. Off the beaten tourist track, there are many islands in the Philippines that remain pristine and serene with lonely stretches of beach untrammelled by the hordes and innocent of prone bodies browning in the sun. In remote mountain regions, the people live as their ancestors have done for many generations, following primordial rituals and traditions in an unending cycle. The islands and islets of the Philippines invite exploration by the adventurous. Its fish-rich seas and inland lakes challenge sport and recreational fishermen; its waters lure sailing buffs and windsurfers; its coral reefs and wealth of marine life delight the scuba diver, snorkeller, marine biologist and underwater photographer alike; its volcanic peaks, rainforests, caves, subterranean rivers, nature reserves and wealth of flora and fauna beckon the mountain climber, trekker, spelunker, botanist, nature lover and scientist. There are championship golf courses in scenic settings, luxury beach resorts, historic places and pilgrimage sites to attract those with specific interests.

For those who want to touch base with the city or big town, there's Metro Manila, Cebu and other destinations with their hotels, high-rise buildings, modern shopping malls and complexes, swinging nightlife, casinos, restaurants and bistros offering a varied range of cuisine.

The Filipino is a blend of Eastern and Western races and cultures and this is what makes him interesting. Fun and laughter come naturally to a Filipino. No matter what his station in life, whether he lives in a *bahay kubo* (nipa hut), a *barong barong* (shack) or a mansion, music and dancing are part of his life. Filipinos are in their element when they are celebrating their festivals. The fiesta is a respite from the daily grind.

The fiesta of the century took place in June 1998 when Filipinos throughout the land celebrated the centennial of Emilio Aguinaldo's proclamation of independence from Spanish colonial rule. There was an outpouring of nationalist sentiment and creativity, and the fiesta mood lingers. Mabuhay!

History

No written records exist of Philippine history prior to the Spanish era. However, archaeological findings and the accounts of early Arab and Chinese traders throw some light on the dim and distant past. One of the most significant archaeological discoveries was made in 1962 by Dr Robert B Fox who found a fossilized skullcap 22,000 years old in the Tabon Caves of western Palawan. In the same cave he found bones of bats, birds and small mammals, some charcoal, hammer stones and a few basalt choppers approximately the same age as the skull. Tabon Man is believed to belong to *homo sapiens*, who came to the Philippines some 55,000 to 45,000 years ago when the land bridges were still in place. Scientists are still searching for the remains of earlier inhabitants whose presence they link with Palaeolithic tools and fossilized bones of extinct animals discovered in Cagayan Valley that date back some 150,000 years.

The Negritos, the dark-skinned, kinky-haired Pygmies who lived by hunting, fishing, and food gathering and who are mentioned in history books as the aborigines of the Philippines, are believed to have come to the islands via the land bridges between 30,000 and 25,000 years ago. These are the forebears of the various tribes today known as Baluga, Atya, Agta, Aeta, Mamanuwa, Batak, Ata and Ati. Thousands of years later, great migrations of peoples swept across the seas and settled in the various islands that make up the Philippine archipelago. The first to arrive by sea were the Indonesians who came between 3,000 and 500 BC. They brought with them Neolithic culture: polished stone implements at first, and later copper and bronze tools and agriculture. The Malays followed between 300 BC and AD 500. They were more advanced culturally, introducing to the country Iron-Age culture: the smelting and manufacture of copper and iron tools and weapons, as well as pottery making, cloth weaving on a hand loom, and the making of ornaments out of glass beads.

FOREIGN INFLUENCES

The archipelago's location along the sea lanes used by trading vessels plying between the South China Sea and the far reaches of the Persian Gulf made the islands a convenient stopping place for Indian, Chinese, Arab, Japanese and Siamese merchants, as well as missionaries, seamen and adventurers. Indian cultural influences filtered into the Philippines between the late 7th and early 16th centuries via immigrants and traders from Indochina, Siam, the Malay Peninsula, Sumatra, Java and the other islands of Indonesia where Indian civilization had spread.

The Philippines

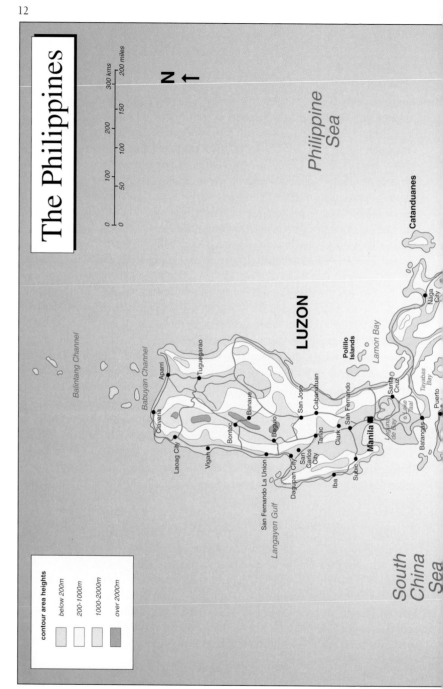

contour area heights

below 200m
200–1000m
1000–2000m
over 2000m

0   100   200   300 kms
0   50   100   150   200 miles

N

Balintang Channel

Babuyan Channel

LUZON

Philippine
Sea

Catanduanes

Aparri
Tuguegarao

Claveria

Laoag City

Vigan

Bontoc
Banaue
Baguio
San Jose
Cabanatuan

San Fernando La Union

Dagupan City
San
Carlos
City
Tarlac
Clark
San Fernando

Iba

Subic

Manila

Laguna
de Bay
Lake
Taal

Santa
Cruz

Batangas

Puerto

Polillo
Islands

Lamon Bay

Tayabas
Bay

Naga
City

Langayen Gulf

South
China
Sea

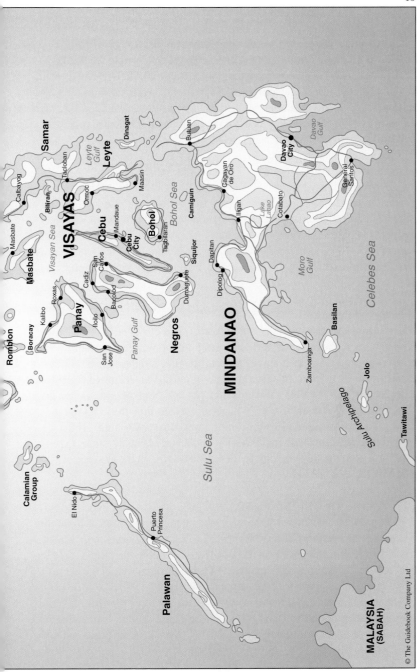

It is not certain when contact with China was established. Some scholars claim it goes back to the Zhou Dynasty (1066–221 BC). By the early part of the Northern Song Dynasty (960–1127), the Philippines was trading with China, and this continued to flourish through the Ming Dynasty (1368–1644). Written accounts in Chinese from the 13th and 14th centuries describe trade between China and Ma-i (also spelt Ma-yi or Mait, the Chinese names for the Philippines). Philippine products such as gold, pearls and tortoiseshell, betel nut, edible bird's nests, cotton (kapok), hemp and yellow wax were exchanged for silk and brocade textiles, coloured beads, fans and umbrellas, porcelainware, iron, tin and lead sinkers for fishnets.

Arab influence arrived at the end of the ninth or the beginning of the tenth century when Arab traders, expelled from central and southern Chinese ports, sought a new route to obtain Chinese goods. Sulu, Palawan and Northern Luzon were on their route to Formosa (Taiwan). Later, Chinese Muslims and Mongols of the Yuan Dynasty (1279–1368) also traded with Sulu. It was not until the end of the 13th century and the beginning of the 14th century, however, that Muslim converts were made.

The recovery in 1995 of the wreck of a 15th century trading vessel, believed to be Chinese, off Pandanan Island in southern Palawan waters, confirms what historians have always believed—that the Philippines was part of a flourishing regional trade and interchange before the arrival of men from the Western hemisphere. The site was surveyed by experts from the National Museum and the French underwater archaeologist Gilbert Fournier, after a pearl diver found coral-encrusted pottery on the sea floor in 1993. In 1995 a team from the National Museum and Ecofarm led by Fournier, salvaged more than 4,700 pieces of artefacts from the wreck; 80 per cent were intact. Most were Vietnamese, others were Thai and Chinese. The stoneware and potteries dated back to the Yuan up to the early Ming dynasties. Experts placed the date of the shipwreck in the early 1400s, based on the presence of a coin which bore the date of 1403.

THE COMING OF THE SPANIARDS

The Philippines became known to the West when Portugal and Spain were competing to acquire new territory and seeking the fabled spices and riches of the Orient. A series of Papal Bulls, culminating in the 1494 Treaty of Tordesillas, had divided the world between the two early superpowers. All lands acquired west of the demarcation line belonged to Spain; all lands east of it to Portugal.

Ferdinand Magellan, a Portuguese explorer in the service of the Spanish king, came upon the islands on 16 March 1521 while seeking a western route to the Spice Islands. After landing on the uninhabited island of Homonhon, he proceeded to the island of Limasawa where he was welcomed by the ruler, Rajah Kolambu. The two men sealed their friendship by drinking from a cup of wine mixed with their blood. The first Mass in Philippine history was celebrated on Easter Sunday, 31 March 1521, when a cross was planted atop a hill. Magellan next headed for Cebu, an island ruled by Rajah Humabon, with a flourishing entrepôt trade. Here Magellan also made a blood compact with Humabon, and on 14 April 1521, Humabon, his wife, and hundreds of his followers were converted to Christianity and baptized. Magellan afterwards planted a wooden cross by the seashore. Fragments of the original cross can be seen today in Cebu. All the chiefs welcomed the Spaniards except for Lapu-Lapu, chieftain of nearby Mactan Island. Whether Magellan decided to subdue the recalcitrant Lapu-Lapu in order to force him to acknowledge Spanish sovereignty, or whether he was drawn into a local dispute by one of the other chieftains is not clear. The fact remains that Magellan and his men confronted Lapu-Lapu on the shores of Mactan on 27 April and there Magellan—'our mirror, our light, our comfort, and our true guide' in the words of his chronicler Antonio Pigafetta—met his death. Lapu-Lapu's victory resulted in the Europeans' loss of prestige. Humabon and his chieftains, angered by the foreigners' rowdy conduct and rape of Cebuano women, massacred a number of them. Those who survived beat a hasty retreat.

Of Magellan's original five ships that had sailed from Spain in September 1519, only one, the *Victoria*, limped back to its home port although it did have the distinction of being the first ship to circumnavigate the globe. The expedition suffered heavy losses but the rich cargo fetched such a good price that the voyage was considered a financial success. This encouraged the Spanish crown to mount four further expeditions between 1525 and 1542. The last, led by Ruy Lopez de Villalobos, resulted in the naming of Samar and Leyte as Las Islas Felipinas, in honour of Prince Felipe of Asturias who later became King Philip II of Spain. The name was subsequently applied to the whole archipelago.

SPANISH COLONIZATION

To establish a permanent stronghold in the Orient, the Spanish king directed his viceroy in New Spain (present-day Mexico) to send an expedition to colonize the islands and convert the natives to Christianity. In 1565 Miguel Lopez de Legaspi, with Fray Andres de Urdaneta as navigator, arrived in Cebu, but the Cebuanos, still hurting from their experience after Magellan's death, gave them a hostile reception. Legaspi and his men were forced to explore other islands in the Visayas, and also Mindanao. In Bohol, he made a blood compact with Rajah Sikatuna. Determined to make Cebu his base, Legaspi then set about conquering the island. The Cebuanos fled to the hills, leaving their kingdom in flames. Miraculously the statue of the

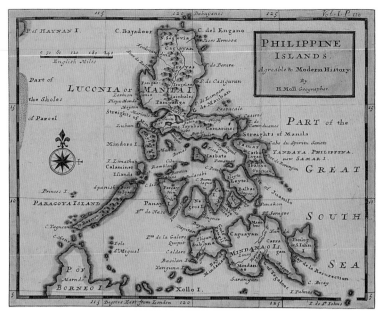

Philippine Islands, H Moll, circa 1720

Infant Jesus, Magellan's baptismal gift to Queen Juana, survived the fire and the Spaniards decided to build a church on the spot where the relic was found. Finally Rajah Tupas, Humabon's son, agreed to cooperate, and after making a blood compact, Spanish sovereignty was recognized. Legaspi set about building and fortifying the kingdom. Fray Urdaneta was told to return to Mexico and on his homeward journey discovered a route via the Pacific Ocean which opened the way for later voyages and the regular galleon run between Manila and Acapulco.

Legaspi was appointed governor general of the new colony, and had orders to explore, conquer and convert other islands. Lack of food on Cebu forced him to look for supplies elsewhere. He turned to the neighbouring island of Panay and in 1569 founded Capiz. Food shortages, however, continued to plague him and when he heard favourable reports of a kingdom further to the north with a fertile inland plain and a good harbour, he ordered Martin de Goiti and his own grandson, Juan de Salcedo, to reconnoitre that area. Entering the harbour in 1570, they discovered a flourishing kingdom called Maynilad on the south bank of a river near the sea. It was protected by wooden palisades and ruled by a young chieftain, Rajah Soliman, who was unwilling to submit to Spanish sovereignty. So in 1571, Legaspi entered Manila Bay with a large force and took Maynilad without bloodshed. He proceeded to rebuild and fortify Maynilad, and established Manila as the capital of the colony. Legaspi's rule was short-lived. In 1572, the adelantado died of a heart attack in Manila. The fortification of the city continued: stone walls were erected, with each succeeding governor strengthening or modifying the fortifications. The walled city became known as Ciudad Murada or Intramuros.

The conquest and colonization of the Philippines grew apace, and within ten years most of the islands had come under Spanish rule. Martin de Goiti subdued Central Luzon, from Bulacan to Pangasinan; Salcedo did the same for the Laguna de Bay area, Tayabas (now Quezon), Zambales, Pangasinan, Ilocos, Cagayan Valley and the Bicol region. At the same time, the friars started their mission of converting the people to Christianity. They not only spread the Gospel and built churches, but also introduced European culture. Church and state were one, and thus the religious orders had both ecclesiastical and political power. The orders founded schools, colleges, universities, asylums, hospitals and orphanages, museums and libraries; set up a printing press and taught Filipinos the art of printing.

Spanish Administration

The Spanish king appointed a governor general and members of the Royal Audiencia (Supreme Court) to rule the islands. The governor had vast executive, military, judicial and religious powers. In the absence of a governor, it was the Royal Audiencia that ruled. In the early years of Spanish conquest, the Philippines was divided into parcels of land called *encomiendas* administered by an *encomendero*—usually a Spanish national—who looked after the needs of the residents within his *encomienda*. Because of abuses in the system, *encomiendas* were abolished throughout the Spanish colonies in 1674 and provinces created in their place.

Between 1565 and 1813, the Philippines was administered by the Viceroy of Mexico. During this time, the galleon trade between Manila and Acapulco made a significant contribution to the progress of the islands. The trade brought silver to the coffers of both church and state as payment for the silk, spices, ivory, porcelain, gemstones and other Oriental goods that the ships carried to the West. Fortunes rose and fell with every sailing of a galleon. The galleon trade came to an end when the Mexican war of independence broke out, dealing a severe blow to the economy. After the Mexican War, the Philippines came under the direct control of Madrid.

Colonial Wars and Native Uprisings

During their 333-year rule, the Spanish faced threats to their hegemony from without and within. The Portuguese, claiming the islands belonged to them under the Treaty of Tordesillas, harassed coastal communities. This only ended when Spain

THE GALLEON TRADE

For about 250 years, galleons (massive wooden-hulled sailing vessels) plied the perilous seas between the Philippines and Mexico, carrying precious cargo from the East and silver from the West. At the centre of this international trade was Manila, where the riches of China, Siam, the Moluccas, Malaya, Borneo, Japan, India, Cambodia, Cochin China and the Philippines arrived for loading onto the galleons bound for Acapulco. The finest Chinese porcelain, sumptuous silks, rich damasks and brocades; diamonds, pearls, rubies, sapphires, topazes and other gemstones; filigree jewellery and gold chains; ivory and jade figurines and carvings; camphor and sandalwood chests; woodcarvings, ebony, ivory, musk, civet and other essences; cinnamon, cloves, nutmeg and other spices; lacquered desks, amber, bronze and copper, Bengal taffetas, cotton cloth, indigo, coconut shell products and sago flour were carried in the holds of the galleons. In Acapulco, they were unloaded and transshipped to further destinations in Europe and the Americas. On their return voyage, the galleons bulged with Mexican silver and bullion in payment for the goods.

The early galleons were 300-500 tonners, but as the trade flourished and the demand for more cargo space grew, their size increased to 1,000 tons until finally 2,000 tonners were ploughing the seas carrying passengers and cargo worth a king's ransom. Space in the holds was allotted to individuals and institutions, both civil and religious, through the granting of permits, and because the galleon trade was highly lucrative the buying and selling of permits for the spaces was rampant. Corruption on both ends of the galleon run was a fact of life. Merchandise was underdeclared or misdeclared as money filled the pockets of the unscrupulous. The galleon trade became a matter of life or death for governments, institutions and individuals. Fortunes were made or lost with each voyage. The west-bound galleons timed their departure from Manila sometime around July to take advantage of favourable weather. The return voyage was undertaken in the early months of the following year. The journey was often fraught with danger from typhoons, hidden shoals and rocks, as well as from pirates. In the history of the galleon run, some 40 ships were either lost at sea or shipwrecked. The wreck of the Nuestra Señora de la Concepcion was found by divers off Saipan in 1988. The divers recovered an amazing haul, including some exquisite pieces of jewellery made in the Philippines as early as the 17th century. In Philippine waters alone, wreckage from some 25 vessels lie strewn over a wide area. Some of the wrecks can be seen by divers around Puerto Galera, where galleons sought shelter from typhoons.

The galleons also fell prey to pirates. Dutch warships lay in wait at the San Bernardino Strait (a treacherous passage between Samar and Leyte), ready to pounce on any galleon returning to Manila. They never caught any because the galleons, forewarned by fire signals, took other routes.

In 1743, after several months of prowling the Pacific in search of a galleon, the English commodore George Anson was finally rewarded. Positioning his ship the Centurion at the Embocadero (the mouth of the San Bernardino Strait), Anson ordered a 24-hour watch. When the sails of the Nuestra Señora de Covadonga appeared on the horizon, he made ready his muskets and his men. The heavily-laden, lightly-armed galleon was no match for the lean and hungry British seamen. The Covadonga's booty was transferred to the holds of the Centurion by grappling hooks and the galleon itself was sold in China. Anson brought back to England more than one million silver pesos and nearly 36,000 ounces of bullion. It took more than 35 carts to carry the booty from the docks to London.

Napoleon's invasion of Spain, the Mexican wars of independence and the opening of the China trade to other nations sounded the death knell for the galleon trade. By 1815, a colourful chapter in the history of international commerce had ended.

Magellan's Cross

and Portugal were united under one king—Philip II of Spain—in 1580. The Chinese warlord Lima-hong attacked Manila with 3,000 men and 64 junks, but was routed. Retreating to Pangasinan, his escape route was blocked by Juan de Salcedo, but the wily pirate dug a channel to the sea and escaped unnoticed with his men one moonless night, never to be seen again. To expand the former Portuguese possessions they had wrested from the Spanish, the Dutch made several attempts to conquer the islands between 1600 and 1647 but were repulsed each time. The British, too, sent an expeditionary force to the Philippines from India in 1762, during the Seven Years' War between England and Spain. General William Draper and his British and Indian troops occupied Manila and the suburbs for 20 months. Manila reverted to Spain under the Treaty of Paris in 1764.

Filipinos and Chinese alike rose up in arms from time to time to protest against oppression, enforced tribute or forced labour. Some uprisings were agrarian in nature, while others stemmed from religious causes or were attempts to institute civil reforms. Some conspiracies were nipped in the bud by tip-offs; others erupted into violence and were brutally quelled.

THE RISE OF NATIONALISM

The brief British occupation gave impetus to the freedom movement. Nationalism was further fuelled by events in the 19th century, when the opening of the Philippines to the world enlarged the country's horizons not only in trade but through the importation of foreign ideas and culture. An enlightened Filipino middle class started to emerge and the opening of the Suez Canal accelerated the flow of communications and liberal ideas. The clamour for civil and religious reforms escalated. The execution in 1872 of three Filipino priests—Fathers Gomez, Burgos and Zamora—unjustly accused by the authorities of fomenting a mutiny in Cavite, fanned the flames of nationalism. Some sought to bring about social and political reform through peaceful means. These included intellectuals educated in Europe such as Jose Rizal, Marcelo H del Pilar and Graciano Lopez Jaena. Others, like Andres Bonifacio, opted for violent means. When Katipunan, the revolutionary society Bonifacio founded, was discovered by the authorities, and many of its members rounded up, tortured and executed, he gave the 'Cry of Pugad Lawin' on 23 August 1896, which signalled the start of the Philippine Revolution. Emilio Aguinaldo led the uprising in Cavite. Inspired by Aguinaldo's victories, the revolutionaries came to regard him as their leader.

The execution of Jose Rizal by firing squad at dawn on 30 December 1896 for alleged rebellion and sedition strengthened the Filipinos' resolve to gain independence from Spain. In the ensuing months, the rivalry between Bonifacio and Aguinaldo for leadership split the revolutionaries into two factions. Aguinaldo suggested scrapping the Katipunan and setting up a revolutionary government. As Aguinaldo gained the upper hand, Bonifacio fell out of grace and in 1897 was condemned to death by a revolutionary court which found him guilty of sedition. The tide of battle turned against the revolutionaries after Bonifacio's death. A peace pact was negotiated between the Spanish authorities and the revolutionaries and Aguinaldo went into

Painting depicting the baptism of Rajah Humabon, his wife and followers, Cebu

voluntary exile in Hong Kong. However, the terms of the peace pact were not honoured by either side, and the struggle for independence continued. Upon his return from Hong Kong, Aguinaldo set up a revolutionary government and on 12 June 1898, from his balcony in Kawit, Cavite, he proclaimed independence from Spanish rule.

Meanwhile events in the New World were coming to a head. Cuba, a Spanish colony, was also fighting for independence. The United States stepped in to help the Cubans, precipitating the Spanish-American war. It was by design rather than accident that an American squadron under Commodore George Dewey was in Asia when hostilities were proclaimed, and on 1 May 1898, he defeated the Spanish fleet. In August of that year, the Americans, aided by Filipinos fighting for the end of Spanish rule, captured Manila. The Filipinos were soon to discover that they had merely exchanged one colonizer for another.

To avoid a clash with the Americans, Aguinaldo moved his headquarters and the capital of the revolutionary government to Bulacan. A revolutionary congress assembled at the church of Barasoain under the presidency of Pedro Paterno on 15 September 1898 and on 29 September the Malolos Congress ratified the independence proclaimed at Kawit, Cavite that June. A constitution was later prepared by a committee headed by Felipe G Calderon. Known as the Malolos Constitution, it was promulgated on 21 January 1899 and on 23 January the First Philippine Republic was inaugurated at Malolos.

THE AMERICAN ERA

While Emilio Aguinaldo continued to fight for independence, the Philippines was ceded by Spain to the United States under the Treaty of Paris on 10 December 1898. An incident on the bridge of San Juan del Monte where an American soldier shot and killed a Filipino triggered off the Philippine-American War. The pacification of the country was a bloody affair. Many innocent people were killed as the forces spread out to conquer and rule. Aguinaldo was captured on 23 March 1901, ending the first Philippine Republic; however, guerrilla warfare dragged on until 1903. On 4 July 1901, a civil government was inaugurated with William H Taft as the first governor. To appease Filipinos who were still intent on self-government, the Philippine Bill of 1902 was passed providing for the establishment of an elected Philippine assembly. Sergio Osmeña was elected speaker and Manuel L Quezon majority floor leader.

Two Filipinos were sent to the United States to serve as resident commissioners in Congress, and other Filipinos were appointed to civil service positions in the Philippines as part of their training for self-rule. The Jones Law of 1916, otherwise known as the Philippine Autonomy Act, contained a bill of rights. The Americans established a system of government and laws, education, trade and commerce. In 1934, the Tydings-McDuffie Act provided for a constitution to be drawn up. A commonwealth government was set up in 1935 with Manuel L Quezon as president. At the end of a ten-year transition period, the Americans were to hand over the reins of government to Filipinos; but before the ten years were up world events intervened.

WORLD WAR II

On 8 December 1941 (7 December at Pearl Harbour), the Japanese bombed the Philippines. Weeks later, General Douglas MacArthur withdrew to Corregidor and set up his army headquarters at Malinta Tunnel, together with the government of President Quezon. The Japanese entered Manila on 2 January 1942 and began their conquest of the islands. Filipino and American forces valiantly resisted the advancing enemy but were turned back. Bataan fell on 9 April 1942. Thousands of prisoners of war were marched to the concentration camp at Capas in Tarlac but many died of starvation and disease along the way and only a few made it to camp. History remembers this as the 'Death March'. Before the fall of Bataan, MacArthur left for Australia with the promise 'I shall return', leaving Gen Jonathan Wainwright in command. The Filipinos and Americans made their last stand on Corregidor. After 27 days of heavy artillery barrage and bombardment, the forces, now running low on water, food, ammunition and supplies were forced to surrender, in Wainwright's words, 'in sorrow but not in shame'.

The three years of Japanese occupation were marked by privation and acts of brutality. A puppet government under Jose P Laurel was set up. Meanwhile an active underground guerilla movement was growing. The war of liberation began in October 1944 when General MacArthur landed his forces in Leyte Gulf and started his northward sweep to liberate the rest of the country. Sergio Osmeña was proclaimed president by General MacArthur after the death of Manuel Quezon. Philippine history has seen some fierce naval and land battles. In some places, space was fought for inch by inch and dearly won.

Manila was heavily bombed by the advancing American forces in February 1945. General Homma's Japanese forces were bottled up in the Mountain Province, trying to fight their way north to Aparri and escape by sea. But the end was near. Finally Homma was forced to surrender.

THE POSTWAR YEARS

The war left the Philippines in ruins. Rebuilding the country became a monumental task. Instead of allowing Uncle Sam to repair the damage, as he did in other countries laid low by war, the proud Filipinos insisted on their claim to independence.

And barely a year after the war's end, the Stars and Stripes was lowered from the flagpole in Rizal Park and the Filipino flag flew proudly alone. The Filipinos were free of colonial rule at last.

The task of nation-building lay ahead. As in any country trying to rise from the ruins of war, it was inevitable that carpetbaggers and opportunists should appear on the scene. There was a trade in surplus war goods and the rise of the so-called 'ten-percenters'. Officials who wanted to get rich quick were not averse to being bribed. Corruption and influence peddling reared their ugly heads. When Manual Roxas, president of the postwar Republic, was felled by an assassin's bullet, his vice president, Elpidio Quirino, took over. The next president, Ramon Magsaysay was killed in a plane crash. He was followed in office by Carlos Garcia, Diosdado Macapagal and Ferdinand Marcos.

THE MARCOS ERA

Marcos was a promising congressman when he allied his political fortunes with the influential Romualdez family by marrying their kin, Imelda Romualdez, a tall, fresh-faced, unsophisticated girl who had grown up in the provinces. When the congressman finally made it to the presidency in 1965, the 'Rose of Tacloban', as Imelda was known, was catapulted into the limelight. Unprepared for her new role, she used to suffer massive headaches, her hands in a constant sweat. But Imelda quickly became accustomed to being First Lady and emerged from her fragile chrysalis to become what the world press described as the 'Steel Butterfly'. She mastered the art of politics and attracted her own coterie of followers and sycophants. One presidential term led to another and because the constitution did not allow for a third term, Marcos (claiming deteriorating law and order and an alleged threat of communist insurgency) declared martial law thereby assuring his rule. Marcos governed the country from 1965 to 1986.

Martial law meant the suspension of freedoms. The old constitution was abolished. Many publications and radio and TV stations were closed and only a few were permitted to operate within certain parameters. People who were suspected of communist leanings were rounded up, incarcerated and questioned. Journalists were thrown into military jails and subjected to interrogation. Among those detained was Senator Benigno Aquino who, for 'humanitarian reasons' was later allowed to leave for the United States with his family to undergo a coronary bypass operation. Industries and businesses owned by Marcos' political opponents were confiscated and taken over by the government. For a while, law and order was restored and, because no dissent was allowed, the government could go ahead and do things its own way without fear of interference. Some infrastructural improvements were made, and a new constitution was ratified, providing for a modified form of parliamentary government. The economy appeared ready to take off, but as the years went by, the promise remained unfulfilled as the gap between rich and poor widened. Discontent was rife as prices continued to rise and the quality of life deteriorated. For those close to the powers that be, life was a bed of roses. The economy, fostered by 'crony capitalism', was being stifled.

PEOPLE POWER

Martial law was lifted in 1981 but there was no end in sight for the Marcos' rule. In the meantime opposition groups were being organized and obtaining support from abroad. These civic organizations operated out of the United States among Filipino expatriates. When Senator Aquino requested a dialogue with the government, he was warned not to return as his safety could not be guaranteed. Nevertheless he decided to come back and when his plane landed at Manila International Airport, he was gunned down on the tarmac. His assassination in August 1983 triggered the people to unite. When the parliamentary elections took place in 1984, the growing opposition was reinforced by the action of concerned citizens and organizations such as NAMFREL (National Movement for Free Elections) which oversaw the elections. An aroused citizenry clamoured for change and in the presidential elections scheduled for February 1986, Aquino's widow Corazon, then a housewife, rose to the challenge and agreed to run against the incumbent Marcos. Both sides claimed victory and there was evidence of massive vote rigging. By then, popular sentiment was running high against the administration and in a show of people power, watched by the whole world on television, the 20-year rule of Marcos ended. The Marcos family went into exile in Hawaii, and in September 1989, Marcos died in Honolulu. Appeals from the Marcos family to return to the Philippines to bury Marcos were denied on the grounds it might destabilize the country's peace. In 1993, however, permission was finally granted for Marcos's body to be returned.

Early 19th-century costume made famous by Imelda Marcos

In Cold Blood

The night before boarding their plane to Manila, Aquino and Kashiwahara were talking in a room at the Grand Hotel overlooking Taipei. Aquino said, "I just got a report from Manila. I may get hit at the airport when I land, and then they will hit the hit man. That's why I'm going to wear this"—he held up a bulletproof vest. "But you know," he went on,"if they get me in the head I'm a goner."

Aquino and ten journalists, plus two Japanese television crews, boarded China Airlines Flight 811 at Chiang Kai-shek Airport. The plane landed at 1:05 p.m. In the terminal there was a welcoming crowd of ten thousand, complete with a band playing Tie a Yellow Ribbon.

Other people were waiting for him as well. By the previous day, all of them knew when he was arriving, and on which aircraft. Tourism Minister José Aspiras, one of the men closest to Imelda, had exchanged cables with the China Airlines office in Taipei and knew every detail. Certain people in the regime seemed to make it a point to absent themselves. Imelda Marcos was having a very long and highly visible lunch with friends at the Via Mare seafood restaurant near the Cultural Center. Fabian Ver was out of sight at secret police headquarters in Fort Bonifacio. Defense Minister Enrile was playing golf at Wack Wack. With President Marcos recovering from surgery, Enrile at the links, and Imelda out to lunch, the levers of government were being worked by Fabian Ver, Tourism Minister Aspiras, Information Minister Gregorio Cendana, and top crony Eduardo Cojuangco, plus the generals loyal to Ver who were commanding the main security forces. Since around 6:00 a.m., Cendana and Aspiras had been at the airport, waiting. Cojuangco hovered nearby.

Something peculiar was going on. U.S. Air Force radar operators at two air-defense installations on Luzon were abruptly replaced by a full battle staff of Filipinos. Two fully armed Filipino F-5 jet fighters were scrambled to find Aquino's airliner and force it down at Basa Air Base, 35 miles north of Manila, but it was cloudy and they could not find it. The Filipino ground radar operators took over the hunt. A second flight of F-5 fighters was scrambled to try again. They also failed. The fifth ranking officer in the Philippine Air Force, Colonel Umberto Capawan, was in charge of the main control room at Villamor Air

Base next to Manila International Airport. He was a member of Fabian Ver's inner circle. At Wallace Air Station north of Manila, a U.S. Air Force major asked his American superior what was happening. The superior answered, "We think we know what's going on." He did not elaborate.

When the China Airlines flight landed at Manila International and rolled up to the landing bay at Gate 8, one thousand soldiers from the Metropolitan Command (METROCOM) were in positions around the airport and on the tarmac. A blue van from the Aviation Security Command (AVSECOM) drew up and disgorged another group of soldiers, who took up positions around the front part of the CAL plane. When its left front door was opened and joined to the accordian chute feeding into Gate 8, three uniformed security men in shirtsleeves climbed aboard—two from AVSECOM and one from METRO-COM. They took Aquino by the arms, felt to see if he wore body armor, then hustled him off the plane, preventing any journalists from accompanying them.

Instead of proceeding straight down the tunnel to the terminal, where other journalists were waiting, the three security men steered Aquino through a side door and down metal stairs leading to the tarmac. A government press aide working for Cendana immediately blocked the doorway so the journalists scrambling off the plane could not see down the ladder. Before Aquino's feet could touch Philippine soil, a shot rang out. One of the three security men escorting Aquino down the steps had shot him in the back of the head at point-blank range. Inside the blue van, other security men quickly picked up the dead body of Rolando Galman and threw it onto the tarmac next to Aquino's still form. These soldiers immediately began firing bullets into Galman, as if they were just now killing him. Galman had been dead quite a while. He was now lying on his stomach but there was dried blood from earlier bullet holes running the opposite direction, uphill, indicating that he had been lying on his back when he was actually killed. The Marcos government would announce that Galman had appeared at the aircraft from nowhere and had murdered Aquino as part of a Communist conspiracy, and only then had Galman been slain by the security men "protecting" Aquino.

Sterling Seagrave, The Marcos Dynasty, 1988

Denied of a state burial at the Libingan ng mga Bayani where past presidents and Filipino war heroes have been laid to rest, Marcos' embalmed body lies inside a glass coffin, on view to the public in the Marcos Mausoleum in his home province of Ilocos Norte. Newly elected President Joseph Estrada stated that he would allow the remains of the former president to be interred at the Libingan ng mga Bayani but this is strongly opposed by members of an organization called Kilosbayan.

On her return to the Philippines, Mrs Marcos lost no time in proclaiming her candidacy for the presidency in the national elections of May 1992 but made a poor showing. In the 1995 general elections, she ran for Congress and won. Disqualified by the Commission on Elections (Comelec) for failure to meet a poll requirement, her victory was later confirmed by the Supreme Court, reversing the Comelec decision. The congresswoman from Leyte renewed her bid for the presidency in the May 1998 general elections, and again failed. Her daughter Imee and son Ferdinand (Bongbong), however, were luckier. Imee won a seat in Congress and Bongbong was elected governor of Ilocos Norte. Meanwhile, Government efforts to regain control of the millions of dollars stashed away in Switzerland during the Marcos regime continue.

THE AQUINO YEARS

Public euphoria over Corazon Aquino's victory did not last long. Saddled by economic and political problems inherited from the Marcos era, the new President had the added burdens of dealing with troubles from members of her cabinet early on, splinter groups in the military establishment destabilising the country with six attempts at a coup d'etat, the clamour to end the US military bases agreement, and massive natural calamities and disasters. Sceptics doubted whether she would last in office but she weathered all the storms of her administration and after six years of rule, described by her as difficult and frustrating years, she stepped down in June 1992 to make way for a new administration led by her former defense secretary—a West Pointer and one-time Armed Forces Chief of Staff, Fidel Valdez Ramos.

For 'giving a radiant moral force to the non-violent movement for democracy in the Philippines and around the world', Mrs Aquino received in 1998 the Ramon Magsaysay Award for International Understanding. The awards in honour of the late President Ramon Magsaysay are the Asian equivalent of the Nobel prize and are given annually to deserving individuals in the region in the fields of community leadership, public service, government service, journalism, literature and communication arts and international understanding.

THE RAMOS ADMINISTRATION

FVR, as Mr Ramos was known, was committed to the same democratic principles guaranteeing human rights and freedoms which his predecessor restored after the 20-year Marcos rule. Under his presidency (1992–1998), the Philippines enjoyed political stability, peace and economic growth. His administration instituted policy reforms which brought about the liberalization of the banking sector, privatization of government corporations, deregulation of the telecommunications industry, a social reform programme committed to lifting the poverty level, the opening up of the country to foreign investments, and an improvement in the country's industrial infrastructure. The successful hosting by the Philippines in November 1996 of the Asia Pacific Economic Cooperation

Ramos' Inauguration, 30 June 1992

(APEC) Forum which drew the attendance of 18 member economies and their heads of state and high-level ministers was chiefly credited to the President's leadership. As part of his diplomatic initiatives, Mr Ramos made 34 overseas journeys, visiting 61 countries during his six-year term. Globalization was his war cry as he encouraged Filipinos to 'pole-vault' the country into the 21st century.

It was during his term of office that the Philippines marked the centennial of its proclamation of independence from Spain. He considers the centennial celebrations as the centrepiece of his administration. Before he stepped down, President Ramos received in Senegal the 1997 Felix Houphouet-Boigny Peace Prize of the United Nations Educational, Scientific and Cultural Organization for negotiating peace with the Muslim rebels in Mindanao. He shared the award with Chairman Nur Misuari of the Moro National Liberation Front (MNLF). President Ramos stepped down on 30 June 1998 to give way to his successor, Joseph Estrada.

THE ESTRADA PRESIDENCY

By an overwhelming mandate of the people who went to the polls on 11 May 1998, Joseph 'Erap' Estrada, became the 13th President of the Philippine Republic, beating ten other presidential candidates. Born Joseph Ejercito, he assumed the name Joseph Estrada for his screen persona. Friends called him Erap which is Pare spelled backwards (Pare in popular Filipino parlance means Buddy and is similar to the Australian's 'mate'). Like his inspiration, former US president Ronald Reagan, he gave up his movie career to become a politician. He first ran for mayor of the municipality of San Juan in Metro Manila in 1967, a post he held for 16 years. He was elected senator in 1987 and vice president in 1992. The new President broke with tradition when he and his Vice President Gloria Macapagal Arroyo took their oaths of office at historic Barasoain Church. Later in the afternoon he delivered his inaugural address, in Filipino language—another first—at the Quirino Grandstand in Rizal Park where presidents before him took their oaths of office. A military and civic parade was a feature of the inaugural rites. Mr Estrada promised to continue the free market policies of the Ramos administration. He outlined a ten-point programme which would be the focus of his administration. Among these are improving the agriculture sector, streamlining bureaucracy, eliminating graft and corruption, implementing law and order and improving the standard of living as per his campaign promise of 'Erap para sa mahirap' (Erap for the poor).

Geography

According to Philippine mythology, several million years ago, the sea and the sky were engaged in a fierce battle. The quarrel was incited by a giant bird seeking a dry place to rest and roost. The sea raged at the sky, throwing mighty waves at it, and the sky hurled down islands and rocks to subdue the seething sea. The sheer number and weight of the islands and rocks forced the sea to retreat. Thus the bird found a home and the Philippine archipelago was born.

The Philippine archipelago consists of 7,107 islands and islets, stretching some 1,850 kilometres (1,150 miles) from north to south and 1,107 kilometres (1,688 miles) from west to east at its widest point. The total land area is approximately 300,000 square kilometres (115,830 square miles), slightly larger than the United Kingdom, and roughly the same size as Italy. On the map, it sprawls between the Asian mainland and Australia, between latitudes 21° and 5° N and longitudes 116° and 127° E. Its geographical boundaries are the Bashi Channel in the north and the Sulu and Celebes Seas in the south. The South China Sea defines its western borders while the Pacific Ocean marks its eastern limits. Some 240 kilometres (150 miles) beyond the northernmost tip of the Batanes group lies Taiwan, and 24 kilometres (15 miles) beyond the southernmost point is the coast of Borneo.

LUZON, THE VISAYAS, MINDANAO

There are three main island groupings in the Philippines: Luzon, the Visayas and Mindanao. Luzon, the biggest island where the capital Manila is situated, forms the northern region, together with outlying islands and islets, including Mindoro, Marinduque, Romblon, Masbate and Palawan. The Visayan islands form the central region and include Cebu, Bohol, Negros, Panay, Samar and Leyte. Mindanao, the second largest island, forms the southern region, together with Camiguin, Basilan and the Sulu Archipelago. Less than 3,000 of the Philippine islands have names and only about 2,000 are inhabited.

Scientists believe that the land mass that is now the Philippines was once a part of the Asian continent which extended as far as Australia. The break-up of the continent occurred sometime during the end of the Cretaceous period (135 million to 75 million years ago) when Australia was separated from the mainland. A further break-up of the continent took place during the Tertiary period of the Cenozoic era (two million to 60 million years ago). The Philippine Archipelago as we know it today was shaped by intense volcanic activity and profound tectonic changes that occurred during the Miocene (about 16 million years ago) and the succeeding Pliocene ages (some 11 million years ago) when new mountains rose up and other parts of the island sank into the sea. Geological studies indicate that during the Miocene period, the Baguio highlands were thrust up from the sea, the Cordilleras were formed and lowland forests rose to become highland forests. More islands merged or separated during the late Pliocene and Pleistocene periods. Mindanao may have been four or five islands which coalesced into one, while the Sulu Archipelago emerged as a chain of tiny coralline islands. Zambales and the Bataan Peninsula formed an island separate from Luzon, while Marinduque was part of Luzon. Samar and Leyte were connected and at one time Samar was joined to the tip of the Bicol region.

Luzon was once linked with Taiwan, and land bridges joined Palawan, Sulu and parts of Mindanao with Borneo, Java, Sumatra and Sulawesi. The rising and falling of the seas during the glacial and interglacial periods have caused the land bridges to disappear and reappear until finally, at the end of the last ice age about 10,000 years ago, all the land corridors were submerged by the sea. Shallower seas off Palawan and western Mindanao bear out the theory of a submerged continental shelf. East of Mindanao is the Philippine Trench or Mindanao Trough; here the sea is 10,830 metres (35,531 feet) deep.

TOPOGRAPHY

The topography of the Philippines is characterized by narrow coastal plains, rich interior valleys, rolling hills and high mountains. Major lowland plains are the Central Plain and Cagayan Valley in Luzon, and the Agusan Valley and Cotabato Valley in Mindanao. Mountain ranges include the Cordillera and Sierra Madre in Luzon. Mt Apo in Mindanao, a dormant volcano, lords it over the other mountains, rising to a height of 3,143 metres (10,311 feet) above sea level. Mt Pulog in Luzon is the second highest mountain, at 2,930 metres (9,613 feet). The Philippines' volcanic origins are evident from an extensive range of volcanic mountains and peaks that runs the entire length of the archipelago. Of the 220 volcanoes in the Philippines 23 are considered active. Four of the six most active volcanoes are on Luzon Island. These are Mt Mayon, noted for its perfect symmetry, in Albay province; Taal Volcano, a well-known tourist attraction in Batangas; Mt Bulusan in Sorsogon province; and Mt Pinatubo, dormant for around 450 years, which sprang to life in 1991. The others are Mt Hibok-Hibok on Camiguin Island and Mt Kanlaon on Negros Island. Recently, Mt Parker in Mindanao also sprang to life after centuries of dormancy. Numerous hot springs, ranging from tepid to boiling, bubble up from the earth.

Seen from the air, the Philippines presents a picture of emerald islands in the sun, ringed by palm-fringed white sand beaches lapped by turquoise seas. Scenic bays, gulfs and natural harbours punctuate the archipelago's irregular coastline, while waterfalls and swift-running streams cascade down mountains. Rivers wind across the plains and cut deep gorges in valleys. The Cagayan River in Luzon is the longest, snaking for 353 kilometres (219 miles) across the provinces of Nueva Viscaya, Isabela and Cagayan, and finally flowing into the South China Sea at Aparri, Cagayan. Other big rivers are the Rio Grande and Agno River in Luzon, the Rio Grande de Mindanao and Agusan River in Mindanao. Of the 59 lakes in the country, the largest is Laguna de Bay, measuring 922 square kilometres (356 square miles).

People

In terms of blood lines, present-day Filipinos are a complex lot. Most Filipinos come from Malayo-Indonesian stock, with varying infusions of Chinese, Spanish, American and other European, South American and Asian blood. There are more than 100 ethno-linguistic groups in the country. The majority of Filipinos, or Pinoys, as they call themselves, are Christians. They predominate in Luzon and the Visayas and now make up the dominant population of Mindanao. Ethnically these are the Tagalogs, Cebuanos, Ilocanos, Ilonggos, Bicolanos, Warays, Pampangueños and Pangasinenses.

Ifugao tribal man in full regalia

Most Muslims make their home in Mindanao, and are concentrated in the Sulu Archipelago, the Lanao provinces, Cotabato and Zamboanga. The Maranaos, Maguindanaos and Sanggils live on the main island while Yakans live on Basilan Island; Taosugs are found in Jolo, Samals in Tawi-Tawi and adjacent islands, and the Jama Mapun in Cagayan de Sulu. Filipino Muslims are the descendants of converts to Islam and in terms of lifestyle, dress and manner are more closely related to Indonesians, Malaysians and Bruneians than to the Christian majority.

CULTURAL COMMUNITIES

The cultural minorities in the Philippines are descended from the early migrants who came by sea and the Negritos who travelled overland from Borneo. They fled to the mountains or remote coastal foothills to avoid being converted to Islam or Christianity. The pagan hill tribes include the Ifugaos, Bontocs, Kalingas, Ibalois, Isnegs and Tingguians who live in the Central Cordilleras of Luzon, and the Mangyans of Mindoro and Palawan. In Mindanao, they include the Manobo, Bukidnon, Subanon, Higaonon, Mandaya, Bagobo, Ismal, Tagakaolo, Tiruray, Bilaan, T'boli and Tasaday tribes. The hill tribes speak Malayo-Polynesian dialects. Since there is little intermarriage, they have retained their blood lines and folk ways. Some of these communities are Christian but underneath a thin layer of Western religion many retain their ancient lifestyles.

The short, dark-skinned, kinky-haired Negritos are spread geographically throughout the islands but their greatest concentration is in the forests of Luzon. They include the Aetas and Balugas of Zambales, Bataan, western Pangasinan, Tarlac and Pampanga; the Atas or Pugots of Cagayan, Isabela and Quirino; the Dumagats of Aurora, Quezon and Rizal; the Agtas of Camarines; the Atis of Panay and Negros; the Mamanuwa of Surigao and Agusan del Norte; and the Bataks of Palawan. These nomadic hunters, fishermen and food gatherers are believed to be related to similar peoples living in the Malay Peninsula, Indonesia, New Guinea and the Andaman Islands. Their traditional way of life is increasingly being threatened as they come into contact with the culture of the Christian Filipinos. In parts of the country, the government has set up reservations or villages where they can improve their livelihood while retaining their traditions.

ETHNIC CHINESE

The Chinese started arriving in the Philippines as traders before the Spaniards, and were sometimes referred to as *sanglays* (from the Amoy word *xeng-li* or trader). In 1571, there were only 150 Chinese living in the Parian, outside the Spanish walled city of Intramuros, but by 1603, their number had grown to 30,000. The early immigrants were mostly lower-class males from Fujian province, many of whom married Filipinas. Some, however, married their own kind. Their children spoke Chinese; they attended Chinese schools and followed Chinese customs. Immigration from mainland China continued through the American era and ceased only in 1952. The Chinese acted as middlemen in the commerce between the natives and the Spaniards and were skilled artisans and craftsmen. Their biggest impact was in commerce and trade. Their offspring have gained significant economic, social and political stature.

INTERMARRIAGE

Intermarriage between lowland Filipinos and other nationalities has been taking place since early times. The first recorded intermarriage in the Catholic faith was the wedding of Rajah Tupas' widowed niece to a Greek ship caulker who had sailed to the Philippines with Miguel Lopez de Legaspi. There are also accounts of a Mexican who had arrived on an earlier expedition and stayed behind to marry a Filipina. A *mestizo* (male) or *mestiza* (female), is the light-complexioned offspring of a Filipino and a Caucasian. In Spanish times, it referred to the children of Spanish fathers and Filipino mothers. *Mestizos* were held in high regard, and occupied positions of influence. Eurasians and Amerasians are considered to be *mestizos*, but today the term is also used for the offspring of mixed marriages.

WOMEN

Filipino women are held in high regard in Philippine society and participate actively in decision-making. Filipinas were given the right of suffrage long before some of their Eastern and Western sisters. They have entered professions that in other countries are traditionally reserved for men. There are female members of the cabinet, senate and congress, the diplomatic and consular corps, women judges, governors and administrators. One woman—Corazon Cojuangco Aquino—rose from the rank of housewife to become the first woman to be elected President of the Philippines.

In the 1998 general elections, two women were among the contenders for Vice President. The bright and diminutive Senator Gloria Macapagal Arroyo, daughter of former President Diosdado Macapagal, was a runaway favourite, leading her opponents by a wide margin. In addition to her duties as Vice President, she has been given the portfolio of Secretary for Social Welfare and Development. Another woman—Loren Legarda Leviste—a broadcast journalist who was a newcomer in the political arena, was the front-runner in the senatorial race. Women have been admitted to the once all-male Philippine Military Academy, and are commissioned officers in the Philippine Navy. Filipinas also hold positions of responsibility in United Nations agencies and commissions and international organizations.

POPULATION

In 1591, just 26 years after Spain started the colonization of the islands, the total population of the archipelago was only 667,612. In the first few years of American rule, the population was recorded at 7,635,426. This figure had grown to 19,234,182 by 1948, and 68,616,536 in 1995, according to the National Statistics Office. Today, the population stands at around 71 million, with an annual growth rate of 2.1 per cent. In this predominantly Catholic country, the bishops have conceded that population regulation may be advocated under certain circumstances, but the Church in the Philippines is opposed to artificial contraception, sterilization and abortion as means of curbing population growth.

FILIPINO TRAITS

Filipinos are a gregarious, sociable lot; they are lively, friendly and hospitable. They sing and dance at the drop of a hat, laugh readily, and have a communal sense of fun. Some social characteristics have both plusses and minuses. For example, their attitude of *bahala na* ('come what may') enables them to meet difficulties and hardships with resignation, leaving it up to the Almighty to sort things out; but it can also result in overconfidence that things will work out in their interest, without much input on their part. 'Face' is a widespread Asian phenomenon. One must maintain 'face' or *amor propio* at all times, otherwise it is *nakakahiya* (shameful) as it redounds on family honour and virtue. It is a social *faux pas* to insult another and cause him to lose face. Filipinos are reluctant to say outright what they think may hurt or disappoint others, so they sometimes beat around the bush or indulge in euphemisms. They may also use third parties to convey their wishes to avoid being direct.

The Filipino's *mañana* habit can be irritating to those who are time-bound. He can procrastinate until tomorrow, but if he has no time to do it properly tomorrow, then *bahala na*. Not all Filipinos have this bad habit. However, one must remember that in the Philippines time is not of the essence for many. Few people are punctual for social engagements. In fact one is not expected to turn up precisely on time at a party. It's always best to check what time the host or hostess actually expects you to arrive.

FILIPINOS ABROAD

Filipinos are adventurous people. You find them in various parts of the world, some even in far-flung places thousands of miles from home. They are there either as tourists, students, professionals in their line of work, entertainers, migrant and contract workers or permanent residents. It is reported that half of the seamen on board merchant ships worldwide are Filipinos. For economic reasons, millions of

Who Am I?

I look at my reflection in the pool and I see a brown man with an inquiring face, eager to know, to taste all the juices of the earth. I came upon myself not knowing wherefrom I came, but I do suspect it was not from an eternal womb, the hollow of a bamboo? Or of the sky? I am alone, yet I know there are likenesses of me, with the same bone and muscle, and hungers that cannot be assuaged. I must also stand alone, for this is what all men must do, if they are to prevail in the wilderness.

I was made to wander; if I had wings I would have soared to the highest my wings could propel me, but with my feet, I must now go as far as they can lead me.

I have seen this face, and it belongs only to me, but I will also recognize it everywhere, for it is the face of a traveller, a seeker, even if he moves not a muscle or an eye, for the mind is what travels farther than what the flesh with all its frailty can reach.

But where will I go and what will I become? Is there a niche somewhere in the desert or in the jungle into which I can fit? And where I belong, where I will die, this the surcease I have always sought?

F Sionil José, Viajero, 1993

men and women have left home temporarily to become Overseas Foreign Workers. OFWs have been hailed as 'heroes' by the government because their remittances, running into billions of dollars annually, have substantially contributed to the economy. Along with the stories of success, however, come tales of tragedy and woe.

Religion

CHRISTIANITY

The Philippines is the only predominantly Christian country in Asia: 92 per cent of the population are Christian. Roman Catholics account for about 83 per cent and Protestants for 9 per cent. Christianity was introduced by the Spaniards during the visit of Ferdinand Magellan in 1521. The first converts were the Cebuanos. The 'conversion of the heathen peoples to Christianity' was one of the principal aims of Spanish colonization. On the expedition of 1565 led by Miguel Lopez de Legaspi, Augustinian friars accompanied him. The systematic conversion of the Filipinos was accomplished by a succession of missionary orders. After the Augustinians came the Franciscans, followed by the Jesuits, then the Dominicans and later the Recollects. The religious orders not only brought the faith to the natives but European culture as well. They not only built churches but hospitals and orphanages, schools and universities, the weather observatory and printing press; they also introduced many other things that changed Filipino culture and lifestyle.

Protestant missionaries arrived in the early 1900s, during the American era, to spread the Gospel. Filipino Protestant sects also sprang up in the early 20th century, notably the Philippine Independent Church (Aglipay) and the Iglesia ni Cristo (Church of Christ). This charismatic movement, with its emphasis on Christian values and a Spirit-led, Spirit-filled life, is gaining a following in the Philippines.

ISLAM

Muslims are concentrated in Mindanao, notably Lanao del Sur, Maguindanao, the Sulu Archipelago and Basilan Island, but are also found in other Christian-dominated areas of Mindanao, such as Lanao del Norte, Cotabato and Zamboanga. Muslims visited Sulu at the end of the 13th century and the beginning of the 14th century and made converts. Two men are linked with the Islamization of the Philippines— Sharif Muhammad Kabungsuwan and Sharif Abu Bakr. The former, a soldier-trader-missionary from Malacca, founded the Maguindanao sultanate in Cotabato in 1475. The latter, an Arab from Mecca who lived in Johore and later went to Sulu where he

Augustinian Church, San Pablo

married Raja Baguinda's daughter, founded the Sultanate of Sulu. Sharif Abu Bakr introduced the Sharia holy law and Arabic script and set up hierarchic rule. The spread of Islam continued northwards and had the Spaniards not arrived on the scene, the Philippines might have fallen under Islamic influence. Manila, Tondo and parts of Pampanga and Ilocos were already Muslim kingdoms in the 16th century.

OTHERS

The early pagan inhabitants of the Philippines escaped being converted to Christianity or Islam because they fled to the mountains. Hence, the descendants of the Negritos and the cultural minorities and highland tribes still retain their animistic beliefs. There are small numbers of Buddhists, Taoists and adherents of other religions.

Government

The Philippines is a democratic and republican state with three co-equal branches of government: the executive, legislative, and judicial. The executive branch is headed by the president who is directly elected by a simple majority for a single term of six years. A bicameral legislature consists of the House of Representatives with not more than 250 members elected for a three-year term, and the Senate with 24 members elected at large every six years. Judicial power is vested in the Supreme Court and lower courts. Administratively, the country is divided into 13 regions and three autonomous regions—the Cordillera Autonomous Region (CAR), the Autonomous Region of Muslim Mindanao (ARMM) and the National Capital Region (NCR). The seat of power is in Metropolitan Manila. There are 78 provinces headed by governors. The most basic unit of government is the barangay or village.

The constitutional provision of a six-year term with no reelection for the presidency came in for debate when a citizens' initiative in 1997 called 'Pirma' (signature) sought to reform the constitution by gathering millions of signatures in support of a charter change or 'cha-cha'. Because of its timing—just months away from the general elections in May 1998—the movement failed. Cha-cha was seen by some as a move to extend President Ramos' term of office. However, amendments to the 1987 constitution are seen as vital as the country prepares for the 21st century. In view of this, a body to study constitutional reforms has been proposed. When president Ramos was asked by *Time* magazine what he thought about allowing the president to run for a second term, he replied: 'That is up to the next constitutional body to look at. I have always said that six years for a good president maybe is not long enough, but six years is too long for a bad president.'

Politics is a game Filipinos love to play. It has permeated every level of society and spawned political dynasties. Governors, city and municipal mayors, congressmen and senators could be husbands and wives, brothers and sisters, father or mother and sons or daughters, or cousins, uncles and grandfathers. Politics has split families and incurred bitter rivalries among relatives. Political gossip is a favourite pastime. It is exchanged in coffee shops, hotel lobbies and cocktail lounges, on street corners—town and country—where politicians, the media, businessmen, eavesdroppers and nearly everyone else congregate to circulate the latest rumours and scandals.

FOREIGN POLICY

The promotion of peace, equality, justice, co-operation and amity with all nations is at the heart of Philippine foreign policy. The Philippines is a charter member of the United Nations and a signatory to various UN conventions. It participates in the UN system and its international organizations. It is a founding member of the Association of Southeast Asian Nations (ASEAN), a regional body created to promote economic growth, social progress and cultural development in the region. The other member states are Indonesia, Malaysia, Singapore, Thailand, Brunei Darussalam, Vietnam, Myanmar and Laos.

Economy

The Philippines is blessed with a goodly share of natural resources. Its forests yield such precious hardwoods as the species of dipterocarp (Philippine mahogany) and molave (narra, tindalo, ipil, etc). Forest products of economic value include rattan, resin and bamboo, as well as gums, seed oils, essential oils, wild food plants and natural dyes. Its mountains, plains, coasts and offshore areas hide mineral treasures: gold, silver, platinum, palladium, copper, zinc, nickel, lead, molybdenum, chromite, iron, cobalt and manganese, much of it untapped. The Philippines is one of the world's producers of gold, chromite and copper. Asbestos, barite, bentonite, cement raw materials, clay, coal, diatomite, dolomite, feldspar, guano, gypsum, limestone, magnesite, marble, mica, natural gas, perlite, phosphate rock, pyrite, rock asphalt, silica, sand, sulphur and talc are among its valuable non-metals. Tuna, mackerel, garoupa, anchovies, round herring, sardines, threadfin bream, mullet and bass as well as molluscs and crustaceans are found in Philippine seas, rivers and lakes. The country's fertile volcanic soil and climate favour such agricultural crops as rice, maize, coconut, sugarcane, bananas, pineapples, mangoes, abaca and hemp.

ECONOMIC OUTLOOK

The National Economic and Development Authority (NEDA) is the government body responsible for socio-economic planning and coordinating the implementation of development plans. It reports directly to the President. The policy reforms introduced by the Ramos administration have done much to improve the economy.

But the currency crisis that affected Asian economies and the adverse effects of El Niño, have slowed down economic development. However, the Philippine economy was not as badly shaken as those of other Southeast Asian nations. GNP growth for 1998 was forecast at between 2.8 and 3.0 per cent. A brighter outlook is seen for 1999. President Joseph Estrada has assured the business community that he will continue the economic reforms begun by his predecessor.

The Sarimanok, legendary symbol of rooster and fish

INVESTMENT OPPORTUNITIES

The peaceful Philippine elections of May 1998 sent out a signal to the international community that the country is a safe haven for foreign investments. Many foreign companies in the past few years have taken advantage of investment opportunities and have set up plants and factories, even regional headquarters, in the Philippines. The existence of an English-speaking, educated and skilled manpower resource is a plus factor. Natural resources, good health care and a high standard of living at low cost also make the Philippines an attractive place for business.

SPECIAL ECONOMIC ZONES

Selected areas in the country have been set up as Special Economic Zones. These contain one or all of the following: an Industrial Estate, an Export Processing Zone, a Free Trade Zone and a Finance and Trade Zone. Export receipts from the country's economic zones account for almost half of the country's total export earnings. Private economic zones outpace government-run zones. Of the four regular zones under the Philippine Economic Zone Authority, the Baguio Export Processing Zone remains the biggest exporter, followed by the Mactan Export Processing Zone, the Cavite Export Processing Zone and the Bataan Export Processing Zone. Other ecozones are located in various parts of the country, including Subic Bay, Clark Field and Cagayan province.

Electronics and their components, apparel, and clothing accessories are the top export earners in the country. Other winners are input/output/peripheral units, ignition wiring and other wiring sets, coconut oil, woodcraft and furniture, metal components, gold, fresh bananas, mineral products, petroleum products and forest products. Other sectors that contribute to the export market are processed fruits, construction materials, marble, computers, ceramics, jewellery, shrimps and prawns, gifts and toys and housewares. The Philippines is a charter member of the World Trade Organization.

Food and Drink

Philippine cuisine has numerous indigenous and foreign influences. Throughout the centuries, the islands have incorporated the cuisine of the early Malay settlers, Arab and Chinese traders, and Spanish and American colonizers, along with other Oriental and Occidental accents and flavours. The strongest culinary influence is from Spain which ruled the Philippines for almost 400 years. Food historians claim that 80 per cent of Philippine dishes are of Spanish origin. Because the Spaniards formed

PHILIPPINE CENTENNIAL

In the closing decade of the 19th century, Filipino nationalist aspirations led to a revolutionary movement which culminated in the proclamation of independence from Spanish colonial rule on 12 June 1898, and the establishment of the First Philippine Republic in 1899.

The 100th anniversary in 1998 of that first proclamation of independence was the focus of celebration throughout the islands and in various parts of the world where there were large communities of Filipinos. An outpouring of nationalist sentiment and artistic creativity marked the Philippines' centennial celebration. Messages and greetings poured in from around the world—from Pope John Paul II, UN Secretary General Kofi Annan, Queen Elizabeth II, US President Bill Clinton and various heads of state, some of whom personally attended the special three-day celebrations. There were mammoth parades, firework displays, a Centennial Ball highlighted by an auction of prized collections and memorabilia, and the Centennial Gowns Parade in which the country's couturiers showed the beauty and elegance of Filipino gowns through ten decades of fashion. Never before had Filipinos witnessed such spectacles or participated in nationwide festivities on such a scale. Historic shrines, statues and markers were unveiled; the National Museum of the Filipino People in Manila and Expo Filipino at Clark in Pampanga were inaugurated. There was street dancing and food festivals, gala concerts and theatre presentations featuring original Filipino compositions and works, a spate of book launches and a week-long film festival, as well as sculpture and painting exhibitions, kite-flying contests showing colourful centennial designs, centennial runs, caravans and treks. There was also a parade on the Pasig River to mark the lighting of seven rehabilitated and spruced up bridges spanning the river.

CENTENNIAL FREEDOM TRAIL

The National Centennial Commission designated a network of historic sites that form the Centennial Freedom Trail so that those who are interested in Philippine history can retrace the trail blazed by those who struggled for freedom. Linked to climactic events between 1896 and 1898 are: Pugad Lawin in Quezon City where the revolution began; Pinaglabanan, San Juan—site of the first battle; Binakayan, Kawit, Cavite—site of the first victory; Dapitan in Zamboanga del Norte where Jose Rizal was exiled; Fort Santiago where he was incarcerated; Rizal Park, then known as Bagumbayan Field where he was executed by firing squad; the Aguinaldo Shrine in Kawit, Cavite where Philippine Independence was first proclaimed; the Barasoain Church in Malolos, where the first Constitution was ratified and the first Philippine Republic was proclaimed. Statues, markers and shrines dedicated to lesser-known heroes and heroines who gave their lives so that Filipinos could be free, were also unveiled during the centennial celebrations.

Activities and festivities began in 1996—the Year of Filipino Heroes—when the country paid tribute to all Filipinos who contributed, directly or indirectly, to the cause of freedom, justice, Philippine independence and nationhood. The year marked the centenaries of two momentous events in Philippine history: the Cry of Pugad Lawin, marking the start of the Philippine Revolution, and the martyrdom of Dr Jose Rizal. The following year commemorated the spread of the revolution from Luzon to the Visayas and Mindanao in 1897 and the martyrdom of hundreds of Filipinos executed in Bagumbayan Field (now Rizal Park). It also marked the 100th anniversary of the death of Andres Bonifacio, Father of the Philippine Revolution.

The Philippine Centennial is an event Filipinos will long remember.

the élite, dishes adapted by upper-class Filipinos were also Spanish-inspired. Thus many of the party and fiesta dishes and those served for special occasions bear names like *relleno, morcon, paella, callos, embutido, caldereta*, etc.

Chinese influence is evident in noodle dishes (*bihon, miki, sotanghon, mami, lomi, miswa*) which go by the general name of *pancit*. Noodle restaurants are called *panciterias* (another Spanish derivation), a term that usually refers to a Chinese eatery. *Pancit Canton* is a favourite of Filipinos when ordering Chinese food, along with *lumpia shanghai* (small spring rolls filled with minced meat and dipped in sweet sauce). Even Chinese dishes have Hispanicized names—*morisqueta tostada* is Yangzhou fried rice, *torta de cangrejo* is crab omelette, *camaron rebozado* is shrimp fried in batter. *Pancit Molo*, an adaptation of wonton soup, is a speciality of the town of Molo in Iloilo. *Pancit luglog, pancit malabon, pancit palabok* are all variations upon the noodle theme. The difference lies in the type of noodle used and the garnishings and flavourings. *Arroz caldo*—rice porridge with slices of chicken meat garnished with chopped spring onions, or *goto*—rice porridge with tripe—are the local versions of the Chinese congee. A less glamorous name for it is *lugaw*. This is a dish which can be ordered in fast-food shops or *carinderias* and is popular with people on a budget. *Siopao* is a steamed bun filled with meat which is usually ordered with *pancit mami*-noodles in soup-to make a filling snack or meal. Chinese sweets popular among Filipinos include *hopia*-flaky pastry with fillings of mashed red or green beans, lotus seed and the like. In Chinatown, small shops sell boxes of piping-hot *hopia* in the afternoons.

Unlike their Southeast Asian neighbours, most Filipinos do not eat chilli-hot dishes, although dishes from the Bicol region are distinguished by their use of chilli and coconut milk, similar to Indonesian, Malay and Thai food. 'Bicol Express' is a fiery dish of pork strips sautéed in garlic, onions, ginger and turmeric, mixed with *bagoong alamang* (salted and fermented shrimp sauce), coconut cream, chopped chillis and hot green and red peppers. Muslim food retains the flavour of its Malay origins. It is spicy and uses coconut milk, chillis, cassava and rice. Many Philippine desserts, particularly those made of rice and coconut, are similar to those of Indonesia and Malaysia. Among these are *biko* and *suman*, sticky rice cooked with coconut milk and sugar and wrapped in banana or *pandan* leaves; *bibingka, puto* and *kutsinta* which are different types of rice cakes, and *bukayo*, a crunchy sweet made of grated coconut cooked in molasses and pressed into bars. Filipino cooking, like other Oriental preparations, involves a lot of chopping and labour-intensive preparation. Rice is the main staple; corn is a substitute in other places. Filipinos prefer to have the entire meal laid out on the table when they eat, rather than have the dishes served one by one. This results in some food being served long after it is piping hot. Filipinos eat with forks and spoons, but in rural areas some people prefer to eat with their hands. *Patis* and *bagoong*, fermented fish or shrimp sauce, similar to those produced by the Vietnamese and Thais, are used to flavour food when cooking and are served as sauces for a variety of dishes such as *kare-kare* or appetisers such as chopped green mangoes.

WHAT TO ORDER

The name of a dish often suggests how it's prepared. *Prito* means fried; *gisa, ginisa* or *gisado* means sautéed. *Ihaw* or *inihaw* means grilled or broiled. *Adobo* is to sautée in vinegar and garlic. *Paksiw* means to stew in sour fruit or vinegar; *ginataan* is anything cooked in coconut milk (*gata*). *Sinigang* is like a bouillabaisse, but thinner in consistency, and uses either fish, prawns or meat with vegetables. It is usually made sour by adding some acidic fruit like tamarind or small green *kamias*.

Much of the fun of visiting another country is trying out its cuisine and sampling regional specialities. Be bold! Worth trying is *adobo*, a dish showing Spanish and Mexican influences but with regional variations. Pork, or a combination of pork and chicken, is stewed in a mixture of vinegar, bay leaf, peppercorns and garlic over a slow fire. Some vegetables and seafood are also cooked *adobo*-style. *Lechon*, pig roasted on a spit, is a fiesta favourite. The crisp and succulent skin is eaten with a sweetish sauce of liver paste. *Kare-kare*, mainly oxtail and eggplants with other vegetables stewed in a rich sauce of ground peanut and toasted ground rice is also found in many Filipino restaurant menus. *Bistek Pilipino* is thin slices of beef marinated in soy sauce and lemon juice and cooked with plenty of onions. *Tinola* is chicken stew. With all the water around the Philippines, fish and seafood are plentiful and fresh. *Bangus* (milkfish), *lapu-lapu* (garoupa or grouper), *tanguingue* and blue marlin are excellent fish. Try the latter grilled with a squeeze of lemon or *calamansi*. *Maliputo* is a tiny freshwater fish with a delicate taste. Seafood is a speciality in many Filipino restaurants. *Hipon* (shrimps), *sugpo* (prawns), lobsters, crayfish and crabs are served in a variety of ways. *Sinigang na sugpo* or *sinigang na hipon* are Filipino favourites. The coconut crab called *tatus* has a rich, nutty flavour and the meat is succulent. The provinces of Pampanga, Iloilo and Negros are also well-known for their cuisine. *Lumpia ubod* (heart of palm) is an Ilonggo spring roll in a soft, crepe-like wrapper stuffed with fresh *ubod* as its main ingredient. Another regional dish is *laing* (pronounced *lah-ing*), a southern speciality of taro leaves simmered in coconut milk and chopped shrimp.

Filipinos flavour their food with dipping sauces (*sawsawan*) according to individual taste. *Bagoong, patis*, vinegar, soya sauce, ketchup and chilli sauce are the usual *sawsawan*. With a squeeze of *calamansi* in the soy sauce or *patis*, a touch of mustard, chilli, or minced garlic in the vinegar, new flavours are created. Filipinos also like sour accompaniments to their food, such as chopped green mangoes mixed with shrimp *bagoong*, or pickled shredded papaya (*achara*).

Visitors can try Philippine food in a variety of settings from smart restaurants and hotel dining rooms to street stalls, fast-food shops and *carinderias*. Eating places that advertise *ihaw-ihaw* serve grilled or barbecued foods, principally meat or seafood. The *turo-turo* (you point to what you want to order) system prevails in *carinderias* or small eateries serving precooked foods. If you happen to be in Metro Manila or the provinces when they hold their food festivals, this is a good opportunity to try the Philippines' regional dishes.

MERIENDA AND SNACKS

The *merienda* is an important Filipino culinary institution. It is a snack taken mid-morning or mid-afternoon. The afternoon *merienda* can include quite a spread of traditional fare, such as *bibingka*, *halo-halo*, *pancit luglog*, *puto* and other typically Filipino pastries and sweets. For those brought up in the Spanish tradition, there's *churros y chocolate*. Melt-in-your-mouth sugared puff pastries (*churros*) are dunked in rich thick chocolate served in small cups. The *bibingka* is a cake made of flour (usually rice flour but also cassava flour), eggs and coconut milk baked in a pan lined with banana leaves to impart a faint fragrance. Some *bibingkas* are baked with salted red eggs and topped with a square of goat cheese placed during the last minutes of baking. It is eaten with freshly grated coconut. There are special *bibingkahan*, places where *bibingkas* are baked and served. *Ginataan* taken at *merienda* is a mixture of diced tubers such as *gabi*, *ube* and *camote* (sweet potato), sliced plantain, strips of breadfruit and some sago or tapioca all cooked together in thick coconut milk with sugar to taste. Coconut is an important ingredient in the preparation of many sweets and desserts. Various types of rice cakes, glutinous and non-glutinous, are also *merienda* fare, as well as fiesta fare. *Pandan* cake from the pandanus plant has a delicate flavour. *Ube*, a violet-coloured tuber, is also used to make cakes, ice creams and jam. *Turron*, banana encased in a spring roll wrapper and fried, is popular as a snack or dessert. It is sometimes encased with a slice of jackfruit or *langka*.

Bakeries are found all over the country. Some turn out excellent breads, Western-style cakes and pastries. Hard rolls (*pan de sal*) are traditionally eaten for breakfast. *Ensaymadas*, which are sugared sweet rolls with cheese topping, can be taken at breakfast or tea.

PHILIPPINE FRUIT

Feast on tropical fruit while in the Philippines. Some fruits are available all year round, others are more seasonal. The markets are good places to buy fruit. The

Philippines has many varieties of bananas, most of which are only available locally as they cannot stand long-haul travel. The *lacatan* is fragrant and sweet and is a year-round fruit. Try other varieties. The Philippines exports a lot of mangoes. They are fleshy, sweet and succulent and can be enjoyed most months of the year. Mangoes are also sold in dried form. Pineapples are sweet and juicy. Other fruits are papayas or pawpaws, chicos, *atis* (custard apple), *guayabano* (soursop), pomelos, rambutan, lanzones, etc. The flesh of the young coconut (*buko*) is a refreshing snack.

THIRST-QUENCHERS AND COOLERS

Taking time off from the Ati-Atihan festival

Teetotallers who want something different from carbonated soft drinks will have a wonderful time in the Philippines trying various fruit juices and fruit shakes. Small green lemons known as *calamansi* have a sharp and tangy flavour and are excellent either as a hot or iced beverage. *Calamansi* and soda is a refreshing drink. Other delightful thirst-quenchers are the juices of ripe mango, green mango, pineapple, *guayabano*, watermelon and melon. Or try Four Seasons, a mixture of the juice of four fruits. Coconut water from the young green coconut is another favourite. In the countryside it is often served in its unhusked shell. Hotel bartenders specialize in concocting drinks with fruity flavours.

Fermented drinks produced in the Philippines include *tuba* from the sap of coconut, *buri* or nipa palms. When the sap is distilled it becomes a potent liquor called *lambanog*. *Layaw* is made from a very strong maize spirit and is usually found in the Cagayan Valley. The mountain tribes in the Cordilleras ferment rice to make *tapuy* wine, while *basi* is sugar cane wine made by the Ilocanos and Kalingas. Grape wine is also produced in Cebu and the Ilocos. There's also a white wine made from *casuy*-cashew. Aged Philippine rum is well known and inexpensive. Then there's San Miguel beer, the best-known national brand. A wide selection of alcoholic drinks is available in supermarkets.

ICE CREAM AND HALO-HALO

Lovers of ice-cream are in for a treat in the Philippines, with a great variety of flavours to choose from. *Macapuno* and *Ube* are among the best flavours. The Brussels-based Monde Selection has awarded the Palm d'Or (Gold Palm Leaves), the highest accolade given for ice creams of distinction, to Magnolia's Ube Supreme and Caramel 'n Cream. Arce ice cream uses *carabao* milk which imparts a distinctive taste to its products.

Ice-cream is readily available in the big shopping malls. Ambulatory vendors sell by the scoop. Ice cream packed in dry ice is a popular take-home purchase for tourists. Check with the airline personnel at the Ninoy Aquino International Airport departure lounge. The dry ice keeps the ice-cream frozen for about nine hours.

Halo-halo is a great favourite among Filipinos, particularly during the hot summer months when it is a refreshing treat. This is a layered concoction of various ingredients—caramel custard, diced gelatin, candied beans, preserved jackfruit, *macapuno* or *kaong*, *ube* jam—topped with shaved ice and milk.
For the special *halo-halo*, a scoop of ice cream is added.

VARIETY: THE SPICE OF LIFE

Restaurants, cafés and bistros serving a range of cuisines from Philippine to Chinese, Japanese, Korean, Thai, Indian, French, Spanish, Mexican, Italian, American, German, Swiss and Austrian are found in Metro Manila and the big cities and towns in the Philippines. Hamburgers and hot dogs with all the trimmings, pizzas thick and thin with various toppings, spaghetti, sticks of barbecued meat, noodles, rice with different toppings are available in fast-food shops and snack kiosks.

Arts and Culture

The Philippines has an active artistic and cultural life. There are concerts and recitals, theatre and drama productions on stage and television, painting and art exhibitions, museum displays, lectures and discussions, dance performances and workshops, film festivals, and literary contests on-going at any given time in cities and towns.

In Metro Manila, for instance, free performances are held during their season in several venues: at the Rizal Park open-air auditorium on Sunday afternoons at 5 o'clock; at the old Paco Park on Friday evenings at 6 o'clock; in various venues within Intramuros every other week on Fridays and Saturdays at 6.30 pm; at the Quezon Memorial Circle's Liwasang Aurora in Quezon City on Sundays at 6 pm. There are also special events held from time to time at Nayong Pilipino near the airport, and other venues.

Like a pearl, Philippine culture has grown through a long and slow process of accretion. Indian, Chinese, Arabic Spanish, American and other foreign influences have added lustre to the pearl. As a result, Philippine art, literature, beliefs, customs and traditions, morals, knowledge and laws have been significantly enriched. The preservation, enrichment, and dynamic evolution of a Filipino national culture based on the principle of unity in diversity and nurtured in a climate of free artistic and intellectual expression is guaranteed in the Philippine Constitution.

It is the National Commission for Culture and the Arts that is empowered to develop, promote, disseminate and preserve the Filipino arts and cultural heritage. The framework for cultural development in the country up to the year 2000 is contained in the Philippine Development Plan for Culture and the Arts. The Cultural Centre co-ordinates artisic and cultural activities. It not only promotes local artists but also brings in outstanding foreign performers. Within the complex are the Main Theatre, art galleries, a museum and library, Folk Arts Theatre and Film Theatre. The Centre serves as a national venue and showcase for the works of Filipino artists in the fields of dance, drama, music and the visual arts. The National Museum, together with the National Library, are the official repositories of the country's historical and cultural heritage.

To encourage the growth of the arts, talented young Filipinos who show great promise are admitted as scholars to the government-run Philippine High School for the Arts, established in 1977. In the serene and wooded surroundings of Mount Makiling in Los Banos, Laguna, the young scholars are trained to fulfil their talents to be able to compete in the international art world. Scholars specialize in theatre, ballet, folk dance, classical music, creative writing and painting. The most talented and most promising young Filipino artists in the musical arts are discovered in the National Music Competitions for Young Artists held yearly at the Cultural Centre of the Philippines.

For up-to-date information on cultural events in the country, consult the newspapers and tourist publications.

MUSIC

The Philippines has a diverse musical culture that blends Eastern and Western influences. Traditional Philippine music is made up of the indigenous music of pre-Hispanic times and music derived from the Spanish era. An example of the former is the music produced by the cultural minorities with gongs and bamboo nose flutes. The Mangyan *git-git* (a violin with strings made of human hair), the T'boli *hagalong* (a two-stringed lute) and the Muslim *kulintang*, a set of pitched brass or bronze gongs usually played on festive occasions, are examples of ethnic musical instruments still in use in the country. Spanish music—both religious and secular—has influenced the *kundiman* of the Tagalogs, the *balitaw* of the Visayans and the *dal'lot* of the Ilocanos. These are often sentimental and melodic tunes accompanied by a guitar.

Filipinos have an innate sense of rhythm and music is very much part of their daily lives. Many children learn to play the piano, violin or some other musical instrument at a young age. The more talented go on to a conservatory of music or study abroad and gain recognition as concert pianists, vocalists, violinists, recording artists and conductors. They participate in international music competitions and music festivals. Filipinos have distinguished themselves as members of the cast in the long-running West End production of the Cameron Mackintosh musical *Miss Saigon* and many have gone on to perform on Broadway, in Germany and Australia. Lea Salonga, then a 17-year-old member of Repertory Philippines, after a worldwide talent search won the lead role of Kim in the West End and later the Broadway productions, for which she received the Lawrence Olivier, Drama Desk, Outer Critics' Circle and Tony awards. She later played Eponine on Broadway in *Les Miserables*. Lea also lent her singing voice to the female lead characters in two Walt Disney animated features—*Aladdin* and *Mulan*, the latter based on one of China's most popular legends.

Filipinos enjoy a wide range of music, from classical to folk, pop, rock and jazz. There are symphony orchestras and chamber groups, jazz, pop and rock bands and combos, and ensembles playing native instruments in the cities and towns. Filipino bands and entertainers are making a name for themselves in various parts of Asia. Filipino compositions in Tagalog and English sung by popular Filipino vocalists enjoy a vast following. Ryan Cayabcab is well-known for his musical compositions. Freddie Aguilar's composition, *Anak* (Child), has been translated into 40 languages worldwide. In the field of classical music, contemporary Filipino composers are using Western idioms to interpret folk themes and legends. Jose Maceda, an ethnomusicologist and composer, shows this in his *avant garde* compositions while Lucrecia Kasilag and Lucio San Pedro, National Artists for Music, and younger composers are producing works with a distinct cultural personality. A Kundiman Festival

(preceding pages) Members of a marching band relax after a parade

is held yearly at the Folk Arts Centre in Manila. Regional winners singing the plaintive Philippine love songs vie for the national championship.

Concerts and recitals by the Philippine Philharmonic Orchestra, Philippine Madrigal Singers, and other Philippine musical groups, as well as by visiting international artists are regularly presented at the Cultural Centre in Manila and other big cities in the Philippines. The International Bamboo Organ Festival held in February each year attracts overseas participation.

DANCE

Dance in its various forms—from the indigenous folk dances of tribal, Muslim and non-Christian Filipinos to dances of Christian and lowland Filipinos; from classical ballet to jazz and modern dance; from ballroom dancing to sport and power dancing—all find expression in the Philippines. The dances of the Philippines are many and diverse. In their purest form the dances of cultural minorities and 'pagan' groups are living documentaries of the most significant aspects of community life, from birth to death. Two women—Francisca Reyes Aquino and Leonor Orosa Goquinco—have done much to preserve the country's traditional folk dances—Aquino by her research and documentation, and Goquingco by elevating the folk dance to the stage in her Filipinescas dance troupe. Goquingco's choreographic works have gained her recognition as a national Artist for Dance. The growth of ballet in the Philippines has been influenced by the Philippine performances of Anna Pavlova, Mia Slavenska, Alexandra Danilova, Dame Margot Fonteyn, Natalia Makarova, Maya Plissetskaya and the stars of the Bolshoi.

Various dance studios, ballet groups and folk dance troupes have brought Philippine dance to the world. One of the most oustanding and earliest exponents of Philippine dance, the Bayanihan Philippine Dance Company was organized in 1957 to represent the Philippines in the Brussels International Exposition, and is today hailed as one of the best dance groups in the world of theatre. Since its foundation, it has undertaken ten world tours. Other dance groups have followed in Bayanihan's footsteps. The Ramon Obusan Folkloric Group also represented the Philippines in various festivals in Europe and Asia. The Integrated Performing Arts Guild, a dance theatre company founded 40 years ago, sets Mindanao folk tales and epics to dance. It now boasts a repertoire of over 40 full-length productions and has received various national awards and endowments.

Ballet Philippines remains at the forefront of modern dance in Asia. It performed at the 1998 World Expo in Portugal and toured Germany, England, Switzerland, Japan, United States and Canada bringing award-winning, original Filipino dance pieces as part of its Centennial Tour. Ballet Manila, organized by Liza Macuja, once a

soloist of the Leningrad-Kirov Ballet, is the premiere classical ballet company in the country. The troupe performed to enthusiastic crowds in Krasnoyarsk in Siberia in 1995. In the Philippines, it is presenting original Filipino ballets and dance dramas especially created for the country's centennial celebrations. Other dance groups include Philippine Ballet Theatre, Ballet Philippines II. Ballet camps participated in by ballet schools, academies and directors, and summer dance workshops are part of the dance scene. Power and sport dances also have their following, while ballroom dancing exhibitions and contests are held regularly.

THEATRE

The Philippines shares with Indonesia and Malaysia a traditional form of Asian theatre, that of shadow puppets (*wayang*). Called the *carillo*, and performed with papier-mâché figures, it was one of the earliest local forms of theatre. The Spaniards introduced *cenaculos*, religious plays based on the passion and death of Jesus performed on stage during fiestas. These are still a feature of Holy Week observance in Bulacan, Nueva Ecija and Pampanga. The Moriones Festival, a highlight of the Easter rites in Marinduque, and Panuluyan, a re-enactment of the search for shelter by Joseph and Mary on Christmas Eve, held in Kawit, Cavite, are examples of street theatre still in vogue today.

Also part of traditional Philippine theatre are the *Moro-moros*, dramas highlighting Christian and Muslim conflicts and comedias or *komedya*—romantic tales of love and honour. Written in vernacular verse, these are staged against a backdrop of a medieval castle or palace and performed to the music of a brass band. The *moro-moro* and *komedya* used to be one of the main features of a town fiesta. This has largely died out but theatre groups are reviving these traditional plays. The San Dionisio theatre group in Parañaque, Metro Manila still stages these dramas. The *yawa-yawa*, a vernacular play depicting the life of San Miguel (Saint Michael the Archangel) in song and dance, was a highlight of the Iligan City fiesta. Another popular form of entertainment was the *zarzuela*, a light operetta or romantic musical comedy introduced by the Spaniards in the 19th century. The story, language and music were Filipinized and the *zarzuela* or *sarswela* became a vehicle for social and political satire directed against the Spaniards and Americans. It peaked in popularity in the 1920s but today is enjoying a revival by contemporary theatre groups.

There are various theatre groups in the Philippines, from Northern Luzon all the way down to Mindanao. In Metro Manila, the professional theatre groups are: The Philippine Educational Theatre Association (PETA), founded in 1967 by Cecile Guidote Alvarez, which performs mostly Filipino plays at the open-air theatre at Fort Santiago; Rody Vera is its artistic director. Repertory Philippines, founded in

A massive crowd gathers in front of the Quiapo Church in Manila for the annual January fiesta

1962 by Zeneida Amador, its current artistic director, stages mainly Broadway and London West End hits at the William J Shaw Theatre in Shangri-la Plaza, its home. School-based groups include Dulaang UP from the University of the Philippines; Teatrong Mulat, a puppet theatre based also at the UP, and Tanghalang Ateneo of the Ateneo University. The San Dionisio troupe in Parañaque and Dalampasigan in Pasig are community theatre groups while Teatro Pabrika is a theatre group of workers from labour unions. All the groups have a regular season. Productions range from original plays with a historical focus or adaptations from folk or modern literature, revivals of *sarswela*, *komedya* and drama, experimental plays, ethnic-based or Broadway-type musicals and Western dramas. The 100th anniversary of the Philippine proclamation of independence has inspired the production of historic plays, dance dramas, and musical productions presented on stage and television.

The Philippines also participates in international and regional drama and theatre festivals and is actively involved with international programmes.

CINEMA

The cinema is the most popular form of entertainment in the country. Filipinos are avid movie-goers and the film industry finds a mass market. Local film stars have a vast following. Cinema houses are now an integral part of the modern shopping mall. People can enter anytime during the screening and can stay on for as many screenings as they wish. Tickets are inexpensive.

Filipinos were introduced to European film shorts and excerpts from musicals in 1897 but it was not until 1912 that the first Filipino film based on the life of Jose Rizal, the country's national hero, was shown. Jose Nepomuceno and Vicente Salumbides were the early filmmakers. Nepomuceno produced his first feature film—*Dalagang Bukid* (Country Damsel)—in 1919. He was a dominant figure in the film industry for the next 25 years. The first 'talkie' was shown in 1929. A British engineer arrived in Manila with 35 cases of equipment and 35,000 feet of film. Immediately after the showing, Manilans succumbed to the talkie fever. The first film made in the Philippines to feature optically recorded sound was *Ang Aswang* (The Witch) released in 1932. Colour films were introduced in the 1930s. The year before World War II was one of Philippine cinema's great periods with musicals, melodramas, horror films, South Sea dramas and films with a nationalistic slant. The period also saw the rise of the big stars. Mainly Japanese propaganda films were produced during the war years. The 1950s was the era of the big studios. LVN, Sampaguita and Premier were the top filmmakers. The star system flourished at that time. Independent producers began to challenge the supremacy of the big studios in the 1960s. Hit by labour problems, the film studios one by one collapsed. A genre of films known as *bomba* or sex films became popular in the late 60s. When the films turned pornographic, there was a civic protest which resulted in the implementation of a new code prohibiting explicit sexual scenes on film.

Films of significance were produced in the mid 70s and 80s by a group of directors: Lino Brocka, Ishmael Bernal, Eddie Romero, Cesar Castillo, Gerardo de Leon, Peque Gallaga, Mike de Leon and others. The late Lino Brocka's films blended popular entertainment, realism and social comment. Some of his films were seen at Cannes and other film festivals in France, namely Nantes and Paris. A retrospective of the best in Philippine cinema was the local film industry's salute to the nation as it celebrated the 100th anniversary of independence.

LITERATURE

The ancient Filipinos had a strong oral tradition. Folk epics, creation myths, legends and fables, and songs and poems relating the deeds of gods and heroes were handed down from generation to generation. The Ilocano *Lam-ang*, the Bicolano *Ibalong*, the Ifugao *Hudhud* and *Alim*, and the Maranao *Darangan* are among the epics. The story and characters of some of the epics show similarities with the *Ramayana*, the *Mahabharata* and other Indian epics. Scholars claim that the Tagalog tale of the monkey and the turtle, the tale of the hawk and the hen of the Visayans, and even the adventures of the legendary Juan Tamad, show Indian influence. Little remains of the written literature of the pre-Hispanic era for these were inscribed on bamboo tubes, tree bark and banana leaves. However, some works which were translated by Spanish scholars still exist, such as the Code of Kalantiaw, written in Panay in 1433. An old Spanish manuscript recounting a fragment of a Bicol epic has also been discovered in Iriga, Camarines Sur. The Muslims have their own religious literature, as well as *tarsilas*, genealogies tracing the descent of sultans and royal *datus*.

The *awit* and *corrido*, based on Spanish romances, are forms of metrical verse that were popular during the Spanish era. The most famous writer of this period was Francisco Baltazar (1789–1862) of Bulacan, known by his native name, Balagtas. He wrote *Florante at Laura*, an allegorical Tagalog poem about the Christian victory over the Moors which contains a veiled protest against Spanish misrule. *Urbana at Feliza* was written by a Tagalog priest, Don Modesto de Castro, in the form of letters written by the characters in the book. Intended for the rising educated Tagalog class, it stressed proper behaviour and etiquette. The book was translated into other Philippine languages such as Visaya, Bicol and Ilocano. M H del Pilar (pen name, Plaridel) from Bulacan was a master satirist whose wit helped stir up revolutionary sentiment. The greatest Filipino novels, Jose Rizal's *Noli Me Tangere* and its sequel *El Filibusterismo*, were published in Spanish and played a major role in precipitating the revolution. These books are available in English at bookstores.

Filipino authors write in English, Pilipino (Tagalog) and regional dialects. Nick Joaquin is the National Artist for Literature. F Sionil José, Carmen Guerrero Nakpil, and Gregorio Brillantes are among the noted contemporary authors writing in English whose works are published abroad. National Achievement Awards in Literature or *Gawad Balagtas* are conferred on writers of fiction, essays, poetry and drama in English, Pilipino and other dialects by the Writers Union of the Philippines or *Unyon ng mga Manunulat sa Pilipinas* (UMPIL). A National Writers.

VISUAL ARTS

The works of early Filipino painters and artists were religious in theme and often featured aspects of indigenous art derived from woodcarvings and textile designs. The first Filipino to paint non-religious themes and to gain renown for his portraits and miniatures was Damian Domingo, a mestizo born at the end of the 18th century. He was appointed professor of the Academy of Drawing, established in Manila in 1821. The academy produced such artists as Juan Arceo, Jose Lozano, Antonio Malantik, Juan Luna and Felix Resurreccion Hidalgo, all of whom gained fame abroad. Luna trained in Madrid and depicted themes of social significance in his paintings. His most famous works include *The Spoliarium*, which won a gold medal

The statue of General Pio del Pilar in Makati

in Madrid and is at the Hall of Masters in the National Museum in Manila, *The Death of Cleopatra*, *The Battle of Lepanto*, and *People and Kings*. Other works by Luna, such as *Una Bulaqueña* and *El Pacto de Sangre* (The Blood Compact) are in the collection of the Malacañang Museum. Luna's birthplace in Badoc, Ilocos Norte, is now a museum and contains copies of his paintings. Hidalgo lived in Paris and painted impressionistic land- and seascapes. Filipino genre painting of the mid- to late 19th century portrayed landscapes, rural life and figures that reflected growing nationalistic sentiments. The most celebrated artist of this time was Fernando Amorsolo, the first National Artist, famous for his landscapes. Amorsolo's *Harvest Scene* is part of the Malacañang Palace collection. Another genre painter whose murals—*Pista sa Nayon* and *Sanduguan*—have adorned the state dining room of Malacañang is Carlos 'Botong' Francisco.

Victorio Edades, Galo B Ocampo, Carlos V Francisco, Diosdado Lorenzo, Vicente Manansala, H R Ocampo, Cesar Legaspi, Anita Magsaysay Ho are among the modernist painters. The Philippines' prominent artists work in a wide range of styles and media. Notable sculptors are Nap Abueva, Renato Rocha, Edgardo Castrillo, Solomon Saprid, and Guillermo Tolentino, whose imposing bronze monuments include a depiction of a revolutionary event, *Cry of Pugad Lawin*, and *The Oblation*, a symbol of freedom at the entrance to the University of the Philippines in Quezon City.

Art galleries in Manila feature the works of contemporary painters and sculptors. The Ateneo Art Gallery at Ateneo University houses an exemplary modern art collection. There are permanent and changing exhibitions at the Metropolitan Museum of Manila on Roxas Blvd, Ayala Museum in Makati, National Museum on Burgos Street, the Cultural Centre complex on Roxas Boulevard, and the galleries of the National Commission on Culture and the Arts in Intramuros. Privately owned sales galleries exhibit the works of established as well as up-and-coming painters and sculptors. The Luz Gallery, Genesis Gallery, Galeria de las Islas, Finale Art File, Hiraya Gallery are among these. The Artwalk on the fourth level of the Megamall in Mandaluyong EDSA has a row of sales galleries with changing exhibits. *Kanlungan ng Sining* (Artists' Haven) is an environmental art gallery at Rizal Park dedicated to the works of Filipino artists. Members of the Art Association of the Philippines use this as a venue for their works. There are also sidewalk galleries in the Tourist Belt of Ermita. In Angono, Rizal province, there is a thriving colony of artists whose works are exhibited not only in the Philippines but overseas. The Blanco and Miranda families are examples (see also page 191).

Cinema Paradiso

Well, we went last night to a cinematograph show, which has established itself in a big empty basement in the Calle Real, with a large sign outside, made of glass letters lighted behind with electricity, all in the most approved European style. The 'show' lasts for half-an-hour, going on from six in the evening to about ten o'clock at night, and the proprietor makes about 300 pesos a week out of it, for he has very few expenses, and it is the sort of thing these people love. They come out when the show is over, stand about and expectorate for a few minutes, and then pay their cents and go in again and enjoy the same thing about five times running, probably without the faintest idea what it is all about from start to finish.

Everything in the hall was boarded up to prevent any stray, non-paying enthusiast from getting a free peep; but all the same I saw several little brown forms in fluttering muslin shirts, outside, where the wall formed a side street, with eyes glued to the chinks of a door in rapt attention; though I don't suppose the little chaps could really see anything but the extreme edge of the back row of benches.

In the hall we were saved from suffocation by two electric fans, and kept awake by a Filipino playing a cracked old piano with astonishing dexterity, rattling out the sort of tunes you hear in a circus and nowhere else on earth. I could not help wondering where he had picked them up, till it suddenly dawned on me that one, at least, gave me a faint hint that perhaps the performer might once have heard Hiawatha on a penny flute; so I concluded that he was playing 'variations.' Pianos never sound very well out here, and I am told it is difficult to keep them bearable at all, for the chords have an unmusical way of going rusty in the damp season, or else snapping with a loud ping.

The moving pictures were not at all bad, rather jumpy at times, but the subjects really quite entertaining, and all the slides, from the appearance of the figures on them, made in Germany, I imagine. The series wound up with an interminable fairy tale in coloured pictures, really a sort of short play, and in this one could see the German element still more apparent, in the castles, the ancient costumes, and the whole composition of the thing. I don't suppose the natives in the audience had the wildest idea what it was all about, or what the king and queen, the good fairy, and the wicked godmother were meant to be, probably taking the whole story for some episode in the life of a saint.

The audience were really more amusing to me than the pictures, and I was quite pleased each time the light went up so that I could have a good look at them. In the front rows, which were cheap, as they were so close to the screen, sat the poorer people in little family groups, with clean camisas and large cigars, the women's hair looking like black spun glass. Our places were raised a little above them, and were patronised by the swells who had paid forty cents-a-shilling. Amongst the elect were one or two English and other foreigners; some fat Chinamen, with their pigtails done up in chignons, and wearing open-work German straw hats, accompanied by their native wives and little slant-eyed children; a few missionaries and schoolma'ams in coloured blouses and untidy coiffures à la Gibson Girl; and one or two U.S.A. soldiers, with thick hair parted in the middle, standing treat to their Filipina girls-these last in pretty camisas, and very shy and happy. A funny little Filipino boy near us, rigged up in a knickerbocker suit and an immense yellow oil-skin motor-cap, was rather frightened at old Tuyay, who had insisted on coming to the show and sitting at our feet. When she sniffed the bare legs of this very small 'brown brother', he lost all his dignity and importance, and clung blubbering to his little flat-faced mother. Poor old Tuyay was dreadfully offended; she came and crawled right under C–'s chair, where she lay immovable till the performance was over.

Mrs Campbell Dauncey, The Philippines;
An Account of Their People, Progress, and Condition

Flora and Fauna

The Philippines is one of the richest countries in the world when it comes to biological diversity—that is, the variety of flora, fauna and living organisms that form the terrestrial, wetland and marine ecosystems. Indeed, Nature dealt the Philippines a lavish hand when distributing its wildlife resources. The archipelago's forests, mangrove swamps, and coastal strands are the habitat of at least 12,000 plant species and 22 species of beach vegetation; 230–240 species of mammals; 186 species of reptiles, 556 species of birds; 16,704 species of insects and 850 species of butterflies. Its waters are home to 2,175 fish species; 98 species of amphibians; about 488 species of hard and soft coral; and over 21,000 species of shells. Half of the species of plants and animals found here are endemic. Human need and greed and the steady exploitation of the natural resources have resulted in the degradation of forests, swamps and coral reefs. This loss of habitat has meant the disappearance of many species and many more are threatened with extinction. Some 18 species are on the endangered list.

FLORA

In their flowering season shrubs, herbs, vines and trees create a vivid, unforgettable canvas of colours in town and country.

The Philippines' warm tropical climate and fertile volcanic soil encourages the growth of many genera and species of plants. Of the plant species found in the country, more than 8,120 are flowering plants. The rest are ferns, fern allies, mosses, liverworts, fungi, algae, and lichens.

Among the more common flowering vines are the *sampaguita* (*Jasminum sambac*), bougainvillaea, *dama de noche* (*Cestrum nocturnum*) and *cadena de amor* (*Antigonon leptopus*). The *sampaguita*, with its fragrant, tiny, white star-shaped blooms, is the Philippines' national flower and is associated with many legends. Strung into garlands, it is sold

The Philippine Tarsier

on the streets by itiner-
ant vendors, given as
welcome leis to impor-
tant visitors arriving at
the airport or to hon-
oured guests at festi-
vals or formal
gatherings. It is be-
lieved to have been
introduced during
prehistoric times,
probably when the
Philippines was part of

the Asian landmass, since the plant is also found in India and other parts of Asia.

Bougainvillaea grow in abundance on the islands—there are about 50 varieties—
and they flaunt their clusters of blossoms in colours ranging from white, yellow,
pale lavender, blue and pink to tan, orange, magenta, red and deep purple.

The hibiscus or gumamela, with its huge showy flowers, also thrives in the
islands. Flowering throughout the year, it is used in landscaping, especially on golf
courses, resorts, and in hotel grounds. Eleven new hybrids have been produced by
Dr Reynold Pimentel and his team from the Institute of Plant Breeding in UP Los
Baños to honour ten Filipino women who played a role in the country's struggle for
freedom.

Of the 1,000 species of orchids growing on the islands, 84 per cent are endemic.
They range from cattleyas to dendrobiums, phalaenopsis and vandas. Among them

are the butterfly orchid,
the well-known *waling-
waling*, (*Vanda sanderi-
ana*) found in
Mindanao, whose long-
lasting cluster of
blooms measures up to
12.5 cm (5 inches)
across and the rare
Phalaenopsis grandiflora
from Palawan and
Phalaenopsis lindenii
from the Cordilleras.

Various species of orchids grow abundantly in the Philippines

The destruction of forests has caused the loss of orchid species and sadly, many orchid producers still take species from the forest instead of growing them commercially. At the 9th Asean Orchid Congress hosted by the Philippines in 1994, the second time the prestigious event was held in the country, the appeal for the conservation of orchid species was again sounded. The Congress also called for a new survey of existing species and the setting up of a national orchidarium in each of the participating countries. The Philippines has an active orchid society, and there are also various horticultural clubs.

Philippine flora shows strong links with that of Borneo, Java, Sumatra, Australia and even the Himalayas. Sixteen genera of plants native to Australia are found in the Philippines. One of the few representatives of the family *myrtaceae* (eg myrtle, clove, guava, eucalyptus) outside Australia, for example, is found in Mindanao. The Benguet pine growing in the Mountain Provinces suggests Himalayan or Asiatic origins. The Philippines has many plants in common with Borneo, Java, Celebes and Sumatra. Some 60 species of flora found in Palawan, Mindoro, and western and central Mindanao are also found in Borneo. These floral migrations took place when the land bridges were still in place.

FAUNA

Most of the animals on the islands are relatively small. The largest species in the country is the Philippine Tamaraw (*Bubalus mindorensis*) which is related to the dwarf water buffalo found in the Celebes. The *tamaraw* is on the international list of endangered species and is now protected in wildlife sanctuaries in the mountains of Mindoro. There is an ongoing Tamaraw Conservation Programme. The Philippine Spotted Deer (*Cervus alfredi*) is another threatened species. Other Philippine fauna are nocturnal flying lemurs, the rare cloud rat found in the mountains of Northern Luzon, Marinduque and Mindoro, clawless otters, Scaly Anteater (*Paramanis cullonensis*), Palawan Bearcat (*Arctictis binturong*), Little Leopard Cat (*Felix bengalensis*), as well as the Calamian deer and Philippine Mouse Deer (*Tragulus napu*) and Philippine Tarsier (*Tarsius syrichta*).

Of the reptiles which are well represented, there are many species of lizards (including iguanas and monitor lizards), snakes (king cobra, pythons) and crocodiles, such as the endemic, endangered Philippine Crocodile (*Crocodylus porosus*).

BIRDS

The Philippines' bird population is spread over four distinct geographical areas: the eastern chain of islands stretching from Luzon to Mindanao; the central Visayas; the outlying islands such as northern Batanes, Babuyan and Mindoro; and the Sulu archipelago and Palawan. Of the 556 species in the Philippines, 160 are endemic. Many subspecies have also evolved over the centuries, and now some 63 species are known as 'single-island endemics'. Philippine birds may be classified into the following categories: marine and shoreland, swampland, forest, urban, grassland, agricultural and village birds.

Among Philippine birds are the Philippine hawk eagle, Philippine cockatoo, Philippine mallard, wandering whistling duck, Great Scops owl, Luzon bleeding heart, greater painted snipe, Koch's Pitta, and Rufous hornbill. The swamps of Cagayan Valley, Central Plain and Bicol are the habitats of the rare Eastern Sarus or Sharpe's crane. The world's smallest falcon is the Philippine falconet or pygmy falcon. Many rare and unique species of birds are found in the forests, mangrove swamps and grasslands of Palawan, a bird-watcher's paradise, such as the endangered Palawan peacock pheasant which has been successfully bred in captivity. Its avifauna show strong links with Borneo and Malaysia.

The most famous of the feathered species in the archipelago is the Philippine eagle (*Pithecophaga jefferyi*), commonly known as the *haribon* (meaning, king of birds). This is the country's national bird, and the world's second largest species of eagle. It has a wing span of two metres (6.5 feet), stands one metre (3.3 feet) high and weighs from four to eight kilos (8.8–17.6 pounds). Its sight is said to be eight times more acute than man's. It can pounce with deadly accuracy and break the neck of an 18-kilogram (40-pound) monkey, carrying it off to its eyrie, or crack the skull of a cobra. This king of birds once reigned supreme in the rainforests of Mindanao, but it has been extensively hunted and trapped, and its habitat systematically destroyed by deforestation and slash-and-burn agriculture. From an estimated population of 10,000 some years ago, only about 300 remain. The bird has been declared an endangered species by the International Union for the Conservation of Nature and Natural Resources.

Efforts to save the eagle in the wild and to breed it in captivity is ongoing at the Philippine Eagle Centre on the slopes of Mt Apo in Davao. Sixteen eagles (male and female) are in captivity; and 58 eagles in the wild are being monitored. The eagle's monogamous habit (it will not mate with another eagle once it loses its natural partner) and its rather slow reproductive cycle means a long process for the breeding programme to bear results. After 15 years of effort by Mr Dominador Tadena using in-vitro fertilization, two female eaglets were successfully hatched at the Eagle Centre in 1992. Sadly, the mother eagle died of cardio-pulmonary arrest in 1994 at the age of 25 years.

■ BIRD-WATCHING

Ornithologists have good opportunities to sight a variety of birds due to the abundance of shoreline, grassland, mountains and forests. Even in the urban areas, orioles, mynahs, kingfishers, bulbuls and warblers make their presence known with their songs and chatter or a flash of plumage as they catch the sunlight. In addition to catching sight of Philippine species, bird-watchers may also see a number of other species as the Philippines is on the migration path of birds and its islands are resting places for several species of birds.

Places where bird populations are concentrated are Quezon National Park, the Tubbataha Reefs, Candaba Marsh in Pampanga, Pagsanjan River delta at Lumban on Laguna de Bay, Lake Naujan in Mindoro, St Paul Subterranean River National Park and the offshore islands of Palawan, Mt Kanlaon National Park in Negros, Pontong Lake near Santadar and Pacijan Island, Cebu, Mt Apo National Park in Davao, and Batanes. Birdlife is prolific along the shorelines. Because of the importance of shorelines and atolls as breeding grounds and habitats for shore and sea birds, some areas have been designated as nature reserves.

On the North Islet of Tubbataha Reef Marine Park thousands of sea birds, such as boobies and terns, and endangered sea turtles converge every year to lay their eggs. This spectacular marine park has been declared a World Heritage Site by the UNESCO not only to preserve its special ecosystem but also for its scientific value.

A comprehensive study of the Philippines' bird population still has to be conducted. Deforestation and poaching have diminished populations and several species are now either endangered, threatened or vulnerable. The Philippine eagle, the green-winged ground dove, black-naped oriole, white-breasted sea eagle, gray-headed fishing eagle are among the endangered species.

BUTTERFLIES AND MOTHS

Butterflies and moths abound, particularly in Palawan, Mindanao and Sulu. Of the 850 species, the most spectacular are the giant *Papilio trojano*, a black-and-green butterfly with a wing span of 18 cm (7 inches) found only in Palawan; the black and yellow male *Troides magallanes*; and the huge Atlas moth measuring 24 cm (9.4 inches) from wing tip to wing tip.

MARINE FAUNA

Fed by the currents of the Sea of Japan, the South China Sea, the Indian Ocean, the Pacific Ocean and the Celebes Sea, Philippine waters harbour a wealth of marine life representative of the whole Indo-Pacific region, from spectacular

Thatched nipa huts strung along White Beach on Boracay Island

coral species to sponges and gorgonians, from pelagic fish to reef fish and shells. Freshwater lakes, rivers and streams also are home to a variety of creatures. Commercial fish such as roundscad, sardines, frigate tuna, anchovies, slipmouth, yellowfish, big-eyed scad, threadfin bream, round herring, skipjack, mullet, fusilier, garoupa, cavalla and mackerel are found in Philippine seas. Shrimps, crabs, prawns and mussels abound. Sport fishermen go after marlin, swordfish, sailfish and tuna. Tiny fish such as the *tabios*, a species of goby, and tiny translucent dwarf pygmy goby are endemic. Marine turtles (known locally as *pawikan*) include the green sea turtle, hawksbill, loggerhead, Olive Ridley and leatherback.

The Philippines has thousands of shells, many unique to the country, ranging in size from the tiny picidum to the giant clam which grows to 1.4 metres (4.6 feet). The rare golden cowrie, the magnificent *Conus gloriamaris* or Glory of the Sea is also found. Shells abound in Sorsogon, Eastern Samar, Palawan, Sulu and Tayabas Bay (Quezon). Natural pearls, noted for their size and lustre, are harvested from oysters and clams obtained by deep-sea divers.

CONSERVATION PROGRAMME

Recognising the critical importance of protecting and maintaining the natural biological and physical diversities of the environment, a law was passed in 1992 providing for the establishment of a National Integrated Protected Areas System (NIPAS) for the protection of the country's national parks. Classified as protected areas are strict nature reserves, natural parks, natural monuments, wildlife sanctuaries, protected landscapes and seascapes, resource reserves, natural biotic areas and other categories established by law, conventions or international agreements in which the Philippine Government is a signatory. The Department of Environment and Natural Resources (DENR), through the Protected Areas and Wildlife Bureau (PAWB), is mandated to oversee the establishment, management and development of protected areas and conservation of wildlife resources in the country. The country's 60 national parks, four marine parks, eight game refuges and bird sanctuaries and ten wilderness areas are covered by NIPAS. Ten priority sites have been identified for the initial implementation of the law. These are, from north to south: the Batanes Protected Landscape and Seascape, Northern Sierra Madre Nature Park, Subic-Bataan Protected Area, Apo Reef Marine Nature Park, Mt Kanlaon Nature Park, Siargao Wildlife Sanctuary, Agusan Marsh Wildlife Sanctuary, Mt Kitanglad Nature Park, Turtle Island Marine Nature Park and Mt Apo Nature Park. Funded by the World Bank, these sites are managed by a national NGO network. Two in-situ conservation projects conducted by the DENR-PAWB involve the *pawikan* (sea turtle) and dugong (sea cow) in Taganak, Tawi-Tawi in the Sulu Archipelago, and the Calauit Game Preserve and Wildlife Sanctuary in Northern Palawan. Projects to save the Philippine eagle, Philippine raptors, spotted deer, tamaraw, cockatoo, calamian deer, fruit bat and Visayan warty pig are ongoing in various sites.

Many non-government organizations are active in conservation efforts. However, there is still much to be done in terms of educating the public about biodiversity conservation and sustainable development.

Sports and Recreation

The Philippines has a coastline longer than that of the United States, and is surrounded by warm tropical seas teeming with a rich variety of marine life. Scuba diving here is world-class, and sport and recreational fishing have a large following (see Sporting Life, page 289). Sailing is a challenging sport here because of the tropical storms and typhoons that occur frequently in the region, but it is also a rewarding experience. Sailing is best from December to February. Yachts cruising along the western side of Palawan find the scenery spectacular with snorkelling and scuba-diving definite pluses. The biennial South China Sea Race between Hong Kong and the Philippines is a major event, and other regattas are held regularly by the Manila Yacht Club and Subic Bay Yacht Club. Powerboat races and contests of native craft such as *paraws*, *vintas*, and *bancas* are also held at provincial festivals. The existence of good boat-building facilities in the country is a plus factor. In Bataan and Cebu there are commercial firms engaged in building made-to-measure sailing yachts which are strong and durable at less cost than elsewhere. Surfing is an undeveloped sport. Siargao is a surfing destination and the province of La Union is attracting some surfers from Hawaii and Japan from November to February. Aurora on the eastern side of Luzon has also a good potential for the sport. Windsurfing can be enjoyed at many beach resorts but those with the best equipment are in Anilao (Batangas), Dakak (Zamboanga), and Boracay (Aklan). Lake Caliraya (Laguna) is also frequented by aficionados of the sport. Beach-lovers who merely want to soak up sun have a choice of thousands of beaches—sand varies from powdery white to coarse black volcanic—spread throughout the archipelago. The only consideration is distance from a city

Landlubbers too can indulge in a variety of sports year-round. Mountaineering, trekking and caving are sports enjoyed by a growing number of enthusiasts. Visitors in search of wilderness and adventure tours have found the Philippines to be a good destination. Horse-racing, horseback riding and polo have their own followers.

Golf is a year-round activity in the Philippines. In the 1990s a number of championship courses designed by the world's golfing greats and featuring modern club facilities and amenities have been built or renovated and more are in the process of development. These are mostly membership clubs but there are reciprocal arrangements with other clubs abroad. Visitors can also play when accompanied by members.

Football, basketball and other ball games enjoy a large following. Basketball is particularly popular among Filipino men and boys and is played in back lots, neighbourhood plazas and school gymnasiums. The big leagues compete for national championships at the Rizal Stadium and Araneta Coliseum, and provincial teams play at regional meets. Pelota, badminton, bowling and pool have their enthusiasts. A left-handed Filipino bowler, Paeng Nepomuceno, is a three-time World Cup champion in bowling, the first earned at the age of 19 in Teheran (1976), the second in 1980 and the third in November 1992 in Le Mans, France.

Filipinos love boxing and the country has produced world-class boxers in the light-flyweight, featherweight and welter-weight divisions who have earned distinctions and medals in world boxing tournaments and Olympiads. Mansueto 'Onyok' Velasco came home to a hero's welcome after bagging the silver medal at the 1996 Summer Olympics in Atlanta. A left-handed bowler, Paeng Nepomuceno, is a three-time World Cup champion in bowling, the first earned at the age of 19 in Teheran (1976), the second in 1980 and the third in November 1992 in Le Mans, France. He also won the world amateur bowling championship in Las Vegas in 1984. Horse racing, horseback riding and polo are other sports with their own avid followers.

Cardinal fish race out from the reef, Batangas

Chess is followed with great interest (see Rizal Park, page 108). Baguio was the venue for the World Chess Championship between Viktor Korchnoi and Anatoly Karpov in 1978. The World's Interzonal Tournament was held in Manila in 1990. In June 1992, the Philippines hosted the World Chess Olympics at which world chess champion Gary Kasparov won over his rival from Uzbekistan. The 19-day tournament was participated in by more than 100 countries. The Philippines has many good chess players, including international grandmasters Eugenio Torre and Rosendo Balinas Jr.

The native games that Filipinos play are *sipa*, in which the players use their legs, feet and knees to kick a hollow woven rattan ball and *arnis de mano*, an ancient Filipino martial art originally used for self-defence. As in fencing, *arnis* players use hardwood sticks to parry and block their opponent's attack. Cockfighting is another ancient Filipino sport as well as entertainment which flourishes today, despite early attempts by the Spaniards to ban it. Stag Derbies, as large-scale cockfights are called, draw enthusiasts from all over the Philippines. The stakes run into thousands of pesos. Filipinos also play mahjong, *sungka* and *dama*. Mahjong was introduced by the Chinese. *Sungka* is played by two people using a wooden board with 14 hollows in it. Seashells or small stones are moved from one hollow to another. *Dama* is a simple form of draughts which is often played on street corners.

Facts for the Traveller

Climate

Two distinct seasons—dry and wet—prevail over much of the Philippines. The days are generally warm, cooled by sea breezes, but at the height of summer the days turn sweleringly hot, cooling down by evening. The northeast monsoon brings mainly dry, warm weather from November to May, with March and April the hottest months. The southwest monsoon brings the rains from June to October, with July and August the wettest months. However climatic variations do occur within the archipelago. The western part (which includes Manila, Mindoro, Palawan, Panay and Negros) has marked dry and wet seasons. In the central part (the Cagayan Valley, across Cebu to northern Mindanao) the seasons are less distinct, but it is relatively dry from November to April. The southeast coast (from Quezon province to Bicol, Samar, Leyte and eastern Mindanao) has its heaviest rainfall from November to February, whereas rainfall is more uniformly distributed in the Batanes Islands and northeastern Luzon, Bohol and most of central Mindanao.

Tropical cyclones known as typhoons occur during the rainy season. Their frequency, intensity and path differ from one year to the next but they are more frequent in the north. South of latitude 10°N they are relatively rare. Storm and typhoon signals warn people of the onset of typhoons. Signal No 1 means a typhoon is within 72 hours of striking the country. Signal No 2, within 48 hours; and Signal No 3 means the typhoon will hit within 36 hours. This signal precipitates the closing of schools, government offices and businesses. The weather is monitored by the Philippine Atmospheric, Geophysical and Astronomical Services Administration (PAGASA).

WHEN TO GO

For warm, sunny days and balmy nights, the most pleasant time to visit the Philippines is from November to February, except along the Pacific coast which can be wet at this time. Temperatures range from 20° to 28°C (68° to 82°F). Christmas is celebrated throughout the country and major festivals such as Ati-Atihan, Sinulog and Dinagyang take place in January. The Philippine summer is from March to May—hot, dry months when daytime temperatures in the lowlands range from 30° to 36°C (86° to 97°F) and night-time temperatures from 21° to 24°C (70° to 76°F). Relative humidity varies between 71 per cent and 85 per cent. Respite from the heat and humidity is sought in the mountains and highlands which draw day-trippers, weekenders and holiday-makers. This is also the season of harvest festivals, the Moriones Festival, Santacruzan and Flores de Mayo. June is the start of the rainy season, with July and August usually the wettest months. Typhoons, called locally *bagyo*, occur between June and November. But even during the rainy season, some parts of the country may be relatively dry. River festivals are prevalent at this time of year. Scuba-diving, golf and fishing, sightseeing, shopping and festivals can be enjoyed year-round.

WHAT TO PACK

Lightweight, washable clothes that don't easily show the dirt, in natural fibres such as cotton are the best to pack. Take plenty of cotton-knit T-shirts, jeans or cotton trousers, shorts, swimsuits (two if you will be in the water a lot), and a sun hat. Casual dress is the rule in most places but if you anticipate going to smart places or being invited to formal occasions then include some dressy outfits (for women) or lightweight suit and tie for men. Filipino men favour the *barong tagalog*, a cream- or eggshell-coloured long sleeved, embroidered shirt of fine *jusi* (a natural fibre) for formal occasions. Visiting heads of state who arrived in the Philippines for the APEC forum were each presented with a silk *barong* especially designed for each one of them. *Barongs* are available off-the-rack from the big department stores or a tailor can rush you one if you need it. There are also many couturiers in Manila who make formal outfits for women.

For women travellers, experts advise packing lightly and carrying one big bag, which eliminates the problem of lost luggage. The tropical Philippines is ablaze with colour, so feel free to go wild with colours. Your choice of outfits will depend on your planned activities and the places you visit. Filipino women like to keep up with the latest fashions and in smart places in Manila and the bigger cities they tend to dress up. It's good to pack a light cardigan and shawl for cool nights in the mountains or air-conditioned places if you are susceptible to drafts. Divided skirts or culottes are versatile. Scarves can double up as sashes and a big rectangular scarf can be worn like a sarong or a wraparound skirt over a bikini or swimsuit. Shops in Manila carry a range of ready-to-wear outfits suitable for town or country, and sportswear. You may also consider having a dress designed for you and made by one of the well-known local couturiers. Footwear should be comfortable, and allow some breathing space for your feet, which will expand in the heat. Rubber thongs are good for the beach but canvas shoes with rubber soles are better for clambering over rocks and coral-strewn shores.

If you will be in the mountains, out at sea fishing, or in the country during the rainy season, take a water-proof jacket with a hood. A cardigan and socks may also be useful. A small folding umbrella, a flashlight and batteries, a transistor radio-cum-cassette player which can double as an alarm clock, and a mini dual-voltage hair dryer are useful. Mosquito repellent, ointments for insect bites, headache pills and band-aids are also good to bring. Electricity in the Philippines is 220 V, 60 cycles (but in some localities, like Baguio, the voltage is 110). Bring a US-style two-prong adaptor. A small packet of detergent, sponge, laundry line, Swiss army knife and collapsible tooth glass are good if you are visiting remote areas. Bring enough prescription medication to last you the trip, vitamins, cosmetics, skin-and hair-care products, if you are particular, otherwise supermarkets and department stores stock well-known brands of toothpaste, soap, shampoo, cosmetics, sun block and tanning

The Filipino jeepney; pop- and folk-art on wheels

lotions. Chemists or pharmacies also carry generic patent medicines and prescription drugs.

Getting There

By air, Manila is the main port of entry in Luzon, with other international airports at Clark in Pampanga and Laoag in Ilocos Norte. International carriers operating services to the Philippines include: Air France, Air New Zealand, Air Niugini, Alitalia, Asiana Airlines, British Airways, Cathay Pacific Airways, China Airlines, Continental Micronesia, Egypt Air, Emirates, Eva Airways, Garuda, Gulf Air, Japan Airlines, KLM, Korean Airlines, Kuwait Airways, Malaysia Airlines, Northwest Airlines, Pakistan Airlines, Qantas Airways, Royal Brunei Airlines, Saudia Airlines, Singapore Airlines, Swissair, Thai International and United Airlines.

VISAS

Most pleasure travellers do not need a visa to enter the Philippines, but must possess a valid travel document and an onward air ticket showing entry to the next country of destination. Permitted lengths of stay range from seven days to 21 days. Visitors who wish to extend their stay beyond the permitted period must apply at the Bureau of Immigration in Manila or must obtain the appropriate visa good for 59 days' stay from any Philippine Foreign Service establishment abroad. Chinese nationals holding PRC and Taiwanese passports, including those holding Certificates/Documents of Identity must obtain a visa before proceeding to the Philippines.

Stateless persons or nationals of other countries not qualifying for the no-visa entry privilege for a seven or 21-day stay must apply for a visa in their country of origin or place of legal residence subject to compliance with prescribed requirements. For more specific information, travellers are advised to check with the nearest Philippine embassy or consulate.

HEALTH

Unless you are coming from a cholera-infected or yellow fever region, no vaccination is required. If you anticipate going to Palawan, Mindoro or other remote areas where there is a risk of contracting malaria, you might consider taking a malaria prophylactic in advance. Seek advice from your doctor. The Bureau of Quarantine in Manila also gives booster shots for cholera and smallpox for those who require it. Tap water is generally safe to drink in Manila. If in doubt, drink boiled or bottled mineral or distilled water. The health care system in the Philippines is generally good and the fees reasonable. It is advisable to carry health and accident insurance. Most deluxe hotels provide medical services.

CUSTOMS

The normal duty-free allowance is two bottles of wine or spirits (not more than one litre per bottle); two tins of smoking tobacco or up to 400 cigarettes; a small quantity of perfume; and reasonable amounts of clothing and jewellery for personal use. Narcotics and synthetic drugs, firearms and weapons of war, as well as various types of explosives are prohibited except when authorized by law. These items can be confiscated and the traveller asked to pay a steep fine or face charges, depending on the offence. A customs declaration form must be filled out upon arrival and presented to the customs official.

MONEY

There is no restriction on the amount of foreign currency one can bring into the country but there's a restriction on Philippine currency taken in and out of the country. Check with the nearest Philippine consulate or embassy on the permitted amount. The Philippine peso is divided into 100 centavos. Bank notes come in denominations of 5, 10, 20, 50, 100, 500 and 1,000 pesos. Coins are in 5, 10, 20, and 50 centavo denominations, and 1,5, and 10 pesos. There is a bank in the airport if you wish to convert foreign currency. The exchange rate fluctuates between P39 to P42 to one US dollar; around P64 to P69 to one pound sterling. Commercial bank, authorized money changers, hotels and other tourist establishments also change traveller's cheques. American dollars are easier and more convenient to change. Never deal with street vendors or non-accredited money changers. To be safe, stick with the banks or hotels, although their rates may be less favourable. Major credit cards such as American Express, MasterCharge, Visa and Diners Club are accepted by the majority of hotels in Manila and resorts, large restaurants and shops.

Banks are open Mondays to Fridays from 9 am to 3 pm, except on public and official holidays. It is advisable to have your passport with you for identification when banking in the Philippines. The commercial banking system in the Philippines comprises some 21 domestic expanded commercial banks (EKBs) and 15 non-EKBs, plus a special government bank. There are 13 non-EKB foreign banks in the Philippines. These are: ANZ Banking Corporation, Bangkok Bank Public Co Ltd, Bank of America NT & SA, Bank of Tokyo Ltd, Chase Manhattan Bank, Citibank NA, Deutsche Bank AG, Development Bank of Singapore Ltd, The Fuji Bank Ltd, The Hongkong and Shanghai Banking Corp, International Commercial Bank of China, Korea Exchange Bank, and Standard Chartered Bank.

Communications

The past few years have seen the introduction of new technologies and the opening up of the country's telecommunications system to more players. Consumers are getting a wider range of services and are benefiting from the entry of more operators in the cellular telephone, pager, trunk radio business and long distance service. Under the National Telephone Programme, digital telephone lines are being installed in Luzon, Visayas and Mindanao. Nine International Gateway Facilities operators now offer international long distance service. The competition among these operators is bringing down the cost of long-distance calls.

Telephone calls can be made from public, coin-operated booths. There are also card phones. Pre-paid Foncards are available from PLDT. Most first-class hotels have IDD or DDD phones in the rooms. You can dial direct to 135 countries worldwide and 34 cities and provinces nationwide. DDD rates are roughly 30 per cent lower than

Philippine handicrafts include a wide variety of basketware

operator-assisted rates. There is a service charge on long distance calls made from hotels.

MAIL

Post offices are open Mondays to Fridays from 8 am to 5 pm and are closed on Saturdays, Sundays and public holidays. In Metro Manila, the main post office is on the south bank of the Pasig River; branches are located in various parts of the metropolis. Courier services are also available. Federal Express and DHL have set up their Asia-Pacific operations in the Philippines.

MEDIA

Press freedom is guaranteed in the constitution of the Philippines, and the media has exercised that freedom to the full, except during the years of martial law under the Marcos regime. Metro Manila newspapers include the English-language *Manila Bulletin, Philippine Star, Philippine Daily Inquirer, Manila Standard, Manila Chronicle, Manila Times, Business World, Malaya* and others. International and regional publications such as *Time, Newsweek, AsiaWeek, The International Herald Tribune* and *The Asian Wall Street Journal* are also available at newsstands.

Several AM and FM radio stations broadcast from 6 am to midnight in English and Pilipino. Shortwave radios can pick up Voice of America, BBC World Service and Radio Australia.

Television networks show English-language and Pilipino programmes. These include local and foreign newscasts, sporting events, variety shows, serials and soap operas.

LANGUAGE

The Philippines has more than 100 ethno-linguistic groups. Eight major dialects are spoken by about 90 per cent of the population. Tagalog, prevalent in Manila and Central Luzon, is spoken in 29.66 per cent of private households; Cebuano, common in Cebu, Bohol, Negros Oriental and most of Mindanao, is spoken by 24.20 per cent of all households; Ilocano, widespread in Northern Luzon, is the language of 10.30 per cent of all households; Hiligaynon or Ilonggo, spoken in Panay and Negros Occidental, is the dialect of 9.16 per cent; Bicol, the dialect in Southern Luzon, is spoken by 5.57 per cent. The other major dialects are Waray-Waray, Pampango and Pangasinan. The official languages are English and Pilipino—the national language based on Tagalog. English is widely used as the medium of communication. The literacy rate is high. Filipinos place great importance on education and even the poorest families strive to achieve tertiary education.

JEEPNEYS

Much has been written about the Philippine jeepney. It has been eulogised and criticised; paraded and displayed in world capitals as an example of Philippine folk- and pop-art on wheels. As a means of public transport, the jeepney is a postwar phenomenon, created with Filipino ingenuity out of surplus army jeeps. The original prototypes have evolved into vehicles with fancy bodywork in wood and chrome, painted in gaudy colours and carrying numerous embellishments. Cavalcades of metal horses ride on their hoods, pennants flutter from their aerials, and frills and furbelows festoon their interiors. Sarao has become a name known in the jeepney world for turning out these colourful vehicles. While practically all fancy jeepneys originate from the same factory, no two are ever alike. Each has its own individual quirkiness and personality, derived as much from the owner's whim as the driver's fancy. One driver may garland the rearview mirror with a lei of *sampaguita* flowers; another may hang Rosary beads. Curtains may be of lace or plastic, or there may be none at all. A stack of cassettes may find space in the dashboard, along with the coin box. Anything goes in a jeepney.

The jeepney has evolved from its gaudier days. Today's jeepney is a more sombre vehicle. Perhaps it is a sign of the times. Fewer jeepneys now display horses on their hoods. Occasionally you may see one, or at the most three, metal horses but generally they have disappeared. Gone too are the fluttering frills that once decorated many a jeepney's grill like cheerleaders' pompoms. The admonitions, incantations, slogans and other writings painted on the front, sides and rear of the vehicle, in addition to the routes and destinations are still in evidence.

Shopping

For the inveterate shopper, a foray into the shopping malls and commercial complexes, bazaars and markets of the Philippines can be both exhilarating and rewarding. Local products range from arts and crafts, ready-to-wear apparel and knitwear, woven and embroidered products, shoes, bags and fashion accessories to housewares, home furnishings and furniture. The Philippines is also famous for its rum, beer and native delicacies such as *pili* nut and durian candies, dried and candied

But the messages too have changed. "Praise the Lord", "God bless us", and similar prayers can be seen painted in the rear mudguards or sides. Though less outrageous in appearance, jeepneys are as ubiquitous today as they were in the good old days—serving the masses who need fast transport. To ride in a jeepney is an experience to be attempted only by those who do not mind being squeezed into a tiny space; who have the ability to recognize the landmarks and signs outside and know when to get out, and the agility to jump out when the moment to alight comes.

In spite of repeated threats to remove them from the streets, they have endured. Indeed, jeepneys have become a way of life in the Philippines.

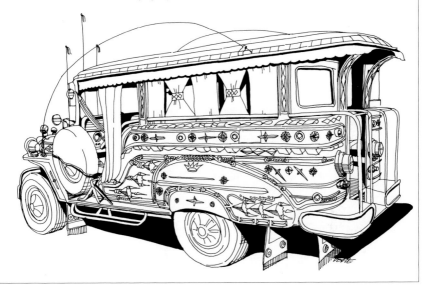

fruit (pineapple, mango, banana) and preserves. You may also consider antiques, gold and silver jewellery, pearls, excavated porcelain, and local paintings.

Many items for the home such as embroidered table linens in natural fibres like ramie and *jusi*, place mats and napkin holders, wooden bowls and trays inlaid with mother-of-pearl or ox bone, *capiz* shell chandeliers and Tiffany lamps, macramé plant holders and jewellery boxes, are ideal gift and souvenir items. There are also fashion accessories made of seashells, mother-of-pearl, coral and *carabao* horn; embroidered shirts and dresses; ethnic woven cloths and garments; artificial plants and handmade silk flowers. Have a look at what's on offer at the shopping malls and markets.

You will find traditional handicrafts in nearly every city and town. Metro Manila, Cebu, Baguio, Davao, Bacolod and the bigger cities and towns of course offer a wider range of merchandise. Check what is the speciality of the province or region—woven mats and blankets, baskets, carvings, embroidery, brassware, etc. These can be obtained at a much lower price in the province. Sometimes, they are only sold in that particular province or region.

Bargaining is allowed in open markets and bazaars but take care to ask first from the vendor whether discounting is acceptable. If so, quote a price that you think is reasonable or a fraction below the normal market value of the item. If in doubt about your bargaining ability, ask for the lowest price, or how much of a discount or *tawad* the vendor will give you. If you think it's worth buying the item even without discount, conclude the deal. If you are not willing to pay the vendors 'final' price, simply tell him you don't agree and walk away.

When shopping in markets and crowded places, beware of pickpockets and watch your wallet and personal belongings.

Department stores have fixed prices. Major credit cards are accepted but some stores want to see your passport, driver's licence or other identification before accepting payment with the credit card. If you buy sale items with a credit card, you may be asked to pay the original, non-discounted price.

A herbal medicine stall in Quiapo, Manila

Travelling Around the Philippines

Although the Philippines is a scattering of islands and islets, no area is so remote
that it cannot be reached by some means of public transport by land, sea or air. On
long distance travel, check whether the transport company accepts credit cards.
Otherwise payment is on cash basis. Keep plenty of loose change and small-denomi-
nation bills if you anticipate taking taxis, jeepneys and tricycles. For a list of transport companies, turn to page 338.

On Land

Buses are the most common type of public land transport for long haul travel. Several bus companies are franchised to operate in various parts of the country. They
range from first class to third class. Air-conditioned buses naturally charge a higher
fare than non air-conditioned ones. It is possible to travel overland to the Visayas
and Mindanao via the Pan Philippine Highway, with connecting ferry services

between Sorsogon and Samar, Leyte and Surigao. Buses to outlying islands in the Bicol region also connect by ferry to Masbate and Catanduanes.

For short-distance travel, the most common mode of transport within cities and towns are jeepneys and tricycles. The jeepney is a postwar phenomenon, created by Filipino ingenuity out of surplus American army jeeps. The early models sported fancy bodywork. Painted in carnival colours they carried numerous embellishments according to the owner's whim and the driver's fancy. The jeepney was the best example of folk art on wheels. It has evolved from its gaudier days into a more sombre vehicle, still with the slogans and admonitions but without the frills and gew-gaws of yesteryear. The sheer number of jeepneys running on city streets, especially in Metro Manila, contributes to the city's clogged traffic. In spite of repeated threats to remove them from the streets, they have endured. Commuters find them a convenient way of moving about.

Jeepneys run on designated routes within cities and large towns and shuttle between towns in the provinces. Tricycles—motorized bicycles with sidecars seating two passengers—ply short feeder routes or function as taxis especially in the provinces. Metered taxis operate in Manila and Cebu. Non-metered Public Utility (PU) vehicles serve as taxis in some provincial towns but charge a flat fare which has to be negotiated beforehand, depending on the distance covered. There are several car hire companies such as Avis and Hertz. The Yellow Pages directory gives addresses and telephone numbers of vehicles for hire, as well as bus companies. The Tourist Information section of the Department of Tourism will also give advice on land transport.

Trains operate between Metro Manila and the Bicol region. The journey by rail is now more comfortable on board the air-conditioned coaches of Philippine National Railways (PNR). Tracks and railway structures along the 478-kilometre (297-mile) Southern Line have been upgraded and rehabilitated. This has cut down the travel time. PNR trains now run as far as Legaspi in Albay province. Extending the line to Matnog in the province of Sorsogon, is in the railway's master plan. Trains leave the main terminus at Tayuman Street in Manila at 4.05 pm and 7.30 pm daily.

Operating within Metro Manila is the Light Rail Transit (LRT) system. The elevated train crosses the heart of Manila. LRT 2 and 3 are under construction. More lines are planned.

BY SEA

Ships, ferries, launches and pump boats are common means of inter-island transport. Travelling by ship offers a cheaper mode of travel from Manila to the Visayas

(previous page) Clear waters, Hundred Isles, Pangasinan Province

and Mindanao, and vice versa, compared to air travel. The convenience and ease of booking and the leisurely pace are seen by many passengers as a plus. Ships and ferries vary in terms of service, regularity and comfort. Some shipping lines offer first-class accommodation and amenities; others provide the basics with no frills. With the acquisition of more modern vessels, shipping companies have increased their passenger capacity.

Pump boats or outrigger *bancas* equipped with outboard or inboard motors are generally used for short distances along the coastlines or between neighbouring islands. Schedules are flexible and sailing times depend on the season, the weather and the tide. Launches are used for longer journeys between small ports and may or may not operate according to schedules. Ferry boats also negotiate crossings between islands. Travel time may be anywhere from 30 minutes to several hours.

Inter-island vessels dock at the North Harbour in Manila. Most shipping companies maintain offices in the North Harbour but have branches or ticket agents in Binondo (San Fernando St), Ermita and Makati.

Major shipping lines include WG&A Philippines (William, Gothong and Aboitiz), Negros Navigation, Sulpicio Lines, Viva Shipping Lines, Moreta Shipping and others operating out of Cebu such as Escaño Lines and George and Peter Lines. There are new, luxury vessels that offer a range of passenger comfort and amenities. WG&A, Negros Navigation and Sulpicio operate such vessels. Check the *Manila Standard* and *Manila Bulletin* for sailing schedules.

BY AIR

Domestic air services are operated by Philippine Airlines, Cebu Pacific, Grand Air, Air Philippines, Asian Spirit and Astro Air. Most flights tend to be fully booked just before or after major holidays and festivals, such as the Christmas season and Easter. Last-minute seats can be hard to obtain. Book your flight in advance and fix your departure date instead of leaving it open. Reconfirm your flight as soon as you arrive at your destination. Allow plenty of time to check in. Flights close about 45 minutes before the scheduled departure time. If you don't show up before then, your seat may be given to another passenger on the waiting list, even if you have a confirmed booking on that flight. No-shows may also be fined. In addition to scheduled services, charter flights are also available. Some airlines offer reduced fares to island destinations if tickets are purchased in advance. Ask for their special promotional fares. Tickets may be purchased four days, eight days, two weeks or one month in advance to take advantage of the lower fares. Tour packages are also available.

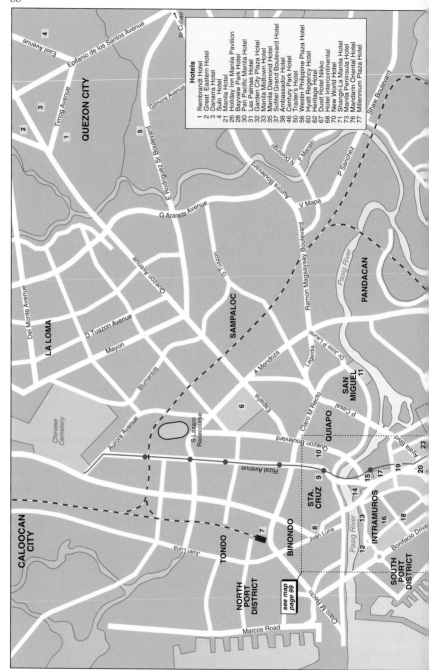

Hotels
1 Rembrandt Hotel
2 Great Eastern Hotel
3 Danarra Hotel
4 Sulo Hotel
21 Manila Hotel
26 Holiday Inn Manila Pavilion
28 Bayview Park Hotel
30 Pan Pacific Manila Hotel
31 Las Palmas Hotel
32 Garden City Plaza Hotel
33 Manila Midtown Hotel
35 Manila Diamond Hotel
37 Sofitel Grand Boulevard Hotel
38 Ambassador Hotel
46 Century Park Hotel
50 Trader's Hotel
56 Westin Philippine Plaza Hotel
60 Hyatt Regency Hotel
62 Heritage Hotel
67 Dusit Hotel Nikko
68 Hotel Intercontinental
70 New World Hotel
71 Shangri-La Manila Hotel
73 Manila Peninsula Hotel
76 Mandarin Oriental Hotel
77 Millennium Plaza Hotel

see map page 99

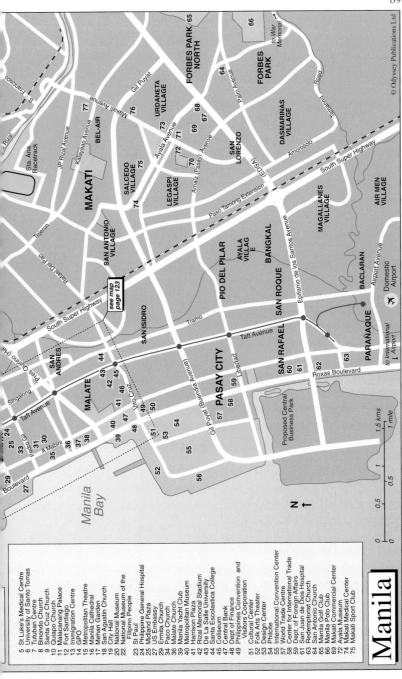

Manila

5 St Luke's Medical Centre
6 University of Santo Tomas
7 Tutuban Centre
8 Binondo Church
9 Santa Cruz Church
10 Quiapo Church
11 Malacañang Palace
12 Fort Santiago
13 Immigration Centre
14 GPO
15 Metropolitan Theatre
16 Manila Cathedral
17 Mehan Garden
18 San Agustin Church
19 City Hall
20 National Museum
22 National Museum of the
   Filipino People
23 St Paul
24 Philippine General Hospital
25 Midland Plaza
27 US Embassy
29 Ermita Church
34 Paco Church
36 Malate Church
39 Manila Yacht Club
40 Metropolitan Museum
41 Harrison Plaza
42 Rizal Memorial Stadium
43 De La Salle University
44 Santa Escolastica College
45 Coliseum
47 Central Bank
48 Dept of Finance
49 Philippines Convention and
   Visitors Corporation
51 Cultural Center
52 Folk Arts Theater
53 Design Center
54 Philcite
55 International Convention Center
57 World Trade Centre
58 Center for International Trade
59 Dept. of Foreign Affairs
61 San Juan de Dios Hospital
62 Redemptorist Church
64 San Antonio Church
65 Manila Golf Club
66 Manila Polo Club
69 Makati Commercial Center
72 Ayala Museum
74 Makati Medical Center
75 Makati Sport Club

Metro Manila

Sandwiched between the Central Plain and the Southern Tagalog region is the National Capital Region (NCR), an urban sprawl consisting of the cities of Manila, Quezon City, Pasay City, Caloocan City, Makati, Mandaluyong, Marikina, Muntinglupa, Novaliches, Parañaque and Pasig, plus the municipalities of San Juan, Las Piñas, Malabon, Navotas, Pateros, Taguig and Valenzuela. This crowded conurbation covering an area of 678.2 square kilometres (262 square miles) is Metro Manila. About ten million souls live in this megalopolis, bounded by Manila Bay on the west and surrounded by the provinces of Bulacan, Rizal, Laguna and Cavite. The Pasig River bisects it and forms a waterway linking the inland lake of Laguna de Bay to the sea.

The heart of the Philippines beats in Metro Manila. It is the seat of government; the centre of the arts and education; the commercial, industrial, business and financial hub of the nation; the main gateway to the Philippines. Lusty and lively, it is a city of contrasts and contradictions. Within its boundaries live the richest and the poorest in the land.

For millions of Filipinos in the provinces, Manila is the city of their dreams. Hundreds leave behind their easy-going lives in the provinces to study in Manila, look for jobs, to or seek fame and fortune. Some are successful, others are not so lucky. Pride forbids them from going home. Instead they try to make a new life for themselves in hardship. The urban pull is exerting tremendous economic and social pressures on a city already bursting at the seams with people.

Before the financial crisis hit Asia, the country was in the midst of a real estate boom. Office towers, mixed-use commercial centres, shopping malls, condominiums, apartelles, townhouses, medium- and high-rise buildings were springing up everywhere, changing the skyline over Metro Manila, particularly in Makati, Mandaluyong, Pasig, Pasay, Manila and Quezon City. While some projects have been affected by the crunch, others are on-going.

ARRIVAL AND TRANSPORT

International flights coming to the country touch down at the Ninoy Aquino International Airport in Pasay City. First-class hotels have airport pick-up services for arriving guests. Licensed taxis operate from the airport to various points in the Greater Manila area. Fares are calculated according to distance and passengers purchase coupons before they board.

A dense network of road, rail and water transport links the municipalities and cities of Metro Manila. Buses, jeepneys and taxis jostle daily with private cars for space on the roads, creating traffic problems. A ring road, called Epifanio de los Santos Avenue or EDSA for short, runs through Pasay, Makati, Mandaluyong, Quezon City and Caloocan, plus other municipalities along the way, and joins up with the expressways and highways heading north and south of Manila. Traffic is heavy along this multilane motorway. On EDSA, civilians, nuns with their rosaries and an elderly woman in a wheelchair confronted the tanks sent in by Gen Fabian Ver to break up the welling demonstration of People Power in 1986. This signalled the downfall of Marcos' rule. Monuments to this peaceful revolution can be seen along the highway. More roads and skyways are being constructed to improve the flow of traffic. The LRT, Manila's elevated rapid transit system operating between Pasay City in the south and Caloocan City in the north relieves some of the pressure on surface traffic along the busy Taft Avenue and Rizal Avenue corridors. An expansion of the mass transit network is planned to alleviate traffic congestion. Construction of the billion-peso LRT 3, an 18-kilometre stretch along the EDSA corridor from Taft Avenue in Baclaran to the North Triangle near SM North EDSA in Quezon City and LRT 2 (Manila-Katipunan) are underway. The blueprints are complete for Line 4 (Manila-Novaliches), Line 5 (Manila-Shaw Boulevard) and Line 6 (an extension of Line 1 to Zapote).

HOTELS AND ACCOMMODATION

Visitor accommodation in Manila ranges from luxury five-star hotels to budget pensions and inns; from serviced apartment-hotels, or apartelles, to hostels. No matter where you stay, you will be given a warm welcome. Filipinos are among the most hospitable people in the world. Manila's leading hotels regularly undergo refurbishment and renovation. Swimming pools, business centres, fitness centres, shopping arcades, speciality restaurants, telephones, televisions, refrigerators, marble baths (some even have private jacuzzis in the rooms), and 24-hour room service are found in the luxury hotels. Many hotels have in-room safety deposit boxes and some have fax machines in the rooms and computers with Internet facilities. Most of the deluxe hotels are either in the Makati business centre or the Manila Bay area. These include the historic and elegant Manila Hotel, an architectural landmark in the city dating back to colonial times, located at the edge of Manila Bay and overlooking Rizal Park. Also in Manila next to Rizal Park is the Holiday Inn Manila Pavilion. Along Roxas Boulevard, from Rizal Park to Pasay City are the Manila Diamond Hotel, the Hotel Sofitel Grand Boulevard, the Hyatt Regency and the Heritage Hotel. Within the Cultural Centre complex is the Westin Philippine Plaza, and just off the boulevard, near the Rizal Memorial sports complex is the Century Park Hotel. First-class hotels in the Bay area and tourist belt (Ermita-Malate) are Bayview Plaza, Trader's Hotel and Manila Midtown Hotel. Several standard and economy hotels are located in Manila's tourist belt.

The most popular of the standard hotels are Royal Palm Hotel, Hotel Las Palmas, Palm Plaza Hotel, Paragon Tower and City Garden Hotel. The newest deluxe hotel in the area is the Pan Pacific Hotel Manila which boasts butler service. The hotel offers its guests a choice of 30 restaurants and bars in Adriatico Square, a four-floor enclave within the hotel. Guests can order room service from any of the outlets. In the Makati business district, the deluxe hotels are the Manila Peninsula, the Mandarin Oriental, the Hotel Inter-Continental, the Dusit Hotel Nikko, the Shangri-La Manila and New World Hotel. The Century Citadel Inn and Millenium Plaza are standard hotels and El Cielito Tourist Inn is an economy hotel. In the Ortigas Centre in Mandaluyong/Pasig, the deluxe hotels are the Shangri-La EDSA Plaza and the Manila Galleria Suites while the Legend and Byron EDSA are standard hotels. Near the airport is the first-class Mercure Philippine Village Airport Hotel. In Quezon City the Great Eastern is a first class hotel, the Sulo and Rembrandt are standard hotels and Danarra Apartel is an economy hotel. All these hotels are accredited and classified by the Department of Tourism.

FOOD AND DRINK

The diversity of eating establishments in Metro Manila—from speciality restaurants and hotel dining rooms to the food courts within shopping malls, fast food outlets and outdoor barbecue stands—means no visitor need ever go hungry. Philippine dishes, Chinese, Japanese, Korean, Thai, Vietnamese, Mediterranean, Spanish and other European cuisines are all available. The Ermita-Malate area and Remedios Circle have many little restaurants and bistros. Guernica's for Spanish specialities and the Aristocrat further along on Roxas Boulevard are well-established. Robinson's Shopping Mall and the new Food Court—Adriatico Square—within the Pan Pacific Hotel have a variety of offerings. Tomas Morato Street and West Avenue in Quezon City are lined with restaurants. Megamall, Shangri-La Plaza and Robinson's Galleria in Ortigas Centre, Pasig/Mandaluyong; the Greenbelt Mall, Glorietta and Ayala Centre at the Makati Business District, Arnaiz (formerly Pasay Road), and Bel-Air in Makati. Greenhills and Wilson Avenue in San Juan all offer a staggering choice of comestibles, from pizzas, hamburgers, nachos, sushi, sashimi, noodles, congee, and finger-licking fare in fastfood outlets to buffets and full-course meals in more formal settings. Don't forget the hotel restaurants which have their own specialities. You can have a Filipino meal for under P100 in the food court of a shopping mall, or a buffet lunch for under P500. Prices escalate when you dine in restaurants. A bottle

Manila after dark glows with neon signs

of wine would add 25 per cent to the meal. A ten per cent service charge is usually added to the bill, plus a four per cent sales tax on food and an eight per cent sales tax on alcoholic beverages. Tipping is optional.

Chefs change, menus change, restaurants may come and go. Filipinos are very trendy, even when choosing restaurants. So check what's new and noteworthy.

NIGHTLIFE AND ENTERTAINMENT

The Filipino's penchant for music and dancing, fun and parties is reflected in the varied choice of music and entertainment in the city. Metro Manila after dark is a lively scene. There's enough variety to keep party-goers and bar-hoppers busy, whether it is listening to music from vocalists, solo instrumentalists and live bands, dancing to the latest rock, rhythm and blues sounds, singing along at videoke bars, or watching cultural dances or cabaret-type shows at restaurants and clubs.

Long before the mantle of night falls upon the city and the neon lights twinkle on, Metro Manila's nightspots are in action. Happy hours (usually from 5 to 7 pm) in the cocktail lounges and bars mean not only drinks at reduced prices but also live music.

Metro Manila's top hotels are good places to listen to first-rate bands, vocalists and instrumentalists. Some places specialize in country-and-western music; others in rock and pop; still others in jazz or folk music, sentimental ballads and *kundimans*

(Filipino love songs). Other places offer ballroom dancing, cabaret-type entertainment and cultural dances.

Dinner with entertainment featuring Philippine folk dances is a nightly offering at Zamboanga Restaurant (Adriatico corner Pedro Gil, Manila). The hour-long show starts at 8.30 pm.

For an elegant dinner (the cuisine is mostly French-inspired) with music, the Champagne Room in the Manila Hotel (jacket and tie required for men) is one place to go to. The ambience is romantic: candlelight, flowers and a band playing danceable tunes and old-time favourites to send you down memory lane.

RJ Bistro, a watering hole of professionals and businessmen first established in Pasay in 1986, features dancing and live bands playing music from the 1950s onwards. Over the years, other RJ Bistros followed. The Music Museum in Greenhills also attracts top local vocalists and bands.

Ermita's girlie bars and honky-tonks have been cleaned up, but there's still life on The Strip. Trendy Remedios Circle attracts the après-theatre crowd, yuppies and members of the café society. Street entertainment is sometimes provided by local musical groups. Makati offers a choice of nightspots where you can enjoy drinks, dinner and dancing in a party atmosphere. Zu at the Shangri-La in Makati is one of the favourite places for Manilans to party the night away. Euphoria at Hotel Inter-Continental is still popular. Studebaker's is a three-storey nightspot that attracts the expatriate crowd. Then there's Kudos, at the Gallery Building; Mars on San Lorenzo Drive corner Arnaiz (Pasay) Road; Equinox, also on Arnaiz Road and Faces at Parkway Arcade (Legaspi Village). These places are crowded during weekends, so those who want to be assured of a place arrive early. Between 11 pm and 2 am they are jumping with life. If a smoky room, packed sweaty bodies on the dance floor and pulsing lights are not your scene, head for somewhere else. All impose a cover charge which goes up on weekends. Dress code is strict. Definite no-nos are shorts, rubber shoes, jeans and collarless T-shirts. Dress smart casual to be on the safe side.

Those who wish to take a turn at the gaming tables can head for the casinos operated by the Philippine Amusement and Gaming Corporation (Pagcor). Filipino casinos are located at the Holiday Inn Manila Pavilion Hotel (UN Avenue), the Hotel Sofitel Grand Boulevard and the Heritage Hotel (Roxas Boulevard). High-rollers have a choice of baccarat, blackjack, pai-gow, roulette, big and small craps. There are also slot machines for the not-so-serious punters. For entertainment, the Casino's Alegria Lounge on UN Avenue regularly stages adaptations of popular West End and Broadway musicals.

For the night-owl on the prowl, check the newspapers and tourist publications to see what's on in Manila, Pasay City, Makati, and Quezon City during your stay.

Some places impose a minimum charge, others have a cover charge, some have strict dress codes. A tip to bar hoppers: keep a sharp eye on the bill handed to you in the dark, especially if you have had several rounds of drinks. You may be paying for one drink too many. Where you go will depend upon your interest and pocketbook.

SHOPPING

Metro Manila offers many pleasant surprises for both serious shopper and casual browser. The city has the widest selection of goods in the country; these come from all over the Philippines and abroad and cater for every pocketbook. Items can be found in a variety of locations—from the modern, sprawling shopping malls of Makati, Mandaluyong/Pasig, Manila, Quezon City and Pasay City, to bazaars and large markets of Manila's older districts. Rustan's, Shoemart (SM) and Robinson's are the leading department stores in Metro Manila and have branches in other parts of the country. The one-stop shopping centre is a concept that has found favour among Filipinos and this type of shopping complex is now all over Metro Manila and is gaining popularity in the bigger towns and cities in the provinces. In addition to boutiques, department stores and supermarkets, this type of shopping complex also houses cinemas, art galleries, restaurants, snack bars and fast food courts, even an ice skating rink and car park, all under one roof. In Makati, the Greenbelt Mall across the Greenbelt Park, the Ayala Centre containing the Ayala Mall and Glorietta, The Quad and The Landmark are upscale shopping complexes. Megamall and Shangri-La Plaza in Ortigas Centre, Mandaluyong, are popular among shoppers. Megamall, as the name suggests, is a massive complex occupying several city blocks. Shoemart, an ice skating rink and art galleries are found here. Next door is the Shangri-La Plaza, housing Rustan's department store, National Book Store, and William J Shaw theatre, home of Repertory Philippines. Not far from this area is Robinson's Galleria. Further along Ortigas Avenue is Greenhills, another large shopping centre with a huge supermarket called Unimart. Shoppers also search for bargains at the Tianggue, a row of small stalls selling anything from jewellery, clothing and accessories, houseware, furniture, gift items and books. Further down Ortigas are shops selling rattan furniture and wickerwork and, nearing Christmas, special Christmas lanterns.

Cubao is the main shopping area in Quezon City. At the heart of Cubao is the Araneta Centre, the pioneer among the present-day malls. Ali Mall, Rustan's, Shoemart. Farmer's Market and Automatic Centre are found in the area. SM City in North EDSA, Ever Gotesco on Commonwealth Avenue are other large shopping malls.

In the city of Manila, Robinson's Place in Ermita is the newest and most modern shopping centre, occupying seven hectares of prime property next to Midtown Hotel.

A reconstructed Spanish colonial house in Intramuros, Manila

It is built in the same concept as Robinson's Galleria and other huge malls, with a variety of shops and boutiques, a food court, cinemas, amusement centre, bowling centre, department stores, supermarket, drugstore, bookstore. It has four major entrances—at M Adriatico, M Orosa, Pedro Gil and Padre Faura streets. Old landmarks are still found in Ermita. On A. Mabini there's Tesoro's which sells Philippine handicrafts, *barongs* and embroidered *jusi*; and on Padre Faura Street La Solidaridad the bookstore. Then there's Harrison Plaza, next to the Century Park Hotel, housing two department stores, a supermarket, boutiques and shops. Another large shopping mall in Manila is Centrepoint along Santa Mesa (Aurora) Boulevard. Manila's older districts like Quiapo, Santa Cruz and Binondo (Chinatown) have many small retail shops which sell lower-priced merchandise. The area under Quezon Bridge, known as 'Ilalim ng Tulay' sells comparatively inexpensive Philippine handicrafts. Divisoria with its wholesale market and Tutuban Centre (see also page 115) offer a variety of goods for the bargain-hunter.

There are plenty of items that make ideal presents to take home. Philippine ice cream in gallon containers packed in dry ice is popular among Asian tourists. This can be bought at the departure area of Ninoy Aquino International Airport. Check with airline personnel before boarding your flight.

The City of Manila

The city of Manila, lying along the curve of Manila Bay, is the grand dame of Philippine cities. Founded by the Spanish *adelantado* Miguel Lopez de Legaspi in 1571 and conferred the title of Distinguished and Ever Loyal City by a royal decree of King Philip II in 1574, Manila has a colourful, chequered and at times, tumultuous past. Nothing much is known about Manila before her conquest by Spain except that it was a flourishing kingdom on the south bank of the Pasig River ruled by a young rajah—Soliman. The name Manila was probably derived from the Tagalog *may nilad* meaning 'there's *nilad* there', referring to a flowering mangrove plant called *nilad* which grew along the river bank. Manila was a Spanish city for 379 years and an American city for almost 48 years. For 250 years, Manila was at the centre of the lucrative galleon trade, the hub for the transhipment of the treasures of the East in exchange for the silver of the West. The British briefly occupied Manila from 1762–64 and the Japanese from 1942–45. In Manila, East meets West, while the new and the old, the modern and traditional combine to give it its unique character.

The stone entrance to Fort Santiago with a relief carving of St James

For the visitor interested in the city's historic past, Intramuros and Fort Santiago, Rizal Park and Paco Park are worth visiting. Landmarks dating back to the Spanish era are the churches in Intramuros, Ermita, Malate, Quiapo, Santa Cruz, Binondo, and Santa Ana; the University of Santo Tomas founded in 1611, with its massive centuries-old stone arch, and Malacañang Palace, the official residence of Philippine presidents. North of the Pasig River are the old districts of Binondo and San Nicolas—Manila's Chinatown; Divisoria, a huge wholesale market, and the renovated Tutuban railway station which has been transformed into a shopping centre. South of the river is the Tourist Belt of Ermita and Malate with their hotels, restaurants and cafés, handicraft shops, bookshops, airline offices and travel agencies; and Roxas Boulevard with Central Bank, the Cultural Centre complex, and the Convention Centre.

INTRAMUROS

When the Spaniards first sighted Maynilad in 1570 on the south bank of the Pasig River, it was fortified against enemy attack by wooden palisades mounted with cannons. Legaspi claimed it for Spain in 1571 and rebuilt the settlement, which was destroyed by fire. He ordered the construction of a fort at the mouth of the river and new fortifications for the enclosed city. Stone walls started to replace Legaspi's wooden fort during the time of Governor-General Santiago de Vera (in office 1584–90). His successor, Gomez Perez de Dasmariñas, began the systematic fortification of the walls according to plans drawn up in Madrid. The original walls were made of volcanic tufa, earth and brick, and were irregular, in some places only 2.5 metres (8 feet) thick, in others 6 metres (20 feet) wide at the top and 14 metres (46 feet) at the base. Succeeding governors improved or altered the fortifications according to the military needs of the time. Work on the walls and fortifications spanned 251 years up to 1835.

The city within the walls, which came to be known as Intramuros, was enclosed by stone walls 4.5 kilometres (2.8 miles) long, with a fort, bastions, ramparts, and guard towers and surrounded by a moat. It was accessible from the outside through seven gates. Three faced the river—Almacenes, Santo Domingo and Isabel II; two were on the land side—Real and Parian; and two faced the bay—Santa Lucia and Postigo. Drawbridges were lowered at 4 am and raised at 11 pm. Intramuros covered 64 city blocks divided into the barrios of San Antonio, San Gabriel, San Luis and San Carlos. The streets were so laid out that one side was always in the shade. Here were government buildings, the residences of the governor-general and the archbishop, churches, monasteries and the houses of the religious orders; hospitals, hotels, schools, colleges and universities, military barracks, an arsenal, a printing press and the residences of the élite.

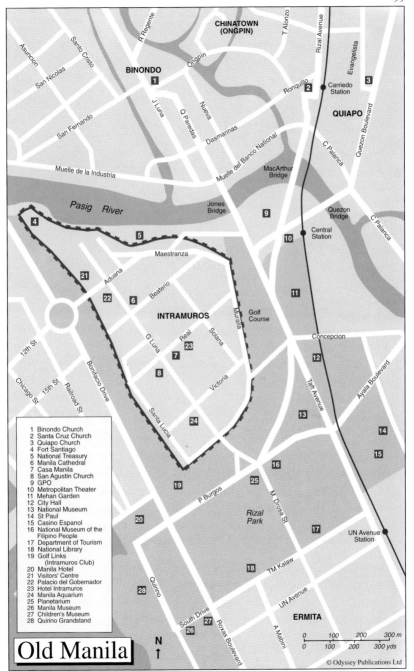

CHINATOWN
(ONGPIN)

BINONDO **1**

QUIAPO

2 Carriedo Station

3

Ronquillo

R Regente

T Alonzo

Rizal Avenue

Evangelista

Asuncion

Santo Cristo

San Nicolas

Ongpin

J Luna

Q Paredes

Nueva

Dasmariñas

San Fernando

Quezon Boulevard

C Palanca

Muelle del Banco National

MacArthur Bridge

Muelle de la Industria

Pasig   River

Jones Bridge

9

Quezon Bridge

C Palanca

4

5

Maestranza

10 Central Station

21

Aduana

22   **6**

Beaterio

INTRAMUROS

11

Golf Course

Muralla

Concepcion

12th St

G Luna

Real

23

Solana

7

12

Bonifacio Drive

15th St

Railroad St

Chicago St

8

Victoria

Santa Lucia

24

Taft Avenue

13

Ayala Boulevard

14

15

16

25

19

P Burgos

M Diosa St

Rizal Park

17 UN Avenue Station

20

18

TM Kalaw

28

Quirino

UN Avenue

A Mabini

ERMITA

South Drive

26   **27**

Roxas Boulevard

1 Binondo Church
2 Santa Cruz Church
3 Quiapo Church
4 Fort Santiago
5 National Treasury
6 Manila Cathedral
7 Casa Manila
8 San Agustin Church
9 GPO
10 Metropolitan Theater
11 Mehan Garden
12 City Hall
13 National Museum
14 St Paul
15 Casino Espanol
16 National Museum of the
    Filipino People
17 Department of Tourism
18 National Library
19 Golf Links
    (Intramuros Club)
20 Manila Hotel
21 Visitors' Centre
22 Palacio del Gobernador
23 Hotel Intramuros
24 Manila Aquarium
25 Planetarium
26 Manila Museum
27 Children's Museum
28 Quirino Grandstand

Old Manila

N ↑

0   100   200   300 m
0   100   200   300 yds

© Odyssey Publications Ltd

Intramuros was the heart and soul of the country for more than 300 years, the seat of civil and ecclesiastical authority and the centre of the highly lucrative galleon trade. Intramuros weathered pirate attacks and an invasion by the Chinese warlord Limahong (or Lin Kao Tien) in 1574, Dutch aggression and blockades in the 17th century, British occupation between 1762 and 1764, and scattered uprisings by Filipinos and Chinese. When the galleon trade ceased in 1815, Manila opened her ports to foreign shipping. Slowly the city's character changed as it expanded outside the confines of the walls. District by district, Manila grew until Intramuros outlived its importance and became a district within the city. Today, the city of Manila is made up of the districts of Intramuros, Ermita, Malate, Pandacan, Paco, Santa Ana, Quiapo, Santa Cruz, Binondo, San Nicolas, Tondo, Divisoria, Port Area, Sampaloc and San Miguel.

Intramuros knew glory and gore, opulence and power. Wars, earthquakes, fires and typhoons have left their mark. In the final days of World War II, bombs pounded Intramuros into rubble, leaving only a few structures that now stand as relics of a bygone era. For a long time Intramuros was a wasteland until the Intramuros Administration (IA) was created in 1979 to restore and develop the Walled City as a historic site and major tourist attraction. The dust and debris of post-war neglect have been removed and over the years the walls, fortifications and gates were repaired and restored. Streets were cobblestoned. Several buildings had their facades renovated and new ones have been constructed, conforming to architectural guidelines established by the IA to preserve and reflect the look and ambience of the Spanish colonial era. Pocket parks and mini gardens add to the pleasure of walking tours. Among the newer sights in Intramuros is the Memorial Sculpture by Peter de Guzman honouring the 100,000 non-combatant victims of war who died during the liberation of Manila in February 1945. The old Aduana Building (the Intendencia) is being rebuilt to house the Spanish collection of the national archives.

Cultural and religious traditions popular during the Spanish era have been revived over the years. One such tradition is the Marian procession in December to

A balloon vendor leans on a tourist calesa at Rizal Park, Manila

mark the feast of the Immaculate Conception. Venerated images of the Blessed Virgin Mary are brought to Manila from different parts of the country to participate in the street procession. Cantar Villansicos, a choral competition of Christmas carols is held also in December while indoor and outdoor displays of the Belen, or Nativity scene, vie for prizes. Buildings are decorated with star lanterns (*faroles* or *parol*) at Christmas time.

Theatrical and musical performances are given free to the public every other weekend on Fridays and Saturdays at 6.30 pm between January and August. Billed as The Intramuros Evenings Performing Arts Series, these take place at four venues: the Puerta Real Gardens, the Baluarte de San Diego Gardens, the Teatrillo Plaza San Luis (at the basement of Casa Manila) and the Manila Cathedral.

■ VISITORS' CENTRE

To appreciate Manila's history, don't miss a visit to Intramuros. A walking tour can give you a good feel for the place. Make your first stop the Intramuros Visitors' Centre. This is located on Plaza Moriones, before the entrance to Fort Santiago, in a reconstructed fortification which used to be the Baluartillo de San Francisco Javier. Its ten chambers were formerly munition chambers. Today they house the Information Office of Intramuros Administration, a photo gallery, an audio-visual chamber, an outdoor café, craft and souvenir shop, and restrooms. An 18-minute documentary in sensurround sound gives a background of Intramuros. A shrine dedicated to Our Lady of Guadalupe is set at the Reducto de San Francisco on the outer walls. This is visible from the first tee of the Club Intramuros golf course which has its clubhouse just outside the walls. The shrine is open daily from 3 to 6 pm. Entrance to the shrine is through a chamber at the end of the Visitors' Centre, on the left hand side of Plaza Moriones outside the stone entrance to Fort Santiago.

■ FORT SANTIAGO

Intramuros takes the form of an unevenly shaped wedge, with Fort Santiago occupying the smallest angle. Declared a national shrine in 1950 (entrance fee: P40 for adults, P15 for students and children), Fort Santiago was the original site of Rajah Soliman's kingdom. The Spaniards named it La Fuerza de Santiago (the Fort of St James), in honour of Spain's patron saint. The entrance to the fort shows a relief carving in stone of San Tiago Matamoro slaying the Moors. Spanish, British, American, and Japanese flags have flown over the fort at various times in its colourful history. The moat and the stone breastwork along the riverside were constructed during the time of Governor-General Santiago de Vera. The fort has been rehabilitated and re-landscaped. Climb on the stone ramparts and parapet for a panoramic view of old Manila and the Pasig River flowing out to Manila Bay. You are standing right on the former site of Rajah Soliman's wooden palisaded kingdom.

The bastion of Santa Barbara, named for the patroness of Spanish artillerymen, was built in 1592 to protect the entrance to the Pasig River. Vaults and a powder magazine were added in 1599 and quarters for the artillerymen and the commandant's house were constructed in 1609. The powder magazine was used as a dungeon and torture chamber for hundreds of prisoners during the Japanese occupation. The dungeon is below the high tide mark which meant that some prisoners incarcerated there were sometimes drowned. The battery was badly damaged during the Battle of Manila in 1945 but was restored between 1951 and 1967 and again in 1991.

The two-storey building on the left, formerly part of the main artillery barracks, is now the Rizal Shrine (open 8 am to 12 noon, 1 to 5 pm daily). Dr Jose Rizal, the Philippines' national hero, was placed here under house arrest for 52 days prior to his execution in Bagumbayan Field (Luneta) on 30 December 1896. On the ground floor is the cell where Rizal slept and where he wrote his poem, *Mi Ultimo Adios* (My Last Farewell). On the first floor is the Rizaliana museum. There is also a small book shop which sells copies of Rizal's novels, *Noli Me Tangere* and *El Filibusterismo*, banned by the Spanish authorities at the time of their publication for their allegedly seditious content. The novels give insight into what Philippine life was like a hundred years ago. Among the events marking the centennial of Rizal's death was the re-enactment of Rizal's walk from Fort Santiago to Luneta.

Also within the fort is the Rajah Soliman Theatre where seasonal plays in English and Pilipino are staged by the Philippine Educational Theatre Association (PETA).

■ PLAZA DE ROMA

Across Aduana Street from Fort Santiago is Plaza de Roma, a small tree-shaded square dominated by a bronze statue dating back to 1834. The statue is that of King Carlos IV who sent smallpox vaccine to the Philippines. Plaza de Roma, known as Plaza Mayor during Spanish times, used to be a venue for bullfights and other public events until its transformation into a garden in 1797. Under the Americans it was renamed Plaza McKinley until the 1960s when it became Plaza de Roma to reciprocate the naming of the Piazza Manila in Rome.

In front of the plaza is the Manila Cathedral, reconstructed in 1958. This is the sixth cathedral built on this site since 1581. Earlier churches were destroyed by fire or earthquake. The cathedral features stained glass windows and mosaics, and incorporates the stone carvings and rosette windows of the old cathedral. On the right-hand side of the square is a pink eight-storey building known as the Palacio del

Gobernador because it was the site of the governor general's palace until its destruction by an earthquake in 1863, when the governor moved his official residence to Malacañang Palace. The building now houses the Intramuros Administration, the Bureau of Treasury, and the Commission on Elections. Further along General Luna Street is San Agustin Church.

■ SAN AGUSTIN CHURCH

San Agustin Church was the only church out of seven in Intramuros that survived the wartime bombardment. The original church of bamboo and nipa, consecrated in 1571, was burnt down during Limahong's invasion. The second, made of wood, also went up in flames when a candle toppled at a governor general's funeral. The present stone church, completed around 1607, has 1.5-metre (5 feet) thick walls and has withstood five earthquakes. Granite lions guard the courtyard entrance and the main door is carved from Philippine hardwood. The interior is painted in *trompe l'oeil* style and features a baroque pulpit, ivory-inlaid *molave* choir stalls and an 18th-century organ. Parisian chandeliers hang from the ceiling. To the left of the main altar, in one of the 14 side chapels lining the nave, is a tomb bearing Legaspi's effigy. Here lie the remains of the *adelantado* and early *conquistadores* such as Martin de Goiti and Juan de Salcedo, as well as early governors and archbishops. San Agustin church is a popular venue for weddings.

Adjoining the church is a monastery garden and museum (open daily from 9 am to 12 noon; 1 to 5 pm; entrance fee: P30/adults, P10/children). The museum houses a notable collection of religious art and artefacts, rare books and manuscripts, photographs and liturgical vestments. Among the items is a six-volume botanical work entitled *Flora de Filipinas*, written in the 18th century by the Augustinian friar Manuel Blanco. Father Blanco's Garden, accessible from a side street at the back of the church, is a popular venue for wedding and other receptions.

■ PLAZA SAN LUIS

Across San Agustin Church is Plaza San Luis, a cultural and commercial complex built in the architectural style of colonial buildings between the 17th and 19th centuries. The area houses art galleries, craft shops, book store, restaurants and café, a boutique hotel and the Casa Manila Museum. The Casa Manila is a lifestyle museum recreating the ambience of a rich man's residence in Binondo at the height of the galleon trade. The architectural plans were drawn up in 1980 by the architect Jose Ramon Faustmann who worked from aerial and period photographs. Adobe stones, timber, bricks and balustrades from demolished period houses were used in its construction, which was completed in 1983. The lavish carvings were created by 50

Sunset over Manila Bay

expert craftsmen from Pampanga and Laguna, while the exquisitely embroidered bed hangings and centrepanes are the work of more than 100 women from Lumban, Laguna. Gilded furniture and furnishings from China and Europe, crystal chandeliers, velvet drapes, painted walls, Persian rugs and carpets, Chinese ceramics, cabinets inlaid with tortoiseshell and ivory and carved *narra* furniture reflect the taste in home furnishings and decor of the time. The floors are made of hardwood, polished to a high sheen. From Calle Real, you pass through the main entrance which is framed by an elaborately carved stone portal and enter the stone-paved passageway used by carriages. This leads to an open patio with a fountain in the middle. Special events take place here during the year such as the annual Christmas carols competition. Wedding receptions and private functions are also held in the patio. Casa Manila is open from 8 am to 6 pm Tuesdays to Saturdays. Admission fee: P40/adults, P15/students and faculty with ID and children under 12. Within the compound is Barbara's, a restaurant capturing the gracious ambience of old Manila. You can actually book the place for a ball.

Around the corner from Casa Manila is another period house displaying the collection of the Intramuros Administration. The changing exhibitions showcase the Philippines' cultural and religious heritage in art pieces, church furnishings, sacred vessels, icons, and other treasures. Most of these are the work of unknown local craftsmen and artisans (woodcarvers, sculptors, metalsmiths, painters) and they reflect the folk art and foreign influences and styles of the times. In the same block is the Hotel Intramuros de Manila, a 25-room boutique hotel designed and furnished like the ancestral homes found in Vigan, Taal and Iloilo. The Hotel and Restaurant Association operates the hotel and a Tourism School with hands-on training for the students.

A short distance from Plaza San Luis is Plazuela de Santa Isabel, a pocket park with a sculpture called Memorare. This is a tribute to Filipinos who died in Intramuros in World War II. In Spanish times, the church and college of Santa Isabel were located here. Tamarind trees (*sampaloc*) used to grow around here. It is said that a house on this site was used as a tryst by a Spanish merchant and a governor general's wife, both of whom met tragic deaths at the hands of the aggrieved husband. The tamarind trees with their sour-sweet fruit, were symbolic of a love that had gone sour.

■ BASTIONS AND GATES

It is possible to walk round the walls and see the gates and bastions. Start with Fort Santiago and from the Visitors Information Centre proceed to Postigo del Palacio, the gate facing Manila Bay. This was built in 1662 and renovated in 1782. Jose Rizal was led through this gate from his cell in Fort Santiago to face a firing squad at

Bagumbayan Field (now Rizal Park) on the morning of his execution. This gate, along Bonifacio Drive, was very near the governor's palace and was used by His Excellency, as well as His Grace, the archbishop, when they wanted to leave or return to Intramuros unseen. Further along is the Santa Lucia gate, constructed in the 18th century. It has two side chambers. One of them has steps leading to a cell now used as a septic tank, and to Malecon Drive, once a popular promenade ground, through a restored cobbled bridge. Here too are the bulwarks of San Jose, San Pedro and San Diego. The historic Manila Hotel is on the other side of Bonifacio Drive. General Douglas MacArthur made this hotel his command post in December 1941 before withdrawing to Corregidor.

The Puerta Real or Royal Gate was used for ceremonial and state occasions, religious processions and parades. The governor general made his official entrance and exit from this gate. After the British invasion of 1762, the gate was relocated in Muralla Street from its former site on Calle del Palacio (now General Luna Street). Because it was narrower and lower, processions were rerouted through the Parian Gate. Two spiral staircases lead up to the restored ramparts. Following Muralla Street you pass several bastions before arriving at Puerta del Parian. This was one of the three main gates to the walled city. Outside the gates Chinese hawkers sold a variety of imported wares. The gate led directly to Calle Real or Royal Street. After the Revellin del Parian and the Baluarte de San Gabriel, you arrive at Puerta Isabel II on Magallanes Drive. The last gate to be built in Intramuros, it was opened in 1862 to ease traffic between Intramuros and Binondo. The statue of the Spanish queen stands in front of the gate. It was installed in its rightful place in 1974, after spending many years in front of the Malate Church. An antiroyalist governor refused to install the statue after completion, and ordered it destroyed. However, after being hidden in a storeroom, the statue was removed to the Ayuntamiento or city council. The chambers flanking the gate were once barracks and arsenals.

■ MANILA AQUARIUM

The wonders of the marine world are displayed at the newly renovated Acuario de Manila at Puerta Real. The marine specimens were gathered from the waters of Batangas, Mindoro, Cebu, Cavite, Batanes, Jolo, Sulu, Palawan, Quezon and other parts of the archipelago. Some of them are rare and seldom seem. Among the exhibits are the stone fish, black tip sharks, cow fish, black lion-fish, blue spotted stingray, moray eel, sea horses and other fish that Filipinos are familiar with. Other displays recreate underwater scenes. The aquarium has a film show on marine life and pictures, drawings and descriptions of turtles, sharks, whales, dolphins and Philippine algae. Open daily from 8 am to 6 pm. Admission P40 for adults, P25 for students and children.

RIZAL PARK

From Intramuros, Rizal Park is a walk away. The park is
bounded by Burgos Street on the north, T M Kalaw Street
on the south, the seawall on the west and Taft Avenue on
the east. This is the city's premier park, dedicated to the
Philippines' national hero, Dr Jose Rizal and the values he
once stood for. It is a favourite place for weekend family
picnics, afternoon strolls and sunset promenades; a lovers' rendezvous, a venue for Sunday concerts and a game
of chess and the setting for a Sound and Light show (*son
et lumière*). The park is popularly known as Luneta after a
small area shaped like a half-moon was cleared outside of
Intramuros and made into an open field.

On the western end of the park fronting Manila Hotel
and near the seawall is the Quirino Grandstand where
presidential inaugurations, political rallies and outdoor
Masses are held. A huge parade was held here in 1998 to
mark the centennial of the proclamation of independence.
It was here that Pope John Paul II addressed the youth of
the world gathered in Manila for World Youth Day 1995.
The promenade along the seawall is a favourite place for
sunset-watchers. Nearby is a restaurant built on stilts over
the waters which affords diners a splendid view. In the
19th century the promenade had a bandstand, a glorieta
in the centre and two circular fountains. It was a tradition
to hold band concerts here. 'The Governor's military band
played in the early evenings, and all Manila came to see
and be seen,' wrote Henry T Ellis, a British author who
visited Manila in 1856. The Heroes Promenade, a tribute
to Filipinos who died for their country, is on the southern
side. Next to it is the San Lorenzo Ruiz Plaza, dominated
by a six-foot tall, 370-kilo statue by Italian sculptor Tom-
maso Gismondi. It was commissioned by Pope John Paul
II as a gift to the Filipino people on the beatification of
Lorenzo Ruiz, protomartyr of the Philippines, who died
for the faith in Japan during the time of the Christian
purges in and around Nagasaki between 1633 and 1637.
The beatification rites were held on this spot on February

Male penitents attempt to touch the Black Nazarene during the Quiapo Fiesta, Manila

18, 1982 by Pope John Paul II, the first time such rites were held outside the Vatican. The statue was unveiled in front of the *narra* tree planted by Pope Paul VI in 1970. The Blessed Lorenzo Ruiz and his fellow martyrs were later canonised at St Peter's Square in Rome on 18 October 1987.

Across the street from San Lorenzo Ruiz Plaza is the Museo ng Maynila (Museum of Manila). Established in June 1997, it occupies the former Army-Navy Club on South Street. The building, constructed in the early 1900s, is undergoing renovation to make it a proper showcase of Manila's rich history. Featured in the museum are rare old photographs and engravings showing Manila from the 1830s to 1930s, archaeological exhibits on loan from the National Museum of excavated pottery and grave ware from the Santa Ana churchyard, a hall especially dedicated to memorabilia of Andres Bonifacio and the Katipunan. The museum is open from 9 am to 4 pm Tuesdays to Saturdays. Admission is free.

Fronting Roxas Boulevard in the central section is the Rizal monument. Jose Rizal's remains were transferred here after they were exhumed from the Paco Park (then a cemetery) in 1912 and are buried beneath this monument. It was in this place, then known as Bagumbayan Field, that Dr Rizal, charged with sedition and inciting to rebellion, was executed by order of the Spanish authorities on 30 December 1896. Twenty-four years earlier, on 17 February 1872, three Filipino priests—Fathers Mariano Gomez, Jose Burgos, and Jacinto Zamora—were also executed here. On the centennial of Rizal's death, a spectacular re-enactment of his execution was held at Rizal Park. A 30-minute sound and light show depicting the Filipino martyr's trial and death by firing squad is presented Wednesdays to Sundays. The first show, from 7 to 7.30 pm is in Tagalog; the English-language show is from 8 to 8.30 pm. The showing is dependent on weather and the number of persons attending. Admission fee is P30 for adults and P10 for students and children. In front of Rizal's monument is a 31-metre-high (102-foot) flagpole which flies the Philippine flag at all times, regardless of the weather. Kilometre 0, the point of reference for land travel in Luzon, is located here. Behind the Rizal monument, near the Rizal fountain, is a bust of Ferdinand Blumentritt, a close friend of Jose Rizal. The Gallery of Heroes, showing the bronze busts of 20 Filipinos who played a role in the country's fight for freedom, flank the central lagoon.

A noteworthy feature of the park is the Chess Plaza, established to ensure the enrichment and promotion of outdoor chess throughout the country. Open from 9 am to 10 pm daily, it is well patronized by chess enthusiasts. Chess sets and timers can be rented by the hour. Anybody can play there, except when there are official tournaments with special schedules. Anatoly Karpov visited the Chess Plaza in April 1998. Other attractions in the park are the Chinese Garden, featuring a replica of the Summer Palace outside Beijing, a lagoon with fountains, a recently enlarged and improved open-air auditorium where live concerts are held every Sunday, a Japanese Garden, a planetarium, a cafeteria managed by deaf-mutes, and a floral clock. An area measuring half a hectare (1.3 acres) close to the cafeteria was redesigned by landscape architect Ildefonso P Santos as an environmental art gallery where Filipino artists can display their works. The architect worked around the old Philippine hardwood trees.

Across Maria Orosa Street in the eastern end of the park is the Orchidarium, (open 9 am to 6 pm; there's a small admission fee). The globe-shaped fountain has been replaced by a monument—Binhi ng Kalayaan—by Ed Castrillo, one of the Philippines' noted contemporary sculptors. Around it is the skating rink (open 6 am to 11 pm; admission P5). A relief map of the Philippines, a garden of tropical plants and a children's playground front Taft Avenue. The Department of Tourism and the National Library are on T M Kalaw Street. On the other side of the Agrifina Circle is the National Museum. The Department of Tourism and the National Library are on T M Kalaw Street. If you walk in the direction of City Hall (with its clock tower) along P Burgos Street, you will reach a white building with a façade designed in the classical revival style. This is the National Museum.

NATIONAL MUSEUM

The National Museum is the official repository of the Philippines' cultural heritage. The museum collection totals more than one million items from the fields of anthropology, archaeology, art, botany, geology and zoology. At present the collections are housed at the old Congress Building fronting P Burgos Street. The Museum, however, is in the process of expansion. It has recently moved its archaeology, anthropology and history sections to their permanent home at the former Finance Building on Agrifina Circle. Constructed by the Americans at the beginning of the 20th century, the building has been restored to its former glory, with its magnificent chandelier and original stained glass windows depicting the seal of the Republic of the Philippines and the Department of Finance. Called the Museum of the Filipino People, it depicts the story of the Filipino people from pre-historic times. Among the exhibits are 2,000-year-old human-shaped clay burial jars made between 5 BC and AD 370 that were found in 1991 in a cave in Maitum, southern Sarangani province in Mindanao. According to an archaeologist, the jars indicated that prehistoric Filipinos had complex cultures which included ancestor worship and burial of the dead. An authentic Ifugao House brought down from the Cordillera mountains is also on display. Ifugao priests called *mumfonis* performed rituals before the transfer and during the installation at the museum to give the house good vibes in its new location.

Philippine Military Academy cadets participating at an Independence Day parade

Made of molave and narra woods, the one-room house features a steep sloping roof of thick *cogon* grass that serves as the outer walls. Not a single nail is used, only rattan bindings and perfect fittings of joints.

Also on exhibition are The Treasures of *San Diego*, one of the most significant discoveries in the history of marine archaeology. The *San Diego* was a Spanish battleship that sank off the coast of Batangas. Its wreckage was found at the sea bottom off Fortune Island in 1992. Recovered by underwater archaeological excavation between February and April 1992 were some 34,000 archaeological items, including stoneware jars, Ming Dynasty Chinese porcelain bowls from the Wanli period (1573–1619), 14 bronze cannon and musket balls, navigational equipment and a variety of objects. The ship was built as a trading vessel in Cebu and was originally named the *San Antonio*. While docked at the port of Cavite for reconditioning and repair, the then Vice Governor General Don Antonio de Morga ordered it converted into a warship and renamed. On 14 December 1660 the *San Diego* was engaged in battle with Dutch ships and was sunk. The Treasures of *San Diego* toured Paris, Madrid, New York and Berlin.

Other cultural treasures at the museum include the fossilized skullcap of Tabon Man of Palawan, approximately 22,000 to 24,000 years old. The Museum of the Filipino People is the first building to be made a permanent home for the museum's collection. The Museum of Natural History, to be housed in what is now the Department of Tourism building, is expected to be ready by 2002. The old Congress Building or Executive House will become the National Museum of Art. Works of outstanding Filipino painters such as Juan Luna, Felix Resurreccion Hidalgo, Fernando Amorsolo, Carlos 'Botong' Francisco and Vicente Manansala are exhibited at the Masters Hall. Juan Luna's massive masterpiece, *Spoliarium*, won the gold medal in the National Fine Arts Exposition in Spain in 1884. Completed in Rome, it depicts fallen gladiators in the Roman Colosseum.

The Planetarium along P Burgos Street is part of the National Museum. Four shows a day are held from Tuesday to Saturday. There are no shows on Sundays and public holidays. The Planetarium is closed on Mondays.

North of the Pasig River

Five bridges span the Pasig River to link Manila's northern and southern districts. These are the Jones Bridge leading to Escolta and Binondo, the MacArthur Bridge leading to Santa Cruz, the Quezon Bridge leading to Quiapo, the Ayala Bridge leading to San Miguel and Malacañang Palace, and the Nagtahan or Mabini Bridge leading to Pandacan.

San Nicolas, Binondo and Tondo, Santa Cruz and Quiapo are old districts. They have seen better days, but those in search of local colour will find plenty to interest them here. The merchandise, fresh fruit and produce, and handicrafts sold in the stores and markets here are less expensive than in the areas frequented by tourists and the more well-heeled residents. When venturing into these crowded, working-class areas, dress simply and forego any display of wealth.

Quiapo and Santa Cruz

Quiapo's principal landmark is the church, built in 1935 on the site of three other churches, the earliest dating back to 1586. Quiapo church houses the Black Nazarene, a lifelike statue of Jesus Christ bearing a cross. The image, carved in dark wood by Mexican Indians, was brought to the Philippines by galleon in the 17th century. Worshippers flock to the church on Fridays. The Holy Week rituals and the evening procession of the Black Nazarene, borne on the shoulders of male devotees, when Quiapo celebrates its feast in the month of January draw massive crowds. Quiapo's Plaza Miranda was the scene of political rallies and electoral campaign speeches. One of the dominant features of Quiapo's skyline is the dome of a mosque and its minaret. There are many stalls under the bridge selling Philippine handicrafts, hence the place is known locally as 'Ilalim ng Tulay' (under the bridge). Fresh fruit is sold in the nearby market.

The side streets near the church are crammed with bazaars selling all sorts of merchandise. Carriedo and Echague are streets that link up with Avenida Rizal in the Santa Cruz district. The Church of Our Lady of Pillar, known simply as Santa Cruz Church, stands on Plaza Santa Cruz at the foot of MacArthur Bridge. The present church, damaged in 1945, was built on the site of the original church, founded by the Jesuits in 1608 to serve Chinese converts. In the side courtyard, the British in 1764 formally surrendered Manila to the Spanish authorities after 20 months of occupation. From the church one can walk to Escolta, once the most fashionable shopping street of prewar Manila. The upstairs coffee shop of Botica Boie was where prominent Manilans met to exchange gossip. Escolta's former clientele have moved elsewhere. Although it is no longer the high street, it maintains its coterie of shops selling shoes, fashion accessories and household wares. From Escolta, Chinatown is just a short walk away.

BINONDO AND SAN NICOLAS

Manila's Chinatown is located in the old districts of San Nicolas and Binondo. Quintin Paredes, Nueva, Gandara, Ongpin and Pinpin Streets form the heart of Chinatown. You know you are there when you see the Chinese gates, the shop signs, the temples, the stores and restaurants which exude an unmistakable Chinese atmosphere. *Calesas*, horse-drawn vehicles, once acknowledged 'kings of the road', no longer reign supreme but still can be found in Chinatown.

Those looking for Chinese herbal medicine, gold jewellery— the kind favoured by Chinese, and traditional Chinese goods such as scrolls, silk embroideries, Chinese porcelain, preserved fruit and meat, and fresh fruit from China come here. Bakeries sell *hopia*, those small round pastry cases filled with bean paste, pork, pineapple, or lotus seed paste. Hopia fanciers come here around 4 pm to collect their orders, still hot from the kitchen. Gandara, Ongpin, T Pinpin and Nueva are the principal shopping streets in Chinatown.

San Nicolas (then known as Baybay, a sitio in Tondo) and Binondo were the places of residence for most Chinese by the end of the 16th century. Previous to that the Chinese lived in the Parian, a lively and noisy settlement just outside the walls of Intramuros, in the area where the General Post Office is today. But as their numbers continued to grow, they became a cause of concern for the authorities. A turn of events climaxed by the assassination of the then Governor Gomez Perez Dasmariñas on the high seas by a Chinese crew when they were going on an expedition against the Moluccas prompted the governor's son and successor, Luis Perez Dasmariña, to expel the Chinese from the Parian. However, in consideration of the Chinese who had been converted to Christianity by the Spanish Dominicans, he bought the islet of Binondo so they could live there after their expulsion. He loved the place so much that he also made a residence there for himself. It was in Binondo that Lorenzo Ruiz, who was to be the Philippines' first saint, was born of a Chinese father and a Filipino mother. The Dominicans built a church, a convent and a hospital here.

The first printing press was installed in Binondo in 1602 which produced the first books in the Philippines using movable type. Father Francisco Blancas de San Jose and the printers Juan de Vera and Tomas Pinpin were credited with this remarkable feat. T Pinpin is today one of the principal streets of Chinatown. In a tree-shaded plaza that recalls the old days of Manila stands the massive church dedicated to Our Lady of the Rosary. This is one of the notable landmarks of Binondo and deserves to be seen. Built in 1587 as a parish for the Chinese, it was one of the earliest Dominican churches in Manila. Fr Diego Aduarte, a noted historian writing about the church in 1630 described it as 'beautiful...very spacious and well lighted, very pleasant, all made of stone, very strong and very attractive'. It was partially destroyed by the British during their occupation of Manila and was heavily damaged in World War II. The church was rebuilt between 1946 and 1971. The western façade and six-storey octagonal bell-tower, however, are original. Restoration and reconstruction work started in January 1977 and was completed in January 1984. In May 1985 it was blessed by the Cardinal. The church was elevated to a minor basilica in 1992. A larger-than-life statue of the martyr San Lorenzo Ruiz, the first Filipino to be canonised by the Vatican, stands in front of the basilica where he served as an altar boy. A plaza is named in his honour at Rizal Park. Not all the landmarks are old: Chinatown now has its own modern cinema and also boasts high-rise buildings.

DIVISORIA AND TUTUBAN CENTRE

This crowded, working-class area bustles with traders and wholesale merchants. Every imaginable type of merchandise catering to a wide socio-economic class is sold here. It is said that half of the goods unloaded in Manila's docks find their way to Divisoria, and many upmarket shops and boutiques in Metro Manila and the provinces source their goods here.

Divisoria, nicknamed Rue de la Div by Lila-Grace Bergoz, is the haunt of the little dressmakers and local couturiers who come here to find what they need among the bolts of cloth and boxloads of fabrics and remnants from the world's fashion capitals. Interior decorators source their materials here too. Goods sold here are far cheaper than similar goods sold in the smarter shopping establishments. Those who enjoy looking for a bargain come to Divisoria to shop. This is where haggling skills come to the fore. It pits the experienced buyer against the seasoned seller. Patience and a nose covering are needed here. If you are allergic to dust and other pollutants, it is best to stay away.

Just a few blocks from Divisoria's markets is Tutuban Centre, a former railway station that was converted into a shopping complex in 1993. Built in 1891, the Tutuban Railway Station is claimed to be the only existing neo-classical, semi-Victorian structure in the Philippines today, and as such is an architectural landmark. The interior has been redesigned and now has wider hallways and the convenience of air-conditioning, escalators and freight elevators or lifts. The cast-iron columns topped by Corinthian capitals have been retained. It is said that these columns were cast in England by the same company that built the Ayala Bridge and Eiffel Tower.

The three-storey central mall, open from 9 am to 8 pm, has 100 retail shops and a food court offering various fast food and bakery outlets and restaurants serving Filipino, Japanese, Chinese and vegetarian food. The main building is connected by air bridges to cluster buildings which have about 1000 small stalls at the Divisoria market selling ready-to-wear apparel, fabrics, and a variety of items at comparatively low prices. You still haggle and bargain but you now shop in air-conditioned comfort. The stalls are open from 9 am to 7 pm. Central Mall II with name brand boutiques was opened more recently. The complex houses four cinemas, a bowling centre, amusement centre and a supermarket.

A plaza named after the revolutionary hero, Andres Bonifacio, forms the façade of Tutuban Centre. Bonifacio was born in the neighbourhood in front of the train station and founded the Katipunan, the first organized revolutionary movement for independence against Spain. The railways were closely linked with the activities of the revolutionaries at the turn of the century. At the lobby of the main building is a mini museum of railway and revolutionary memorabilia. Plaza Bonifacio is now a venue for cultural events such as concerts.

Tutuban was the centre of commerce in old Manila and Tutuban Station, inaugurated in 1891, served as the hub of rail transport in Luzon until the 1960s. A Spanish royal decree establishing a railway system in Luzon was passed in June 1875 and in 1885. An auction was held in Madrid for the concession to build a railway line from Manila to Dagupan City in Pangasinan province. The winning bidder was the British-owned Manila Railway Company, Ltd. The first stone was laid in 1887 by then Governor Emilio Terrero and the first section of the line—a 44-kilometre distance to the banks of Calumpit River in Bulacan province—was opened in 1890.

The railways played an important part during the turbulent closing years of the 19th century when Filipinos fought to gain independence from Spain and in the ensuing Filipino-American war. In October 1896, trains were derailed several times as revolutionaries attacked the supply convoys. The trains were also used to transport revolutionary troops and supplies in 1898. Filipino and American forces fought for control of the railway system in February 1899 and in October 1899, Gen. Emilio Aguinaldo, who had previously proclaimed independence from Spain, ordered the cutting of rail tracks and derailment of the trains.

The Manila Railway Company was renamed Philippine National Railways (PNR) in 1964. In 1989, 22 hectares of the PNR's property on Claro M Recto Avenue was leased long-term to a private developer for commercial development. This area of Manila is undergoing urban renewal and the architects and developers hope to retain the historic significance of the district.

Transport: Jeepneys marked Divisoria will take you there. Or you can board the LRT; get off at Doroteo Jose station and walk to Claro M Recto Street to catch a Divisoria-bound jeepney. Taxis are the easier and more convenient option.

UNIVERSITY OF SANTO TOMAS

Another distinct landmark dating back to Spanish times is the University of Santo Tomas, the oldest university in the Philippines, founded by the third Archbishop of Manila, Msgr Miguel de Benavidez on 23 April 1611. First called the Colegio de Nuestra Señora Rosario, it was located within Intramuros, the walled city, and was originally conceived as a school to prepare young men for the priesthood. It was later renamed Colegio de Sto Tomas in honour of the St Thomas Aquinas. Pope Innocent X elevated it to the rank of university on 20 November 1645, and Pope Leo XIII conferred on it the title Pontifical University on 17 September 1902. Pope Pious XII in 1947 bestowed upon it the title Catholic University of the Philippines. You entered the old campus through a massive stone gate, the Arch of the Centuries, decorated with statues of saints. After the destruction of the original building, the university was relocated in 1927 to its present site on España Street in Sampaloc district. The statue of the founder and the stone portal, were transferred to the present campus. Famous alumni of the university include Jose Rizal, M H del Pilar, A Mabini, Emilio Aguinaldo, the three martyred priests—Gomez, Burgos and Zamora—and Philippine presidents Quezon, Osmeña, Laurel and Macapagal. The campus was used as an allied internment camp by the Japanese during World War II. The university houses the oldest printing press in the country, and its library contains rare manuscripts, books, coins and medals. Its Museum of Natural Science, which has extensive collections in several areas, was the only museum in the country when the Philippine Republic was inaugurated in 1898. It has since been expanded to include the arts when the university acquired works of art by Filipino masters in the

1940s. Closed for renovation in 1997, the UST Museum reopened on 31 July 1998. The university is accessible by jeepneys marked España or UST. Not far from Santo Tomas University is Malacañang Palace on J P Laurel Street. Mendiola Street is nick-named University Belt because Centro Escolar University and San Beda College, among others, are located on this street. The twin-towered, neo-Gothic San Sebastian Church, founded in 1621, is also in this area.

Malacañang Palace

Historic Malacañang Palace by the Pasig River is the official residence of Philippine presidents. It has been the residence of 18 Spanish governors general, 14 American civil governors and nine Philippine presidents starting with President Manuel Quezon. President Marcos was its longest occupant. He stayed there for 20 years and it took a revolution to remove him. President Corazon Aquino broke with tradition when she chose not to reside at the Palace during her incumbency. Instead she made it a museum of the people (Museo ng Malacañang). President Ramos, her successor, also held office at the Palace but opted to stay at the Arlegui residence. When Joseph Estrada was elected President, he decided to make Malacañang once again the official residence of the President. Malacañang is one of the most visited historic landmarks in the country and enjoys the patronage of both foreign and local tourists.

Rich merchants of Manila once maintained vacation homes along the north bank of the river. The site of the present palace was formerly a private resort with a stone house and gardens with a bath. The name Malacañang may have come from the Tagalog, *may lakan diyan* (there are nobles there). Malacañang's first recorded owner was Don Luis Rocha who made his fortune in the galleon trade. The estate was bought from him in 1802 by a Spanish army colonel, Don Jose Miguel Formento. The Spanish government acquired the estate from Formento's heirs in 1825. Posesion de Malacañang, as it was known, was designated as the summer residence of the governor general by the Royal Decree of 27 August 1847. Fourteen Spanish governors, starting with Narciso Claveria y Zaldua, used it as a summer residence. Fleet commanders and visiting dignitaries were entertained here. But when a devastating earthquake in 1863 destroyed many buildings in Intramuros, including the governor's palace, Governor Rafael de Echague moved to the summer residence and ordered the renovation of the stone house and the construction of a two-storey building at the back. There were attempts to reconstruct the palace in Intramuros but these were abandoned when another disastrous earthquake hit the city in 1880. Succeeding chief executives made additions and improvements to the residence during the Spanish regime.

When the Americans took over the colonial government, Malacañang was a

Spanish building with *azoteas*, patios and sliding windows with *capiz*-shell panes. The Americans replaced the wooden structure with concrete and improved the interiors with hardwood panelling. The façade, however, was retained. Plumbing, electricity and a sewer system were installed, as well as a swimming pool and tennis court. Each succeeding occupant made changes in the furnishings to suit their tastes. During the Marcos era, the old palace was extensively renovated and a larger one built under Imelda Marcos's auspices. Malacañang then lost much of its colonial character. The iron canopy, embellished with flowerets and scrolls, and built during the term of American civil governor Francis Burton Harrison (in office 1913–21) was relegated to the junk heap during the demolition but fortunately was rescued from its state of rust and neglect and restored to its original glory. It now stands at the entrance to the Executive Building or Kalayaan Hall as a reminder of a bygone era.

At the time of President Aquino, Malacañang Palace was opened for public viewing. The ceremonial hall, state dining room, drawing rooms and apartments containing paintings and sculptures by Filipino masters, the basement storage room, known as Imelda's department store, containing her shoes (less than 2,000 pairs, not 3,000 as reported), *ternos*, gowns, and gifts were visited by thousands of tourists. The gifts and mementoes which President Aquino received from government and private institutions and foreign dignitaries were housed in the Presidential Gifts Gallery.

One wing of the palace has been renovated and in 1993 was turned into a Philippine Presidential Museum managed by the Malacañang Heritage Foundation. On view are a collection of portraits and memorabilia from past Presidents, starting with the time of Emilio Aguinaldo to President Ramos. Each President's achievements and life history are included in the museum. To complement the permanent Presidential exhibits, special changing exhibition areas have also been designated by the Foundation.

South of the Pasig River

The tourist districts of Ermita and Malate noted for their souvenir shops, hotels, restaurants and vibrant nightlife, Paco with its old park, Santa Ana with its church and archaeological site and San Andres with its fruit market are all south of the river.

ERMITA AND MALATE

Manila's tourist belt encircles the districts of Ermita and Malate. Once genteel residential areas in pre-World War II years, the tourist belt is now filled with

The Inner Sanctum

I couldn't believe I would be able to find the actual Marcos apartments, and I knew there was no point in asking. We went up some servants' stairs, at the foot of which I remember seeing an opened crate with two large green jade plates. They were so large as to be vulgar. On the first floor a door opened, and we found ourselves in the great hall where the press conferences had been held. This was the one bit of the palace the crowd would recognize, as it had so often watched Marcos being televised from here. People ran and sat on his throne and began giving mock press-conferences, issuing orders in his deep voice, falling about with laughter or just gaping at the splendour of the room. It was all fully lit. Nobody had bothered, as they left, to turn out the lights.

I remembered that the first time I had been here, the day after the election, Imelda had slipped in and sat at the side. She must have come from that direction. I went to investigate.

And now, for a short while, I was away from the crowd with just one other person, a shy and absolutely thunderstruck Filipino. We had found our way, we realized, into the Marcoses' private rooms. There was a library, and my companion gazed in wonder at the leather-bound volumes while I admired the collection of art books all carefully catalogued and with their numbers on the spines. This was the reference library for Imelda's world-wide collection of treasures. She must have thumbed through them thinking: 'I'd like one of them', or 'I've got a couple of them in New York', or 'That's in our London house'. And then there was the Blue Drawing Room with its twin portraits of the Marcoses, where I simply remember standing with my companion and saying, "It's beautiful, isn't it." It wasn't that it was beautiful. It looked as if it had been purchased at Harrods. It was just that, after all the crowds and the riots, we had landed up in this peaceful, luxurious den. My companion had never seen anything like it. He didn't take anything. He hardly dared touch the furnishings and trinkets. We both simply could not believe that we were there and the Marcoses weren't.

I wish I could remember it all better. For instance, it seemed to me that in every room I saw, practically on every available surface, there was a signed photograph of Nancy Reagan. But this can hardly be literally true. It just felt as if there was a lot of Nancy in evidence.

Another of the rooms had a grand piano. I sat down.

"Can you play?" said my companion.

"A little, " I exaggerated. I can play Bach's Prelude in C, and this is what I proceeded to do, but my companion had obviously hoped for something more racy. Beside the piano stood a framed photograph of Pham Van Dong, and beside the photograph lay a letter. It was a petition from members of a village, asking for property rights on the land they lived on. It was dated well before the Snap Election. Someone (Marcos himself? The letter was addressed to him), must have opened it, seen it was a petition, popped it back in the envelope and sat down to play a tune. The keys were stiff. I wondered if the piano was brand new.

A soldier came in, carrying a rifle. "Please co-operate," he said. The soldier looked just as overawed by the place as we were. We co-operated.

When I returned down the service stairs, I noticed that the green jade plates had gone, but there was still some Evian water to be had. I was very thirsty, as it happened. But the revolution had asked me to co-operate. So I did.

James Fenton, The Snap Revolution

restaurants, cafés and bistros, cocktail lounges, curio and souvenir shops, travel agencies, hospitals, La Solidardad bookshop, and hotels (Holiday Inn Manila Pavilion, Bayview Plaza, Ambassador, Manila Diamond, Manila Midtown, Pan Pacific Manila), pensions and boutique hotels. The principal streets running north and south are MH del Pilar, going south, A Mabini, going north, Adriatico and Orosa Streets. In front of the American Embassy is a small, tree-shaded square, the Plaza Nuestra Señora de Guia which leads to the Ermita Church (on M H Del Pilar and Flores streets) where Our Lady of Guidance, patroness of the galleons, is enshrined.

In the month of May, the church parishioners hold their 'Bota Flores', a religious festivity consisting of the recital of prayers and singing of hymns in front of the huge sculptured image of Our Lady of Guidance, capped by the celebration of Holy Mass in the church. Bota Flores celebrates the finding of the statue by a Spanish soldier who was with the expeditionary forces of Don Miguel Legaspi. It is said that on 19 May 1571 the soldier saw some natives venerating a small statue enthroned on a pandanus bush. The Spaniards subsequently built a shack over the statue and dedicated it to Our Lady of the Immaculate Conception. This was the first Christian shrine in Manila and the oldest Marian statue in the Philippines. The Spaniards called the place La Ermita.

A leisurely walk in the southerly direction brings one to Remedios Circle, a trendy section of Malate. Around it cluster cafés and bistros, restaurants offering a variety of cuisines, art-deco nightclubs and boutique hotels. Guernica's, a popular Spanish restaurant, is one of the old-timers in the Circle, having opened an outlet here in 1982. On the streets radiating from the circle are restaurants serving Mexican, Chinese, Korean, French, Italian and Filipino food. Nightspots in the vicinity add to the ambience; these are patronized by the after-theatre crowd, artists and yuppies.

A short walk from Remedios Circle is the 16th-century Augustinian Church of Malate, dedicated to Nuestra Señora de Remedios, patroness of women in childbirth. British troops occupied the church during their attack on Intramuros in 1762. On the plaza fronting the church stands a statue of the Virgin and one of Rajah Soliman. Near the church is Aristocrat Restaurant. Next to it is the Hotel Sofitel Grand Boulevard. From the church, San Andres leads to San Andres Market.

PACO PARK

A peaceful oasis shaded by centuries-old trees, the park was formerly a cemetery built by the Dominicans where above-ground burial was practised. Within the circular walls are double rows of niches. The first burials after its completion in 1820 were victims of the cholera epidemic. The last burials took place in 1912. Rizal was

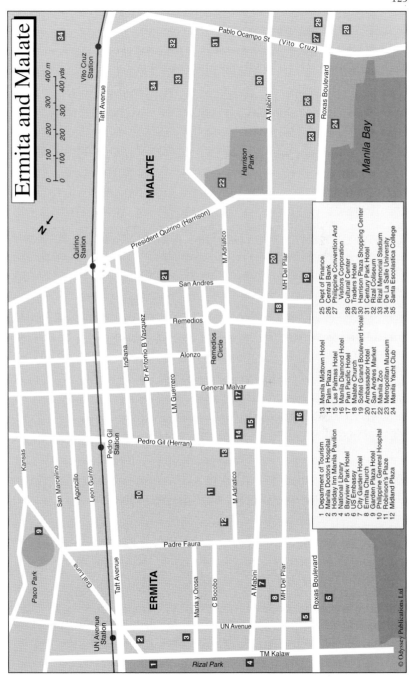

Ermita and Malate

1 Department of Tourism
2 Manila Doctors Hospital
3 Holiday Inn Manila Pavilion
4 National Library
5 Bayview Park Hotel
6 US Embassy
7 City Garden Hotel
8 Ermita Church
9 Garden Plaza Hotel
10 Philippine General Hospital
11 Robinson's Plaza
12 Midland Plaza
13 Manila Midtown Hotel
14 Palm Plaza
15 Las Palmas Hotel
16 Manila Diamond Hotel
17 Pan Pacific Hotel
18 Malate Church
19 Sofitel Grand Boulevard Hotel
20 Ambassador Hotel
21 San Andres Market
22 Manila Zoo
23 Metropolitan Museum
24 Manila Yacht Club
25 Dept of Finance
26 Central Bank
27 Philippine Convention And
   Visitors Corporation
28 Cultural Center
29 Traders Hotel
30 Harrison Plaza Shopping Center
31 Century Park Hotel
32 Rizal Coliseum
33 Rizal Memorial Stadium
34 De La Salle University
35 Santa Escolastica College

© Odyssey Publications Ltd

secretly buried here in 1896 in a mismarked grave. His bones were exhumed in 1912 and transferred to their final resting place beneath the Rizal Monument at Rizal Park. Within the park is a chapel and a fountain. Music lovers come here on Fridays at 6 pm for the 'Paco Park Presents', a weekly series of concerts which feature solo artists, duets and small ensembles. Just outside the park are the economy Park Hotel and standard Garden Plaza Hotel (formerly Hotel Swiss). It was a Swiss national who opened the Old Swiss Inn Restaurant on Roxas Boulevard in 1946 and who later established the Swiss Inn beside Paco Park.

Santa Ana

This riverine community had a flourishing trade with Chinese merchants who dealt in porcelain, silk and precious metals. The Franciscans built their first mission outside Intramuros here in 1578, but the original church was destroyed by an earthquake. It was replaced by the present church with its hexagonal tower, completed in 1725. Excavations of the churchyard and nearby properties showed the area to be a rich archaeological site. The church and surrounding area were built over a cemetery and habitation estimated to be more than 800 years old. Pottery dating from the late Northern Song Dynasty (AD 960–1279), coins and other artefacts were found in the graves. The excavated relics are displayed in situ. Santa Ana was considered a resort area and in the 1870s, regattas were organised by British businessmen. British presence can also be seen from the old family recipes kept by long-time residents which mention English sausages and Stilton cheese. Horse racing was introduced in the late 19th century when the first track was laid down in Santa Ana. There was no grandstand and members had their own private two-storey stands. Lavish food was laid out by the hosts for their guests. The Manila Jockey Club was formed later and horse racing became popular.

Roxas Boulevard

This is the main thoroughfare running north–south along the curve of Manila Bay. Formerly known as Dewey Boulevard, after the American Admiral George Dewey who captured Manila from the Spaniards in 1898, it was the most elegant boulevard in the city before World War II. Stuccoed white mansions and walled villas with well-tended gardens and lawns lined the beach front. This was Millionaire's Row before Forbes Park and Dasmariñas Village in Makati replaced it. Open-top red double-decker buses called *matorco* cruised the long stretch of seafront and were particularly popular among Sunday strollers and promenaders. On Roxas Boulevard are the American Embassy, Philippine Navy Headquarters, Manila Yacht Club, Central Bank, Cultural Centre complex, the Department of Finance, the Department of

Foreign Affairs, condominiums, museums and art galleries, travel agencies, airline offices, the Bay area hotels, restaurants and nightclubs.

Within the Bangko Sentral ng Pilipinas (Central Bank) complex is the Metropolitan Museum with its changing exhibits of local and international art (open 10 am to 6 pm Mondays to Saturdays; closed Sundays and holidays. Admission: P20/adults; P5/students with ID). Occupying a new gallery within the Museum is a collection of the Central Bank's Philippine art acquisitions over the years. Now the public can enjoy and appreciate one of the most comprehensive and significant collections of Filipino paintings in the country. The exhibits change every quarter. Portraits, landscapes, and scenes depicting various aspects of Filipino life are represented. The collection shows great scope and variety, ranging from the works of obscure and unschooled 18th century artists and 19th century masters to the major painters of this century.

The Cultural Centre Complex, built on reclaimed land along Roxas Boulevard, includes the CCP—housing a 2,000-seat concert hall, 400-seat theatre, library, Museum of Philippine Humanities, the Contemporary Art Museum (open 9 am to 5.30 pm, nominal admission fee), and art galleries; the refurbished Convention Centre seating 6,000 in its Plenary Hall (conducted tours available); the Folk Arts Centre; the Westin Philippine Plaza Hotel; the Coconut Palace; the Design Centre, and the Philippine Centre for International Trade and Exhibitions. The complex is a popular venue for international and regional conventions, film festivals and world beauty pageants such as the 1995 Miss Universe contest.

The Coconut Palace is an architecturally unique structure, incorporating a cluster of hexagonal pavilions designed by Francisco Mañosa, one of the Philippines' most innovative architects. The coconut, the country's 'tree of life', is put to imaginative use here. Seventy per cent of the building makes use of the tree; the rest is made of other Philippine materials. Its trapezoidal plan covering a floor area of 3,000 square metres (32,000 square feet) provides the setting for seven private rooms on the first floor and function rooms on the ground floor. Each of the private rooms has a different motif inspired by the arts and crafts of various regions. Originally built as a presidential guesthouse during the Marcos era, it was completed in time for the visit of Pope John Paul II, who never stayed in it.

The street perpendicular to Roxas Boulevard in front of the CCP complex is Pablo Ocampo Sr (formerly Vito Cruz) which leads to the Rizal Memorial a sports complex, Harrison Plaza shopping centre and Century Park Hotel.

PASAY CITY AND PARAÑAQUE
Sen Gil J Puyat (formerly Buendia) marks the boundary between Manila and Pasay

Traditional women's dress worn during the Spanish times in Northern Luzon (top right); the terno, *popularized by Imelda Marcos is the formal wear of Filipino women (bottom left); the* Maria Clara, *a Spanish-influenced costume for women in colonial days (bottom right)*

City. Travelling south along Roxas Boulevard past the Philippine International Trade and Exhibits (Philtrade) complex, World Trade Centre, the Hyatt Regency Hotel, the San Juan de Dios Hospital and the Heritage Hotel on EDSA extension, you reach Baclaran, a district of Parañaque. An outdoor bazaar sells a variety of cheap merchandise. The place is crowded on Wednesdays when devotees of Our Lady of Perpetual Help flock to the Redemptorist Church for the weekly novena. The area around the church fills with makeshift food stands selling barbecue (satay sticks) and the Philippines' beloved *lechon* (spit-roasted suckling pig with its crisp skin). The road to the international airport veers left not far from the church. Close to the airport is Nayong Pilipino.

Parañaque, an old salt-making, fishing and farming town also noted for its embroidery, put itself on the world map in December 1996 when it transformed four hectares of reclaimed land along Manila Bay into a massive open-air amphitheatre with state-of-the-art special effects, lasers, computer-controlled lights and sound system for the two-night concert of pop star Michael Jackson. Along the coastal road to Cavite is the gigantic Coastal Mall Fisherman's Wharf incorporating a fish port and a cluster of bamboo-and-thatched roofed restaurants standing on stilts over the brackish water. People come here for the rustic setting and to enjoy seafood and grilled dishes cooked Filipino style. From here, a side road leads to Las Piñas. Visitors can make a brief stop here to see the unique bamboo organ in the church. Built between 1816 and 1822 by Father Diego Cera, a Spanish priest, the organ measures more than five metres (16 feet) high and four metres (13 feet) wide. There are 174 bamboo pipes, 122 horizontal reeds of soft metal, a five-octave keyboard, and 22 stops arranged in vertical rows. The organ has withstood earthquakes, typhoons and years of neglect, proving the strength and resilience of bamboo. In the early 1970s, the organ was shipped to Germany for restoration. Today, international organists converge on Las Piñas for the annual Bamboo Organ Festival held in February.

NAYONG PILIPINO

The Philippines in miniature is laid out in this 46-hectare complex next to the Mercure Philippine Village Airport Hotel. A major visitor attraction for the past 25 years, Nayong Pilipino (Philippine Village) showcases the country's tourist attractions, arts and culture. The park's mission 'to enshrine the rich national heritage of the Filipino through the authentic depiction of customs and traditions' is reflected in the mural at the park's entrance done by National Artist Napoleon V Abueva.

This one-stop, instant-Philippines tour takes you to seven major Philippine regions: the Tagalog, Ilocos, Cordillera, Bicol, Visayas, Mindanao, and Sulu. Each region has a familiar touristic landmark—typical Tagalog architecture, a replica of the Mayon Volcano and Cagsawa ruins in Bicolandia, Magellan's Cross in Cebu and the Chocolate Hills of Bohol in the Visayas, Samal houses on stilts, a mosque and a *datu*'s residence in the Mindanao section, Ifugao huts and rice terraces in the Cordilleras and a stately Vigan House in Ilocos. Regional arts and crafts are displayed and sold in typical houses. Colourful jeepneys make it convenient for visitors to tour the park.

Of special interest within the park are the Museo ng Buhay Pilipino featuring DM Guevara's collection of Philippine antiques; the Philippine Museum of Ethnology with its permanent and changing displays showing Philippine costumes and the ancient arts of carving, weaving, weaponry and the making of personal ornaments; the Crafts Museum exhibiting Philippine-made pottery and brassware, bags and baskets made from local materials, blankets and fabrics woven in the fashion of *ikat* and *t'nalak*, and indigenous-style jewellery and accessories. Museum hours: 9 am to 6 pm Tuesdays to Sundays, closed Mondays.

There is a six-hectare lagoon for fishing and boating, and an aviary of Philippine birds. The orchidarium has 50 species of orchids including the rare *waling-waling* (*Vanda sanderiana*) of the Philippines. More species are being added to make the orchidarium one of the best in Southeast Asia. There's also a garden of Philippine plants and a children's playground featuring Filipino games.

MAKATI

Metro Manila's modern centrepiece is Makati, the country's financial and commercial hub, surrounded by residential 'villages' where the rich, the famous and the powerful live. Makati is a postwar phenomenon. It rose from what was formerly swampland and a red-light district, as a result of the astute planning of the Ayala-Zobel family. Today it boasts high-rise condominiums and office tower blocks, commercial complexes, smart shopping malls housing boutiques, department stores and supermarkets. Speciality restaurants, fast food outlets, cocktail lounges and bars abound. Five-star hotels. (the Shangri-La, Mandarin, Peninsula, Inter-continental, Dusit Hotel Nikko and New world), banks, airline offices and travel agencies, embassies and consulates, and the Makati Medical Centre are also located here. Nearby, in plush Forbes Park and North Forbes, are the Manila Polo Club and Manila Golf Club. Also a short driving distance away is the American Memorial Cemetery, the Libingan ng mga Bayani, a cemetery and war memorial for Filipino soldiers, and the Villamor Golf Club.

Development and construction continues. The Rockwell Centre, a 15-hectare modern inner-city redevelopment, will consist of residential condominiums, office towers, a retail centre, serviced apartments, a hotel, a lifestyle club and the Ateneo Professional School for business and law. On this site will rise the 34-storey, 407-room Ritz Carlton Hotel.

Amidst the canyons of glass, stone and steel is the Greenbelt Park, a restful patch of greenery where office workers, shoppers and tourists can take a respite from their activities. Within the park is a unique circular chapel which seems to float on water. This is the Chapel of Sto Niño de Paz serving the business district; it is filled with churchgoers during the daily noonday mass. Musicians and bands also provide entertainment for park-goers. Twice a week on Tuesdays and Saturdays, from 7 am to 4 pm, producers of organically grown fruit and vegetables bring their products to be sold at the park. The Ayala Museum is also in Greenbelt Park.

AYALA MUSEUM

Highlights of Philippine history, starting with the hunters of Cagayan Valley (150,000–30,000 BC) to the proclamation of the Philippine Republic in 1946 are featured in a series of three-dimensional dioramas. The wooden figures used in the dioramas were crafted by woodcarvers from Paete in Laguna province. Special lighting heightens the drama of each event. Large-scale models of ships and boats that have figured in Philippine history are featured in a special gallery, while in another gallery the country's archaeological, ethnic and colonial heritage is showcased. Artefacts from Philippine prehistory taken from burial and excavation sites are on display. A third gallery shows changing art exhibits—paintings, sculpture, ethnic arts and handicrafts, prints and photographs by local artists. In addition, the memorabilia of statesman Carlos P Romulo are on view in two adjoining rooms. The museum has also acquired several oil paintings by Fernando Amorsolo. Facilities include an audiovisual room and museum shop. The museum is open Tuesdays to Saturdays from 8 am to 6 pm; admission: P60 for adults, P30 for children and students with ID.

FORT BONIFACIO

The conversion of former American and Philippine military facilities into mixed-use, high-impact development projects is currently being undertaken in various parts of Luzon by the Bases Conversion Development Authority (BCDA) in partnership with the private sector. One of the biggest to be redeveloped is the sprawling Fort Bonifacio close to Makati, together with Villamor Airbase, home for nearly 50 years of composite units of the Armed Forces of the Philippines. Before World War II, Fort Bonifacio was known as Fort McKinley and was the largest American military base in the country. The BCDA bid out 214 hectares of prime land for development. The winning bid was submitted by a Filipino and foreign consortium. Envisioned as a model urban community, Fort Bonifacio will have a core business district with a cluster of 25- to 30-storey 'intelligent' office buildings, upscale residences and a modern 15- to 20-hectare shopping complex. Most of the buildings will be interconnected by aerial bridges for pedestrians. There will be a lot of greenery, making this future urban centre an ecological city. A new golf course to replace the old one will also be constructed. When completed, the core business district will form a growth triangle with the Makati and Ortigas business centres. The development of a 105-hectare unused portion of the Fort Bonifacio reservation into a Heritage Park—a combination of a memorial park and a historical-ecological preserve—is also being undertaken by the BCDA and the Philippine National Bank.

Located within Fort Bonifacio is the Libingan ng mga Bayani, a cemetery and war memorial for Filipino soldiers, and the Philippine Army Museum and Library on MacArthur Avenue. The displays include tanks, war relics and weapons, photographs and dioramas portraying the army's role in war and peace. Hours: 9 am to 4.30 pm daily except Wednesdays.

AMERICAN MILITARY CEMETERY AND WAR MEMORIAL

The American Military Cemetery and War Memorial is a 61.5-hectare (152-acre) plot of land within the Fort Bonifacio complex that was donated by the Philippines in perpetuity to the American Battle Monuments Commission in 1948. This tranquil spot, planted with trees, bushes and shrubs from various parts of Asia, is the final resting place of 17,206 identified American and allied war dead, killed in action during World War II. The well-tended green lawns are accented by rows of tombstones, white crosses and Stars of David. A massive monument also bears the names of 36,279 servicemen whose remains have never been recovered. Within the cemetery is an inter-denominational chapel. Situated some 10 kilometres (6 miles) from the heart of Manila, this is a place of pilgrimage for people from all over the world.

To get there, take McKinley Road, an extension of Ayala Avenue in Makati. The road leads through Forbes Park, past Santuario de San Antonio Church, Manila Golf Club and the Manila Polo Club.

MANDALUYONG/PASIG

Another business centre rivalling Makati has risen in the cities of Mandaluyong and Pasig. The Ortigas Business Centre with its core of high-rise office and commercial buildings, is attracting large corporations and banks. The Asian Development Bank headquarters, the Philippine Stock Exchange, a medical centre, banks, the Shangri-La EDSA Plaza Hotel and Manila Galleria Suites, and two shopping complexes—Megamall and Shangri-La Plaza—are located here. The Shangri-La Hotel recently opened its 14-storey, 218-room Tower wing, connected to the main edifice by an air-conditioned link bridge. Megamall is massive, occupying several city blocks.

Housed under one roof are a car park, the SM department store, supermarket, boutiques, several cinemas, ice skating rink, restaurants, snack bars, art galleries and more. Next door is the Shangri-La Plaza, housing Rustan's department store, National Book Store, shops, restaurants and snack bars. This is the home of Repertory Philippines and the William J Shaw Theatre. Not far from this area is Robinson's Galleria, another huge shopping complex with an art gallery, restaurants, fast food outlets, snack bars and supermarket. Two hotels—the Byron Edsa on Boni Avenue and Legend on Pioneer Street—have opened in recent years. Residential condominiums and apartelles have also mushroomed in the area.

QUEZON CITY

Quezon City, former capital of the Philippines, was named after President Manuel Quezon, its founder. In area it is four times bigger than the city of Manila, with wide boulevards and streets. Quezon City will have the distinction of hosting the World Expo in 2002. The Expo site will be the 25-hectare Quezon Memorial Circle, and the 15-hectare Ninoy Aquino Parks and Wildlife which will then be connected by the light rail transit. The Memorial Circle was constructed shortly after World War II in memory of President Quezon. It is complete with cultural and recreational amenities, food stalls and restaurants, cycling and jogging paths and picnic grounds. During the concert season, cultural presentations, free to the public, are held at the Circle's Liwasang Aurora on Sundays at 6 pm. The Circle is accessible from several points in Metro Manila. Quezon City has several residential subdivisions with lovely homes and gardens, housing estates (called projects), national government offices, schools, colleges and universities (University of the Philippines, Ateneo de Manila University), hotels (Sulo, home of beauty contestants who come to the Philippines for the Miss Asia Pacific pageant, Great Eastern, Rembrandt, Danarra, hospitals (St Luke's Medical Centre, Philippine Heart Centre, Children's Hospital, Veterans Memorial Hospital), churches, television stations and golf courses. The city also boasts numerous restaurants and nightspots along Tomas Morato Street, West Avenue, Quezon Avenue, and Cubao.

City landmarks are the Welcome Pylon at the boundary of Manila and Quezon City, and the Quezon Memorial Circle with its 30-metre-high (98-foot) Quezon Monument and Mausoleum. To the northeast of the circle is the sprawling campus of the University of the Philippines in Diliman, with the statue of *The Oblation* at the entrance. The Ateneo University and Ateneo Art Gallery is in Loyola Heights. Beyond Diliman is Balara Filters, which supplies Manila's drinking water. The Central Bank complex on East Avenue houses the Money Museum with its extensive collection of Philippine banknotes and coins dating back to pre-Spanish times, gold artefacts and foreign banknotes and coins.

The commercial centre is Cubao, with shopping complexes, department stores, the Farmers' Market, cinemas, restaurants, fast-food shops, amusement centre, and the huge Araneta Coliseum, venue for entertainment extravaganzas such as international ice shows and circuses, pop concerts, stag Derbies (big cockfights) and boxing bouts such as the Muhammed Ali–Joe Frazier world championship fight. Also in Cubao, along EDSA, is Nepa-Q Mart, a food centre and market mall. Agri-based products from different provinces in the Philippines, such as organically grown vegetables and fruit, and naturally fermented and aged *bagoong* and *patis* (fish and shrimp sauces), soy sauce and vinegar are found here.

The Santo Domingo Church on Quezon Avenue is the national shrine of Our Lady of the Rosary. In October, the annual La Naval procession takes place to commemorate the Spanish naval victory over a vastly superior Dutch fleet in 1646. The victory is ascribed to the Blessed Virgin's miraculous intervention. Greatly outnumbered, the Spanish and Filipino forces vowed that if they won they would hold a procession in honour of Our Lady. The tradition has been kept alive these past centuries.

MARIKINA CITY

Not far from Quezon City is Marikina the city that shoes built. This riverside town is famous for turning out stylish shoes at affordable prices for Filipinos, thanks to an enterprising Spaniard who encouraged the local farmers to make shoes in their spare time towards the end of the last century. The cobbler's art has been handed down from generation to generation. This has spawned an industry worth three billion pesos in yearly sales. Marikina is home to 20,000 shoemakers and 2,000 shoe factories, turning out around 10,000 pairs of shoes annually. The city recently opened the Marikina Footwear Museum in a 300-year-old building in San Roque which has been restored to its original Spanish design. Imelda Marcos has entrusted her 1,500 pairs of shoes to be exhibited in the museum. Also showcased are shoes donated by President and Mrs Ramos and other past presidents. The city holds a yearly Shoe Festival and Industrial Fair and recently introduced a fashion show of footwear at the newly constructed Riverbend Ballroom at RiverPark—Marikina's new Business District. Shoe making has been endorsed by the city mayor to the Department of Education, Culture and Sports as one of the vocational courses to be offered to schoolchildren.

CALOOCAN CITY AND SUBURBS

This industrial city is on the main route heading north out of Manila. A monument honouring the heroes of the Revolution is a focal point in Caloocan. This is known

Imelda Marcos' bedroom

to jeepney drivers as Monumento. To the south lies the Chinese cemetery. Along the coast are Navotas, one of the largest fishing ports in the country, and Malabon, another fishing centre famous for its *pancit malabon*, a noodle dish. To the north is Valenzuela, site of the San Miguel brewery. The eastern suburb of Pateros is famous for duck breeding and the *balut* (duck egg) industry.

Excursions Outside Manila

A visitor with limited time in the Philippines can conveniently take in a few sights outside Manila. One option is to visit historic Corregidor Island, a popular destination, particularly among war veterans and their families.

CORREGIDOR

Corregidor is a small tadpole-shaped island off the southern tip of the Bataan Peninsula, some 41 kilometres (26 nautical miles) from Manila. Like a sentinel guarding the entrance to Manila Bay, it served as a checkpoint during Spanish times for vessels entering Manila Bay. In centuries past, Chinese and Muslim pirates prowled the seas around Corregidor, and Dutch ships engaged in naval battles with Spanish warships. The Spaniards used Corregidor as a signal post, lighting bonfires to advise

Manila of the arrival of galleons. Later they fortified the island and erected a lighthouse which guided sailors along the rocky coastline. Recognizing its strategic location, the Americans who took over from the Spaniards made Corregidor a military reservation as part of the 'harbour defenses of Manila and Subic Bay'. They strengthened the fortifications and by the early 1920s, some 22 seacoast batteries and an electronically controlled minefield ringed the island. The Americans also fortified the outlying islands of El Fraile, Caballo and Carabao. Corregidor became a bloody battle zone during World War II (see History, page 23). Here thousands of Filipino, American and Japanese soldiers fought and died in 1942 and 1945. Today it is preserved as a national shrine.

Corregidor covers an area of 546.38 hectares (1,530 acres) and is approximately 5.6 kilometres (3.48 miles) long and about 2.4 kilometres (1.49 miles) at its widest point. It is divided geographically into Topside, Middleside, Bottomside, Malinta Tunnel and the Tail. The lowest part of the island where the tail is, lies about 15.2 metres (50 feet) above sea level and the highest point rises up to 191.4 metres (628 feet) above sea level. A great deal of work went into making the island a fitting national shrine. Access roads have been concreted or made into all-weather surface roads. The jungle, which once threatened to devour the remaining relics of bombed and blasted buildings, has been pushed back and is now carefully held at bay. A Pacific War Memorial and a Filipino Heroes Memorial, as well as several monuments around the island have been built to pay tribute to those who fell in battle.

Standing on this island fifty years after the war, with the sun pouring gold on a hushed and green landscape and breezes blowing in from the sea, it is hard to imagine the rain of death and destruction it once endured. But as one travels from Bottomside to Topside, there is a stirring of the ghosts of the past. A larger-than-life statue of General Douglas MacArthur, with his trademark sunglasses and his hand raised, as if to bid farewell to the unseen troops with the promise 'I Shall Return', stands at the Lorcha Dock at Bottomside. There is also a large statue of Commonwealth President Manuel L Quezon who transferred the seat of government at Malinta Tunnel, standing in front of the entrance to the hospital lateral.

■ MIDDLESIDE

Mid-point on the island, popularly called Middleside, at 161.5 metres (530 feet) above sea level, are the ruins of the Middleside Barracks built between 1912 and 1916, the YMCA, hospital, and commissary building. There's a wide swath of green in front of the YMCA ruins where the soldiers used to play baseball. If one Pablito Martinez happens to be your guide, he will tell you the story which you may or may not believe, that the New York Yankees played here and were defeated by the Corregidor team, much to the disgust of a certain Babe Ruth and Lou Gehrig.

Close by is a small aviary and the ruins of an underground water reservoir. Here you see blue and gold macaws from Brazil, successfully bred in captivity; a scarlet macaw and green winged macaw, both from South America, sulphur-crested cockatoos, an umbrella-crested cockatoo, a mustache parakeet from Indonesia, an African grey parrot, and a red-vented cockatoo from Palawan. There are plans to expand the present aviary into a bird park with an orchidarium and a children's playground.

■ TOPSIDE

It is at Topside that the most vivid realities of the war are seen and felt. Every inch of ground tells the story of those thousands of Filipino and American soldiers who fought one of the great delaying actions of World War II. From ninth of April to sixth of May 1942, they held back the enemy amidst artillery barrage and bombing, until ammunition, medicine, food and finally water ran out, forcing the defenders to surrender 'in sadness but not in shame' in the words of their commander Gen Jonathan Wainwright.

All of the modern seacoast artillery was emplaced at Topside which commanded the narrow north and south entrances into Manila Bay. Some of the batteries with their gun emplacements have been preserved. Cleaned of rust and dirt, the restored cannons and mortars gleam a dark olive. The big guns now lie silent; only the voice of the tour guide tells their story. There's Battery Hearn and Battery Smith facing the South China Sea. Battery Hearn had a seacoast gun that could turn 360 degrees and fire in any direction; it had a 27.2-kilometre (17-mile) coverage. But anti-naval guns proved useless for the Bataan campaign. Then there's Battery Grubbs and Battery Morrison facing Bataan; and Batteries Geary and Crockett facing Cavite. Battery Geary's eight 12-inch mortars were considered the most effective anti-personnel weapons of Corregidor, together with Battery Way. A direct hit by Japanese artillery on its centre magazine totally destroyed the Battery on 2 May 1942. At the centre is Battery Way. Its guns delivered the most telling counterfire during the last 27 days of the Battle of Corregidor. The other preserved batteries are Morrison, James, Chenney, Wheeler, and Ramsey. Today, children scramble on the guns and peer through their dark round muzzles under the watchful eye of their parents. Tourists pose beside them for picture-taking.

But it is the sight of the desolate ruins of barracks and buildings that stand as stark reminders of the ugliness of a world torn by war. Once there was life in these buildings. There was laughter, even children's voices. For Topside was the nerve centre of military life at Fort Mills. Here were the harbour defense headquarters, the Milelong barracks, the senior officers' quarters, parade ground, golf course, the chapel, the bachelor officers' quarters, the cinema. It is said that the last film to be shown before the sound track was silenced forever was Gone with the Wind. Gone with the wind now are the parade grounds, the post office, and the golf course. But the Spanish-era lighthouse still stands. It has been rehabilitated, equipped with solar panels and high technology instruments. It is now operated by the Philippine Coast Guard. Those with good legs and stout heart can take the spiral staircase to the top for a bird's eye view of the island and surrounding waters.

■ PACIFIC WAR MEMORIAL

The Pacific War Memorial at Topside was built at the expense of the United States government. Its dome was so constructed that at high noon the sunlight falls directly on the Altar of Valour. An inscription on the side of the altar, made of white Philippine marble, reads: 'Sleep, my sons your duty done...for freedom's light has come. Sleep in the silent depths of the sea, and in your bed of hallowed sod until you hear at dawn the low clear reveille of God.' Marble panels inscribed with records of land, sea and air battles flank a broad esplanade at the end of which is a steel sculpture depicting the Eternal Flame of Valour. The memorial commands a view of Bataan and the surrounding waters. Within the complex is a museum of war memorabilia. Also on display are two cars that belonged to President Quezon. One of these, a

Early morning mist in the Sierra Madre range, Luzon

1937 Cabriolet, was turned over to General MacArthur for his use. The car was also used by Japanese Generals Homma and Yamashita.

■ MALINTA TUNNEL

Located at Bottomside near the docks and warehouses is the Malinta Tunnel, bored out of Malinta Hill by the Americans from 1922 to 1932. The main tunnel is 254.5 metres (835 feet) long and 7.3 metres (24 feet) wide, with 24 laterals. It housed an arsenal and underground hospital, and served as the headquarters of General MacArthur and later General Wainwright until Corregidor fell to the Japanese in May 1942. President Quezon's Government was transferred here on 24 December 1941, weeks after the Japanese bombed Manila. A 30-minute Sound and Light presentation dramatizing the events of the war is one of the highlights of a trip to Corregidor.

■ FILIPINO HEROES MEMORIAL

The Filipino Heroes Memorial occupies a 2.2-hectare (5.43-acre) site on the tail end of the island. It features 14 murals depicting heroic battles fought by Filipinos from the 16th century to modern times. A recent addition to the memorials erected on the island is the monument to the foot soldier inaugurated in June 1995.

Also at Tailside is the Japanese Garden of Peace Park, where visiting Japanese war veterans and their families can honour the memory of their dead. The Musashi Memorial on Bottomside is another Japanese site.

■ ACCOMMODATION

Facilities for staying guests are available at the 31-room Corregidor Hotel which has a restaurant and bar, an outdoor swimming pool and tennis court; the Corregidor Hostel, with 48 dormitory-style beds; and seaside cottages at South Beach which include a clubhouse with two restaurants. There's also a campsite for students, scouts and out-of-school youth at Middleside near the aviary. The island has an airfield, a heliport, mini-mart, a chapel, a small school, and a first-aid clinic. The Corregidor Foundation Inc. supervises and manages the national shrine.

■ GETTING THERE

Sun Cruises operates a daily tour to the island departing at 8 am from the PTA Bay Cruise Terminal, Cultural Centre Complex on Roxas Boulevard. Staff in snappy navy whites are on hand to board tourists. It's a comfortable one-hour ride across Manila Bay on the MV Sun Cruiser. Buses await at the dock to take the visitors around. The US$43 package includes return fare, guided tour of the island and set lunch at the

Corregidor Hotel. The Sound and Light Show (extra P150/adult, P100 children) is optional. (Tel 831-8140 / 524-8410 / 524-0333.)

The MY Tennessee Walker, a floating restaurant with a seating capacity of 200 persons, offers a whole day cruise to the island (P1,056 for adults, P792 for children 12 years and below, inclusive of buffet breakfast, lunch and a tour of the island). The boat leaves the MacArthur Landing at the Manila Hotel at 7.30 am and returns at 5.30 pm. (Call 716-0204 or the Manila Hotel concierge for reservations.)

Luzon

Luzon is the biggest and most populous of the islands in the Philippines. It consists of the Central Plain, the Zambales range and Bataan peninsula, the Cordilleras, the Ilocos coast, Cagayan Valley, the Southern Tagalog region and the Bicol peninsula. The islands of Mindoro, Marinduque, Romblon, Masbate and Palawan, plus the Batanes group in the north and several offshore islands and islets are considered part of Luzon.

Central Luzon

North of Manila lies the Central Plain of Luzon, a vast region of 18,277 square kilometres (7,057 square miles) comprising the provinces of Bataan, Bulacan, Nueva Ecija, Pampanga, Tarlac and Zambales and the cities of Angeles, Olongapo, Cabanatuan, San Jose and Palayan. Driving from Manila north to the Ilocos coast, the flat plains stretch for kilometres around with the hulk of Mt Arayat the only dominant physical feature. The region is practically landlocked. The Zambales mountains in the west separate it from the rest of Northern Luzon and the Caraballo mountains in the east separate it from Cagayan Valley. A chain of volcanoes borders the western side of Luzon. Mt Pinatubo, one of three major volcanic centres, lies in the central portion of the Zambales Range, a mountain belt extending 220 kilometres north-north-west from Lingayen Gulf in the north to Bataan in the south. The other volcanic centres in western Luzon are Mt Mariveles and Mt Natib in Bataan.

Even before the coming of the Spaniards, the area was already thriving. Its navigable waterways made this hinterland accessible to early immigrants and traders from neighbouring kingdoms and countries. The Spanish conquistadores made the region into one big province with Bacolor as its capital, but as time went by, separate provinces were created. Although the Spaniards set up missions, little development took place until the 19th century. With the rise of nationalism, Bulacan, Pampanga, Tarlac and Nueva Ecija were among the eight original provinces to take up arms against Spain signalling the start of the Philippine Revolution. Even under American rule, hostilities and resistance continued. Bataan played a prominent role in World War II and the infamous Death March took place in this region culminating in Tarlac. After World War II, problems of agrarian reform caused political and social unrest, particularly in Pampanga, the hotbed of dissidents. The dissidents are no longer a problem. Acts of nature are.

The Philippines captured world attention in 1991 when Mt Pinatubo, dormant for 450 years, exploded in one of the most violent volcanic outbursts in recent memory. The provinces in Central Luzon received the brunt of the volcano's destructive force. Over time, Pinatubo spewed out an estimated seven cubic kilometres of volcanic debris in the eight river systems of Pampanga, Tarlac and Zambales. Sixty to 70 per cent of their land area is adversely affected by ashfalls and *lahars* (flowing mixtures of volcanic materials and water with the consistency of wet concrete). The activated volcano poses an ever constant threat to the lives and property of the inhabitants of Central Luzon. Heavy rains trigger off mudflows from the volcanic slopes threatening to engulf towns and villages along their path. Pampanga province is particularly vulnerable. The eruption wrought changes to the face of the land and continues to affect the lives and fortunes of thousands of Filipinos.

BULACAN

Bulacan is the gateway to Central and Northern Luzon. It is the cradle of the First Philippine Republic and the birthplace of many heroes of the Philippine Revolution such as the Great Propagandist Marcelo H del Pilar and General Gregorio del Pilar. The province has produced national artists in various fields, such as literature, music, painting and sculpture, film and entertainment, dance and drama. The Filipino poet Francisco Baltazar, popularly known as Balagtas, the writer Jose Corazon de Jesus (Huseng Batute), composers Nicanor Abelardo and Francisco Santiago, and the sculptor Guillermo Tolentino are some of them.

The province is known for its sweets and traditional delicacies— vinegar from Paombong, jewellery and leatherware, clay pots and glazed jars. Bulacan attracts scores of visitors in May. They go for the three-day fiesta at Obando, the Carabao festival in Pulilan and the Santacruzan (see also Festivals, page 277). In July, Bocaue celebrates its river festival, known as Pagoda sa Wawa. Antiques and local artefacts are displayed in the Bocaue Museum. A Jewellery Centre is located at Pandayan in the town of Meycauayan, home to jewellery makers. The centre has a showroom to display jewellery products, an audio-visual and conference room, a gem and assaying laboratory and facilities for the appraisal of jewellery.

Natural attractions in the province include the Sibul Spring and Pandi Mineral and Bath Spring, known for their medicinal waters, and Madlum Cave.

Agriculture, food processing plants, tanneries, textile mills, marble quarries, furniture factories, flower farms, cement industry, ceramics and pottery provide a livelihood for the province. The province supplies marble quarried outside San Miguel and San Ildefonso towns for the manufacture of stone furniture for export.

Rainforest at Subic Bay, Zambales

■ **MALOLOS AND THE BARASOAIN CHURCH**

Bulacan was one of the eight provinces that first took up arms against Spain in the Philippine Revolution of 1896. Three republics were established in the province: Real de Kakarong de Sili in 1896; Biak-na-Bato in 1897, and the Malolos Republic in 1899.

Malolos (44 kilometres/28 miles from Manila) was the seat of the short-lived Philippine Republic proclaimed by Emilio Aguinaldo. From mid-September 1898 to the last week of February 1899, the Malolos Congress met in the Barasoain Church to develop the Philippine Constitution which led to the birth of the Philippine Republic with Malolos as its capital.

The eyes of the Philippines and of the world were on Barasoain Church on 30 June 1998 when Joseph Ejercito Estrada and Gloria Macapagal Arroyo broke with tradition by taking their oaths of office as President and Vice President of the Republic of the Philippines in the historic church. Construction of Barasoain Church was undertaken in 1885 by Rev Fr Francisco Royo, OSA. For the centennial celebration, the church was restored in keeping with its original ecclesiastical design. The convent was converted into a museum.

■ **CASA REAL**

An historic landmark in Malolos, Casa Real is one of the Philippines' major museums of history, and the repository of artefacts and memorabilia from the First Malolos Congress. Declared a national shrine in 1980 by then President Diosdado Macapagal, Casa Real has been restored to its original Spanish architecture. The building has a checkered history. It started life as the town hall of the newly founded town of Malolos in 1580 and at different periods was known as Casa Tribunal, Ayuntamiento and Casa Presidencia Municipal. It was the seat of the Royal Coffer during the Spanish era and home to the National Printing Press for revolutionary newspapers.

The American military government used this as its headquarters. At various points in history, it functioned as a hospital, an annex of the Bulacan High School, an office of the Japanese Chamber of Commerce, a post-war relief distribution centre, and the temporary headquarters of the provincial government. The Telecommunications Office, Philippine National Bank and the Bureau of Posts also had their branch offices here.

The provincial government offices, the Convention Centre, Trade Centre and Cultural Centre are located in the provincial capital complex just off the MacArthur Highway. The province's historical and cultural heritage is displayed in the Bulacan

Museum, located at the Nicanor Abelardo Building (formerly Hiyas ng Bulacan). The Bulacan Tourism Office is also housed here.

Bulacan has 26 resort establishments. Lodging facilities range from nipa huts and cottages to air-conditioned hotel rooms. Most of these accept walk-in customers but making advance reservations is advisable during the summer months. DJ Paradise Resort and Club Royale Resort are among the places to stay in Malolos.

Bulacan is easily accessible by road from Manila and other points in Central Luzon. Several bus lines going north serve the province.

PAMPANGA

Pampanga province is noted for its cuisine, expert wood-carvers and makers of innovative Christmas lanterns, the Philippine Christmas Village near the capital San Fernando and Clark—site of the Philippine Centennial Exposition, Mimosa Leisure Estate and duty-free shops. A native son—Diosdado Macapagal, the 'poor boy from Lubao'—rose to become President of the republic. His daughter, Gloria Macapagal Arroyo, following in his political footsteps, is now Vice President of the Philippines. Pampangueños are famous for their cooking skills, and recipes are handed down from one generation to the next. The popularity of the food is shown by the number of restaurants serving Kapampangan specialities.

The Feast of St John the Baptist and the Apalit River Festival in honour of St Peter, both in June, are occasions to visit relatives and friends in Pampanga. In the past, the fluvial festivals were marked by the inevitable dousing of water on passers-by and guests, all in good fun. Lenten rites re-enacting Christ's crucifixion are held in various municipalities. In December, San Fernando celebrates the province's Foundation Day and stages a Giant Lantern Festival at the Christmas Village, located just outside the town.

The Spaniards founded the province in 1571, but prior to that, traders from other lands were sailing up the Pampanga River bringing not only barter items but their culture. Among the early settlers were people from Sumatra under Prince Balagtas.

Pampanga was one of the worst affected provinces in the destructive eruption in 1991 of Mount Pinatubo in nearby Zambales province. Some areas resemble desolate lunar landscapes where deposits of *lahar* (volcanic mudflows) are heaviest. Bacolor, once the region's proud capital, is sadly ruined by the volcanic ashfall. Its parish church, dating back to 1754, stands half-buried in *lahar*. However, vestiges of the province's Spanish past can still be seen in the centuries-old churches and period houses in towns that have survived the volcano's fury.

144

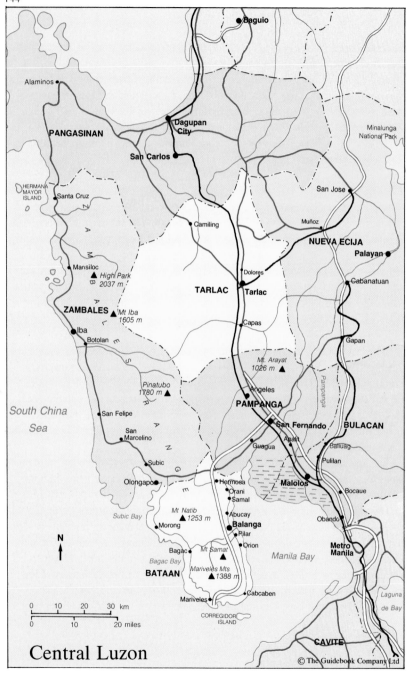

Central Luzon

© The Guidebook Company Ltd

■ **CLARK FIELD**

When Mount Pinatubo erupted, Clark was the largest American Air Force Base outside the USA. Heavily damaged by *lahar* and ashfall, the military facility was turned
over to the Philippine Government in November 1991. It took a natural disaster to
put an end to the debate then raging on whether to renew the lease on the US bases,
then due to expire in September 1991.

Clark rose phoenix-like from the ashes and today thrives as one of the country's
Special Economic Zones (SEZ). Several foreign companies have set up manufacturing plants on the industrial estate. Located within the SEZ is the 177-hectare
Mimosa Leisure Estate, a leisure and recreation centre with a 36-hole championship
golf course set in beautifully landscaped grounds, a clubhouse, a restaurant, driving
range, swimming pools, golf and tennis academies; a casino with Hollywood-themed
gaming rooms and live entertainment; Montevista Hotel and vacation villas, and the
337-room Holiday Inn Resort Clark Field, winner of the 1997 Kalakbay Resort of
the Year AAA award. Just 90 minutes' drive from Manila, Clark is one of the more
popular destinations outside Manila.

Clark is now the permanent home of the Philippine Centennial International
Exposition, inaugurated in June 1998 to commemorate the 100th anniversary
of independence from Spain. The centrepiece of the 60-hectare Expo Filipino is
the Freedom Ring, a structure occupying nine hectares and designed to look like
a Pampanga Christmas lantern. The complex is made up of a 35,000-capacity
amphitheatre, with high-tech equipment, and pavilion/exhibit areas. The Expo
site also features several plazas, pavilions and theme parks. Among these are the
Millennium Hall showcasing the trade and commercial exhibits of Philippine and
foreign groups; Ancient Island depicting the Philippines' pre-colonial past with
indigenous groups such as the Ifugaos, Kalingas, Sama Dilauts and Maranaos
displaying their rituals and crafts; Colonial Plaza recreating the country's Spanish
era. Admission to Expo Filipino is P180 for adults and P110 for the disabled and
senior citizens with ID. Children under three feet in height are admitted free. There
are guided tours to the Exposition site. Optional tours take in the Clark Museum,
Museong Kapampangan, Crystal Factory, Mimosa Leisure Estate and some duty-free
shops.

Clark has an airport with two long runways capable of landing all types of
aircraft. The complex occupies an area of 2,200 hectares and, when fully operational
as an international airport, will serve as the alternate gateway to Metro Manila.

ANGELES CITY

Angeles City, 83 kilometres (52 miles) from Manila and 16 kilometres from the provincial capital of San Fernando, was known in olden times as Kuliat. In the days when Clark was a US servicemen's R&R centre, Angeles was known for its swinging nightlife, but most of the bars are now closed down. In October Angeles celebrates the feast of La Naval in honour of Our Lady of the Rosary who is credited with the miraculous victory of Filipino and Spanish naval forces against the Dutch fleet. The festival is still called Fiestang Kuliat. Trade exhibits, a food festival and street dances mark the celebrations.

Among the standard hotels accredited by the Department of Tourism are the Century Resort Hotel (Villarica compound, Balibago), Clarkton Hotel (Don Juico Ave, Balibago), Maharajah (Texas St, Villasol Subdivision), Marlim Mansions Hotel (Diamond subdivision, McArthur Highway), Oasis Hotel (Clarkville compound), Swagman Narra Hotel (Sy Orosa St, Diamond subdivision) and Vegas International Hotel (Malabanas Rd, Balibago). Economy hotels include Endeavor Lord Hotel (Malabanas Rd), Liberty Hotel (Conching Rd), New Premiere Hotel (Malabanas Rd) and Valle Flores Hotel (Don Bonifacio Subd).

■ CHRISTMAS VILLAGE

This theme park, located some 66 kilometres (41 miles) north of Manila, is in the outskirts of San Fernando, the provincial capital. It's a short drive from Metro Manila and fits into a day excursion. From the highway, the village's distinctive shape and colour—like a giant Christmas lantern—catches the eye. The layout of the grounds is also shaped like a lantern. The traditions associated with Christmas in the Philippines find their expression here.

Among the park's attractions is Village Replica, showing a typical Philippine village celebrating Christmas, and reenacting various regional Yuletide practices, a display of Christmas ornaments from different countries, a collection of baskets from all over the Philippines, and the house that Mount Pinatubo built. The flooring, roofing, wall tiles, bathroom fixtures, kitchen counters, bowls and plates of this one-room house designed by the architect Francisco Mañosa were manufactured by different companies out of the ash, sand and rocks from Mount Pinatubo. The house is unique in that it is the collaborative work of individuals and companies.

Within the theme park are the Gardens of the World, a permanent display of plants from 22 countries. The Tourism Department Office is also located here.

Paskuhan holds regular events during the year such as the Bulaklakan Festival or floral offerings to the Blessed Virgin Mary at the end of May; Pamagsadya, a blessing of small lanterns in December; Abe-Abe Festival, a local version of the Mardi Gras,

A giant lantern in San Fernando, Pampanga

also held in December and the Giant Lantern Festival before Christmas, consisting of competitions and exhibition of giant lanterns from San Fernando. Other entertainment and shows are held during the year.

Pampanga is at the crossroads of transportation. The North Expressway, MacArthur Highway and the Gapan-Olongapo Highway traverse San Fernando.

TARLAC

Tarlac is Central Luzon's melting pot. Tagalogs, Pampangos, Ilocanos and Pangasinenses have settled here. It is the home province of former President Corazon Aquino. Tarlac is noted for its rice and sugar plantations, the Cojuangco-owned Hacienda Luisita with its fine golf course, and Camp O'Donnell in Capas where thousands of prisoners of war were incarcerated during World War II. In the 17th century, Tarlac province was a huge wilderness lying between the rugged mountain ranges and foothills in the west and the crocodile-infested swamps in the east. It took a day by horseback to traverse this area from end to end. Several families from the nearby towns settled here, cleared the jungle and planted sugar, hemp, indigo, tobacco and coconut. To protect the settlers from incursions by hostile natives in the west, the Spanish authorities made the area a military *commandancia* in 1869.

Created out of parts of Pampanga and Pangasinan, Tarlac formally became a province in 1874. Its capital is also named Tarlac.

Native sons, led by General Francisco Makabulos, participated in the fight to gain freedom from Spain by attacking the Spanish garrison. The revolutionary government of President Emilio Aguinaldo was transferred to Tarlac on 12 October 1899. It was in Paniqui that Father Gregorio Aglipay formally broke with Rome and formed the Philippine Independent Church.

There are several historic sites in the province. The Santo Domingo Death March Marker is a giant rock carved out of Mt Samat. It was here where 60,000 Filipino prisoners of war started their journey on foot to Camp O'Donnell, seven kilometres west of Capas town. Thousands died along the way, and thousands more perished in the concentration camp which became their burial ground. Later their bones were transferred to Mt Samat, the national shrine in Bataan province. The Capas Death March Monument is located along the highway, some three kilometres from the town proper. At Camp Servillano Aquino, formerly known as Camp Ord, there is a tree called the Eisenhower Tree, planted on July 4, 1939 by then Lt Col Dwight D Eisenhower. At the time, he was Chief of Staff of Gen Douglas MacArthur, military adviser of the Philippine Commonwealth.

The Maria Clara Museum in Camiling displays mementos of Leonor Rivera, the sweetheart of Jose Rizal, who portrayed her in his novels as Maria Clara, the embodiment of Filipina womanhood. The San Sebastian Cathedral in the capital Tarlac was the site of the revolutionary congress. The provincial capitol is built on top of a hill commanding a view of the town. A monument to General Makabulos stands near it and not far away is Maria Cristina Park.

The small Jecsons Hotel is accredited by the Department of Tourism while several lodging houses and resorts are licensed by the Local Government Unit.

Tarlac, approximately 125 kilometres from Manila, is a 5.5-hour journey from the city and is on the bus route to the Cordilleras and Northern Luzon. Philippine Rabbit has its terminal in Tarlac. Victory Liner, Pantranco, Fariñas Lines, Dangwa and other buses plying the Northern Luzon route pass through Tarlac.

NUEVA ECIJA

Nueva Ecija, occupying the eastern rim of the Central Luzon Plain, is the largest province in Central Luzon. It is the Central Plain's rice basket and is often referred to as the agricultural centre of Luzon because the Philippine Rice Research Institute and the Central Luzon State University are both located outside Muñoz. The province also grows corn, mangoes, tomatoes, onions and sugarcane. A winery in Gapan produces fruit wines made from *duhat* (a native plum) and *bignay* (similar to the blackcurrant).

A Spanish governor, a native of Ecija in Spain, named the province Nueva Ecija. It was made a *commandancia* in 1705. Gapan, founded in 1595 when it was still part of Pampanga, was the site of the first Augustinian mission in Nueva Ecija. The Byzantine-style Catholic Church here and old municipal hall are remnants of that past. Ruins of brick walls in Bongabon attest to the presence of the Augustinians who set up a mission here in 1636. At the turn of the 18th century, the missionary work expanded to Puncan, Carranglan and Pantabangan. Ruins showing identical Augustinian architecture can still be found. The province was among those that rose up in arms against Spain. Nueva Ecija had a brief moment of glory when President Emilio Aguinaldo moved the seat of his revolutionary government to San Isidro. Cabanatuan, Palayan City and San Jose are the three chartered cities of Nueva Ecija. Palayan City is the new provincial capital. Cabanatuan was the epicentre of the killer earthquake in July 1990 that destroyed many parts of Baguio and caused hillsides to collapse.

The province's natural attractions include the Minalungao National Park where one can swim, fish, dive from the cliffs and go caving; General Luna Falls in Rizal, Mt Olivete in Bongabon, with its waterfalls, medicinal springs and caves; the rivers and low-lying hills in Capintalan (Carranglan), ideal for hiking. Also tourist attractions are Diamond Park in San Jose City offering a panoramic view of the countryside and Pantabangan Dam. The guesthouse provides first-class accommodation with carpeted and air-conditioned rooms, a swimming pool and other recreational facilities.

Baliwag Transit, Five Star Transit and Ram Trans operate between Metro Manila and Cabanatuan City and Baliwag Transit also plies the Manila-San Jose route.

BATAAN

Bataan province, located southwest of Pampanga, occupies a peninsula which is an extension of the Zambales range with its volcanic mountains of Natib, Santa Rosa and Silanganan in the north and Mariveles, Limay (Cayapo) and Samat in the south. Located southwest of Pampanga, the peninsula is mountainous, with cliffs and headlands in the west, and coastal towns in the east. Bataan and Subic are priority areas for the implementation of the NIPAS Act, a law passed in 1992 for environmental protection and conservation of national parks. Bataan is one of the major suppliers of fruit to Manila. An export processing zone, an oil refinery and chemical complex, paper mills, shipyards, a quarantine port, and beach resorts are found in the province.

The peninsula's strategic position at the entrance to Manila Bay, exposed to the South China Sea, gave it an important role from early times. Bataan was among the first areas in Luzon to come under Spanish rule when Dominican friars established missions here in 1572. The Dutch plundered the coast and massacred 200 natives in

Abucay in 1647. Filipinos under Spanish command fought back and drove the Dutch away.

■ WORLD WAR II

Bataan is remembered in modern history for the heroic resistance put up by the Filipino-American forces against the invading Japanese in World War II. Some of the fiercest fighting in World War II took place here. Lacking reinforcements and handicapped by malnutrition, illness and lack of medicine, the defenders finally surrendered on 9 April 1942. Emaciated prisoners were marched from Mariveles up the peninsula to the concentration camp in Capas, Tarlac. Thousands perished from disease and brutal treatment along the 112-kilometre (70-mile) Death March route. 'No soil on earth is more deeply consecrated to the cause of human liberty than that on the island of Corregidor and the adjacent Bataan peninsula,' said General MacArthur when he returned on a sentimental journey to the Philippines.

Pugots, descendants of aboriginal Negritos, in the foothills of the Sierra Madre mountains (above); a Negrito family (right)

Bataan's role in the fight for freedom is recorded by the numerous historical markers indicating battle positions, the route of the Death March, and other significant wartime sites throughout the province. The First Line of Defence marker is in the town of Dinalupihan and a Democracy Marker is found in Hermosa near the border with Pampanga. In the town of Pilar, all the major places of interest recall the Battle of Bataan. The Dambana ng Kagitingan (Shrine of Valour) atop Mt Samat honours the memory of those who fought and died during World War II. The shrine, 14 kilometres (9 miles) from Pilar junction, is dominated by a giant steel and concrete cross rising to a height of 95 metres (311 feet) and visible for miles around. On a clear night, the lighted cross can be seen from Roxas Boulevard in Manila across the bay. On the arms of the cross there is a viewing gallery commanding a magnificent vista of the surrounding land and sea. The anniversaries of the Fall of Bataan (9 April) and Corregidor (6 May) are commemorated by wreath-laying ceremonies and Mass. In Balanga, the provincial capital, a Fall of Bataan marker is located, as well as one showing where General Edward King of the US Armed Forces officially surrendered to the Japanese. Boat races, water skiing and other activities take place here in May after the Araw ng Kagitingan ceremony on Mount Samat. Balanga, 124 kilometres (77 miles) from Manila, is centrally located in the peninsula and is a hub of commerce and transport. From Balanga, a scenic 49-kilometre (31-mile) road winds across the peninsula to Bagac and Morong. On Good Friday, penitents carrying crosses can be seen walking along this road. The coast between Balanga and Mariveles is lined with beach resorts.

■ OTHER ATTRACTIONS

The Roosevelt National Park, a dipterocarp forest with natural springs and a game refuge, is located in Dinalupihan and Hermosa. The fishing town of Orani is the site of a Good Friday 'crucifixion'. Offshore islets nearby are inhabited by wild duck and other game birds. Samal, noted for its embroidered handicrafts, holds a *senaculo* (Passion play) on Good Friday. The fishing port of Abucay, birthplace of the first Filipino printer Tomas Pinpin, is the site of a battle marker. Sibul Spring is in Abucay. Mt Natib (1,278 metres/4,193 feet) is one of the three major volcanic centres in the region. Orani is the jump-off point for adventure seekers who wish to go mountain-climbing, rapelling or camping. A trail shelter is available for overnight trekkers. In Orion where he lived and died, there's a monument to Francisco Balagtas, the 'Prince of Tagalog Poets' who wrote *Florante at Laura*. At the southern tip of the peninsula is Mariveles, 171 kilometres (106 miles) from Manila. An early Spanish settlement and former fishing port, it lies in the shadow of Mt Mariveles (1,388 metres/4,554 feet), another volcanic centre in the region. Mariveles has become a major industrial centre and the Philippines' first export processing zone. Points of interest include the marker indicating the start of the Death March, hot sulphur springs and an Aeta settlement. Bagac has fine beaches, a war marker and the Filipino-Japanese Friendship Tower. A few kilometres to the northeast are Pasukulan Falls. South of town is Sun Moon Beach. In the adjacent cove, at Barangay Pasinay, is Montemar Beach Club (with swimming pool, tennis court, nine-hole pitch and putt course, and facilities for water sports). The forest reserve in Morong is the site of the UN Refugee Centre and there are various relics of the refugees' stay here. There is also a *Bangkal barangay* where the Aetas have been resettled and where they continue to maintain their traditional lifestyles and customs. Morong is the jump-off point to other mountains such as Mt Silanganan, with its 24-metre (80-foot) high waterfalls fed by mountain springs and a water pool for swimming. Mountain climbing, trekking, caving and rapelling are among the recommended activities in this area. There are also beach resorts nearby.

Places to stay include The Piazza Hotel (with swimming pool, nightclub/disco) and Villa Imperial in Mariveles; Vista Corregidor in Cabcaben; Alitaptap Hotel, Joyous Fishpond Resort and Buenavista Resort in Balanga; the Montemar Beach Club at Barangay Pasinay in Bagac; Freddielie Resort, Labini Summer Resort and Ann Jolyn in Orani; Villa Edem Beach Resort, Villa Carmen Beach Resort and Joriz Farm in Limay.

Pantranco, Philippine Rabbit, Panther Bus Co, Genesis Bus Co travel from Manila to Bataan.

ZAMBALES

Zambales occupies the western side of Central Luzon, with a long coastline indented by small bays and coves. Most of the towns are located on a narrow coastal strip backed by a range of tall, rugged mountains separating the province from the Central Plain. Rich deposits of chromite lie beneath the Zambales mountains. The province is known for its mangoes, salt-making, rope-making and the production of *bagoong*, fermented fish sauce.

Zambales came under Spanish rule in 1572. Among the early Spanish settlements were Masinloc, founded in 1607; Iba, founded in 1611, and Santa Cruz. The original inhabitants were the Zambals and Aetas. When Tagalogs and Ilocanos started migrating to the province, the Aetas fled to the interior and settled in the area of Mt Pinatubo. The volcanic eruption in 1991 rained death and destruction on a wide scale. Among the hardest hit were the Aetas.

SUBIC/OLONGAPO

Located at the southernmost tip of Zambales province, 127 kilometres (79 miles) north of Manila, is Olongapo City. The Zambales mountains frame its three sides and Subic Bay lies at its base. Noting the natural harbour protected by the surrounding mountains and the strategic location of this deep water bay along the sealanes of trading ships, the Spaniards made Subic Bay a naval port in 1884. Olongapo, then a fishing village on the shores of Subic Bay, was turned into a Spanish naval arsenal and shipyard in 1885. A gate, watch tower, several buildings and a railway connecting the hills of Olongapo and the bay were ordered to be constructed. Subic and Olongapo became American military reservations when the Americans took control of the Philippines at the turn of the century.

Subic was the largest American naval base outside the continental United States, providing the logistical support for the US Seventh Fleet's ships and aircraft. When Mt Pinatubo erupted in 1991 forcing the Americans to abandon Clark Airbase, it was only a matter of time before they would give up Subic too. The formal turnover took place in November 1992 when the last American ship left port. Before the turnover, there was anxiety that the American pullout would leave an economic void in the area. But Olongapo Mayor Richard Gordon was determined that the infrastructure and resources—the extensive dockyards, warehouses, cold storage facilities, airfield, buildings, housing, more than 80 kilometres of good roads, power generator plant—left behind by the departing Seventh Fleet should not go to waste. Gordon's dream was to convert Subic into a special economic and free port zone.

As chairman of the Subic Bay Metropolitan Authority (SBMA), Richard Gordon turned Subic into a success story. Its free trade status, strategic location, excellent infrastructure, modern telecommunications, shipping support facilities and services, abundant water and power supply, airport, highly qualified workforce, efficient security and variety of amenities were drawing investors.

Companies wishing to set up factories had to follow strict environmental rules. Only non-polluting industries were allowed to operate in the free port zone. Subic, with its rainforest and watershed reserve, is one of the ten priority protected areas in the country funded by the World Bank through the Global Environmental Facility. Scientists are conducting a study of its biodiversity.

■ LEISURE AND SPORTS

Subic's scenic setting and excellent facilities make it an ideal holiday resort. One can enjoy various leisure and sporting activities, such as a game of golf at the Binictican Valley Golf Course (make reservations in advance), mini golf, tennis, squash, basketball, bowling, horseback riding, fishing (permit required), diving (to see wrecks of American and Japanese ships), swimming in any of the swimming pools, yachting and boating, bay cruises, aquatic sports, and picnics. The Subic Bay Yacht Club has a recreational centre offering a wide range of water sports activities.

■ ACTIVITIES FOR THE ADVENTUROUS

Jungle and Eco Tours are available for interested visitors. A hike into the heart of the rainforest brings you to the Jungle Environmental Survival Training School (JEST). Trainers demonstrate basic jungle survival skills. The JEST Camp was the training site for US forces preparing for the Vietnam War in the 1960s. Within the JEST compound is a mini zoo and handicraft shop. An overnight stay in the jungle can be arranged; bring your own tent. Or join an Eco Tour (minimum of 10 persons) to the rainforest with an Aeta guide who will bring you to their tribal village to see their customs and dances. Wear proper attire for the forest trek. A two-hour general tour of the former base complex (visitors use their own vehicles but hire a guide) and bay cruises are other options for visitors. Tours are available from 8 am to 3 pm daily. The Tourist Office at Room 11 of Building 229 (SBMA office, tel 252 4229/ 4123) gives you all the necessary information, rates and permits and makes arrangements for tours.

Some visitors make a special trip to Subic just for the duty-free shopping. Shopping malls, PX, commissary and specialty stores offer a range of merchandise. Visitors must obtain a purchase card at the Merchandise Control Office (Building 8211; open 7 am to 3 pm). Show a valid identification with photo (passport, driver's licence, etc).

Accommodation is available at the Subic International Hotel, the Subic Bay

Vigan Cathedral, Ilocos Sur, a former encomienda *of Juan de Salcedo*

Resort and Casino and lodges run by the SBMA. Five buildings that used to be barracks now house visitors. Thirty villas were constructed for the APEC Conference of 18 heads of state in November 1996. The 18-hole Binictican Valley Golf Course was redeveloped into a 27-hole course. Subic caters to a range of tastes in its dining facilities. At the Subic Seafront which used to be the exclusive Officers Club, international and Filipino dishes are served. You can also find Japanese and Chinese restaurants, a fast food court, steakhouse, and a diner serving hotdogs and hamburgers. For those who wish to flirt with Lady Luck at the gaming tables, there's the casino on Waterfront Road and the Casino Filipino in Olongapo City. Olongapo attracts visitors during its Maytime festival, Mardi Gras, Oktoberfest and the city fiesta on the 30th of December. Olongapo is also a jump-off point for year-round dive sites around Subic Bay. There are several hotels, beach resorts and tourist inns.

■ GETTING THERE

Subic is accessible by commuter ferry from Manila, by charter aircraft or by car or bus from Manila. It takes about two to three hours' drive from Manila. Visitors must obtain a gate/car pass at the SBMA Visitors' Centre. Present a valid, laminated ID card, passport or driver's licence and current car registration. Victory Liner and Saulog buses ply the Manila-Olongapo route. Jeepneys and tricycles operate within city limits.

■ **OTHER PLACES**

There are several offshore islands between Olongapo in the south and Santa Cruz in the north where coral reefs and drop-offs make it possible to go snorkelling and scuba-diving. Botolan is the jumping-off point for the sites around Hermana Mayor Island where diving takes place from November to June. There are several resthouses and beach resorts along the shoreline. A *banca* to Gaines Island, which is actually a peninsula, can be hired. San Felipe is a town of potters. Iba, the provincial capital, and birthplace of President Ramon Magsaysay, is 83 kilometres (52 miles) from Olongapo. There are good beaches north of town. Fine snorkelling is available around Magalawan Island. Santa Cruz is the northernmost town in the province, close to the border with Pangasinan.

Northern Luzon

ILOCOS

The Ilocos region, or Region 1 consisting of the provinces of Pangasinan, La Union, Ilocos Sur and Ilocos Norte, occupies the northwestern portion of Luzon. A long and narrow coastal plain backed by mountains, the Ilocos coast is one of rugged beauty with dramatic seascapes, particularly on the northwestern tip. The inhospitable environment has shaped a sturdy, hard-working, entrepreneurial and thrifty people. Ilocanos are noted for their weaving, jewellery making and pottery. The Ilocos provinces have some of the finest examples of 18th-century rococo architecture in the country, exemplified by the Augustinian churches with their lavish ornamentation combining Philippine and Chinese motifs. Most of the religious artwork in the region has been executed by unknown artisans. The region also produces the native wine of Ilocanos called basi, made from fermented sugarcane juice. The region is accessible by bus from Manila and neighbouring provinces. There are local and international flights to Laoag in Ilocos Norte.

PANGASINAN

Pangasinan is a major rice producer, second only to Nueva Ecija. The province is known for salt production (*pang asinan* means "a place where salt is made"), oyster farms, and fish ponds used for *bangus* (milkfish) culture. It is the home province of former President Fidel V Ramos. Filipino and Allied forces led by Gen Douglas MacArthur landed on the beaches of Lingayen Gulf on 9 January 1945 to start the liberation of Luzon from the Japanese. At the back of the provincial Capitol is the Lingayen Gulf War Memorial built to honour the liberation forces. Pangasinan's

major tourist attraction is the Hundred Islands, scattered along the southern shores of the Lingayen Gulf. The area is a national park. The Philippine Tourism Authority operates the Lingayen Gulf Resort Hotel here.The jumping-off point is Alaminos where visitors can board *bancas* to the island of their choice. The prices for boat hire are fixed. The beaches are first-rate, the coral reefs excellent for diving and snorkelling. Camping is recommended on Quezon, Children and Governor's islands.
  Alaminos offers a number of small resort inns. A variety of seashells are sold here. People who want a quiet holiday by the sea head for San Fabian, on the northern coast of Lingayen Gulf. The San Fabian Beach Resort in Barrio Bolasi offers accommodation ranging from dormitory and guestrooms to presidential suites with air-conditioned double rooms, each with a private toilet and bath with hot and cold water. Facilities include a restaurant, pavilion and conference hall. There are picnic sheds and sleeping tents in the vast grounds. Local sportfishermen also fish for *talakitok* (jacks) in the waters around Bolinao. They stop off in Alaminos to buy live shrimp, then on to Bolinao where they hire *bancas* for a half day's fishing.

LA UNION

The gateway to the region is La Union, sandwiched between the South China Sea and the foothills of the Cordillera mountain ranges. La Union became a province in 1850. The capital, San Fernando, is 270 kilometres (168 miles) northwest of Manila. It is hub of transportation and commerce in Northern Luzon. The biennial South China Sea Race from Hong Kong to the Philippines culminates in San Fernando. Proximity to Baguio makes La Union an ideal side trip for those in the mountain resort who wish to enjoy the sun and sea. The province has several beach resorts strung along the coast; the most popular are located in Bauang and Agoo, with newer ones in Caba and San Juan. Swimming, scuba diving, boating, waterskiing and surfing are the favoured sports. Poro Point is a picturesque spot and a jumping-off point for diving areas in the South China Sea and Lingayen Gulf. Surfing enthusiasts go to San Juan to enjoy high waves between November and February. The Agoo Playa Hotel, located in San Nicolas West, Agoo, some 235 kilometres (147 miles) from Manila is also a popular resort.
  Agoo is the oldest town in the province. Established in 1578, it served as the first point of contact with Christianity in the southern Ilocos region. The Museo Iloko at Agoo houses religious art and artefacts. Along the national highway is a shrine to Sto Niño de Pescador, built on the spot where the old church belfry stood. A pilgrimage site in the province is the Shrine of Our Lady of Namacpacan, the patroness of travellers, in St Catherine's Church in Luna, 34 kilometres (21 miles) from San Fernando. Pilgrims have flocked to Apparition Hill in Agoo when it was

reported that the Blessed Virgin Mary, weeping tears of blood, appeared to a 12-year-old boy. Many believers have reported seeing the miracle of a dancing sun.

ILOCOS SUR

The province, along Northern Luzon's western coast, is long and narrow, and backed by mountains with a densely populated coastal plain. The province's major towns are strung out along the coastal highway. Vigan, the capital, is the birthplace of Padre Jose Burgos, one of the three martyr-priests executed in Manila in 1872 for alleged sedition. It is the home province of Gabriela Silang, a revolutionary heroine, and former President Elpidio Quirino. Ilocanos are known for their *pinakbet* (an eggplant dish that is the Philippine version of ratatouille), *bagnet* (roast pork), jars (*burnay*) and clay tiles, woven cloth called *abel*, woodcraft and furniture-making, mat, hat and basket-weaving. Loom-weaving is their most extensive handicraft.

Long before the Spaniards arrived, Ilocanos were already trading with Chinese merchants, and over the centuries, many Chinese settled in Vigan, intermarried and became wealthy. Juan de Salcedo, the grandson of Miguel Lopez de Legaspi, explored the area in 1572 and was made lieutenant governor of the Ilocos region. Spanish missionaries were active in the region, building churches. The parish church of Vigan was founded in 1575, Santa in 1576, Tagudin in 1586, Narvacan in 1587, Bantay, Candon and Sinait in 1591. The churches of Santa Cruz, San Esteban and Magsingal were established in the 17th century. Those of San Juan (Lapog), Santiago, Santo Domingo, Santa Maria, San Ildefonso, Cabugao, Santa Lucia, Santa Catalina and San Vicente were built in the 18th century, while those in Caoayan and Cervantes were constructed in the 19th century. Many of these churches still exist and are interesting to visit.

VIGAN

Vigan, about four kilometres from the coast, on the Mestizo River, is the Philippines' third oldest city, after Cebu and Manila. Unlike the first two cities, it was never fortified. When Juan de Salcedo made it his *encomienda* in 1578, it was already a thriving settlement. He called it Ciudad Fernandina. It became the political, commercial and ecclesiastical capital of northern Luzon. Vigan was the seat of the Diocese of Nueva Segovia after its transfer from Lal-lo, Cagayan in 1758. Diego Silang led a revolt against the Spaniards in 1762, capturing Vigan and defeating the Bishop's forces but was assassinated in 1763. His wife, Gabriela, continued the revolt but was later captured and hung in Vigan.

Some of the best remaining examples of Spanish colonial architecture in the Philippines today can be found in Vigan. The city's Spanish colonial houses, narrow

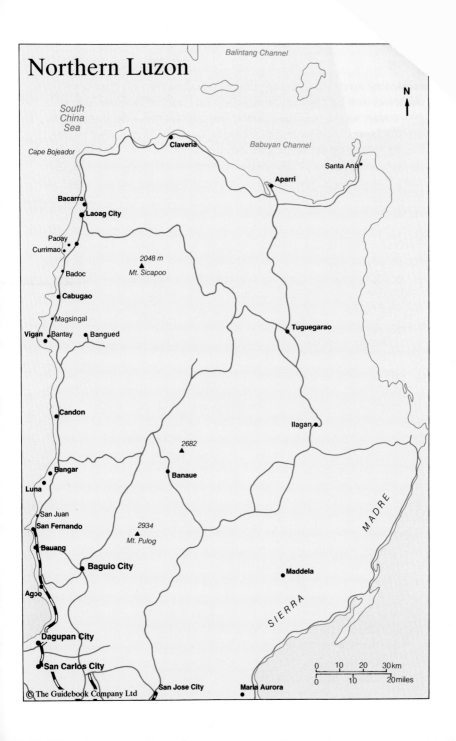

.s and charming plazas are its main attractions. Many of the fine
ouilt by Chinese mestizos at the height of the indigo trade in the
ich created great wealth for many merchants. The nouveau-riche
mestizos became Vigan's élite. The old houses are concentrated in what was the
Chinese mestizo quarter south of the cathedral. Crisologo Street, once the main
shopping street, Plaridel, V de los Reyes, Governor Reyes have notable houses. This
area still retains the genteel charm of a bygone age, when life was slow-paced and
horse-drawn *calesas* clippety-clopped on cobblestone streets. One of the gracious old
houses is the elegant Rosario residence which hosts many visiting dignitaries.
Kaivigan Foundation and SVAHAI (Save Vigan Ancestral Homes Association, Inc)
are spearheading efforts to preserve and restore these old houses. There is now a
move to include Vigan on the UNESCO World Heritage List. About 187 ancestral
homes dating from the 17th to the 19th centuries are included in the plan. The
residence of Padre Jose Burgos is probably the oldest in the list. It is now a museum
and library displaying the mementos of the martyr-priest, along with Ilocano
artefacts and ethnic art of the Tingguians. Among the old houses in need of restoration is the Syquia Mansion, home of former President Elpidio Quirino. His wife was
a Syquia.

Within walking distance from the colonial houses is Plaza Burgos, the Cathedral
of St Paul, the Archbishop's Palace, the Provincial Capitol and the Burgos Museum.
The Palacio del Arzobispado (Archbishop's Palace), constructed in 1783, housed the
ecclesiastical court until 1890. It was occupied by the revolutionists who imprisoned
Bishop Jose Hevia Campomanes in 1896, and used as a garrison by the American
forces under Lt Col James Parker in 1899. Spared from destruction during World
War II, it now houses the ecclesiastical Museum and Archives of the Archdiocese of
Nueva Segovia. Among the priceless collections are the silver altar of repose used by
the cathedral on Maundy Thursday, silver icons and altar ornaments, an ivory statue
of Nuestra Señora de la Caridad or Apo Caridad, Queen of Ilocandia, liturgical
vessels, vestments and ornaments, documents, church furniture, architectural plans,
paintings and sculpture. The Throne Room is located on the second floor.

South of Plaza Burgos is Plaza Leona Florentino, a pocket park dedicated to
Leona Florentino (1849-84), daughter of Vigan, foremost Ilocano poetess, satirist
and playwright. Her works in Spanish and Ilocano were exhibited in expositions in
Madrid in 1887 and Paris in 1889. Close by is the Florentino house and Café Leona
restaurant (open 8 am to 10 pm) serving Ilocano and Filipino dishes

Vigan draws many visitors in February when it celebrates its fiesta and in May
when it holds its Viva Vigan Festival of Arts. A trade fair, photo exhibit, on-the-spot
painting contests, band competitions, tilbury carriage parade and contest, fashion

show, and musical programmes in the town plaza are among the events in the week-long festival. While in Vigan, visitors can watch potters and weavers at work. At Pagburnayan, there is a community of potters whose ancestors came from China. They produce dark jars, called *burnay*, traditional containers of the Ilocano wine known as *basi*. The craft has been handed down from one generation to the next. Barangay Bulala produces the bright red earthenware pots, jars and the Vigan tiles widely used for patios.

■ WHERE TO STAY

The Villa Angela on Quirino Boulevard is a Vigan heritage house built in 1873 that now serves as a hotel. It has six rooms furnished with four-poster beds, family-type bedrooms and dormitory-style accommodation. The actor Tom Cruise slept in the master bedroom when he was in Ilocos for the filming of *Born On The 4th Of July* during the fiesta of Vigan. El Juliana, a 27-room economy hotel, is also on Quirino Boulevard. Vigan Educational Cultural Centre (Mena Crisologo Street) is a homestay site.

Partas buses travel to Vigan, a journey of eight to nine hours from Manila. One can also fly to Laoag, then take a bus to Vigan.

■ OUT-OF-TOWN

From Vigan, one can take excursions to various places. By private transport or hire car, the neighbouring provinces of Abra and Ilocos Norte are just an hour or so's drive away. Historic churches in the province are also within driving distance of the city. About 40 kilometres (30 minutes' drive) from Vigan is the church of Nuestra Señora de la Asuncion in Santa Maria. Used as a fortress in the Revolution of 1896, it is a national monument and a UNESCO World Heritage Site. It is one of four churches in the Philippines selected as the best examples of Philippine baroque architecture blended with unique folk arts. Originally built by the Augustinians as a chapel of Narvacan, it became a parish in 1769, dedicated to Our Lady of the Assumption. The tower was built in 1810 and the main church featuring heavily buttressed walls was built of stone and restored in 1863. Situated 60 metres (197 feet) above the town, it commands a fine view of the surrounding countryside. The church is reached by a winding stone stairway. Another series of stone steps leads to an abandoned cemetery at the foot of the hill.

ILOCOS NORTE

The province is on the northernmost edge of western Luzon with the Babuyan Channel marking its northern boundaries. It has a rugged, rocky terrain and from

Cape Bojeador to the Cagayan boundary, one is treated to dramatic scenery along the coast, particularly on Patapat with its sheer cliffs. Pagudpud is one of its well-known resorts. Like Ilocos Sur, its sister province, Ilocos Norte has many notable churches, legacies of the Spanish era. Ilocos Norte is the home province of the former president Ferdinand Marcos, the renowned painter Juan Luna and his equally famous soldier-writer brother Antonio. Laoag City is its capital and the centre of trade and education.

Among the points of interest are the Church of San Agustin in Paoay, a fortress-like church with massive buttresses to withstand earthquakes. The thick walls are made of coral-rubble faced with brick. It has a separate bell tower that was used as a lookout by Katipuneros during the revolution and local guerrillas in World War II. This 'earthquake baroque' church is a UNESCO World Heritage Site. Several kilometres from the town is Paoay Lake National Park. The 'Malacañang of the North' (so-called because it was the official residence of President Marcos when he was in the North) overlooks the lake. The residence is open to tourists who pay an entrance fee. The beautifully landscaped grounds with masses of bougainvilleae are extensive and well-maintained. A short drive away is the Fort Ilocandia resort hotel with tennis courts and swimming pool and Lake Paoay golf course.

North of Laoag is Bacarra. The truncated bell tower of the Bacarra Church presents an unusual sight. An earthquake caused the dome of the massive square belfry to collapse onto the third storey. It is still poised there. In Laoag, the Renaissance-design St William's Cathedral has a sinking bell tower. Other provincial attractions are the Balay ti Ili, the former home of the Marcos family in Batac, 17 kilometres (10.5 miles) from Laoag, The house is a museum of Marcos memorabilia. Next to it is Marcos' mausoleum where the body lies inside a glass coffin for public viewing. The former dictator has been denied burial at the Libingan ng mga Bayani in Makati, Metro Manila. How long the body will lie there before it is finally buried is not known. The Juan Luna Shrine and Museum in Badoc, south of Laoag is another visitor attraction.

Bus travel from Manila to Laoag takes about nine hours, between Vigan and Laoag about an hour. There are also local flights to Laoag. Daily flights from Taiwan bring tourists and businessmen to Laoag via Laoag International Airport. Aside from Fort Ilocandia Resort Hotel, another popular white beach area is Pagudpud, under an hour's drive from Laoag City. Accommodation in Laoag is available at the Palazzo de Laoag, a standard hotel, and at lesser hotels and pensions.

(preceding pages) Mt Pinatubo

The Batanes Group

Off the coast of mainland Luzon, lying between the Luzon Strait and Balintang Channel, are the outer islands of the Batanes group which form the province of Batanes, about 860 kilometres (534 miles) from Manila. Batan, Itbayat and Sabtang are the biggest of the islands. The northernmost island in the Philippines is Y'ami, also known as the Orchid Island. On a clear day, one can see Taiwan. The island is surrounded by a wealth of marine life; the coconut crab, locally known as *tatus*, abounds here. The Batanes islands are on the sealane between the Philippines and Taiwan, Japan, China and Hong Kong.

The islanders, called Ivatans, are a pre-historic people of Malay stock with a mixture of Chinese and Spanish blood from the early immigrants from Formosa (Taiwan) and the Spaniards who settled on the island. It was during the incumbency of Governor General Jose Basco y Vargas that a Spanish expedition was sent to the islands in 1782. Basco, the provincial capital on the island of Batan, was named after him. Traditionally a seafaring people, the Ivatans are hardy, elemental, friendly, and peace-loving. They live in limestone houses with low doorways and small windows to protect them from the wet and windy weather. Fishing and farming are their livelihood and they grow a lot of root crops, such as taro and sweet potatoes. They also raise cattle, *carabao* and goats. The Ivatans have few modern pleasures in life. The video is one of them. This keeps them in touch with the world outside.

Basco is 280 kilometres (174 miles) north of Aparri in Cagayan province and 190 kilometres (118 miles) south of Taiwan. Basco is the last weather station in the Northern Philippines and therefore is a reference point for all typhoons entering the Philippine area of responsibility. It is not surprising that people think Batanes is constantly battered by typhoons. In these rugged, windswept islands, the landscapes and seascapes are dramatic with towering cliffs pounded by waves, craggy peaks, gorges, pastures atop ridges and emerald farms forming a pattern like patchwork quilt. Spelunking at the Chawa Cave and Crystal Cave in Mahatao; surfing at Madi-wedved in Mahatao; trekking at Marlboro Country and Naidi Hills, mountain-climbing and trail-blazing at Mt Iraya (a dormant volcano) and bird-watching are among the activities for visitors. Most of these are only a few kilometres from Basco.

Basco has pension houses and lodges. The Batanes Homestay Association and St Dominic's Cooperative for Homestay are good contacts. Contact the Tourist Information Office of the Department of Tourism. There are local flights from Manila and Tuguegarao, Cagayan. Ships also call in from the mainland.

Cagayan Valley

Cagayan Valley consists of the provinces of Cagayan, Isabela, Nueva Vizcaya and Quirino. Together with Batanes province, they form Region Two. This is rugged country, with wild seacoasts, thickly wooded mountains and verdant valleys. Tourists have not yet beaten a path to Cagayan Valley. It is still pristine and as such is ideal for ecotourism adventures such as wilderness trekking, camping, mountaineering, spelunking, bird watching, ocean cruising, snorkelling, scuba diving, game fishing. Cagayan Valley has been inhabited since ancient times, as evidenced by archaeological discoveries in caves. Chinese and Japanese were trading with the inhabitants long before the Spanish arrival. The Spaniards founded missions in Camalaniugan and Lallo which became the seat of the Diocese of Nueva Segovia from 1594 until its transfer to Vigan in 1755. Massive, fortress-like churches were built by the Dominicans. Some of the relics of the Spanish past can still be found today. The Cagayan River, the longest watercourse in the country, flows across three provinces: Nueva Vizcaya, Isabela and Cagayan where it finally meets the sea at the delta in Aparri.

CAGAYAN

Cagayan province (capital: Tuguegarao) is at the northeastern tip of mainland Luzon, bounded on the east by the Sierra Madre Mountain range which extends up to the beaches of the coastal towns, on the south by Isabela Province, on the west by the Cordillera Mountains and on the north by the Balintang channel, Babuyan Channel and the China Sea. The offshore islands of Palaui, Fuga and the Babuyan group (Calayan, Dalupiri, Camiguin and Babuyan Claro) are part of the province. Cagayan is a paradise for spelunkers, trekkers and enthusiasts of water sports and fishing. On the western side of Cagayan, reached via the Ilocos coast in one of the most dramatic and scenic drives in the country on Patapat Road are the coastal towns of Sta Praxedes, Claveria, Sanchez Mira, and Pamplona with stretches of black and white sand beaches. The Portabaga Falls in Sta Praxedes is one of the most beautiful in the province. Abulog, Ballesteros, the great river delta at Aparri, all have their own rugged beauty. San Vicente, on the northeastern coast, is the jump-off point for anglers after big game fish in the Pacific. It is the site of international and national gamefishing competitions. Thirty minutes away by boat is Palaui Island with its Spanish era lighthouse. The seas surrounding the island are rich in marine life. Mountain climbing, trekking and scuba diving are ideal sporting activities here. Port Irene in Santa Ana is being developed as an international port of call. At Lallo, the Magapit suspension bridge spans the Cagayan River and links the first and second districts of Cagayan. It is 74 kilometres from Tuguegarao, the provincial capital.

Some 24 kilometres (15 miles) southeast of Tuguegarao is the Callao Caves National Park, accessible via Peñablanca. The 192-hectare park with its multi-chambered caves, massive rock formations, spectacular stalactites and stalagmites, deep canyons and stream is also a recreational resort. The first chamber has been cleared of some of its stalactites and stalagmites to accommodate a chapel. The other caves have yielded prehistoric remains of bones and tools. The provincial museum in Tuguegarao is worth a visit to see the archaeological and geological collections. There are hundreds of caves in the area which are in a pristine state. These caves may be explored with guides from members of the Sierra Madre Outdoor Club (contact Olimpio Muñoz, president tel (087) 844-1621 or Speleo Philippines, Cagayan chapter (call Richard Guzman, Edgardo Tiongson, tel (078) 844 2816, Francis Battung, tel (078) 844 2359, or DOT-Cagayan Valley Region tel (078) 844 1621 or 844 5364. Within the area is the Pinacanauan River, ideal for river rafting or boating and swimming. Mountain climbing, trekking, bird-watching and bonsai exploration are other activities in Peñablanca. Piat is a place of pilgrimage for those with a devotion to the Blessed Virgin. It is the home of Our Lady of Piat, said to be miraculous. Originally

from Acapulco, it travelled to Macau and was brought to Piat in 1630. Our Lady of Piat's feast is celebrated on 2 July. Before that Piat holds the Sambali Festival, a war dance of tribes reunited and converted to Christianity through the intercession of the Lady of Piat. Songs, dances and other activities projecting the culture of the tribes are held every year at the end of June.

A tribal woman from Ifugao Province in Northern Luzon

The biggest Spanish-built church in Cagayan Valley, constructed between 1761 and 1767, is St Peter's Cathedral, seat of the archdiocese of Tuguegarao. It was severely damaged during World War II but was rebuilt under Bishop C Jurgens.

Tuguegarao has several economy hotels, pensions and tourist inns. Hotel Candice, Hotel Ivory and Convention Centre, Pension Roma, Michaela's Hotel and Restaurant are among them. There is also a Homestay programme. Contact the Cagayan Provincial Tourism Council and Provincial Office at (078) 844 1514 for a list of accredited places to stay. There are domestic flights to Tuguegarao while various bus companies operate lines to Cagayan.

ISABELA

Isabela, named after Queen Isabela II of Spain, was made a province in 1856 out of portions of Cagayan and Nueva Vizcaya. Noted for agriculture and the Magat Hydroelectric Dam, Isabela is one of the country's most progressive provinces. Ilagan is its capital. Santiago City, 328 kilometres (205 miles) from Metro Manila and accessible by land transport from any part of Luzon, is the only city in Cagayan Valley and is Region II's industrial centre; it is also the province's food basket. Isabela's natural tourist attractions are the Bonsai Forest at Sumanget, Dinapigue, the Santa Victoria Caves at the Fuyo National Park, and the rainforest at Palanan, one of the world's remaining low-altitude rainforests with its wealth of undocumented endemic flora and fauna and its exceptional biological diversity. It was in Palanan that the American forces captured Gen Emilio Aguinaldo in March 1901, ending the short-lived First Philippine Republic. There is a shrine dedicated to Aguinaldo here. Palanan is accessible by light aircraft from the Cauayan Domestic Airport, or by pumpboat from Santa Ana, Cagayan or Baler, Aurora or by trail hiking from San Mariano, Cauayan and Ilagan in Isabela.

The province also boasts old historic churches. The baroque Church of St Mathias in Tumauini, built in 1753 by the Dominicans, has an interesting embellished facade and a unique cylindrical bell tower. The San Pablo Church founded before Isabela was made a province is said to have the tallest bell tower in Cagayan Valley.

NUEVA VIZCAYA

Nueva Vizcaya is the southern gateway to Cagayan Valley. Bayombong is its capital. Like the rest of Cagayan Valley, it is rugged and mountainous and beckons to adventurers. The Mt Pulog National Park is accessible via Kayapa, some 117 kilometres (83 miles) from Bayombong. Dalton Pass is a vital access point from Manila to Cagayan Valley. Because of its strategic location it became the scene of bloody fighting between Japanese and combined Filipino and American forces in the closing days of World War II. Markers commemorate the sacrifice made by the soldiers who gave

up their lives here. The Dalton Pass National Shrine is located at Santa Fe, 50 kilometres (31 miles) from Bayombong. The salt springs in Salinas are perhaps the most
famous landmark of the province. The Villa Margarita Mountain Resort with its
spring-fed pools, water slides and a citrus plantation, is a good place to stop overnight
on the way to the Banaue rice terraces two hours away. It is at Barangay Busilac,
Bayombong, along the Maharlika Highway and is 260 kilometres (141 miles) from
Manila. The St Dominic Cathedral, the first cathedral in the province, was rebuilt
after being razed twice and has an 18th century Spanish-style facade. Situated in
Bayombong, it is a relic of the province's historic past. More modern is the
provincial capital with its park and man-made lagoon.

QUIRINO

Before September 1971, Quirino was just a sub-province of Nueva Vizcaya with only
four municipalities to its name. Republic Act 6394 changed that and it became a full
province from that time, with Cabarroguis as its capital. The province is named after
the late President Elpidio Quirino. Agriculture is the main industry. Basketry, rattan
craft and dried flower products are small-scale industries. Among the natural tourist
attractions are the Nagbukel Cave, along the highway in Diffun some four kilometres
from Cobarroguis, visited by local tourists during Holy Week; Aglipay Caves, ten
kilometres from the capital, with picnic huts and cottages for overnight accommodation; Governor Rapids, noted for its limestone walls and its swiftly flowing waters
made for white river rafting, swimming and fishing, located in a barrio of Maddela,
some 34 kilometres (21 miles) from Cobarroguis; the Victoria Falls at Barrio Sangbay,
Nagtipunan, about 54 kilometres (34 miles) from Cobarroguis, believed to be the
source of the mighty Cagayan River; and Bisangal Waterfalls, found in a virgin forest
which is a wildlife sanctuary. This is some 35 kilometres (21 miles) from Cobarroguis.

The Cordilleras

Forming a mountainous spine running north to south down to the Central Plain, and
separating the Cagayan Valley from the Ilocos coast is the Cordillera Central massif,
consisting of three mountain ranges. Here live the highland tribes such as the Bontocs,
Ifugaos, Igorots, Kalingas, Isnegs, Kankanays and Tingguians who still retain their age-
old traditions. The provinces of Abra, Apayao, Benguet, Ifugao, Kalinga, and Mountain
Province, and the chartered city of Baguio are located here. Together with 76 municipalities
and 1,173 barangays, they form the Cordillera Administrative Region. The region occupies
seven per cent of the total land mass of the Philippines yet is the least populated. It is rich
in minerals—gold, copper, silver, zinc and non-metallic reserves, and has untapped
geothermal energy resources and underdeveloped hydroelectric resources.

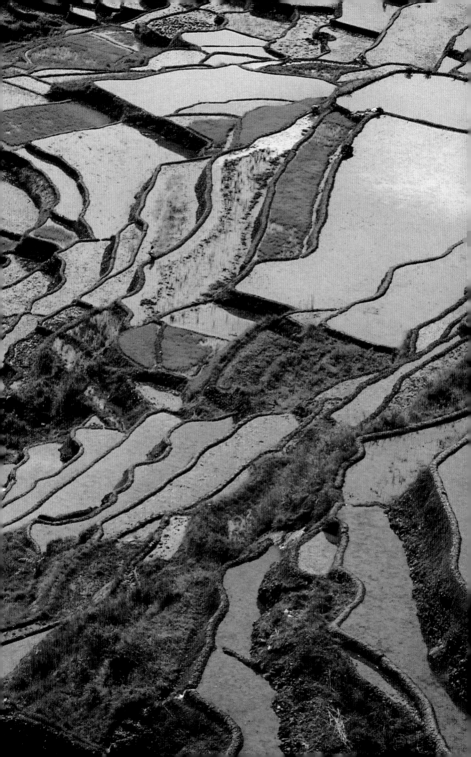

BAGUIO

Nestling among pine forests 1,524 metres (5,000 feet) above sea level is Baguio, the Philippines' summer capital in the province of Benguet. Baguio is noted for its scenic parks and gardens, golf course, tribal woodcarvings and handweaving, silver filigree, basketware, fresh strawberries and vegetables. It is also the home of the Philippine Military Academy and a favourite honeymoon destination among Filipino newly-weds. Its pleasant climate, at least eight degrees cooler than the lowlands, makes it a popular refuge for city and town dwellers who wish to escape from the searing summer heat or to experience crisp weather at Christmas time. Baguio suffered from a massive earthquake in 1990 which devastated many parts of the city. It has recovered from the disaster and has regained its stature as a holiday area. It was a long-held tradition for lowlanders to make their annual exodus during Holy Week to this mountain city.

Before the Americans developed Baguio at the beginning of the century as their vacation resort, it was just a small hamlet of about 20 homes. According to some sources, the name Baguio probably derives from the Igorot word *bag-iw*, meaning moss. It became a town in 1900 and a chartered city in 1909. To reach their mountain retreat, the Americans constructed the winding Kennon road, named after the last engineer who built it—Col Leighton Kennon. Burnham, an American architect, laid the grid for the city, modelled on the layout of Washington DC. Burnham Park, a wooded area at the heart of the city, is named after him. The park has landscaped, flower-filled grounds and orchidarium, children's playground, bicycle lanes and man-made lake. It also has tennis and basketball courts, a football field and an athletic oval.

Baguio has several tourist landmarks: the twin-spired Baguio Cathedral

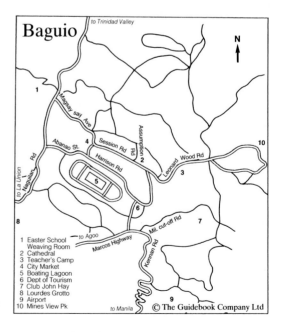

Baguio

N

1 Easter School Weaving Room
2 Cathedral
3 Teacher's Camp
4 City Market
5 Boating Lagoon
6 Dept of Tourism
7 Club John Hay
8 Lourdes Grotto
9 Airport
10 Mines View Pk

to Trinidad Valley
to Agoo
to Manila
Marcos Highway
Magsaysay Ave
Abanao St.
Session Rd
Assumption Rd
Harrison Rd
Leonard Wood Rd
Mil. cut-off Rd
Kennan Rd
to La Union
Naguilan Rd

© The Guidebook Company Ltd

(preceding pages) The Ifugao rice terraces, Northern Luzon

perched at the highest end of Session Road, Baguio's main street; Teacher's Camp, just off Session Road, a venue for meetings and conferences; the Botanical Gardens displaying the rich flora of the Cordilleras and also a collection of Igorot folk art and architecture; Mansion House, the summer residence of Philippine presidents, built in 1908 for American governors general, destroyed during World War II and rebuilt. It has an imposing main gate patterned after Buckingham Palace. About 20 minutes' away from downtown Baguio is the Philippine Military Academy. The Lourdes Grotto enshrining the statue of Our Lady of Lourdes is a pilgrimage site on Mirador Hill, reached by climbing 225 steps. An Ifugao woodcarving village is located five kilometres from the city.

Club John Hay, a former US air base which was handed over to the Philippine Government on the expiry of the American bases lease, is currently being redeveloped by a private consortium into a resort complex with guest cottages, restaurants, playing fields, parks and sports facilities. John Hay, with its golf course set in rolling terrain, is popular among golfers. The Mountain Province Museum with its artefacts and relics showing the cultural heritage, customs and traditions of the Mountain Province is temporarily located within the 506-hectare (1,250-acre) property.

■ PARKS AND VANTAGE POINTS

Located in the suburbs are several scenic parks and vantage points which afford spectacular views. Mines View Park on the city's eastern side commands a panoramic view of the surrounding mountains and valleys. Below are the former gold mines of Benguet Corporation. Wright Park is a pine forest preserve, noted for its horseriding trails and a 100-metre x 5-metre wide (328 feet x 16.4 feet) reflecting lagoon, mirroring the row of pines alongside it. It is reached by climbing a stone stairway at the top of which is a stone pergola. Sunshine Park along Governor Pack Road, has flower gardens. Cultural presentations are held on its covered stage.

■ SHOPPING

Baguio's city market (Magsaysay Ave) has plenty to interest the general shopper, souvenir hunter and camera buff. Mountain people from nearby villages and hills come to buy and sell. The market stalls sell a variety of fresh fruit and vegetables, flowers, and the usual merchandise one would expect to find in a market. Visitors usually go there for the handicrafts, carved wood products, basketware, trinkets, silver crafts, handwoven garments, dried or "everlasting" flowers, fresh fruit, sausages and fruit preserves and jams. Nearby is the Maharlika Livelihood Centre (Abanao Street corner Magsaysay Avenue). There are also other places in town where one can look for handicrafts and gift items, sweets and preserves. Check out Munsayac's

Handicrafts (Leonard Wood Road), Narda's Handicraft (Upper Session Road), Masferre Souvenirs (Ferguson Road). For ethnic weaves, the Easter Weaving School (Guisad Road) sells a variety of Igorot woven products in bold colours and designs. The handicraft shops in the vicinity of Mines View Park also sell woven products, such as bed covers, in the distinctive weave called *abel* from northern Ilocos, as well as bonnets, scarves, ponchos and cardigans in the Igorot style. Those in search of unique gifts and souvenirs will find various items made from handmade paper.

Baguio produces silver filigree jewellery. Hand-crafted silver filigree jewellery and silver products can be found at the Saint Louis University Silver Shop (Assumption Road). Pilak Silver Craft and Gift Shop (37 Leonard Wood Road), Ibay's Silver Shop (Governor Pack Road) and Sun Rose Silver Shop (Leonard Wood Road) are other places one can look into.

Strawberry and blackberry preserves, marmalades, fruit purees, peanut brittle and baked products are sold by the Good Shepherd nuns (the convent is at 8 Gibraltar Road).

■ WHERE TO STAY

The Baguio Country Club offers upscale accommodation. There are also several standard and economy class hotels, tourist inns, apartels, pensions and lodging houses. Among the hotels are the Acapulco Mountain Resort, Baguio Palace Hotel, Casa Henerosa, El Cielito Inn, Elegant Hotel and Restaurant, Forest Inn, Hotel Supreme, Prime Benguet Hotel, Skyrise Hotel and Restaurant, Baguio Vacation Hotel, and Zion Hotel. Inns include Alpine Hotel, Kisad Hotel, Silverstone Inn, Swagman Attic Inn, Villa La Maja Inn and Woods Inn. Club John Hay is temporarily closed for redevelopment.

The bigger restaurants catering to tourists serve international food. The proximity of Trinidad Valley, the vegetable garden of the Philippines, assures a supply of fresh vegetables and fruits, a welcome boon to vegetarians.

■ SPECIAL EVENTS

Baguio holds a Flower Festival in February with a floral parade and other activities. The city celebrates its Foundation Day in September and stages an Arts Festival in November-December. The Easter holidays, particularly during Holy Week, attracts lowlanders to the City of Pines.

■ OUTSIDE THE CITY

La Trinidad, the capital of Benguet province, is six kilometres (four miles) north of Baguio. Called the 'salad bowl' of the Philippines, the fertile valley is dotted with vegetable farms growing cabbage, carrots, beans and fruits such as strawberries. A museum here contains tribal artefacts.

Asin Hot Springs, 1,000 metres (3,280 feet) lower than Baguio towards the coast, enables visitors to enjoy swimming in a warm pool fed by hot sulphuric springs. The place has a hanging bridge traversing a river. Along the way you can see woodcarvers at work.

■ **GETTING THERE**
Check flight schedules to Baguio (flying time: 50 minutes). The airport is at Loakan, 12 kilometres (7.5 miles) from the city. Saulog, Victory Liner, Philippine Rabbit, Dangwa and Dagupan Lines buses operate regular trips from Manila and other places in Luzon passing Naguilian Road and exiting through Marcos Highway, via La Union province. The usual route is via Kennon Road. The trip by bus is around six hours. Jeepneys connect the main towns and travel across the provincial borders and into Cagayan Valley or Abra. From Baguio it is easy to travel to the Ilocos provinces.

MT DATA AND THE RICE TERRACES
The rice terraces, described as 'the eighth wonder of the world', are an impressive sight, like stairways to the clouds. Built millennia ago by hardy Ifugaos, they are an amazing feat of human engineering skill. Whole mountainsides are terraced from top to bottom with rice paddies and are still in use up to the present day. The famous Banaue rice terraces are found in Ifugao (overnight accommodation is available at the Banaue Hotel, Fairview Inn, or Sanafe Lodge), but even finer are the terraces at Batad near Banaue and Maligcong near Bontoc in the Mountain Province. The rice terraces have been declared a UNESCO World Heritage Site.

From Baguio, the journey takes around eight hours over winding roads and hairpin curves affording dramatic scenery along the way.

To break the journey, one can stop at Kilometre 100 in Bauko, Mt Province. Mt Data Hotel is set amidst pine forests 2,256 metres (7,000 feet) above sea level. On cold nights, there is a cozy fire going. Bontoc people entertain guests at the Lounge with their rituals and dances. You may tarry here and take a day tour to explore the nearby town of Sagada, 19 kilometres (12 miles) west of Bontoc central. Sagada is noted for its caves—ancient burial sites, some still seen with hanging coffins. Cave explorations are undertaken by spelunking clubs.

ABRA

This land-locked province, accessible by road from Ilocos and Baguio, has its share of natural attractions, appealing mostly to trekkers, spelunkers, and those in search of adventure in the wilderness. Like other lesser known provinces of the Philippines, Abra is well off the beaten tourist track. Bangued is its capital. Bamboo and rattan craft are the leading industries.

Southern Luzon

Southern Luzon comprises the provinces of Cavite, Laguna, Batangas, Aurora, Rizal and Quezon (collectively known as CALABARZON); the island provinces of Mindoro (Oriental and Occidental), Marinduque, Romblon and Palawan (also known as MIMAROPA), and the Bicol Region. Together they form Region IV. Calabarzon, which is the Southern Tagalog region, is steeped in history, legend and lore. It is also a scenic area of lakes and rivers, lush green fields and mountains, mineral springs and waterfalls, subterranean rivers and caves, rugged seacoasts and fine beaches. The seas, lakes, orchards and fields of Calabarzon supply the markets of the greater Manila area. Artisans and craftsmen from this part of the country are skilled shipbuilders, woodcarvers, smiths, embroiderers and weavers. Their products are sold in Manila's smart shops, and are also exported.

Diving, fishing, snorkelling, swimming, windsurfing, boating, shooting the rapids, hiking, trekking, horseback riding, golf and tennis are among the sports of the region. Those who simply wish to lie on the beach or laze by the pool have a choice of resorts. The destinations are a one- to three-hour drive from Metro Manila. Regular public transport serves these destinations, but you can also hire a limousine from your hotel or a car rental company, or join any of the package tours offered by local operators. Accommodation ranges from basic cottages to deluxe in the upmarket lakeside or seaside resorts. The cuisine can be ethnic and/or continental. Those with time to spare can take a leisurely drive through these provinces. The roads are good, with stretches of superhighways.

Marinduque, better known for its Moriones Festival held during Holy Week; Occidental and Oriental Mindoro, well-known for their excellent dive spots, flora and fauna; Romblon, famous for its marble, and Palawan, with its subterranean river, variety of wildlife and spectacular land and seascapes, are all islands off mainland Luzon. Geographically, Romblon and Palawan are closer to the Visayan islands but administratively they are considered part of Luzon.

CAVITE

Cavite is one of the regional growth centres in the country. It was already a flourishing trading port in the 13th century, frequented by Chinese junks moored at Sangley Point (from *xeng-li*, "trader" in the Amoy dialect). Cavite City was founded the same year as Manila (1571), and had forts, cobblestone streets and colonial houses. It was subjected to Muslim and Dutch attacks. One of the old forts that still stands today is Fort San Felipe built in 1609 to protect the growing city. The British landed here when they invaded Manila. For more than two centuries, Cavite was the centre for building the great galleons that plied the Manila-Acapulco route.

The province played a prominent role in Philippine history. Made a politico-military province in 1614, Cavite was a breeding ground for revolutionaries during the Spanish era and was one of the eight original provinces that rebelled against Spain. The Cavite Revolt of 1872 led to the execution of three Filipino priests, Fathers Gomez, Burgos and Zamora. General Emilio Aguinaldo, president of the short-lived first Philippine Republic, is a son of the province. Andres Bonifacio, also lived here. The rivalry between Aguinaldo and Bonifacio split the revolutionaries into two camps. Maragondon has an old church with a massive carved door and ornate interior. It was here that Andres Bonifacio and his brother were held after a revolutionary military court condemned them for sedition and ordered their executions.

The Aguinaldo Shrine at Kawit and other historic markers, Tagaytay, Puerto Azul and the beaches of Ternate are the most popular destinations in the province.

■ KAWIT

The Aguinaldo Shrine in Kawit, some 23 kilometres (14 miles) from Manila, is one of the province's visitor attractions. It was from the balcony of his house that General Emilio Aguinaldo proclaimed Philippine independence from Spain on 12 June 1898. Here the Philippine flag was raised and the national anthem played for the first time. A re-enactment of the reading of the proclamation was held at the shrine's garden as part of the centennial celebration on 12 June 1998. The house and its tower were restored for the celebration. The shrine contains a museum displaying the general's memorabilia and other historical relics.

Kawit holds a pageant every Christmas Eve called Maytinis, in which the story of Joseph and Mary looking for an inn to stay at is re-enacted.

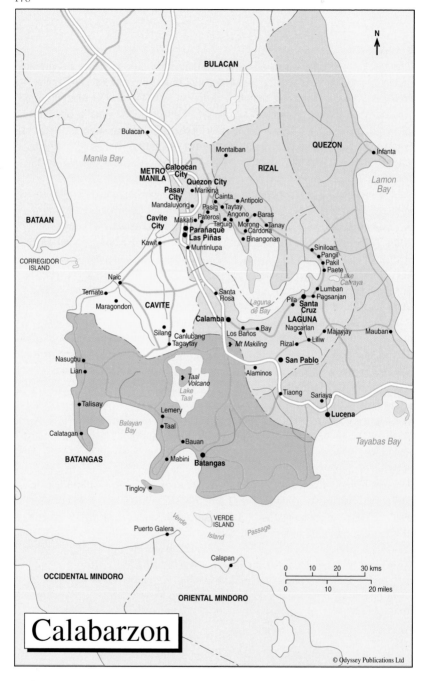

N

BULACAN

Bulacan

Montalban

QUEZON

Infanta

Manila Bay

METRO MANILA

Caloocan City

Quezon City

RIZAL

Lamon Bay

Pasay City

Marikina

Cainta

Antipolo

BATAAN

Mandaluyong

Pasig

Taytay

Pateros

Angono

Baras

Cavite City

Makati

Taguig

Morong

Tanay

Parañaque

Cardona

Las Piñas

Binangonan

Kawit

Muntinlupa

CORREGIDOR ISLAND

Siniloan

Pangil

Pakil

Paete

Naic

Santa Rosa

Lake Caliraya

Ternate

Laguna de Bay

Lumban

Maragondon

CAVITE

Pila

Pagsanjan

Calamba

Bay

Santa Cruz

Silang

Canlubang

Los Baños

Nagcarlan

LAGUNA

Majayjay

Mauban

Tagaytay

Mt Makiling

Rizal

Liliw

Nasugbu

San Pablo

Lian

Taal Volcano

Aminos

Lake Taal

Tiaong

Sariaya

Talisay

Lemery

Lucena

Balayan Bay

Taal

Calatagan

Bauan

Tayabas Bay

BATANGAS

Mabini

Batangas

Tingloy

Verde Island

VERDE ISLAND

Passage

Puerto Galera

Island

Calapan

| 0 | 10 | 20 | 30 kms |

| 0 | 10 | 20 miles |

OCCIDENTAL MINDORO

ORIENTAL MINDORO

Calabarzon

■ TAGAYTAY RIDGE

Tagaytay is a popular day excursion from Manila. Tourists make the 56-kilometre (35-mile), 90-minute trip for spectacular views of Taal Volcano and Lake. Several fruit and flower stalls line the highway to Tagaytay. A flower festival and a pineapple festival are Maytime activities in the city.

Tagaytay Ridge is believed to be the outer rim of an extinct volcano. The scene— 'a crater within a lake within a crater within a lake'—is so serene that it is hard to imagine that death and destruction could come from it. Yet this is one of the most active and deadliest of the archipelago's volcanoes. During eruptions, the pyrotechnics can be watched from the safety of the ridge. Tagaytay's elevation gives it a pleasant climate.

Many Manilans have second homes here to escape the city's summer heat. Residential subdivisions have sprung up, attracting more city dwellers to buy property. Religious orders of nuns have houses here. Tagaytay is popular for conferences and religious retreats. The Development Academy of the Philippines Conference Centre hosts conventions and conferences and rooms are available for delegates. Visitor accommodation is also available at the Taal Vista Hotel, Villa Adelaida, and various other hotels.

High above the ridge is an unfinished structure begun during the Marcos regime and intended as a villa for the state visit of Ronald Reagan. It was never completed. This is the 'Palace in the Sky' as it was then called. Today it is a People's Park. Visitors who don't mind the climb are rewarded with dramatic views.

Close to the People's Park is the Tagaytay Highlands, a 400-hectare (988 acre) golf course and resort complex. The complex has something for everyone. For the golfer, it is the chance to play an exhilarating game amidst scenic surroundings, with challenging sand traps and five man-made lakes. For plant- and animal-lovers, the resort's lush gardens and animal farm are reasons to pay a visit. The attractions at the farm are the miniature animals—potbellied pigs, mini Shetland and Fallabella ponies, mini cattle from Africa, and a wallaby. There are orang-utans, pythons and fainting goats, as well as Japanese bantam chickens, pheasants and peacocks, parrots, and other bird species.

The gardens, on the other hand, are a horticulturist's delight. There are different varieties of ornamental bananas, bamboos, leea, heliconias; Mussaenda hybrids, yellow bells, golden duranta, hybrid tea roses and other ornamental plants. The complex has its own kitchen gardens to provide organically grown vegetables for the resort's restaurants.

■ **BEACH RESORTS**

Cavite's beach resorts are easily accessible from Manila. Puerto Azul, 62 kilometres (39 miles) from Manila past Ternate town, and Caylabne Bay Resort are the most popular. Puerto Azul, set in a forested area, has a golf course, tennis, squash, badminton/pelota courts, a swimming pool and facilities for water sports.

Further on is Caylabne Bay Resort on Caylabne Point. The hour and a half drive from Manila to the resort follows winding mountain roads.

The fishing town of Naic is the embarkation point for sport fishermen after triggerfish, locally called *papacol* or *baget*. The fishing grounds around Carabao Island and Fraile Island are considered excellent, and while fishing can be enjoyed year-round, the best months are from June to September. Boats can be hired at the Seaside Beach Resort.

■ **GOLF**

Cavite is also a golfing destination boasting several championship golf courses. There is Southwoods in Carmona designed by Jack Nicklaus; The Orchard in Dasmariñas designed by Arnold Palmer and Gary Player, and Tagaytay Highlands, all built in the 1990s. The 1995 Johnny Walker Classic was held at The Orchard, drawing the world's top golfers. Splendido Taal, a spectacular course along Tagaytay Ridge, was designed by Greg Norman, while Fred Couples and Bernhard Langer designed the Riviera golf course in Silang.

BATANGAS

Batangas' coastline is indented by bays and coves. The province, south of Cavite, is a favourite weekend retreat for city-dwellers who want to enjoy sun and sea. A range of seaside resorts, from moderate to luxurious, dot the coast. The choice of accommodation depends on your interest. Matabungkay and Calatagan are popular for both the lazy sun-seeker who just wants to lie on the beach and the active sportsperson. Scuba diving, snorkelling and windsurfing are favourite activities. Golfers find challenge in the championship golf course designed by Robert Trent Jones Jr on the headlands of Calatagan overlooking the bay, while deep ravines and steep hills in Batulao, Nasugbu, give the golfer the experience of playing a par 72 game in the Palmer-designed Evercrest golf course. Then there is the 27-hole Mount Malarayat golf course and country club in Lipa City which has a children's pavilion, sports centre and sports lounge as well as equestrian facilities.

Coral gardens attract marine biologists and enthusiasts of underwater photography. The waters around Nasugbu, Balayan Bay and Verde Island are choice dive sites. For the sport fisherman, there is fishing for jacks in the surrounding waters.

Those who like trekking can take a *banca* ride on Taal Lake to Volcano Island or climb Mt Magiting in Anilao, ending the day with a dip in the sea.

Batangas is famous for its embroidery, *balisong* (knives) and an unusual festival featuring a parade of roast pigs (see Festivals, page 277). Lipa City is also a pilgrimage site as the Blessed Virgin, known as the Mediatrix of All Grace, made her appearance to a Carmelite postulant more than 40 years ago. Her apparition was signalled by a shower of rose petals.

Before the arrival of the Spaniards, Indians, Chinese and Arabs lived and traded in the villages lining the Pansipit River. Archaeological excavations in Calatagan have yielded porcelain from the Chinese Yuan and Ming dynasties. Juan de Salcedo, Miguel Lopez de Legaspi's grandson, explored the region in 1570 and made it a Spanish territory. The province was created in 1581. Then known as Bonbon, it extended over a much larger area which included Camarines, Marinduque and Mindoro. Later separated from the outlying regions, it went through several name changes, from Balayan to Taal and finally Batangas. Like Cavite, Batangas was one of the first eight provinces to revolt against Spain. One of the country's national heroes, Apolinario Mabini (the "brains of the Katipunan") was a Batangueño. His home in Tanauan is a national shrine.

Arabica coffee was introduced by Fray Benito Baras in 1740 and between 1814 and 1889 coffee led the country's exports, making the Philippines the world's fourth largest exporter of the bean. A coffee blight in the late 19th century destroyed plantations in Europe, South America, Java and the Philippines. The industry revived only a century later and has never regained its former status.

■ **HERITAGE VILLAGE**

The town of Taal with its colonial ancestral houses, municipal building, the Agoncillo Museum, and the church all give the visitor glimpses of the past. The whole town is being preserved as a heritage village. There are speciality shops selling Taal chocolate and the local fish delicacies, *maliputo* and *tawilis*. Women hand-embroider *barongs* (shirts) and table linen. Taal Church dates back to 1575 and is constructed in baroque style. Caysasay Chapel, reached by descending 123 steps, has a well that is supposed to be miraculous. Townsfolk say the church is frequently visited by the Blessed Virgin Mary.

■ **TAAL LAKE AND VOLCANO**

One of the most picturesque sights in Batangas is Taal Volcano, an island located near the centre of Taal Lake. It is one of the world's lowest volcanoes; its highest point—on the eastern rim of the main crater—is only 311 metres (1020 feet) above

Taal Volcano and Lake seen from Tagaytay Ridge, Luzon

sea level. It is also one of the Philippines' most active volcanoes, with at least 33 recorded eruptions since it first exploded in 1572. Taal Lake originated from the collapse of prehistoric volcanic centres. The underwater topography suggests the presence of about 35 different submerged volcanic landforms. The lake is a rich fishing ground with several varieties of milkfish, carp, *maliputo* and *tawilis*. It is possible to go up to the volcano from Talisay town.

LAGUNA

Laguna, a land of lakes, springs, waterfalls and ancient volcanoes, lies in the transitional zone between the central plain and volcanically active southern Luzon. Makiling and Banahaw, volcanic mountains rich in myth and legend, are part of the landscape. Many towns of Laguna border Laguna de Bay, the largest freshwater lake in the country. Fertile volcanic and alluvial soil supports an agricultural economy. Laguna is a major producer of coconuts, rice and corn. The International Rice Research Institute and the University of the Philippines Colleges of Agriculture and Forestry are located in Los Baños. Calamba is the birthplace of Jose Rizal. Laguna is also known for its *lanzones* fruit, handicrafts, piña and *jusi* embroidery from Lumban and woodcarvings from Paete. Shooting the rapids in Pagsanjan, fishing and windsurfing on Lake Caliraya, golf at the Canlubang estate and Santa Elena golf course in Santa Rosa, trekking on Mt Makiling, swimming in the hot springs of Pansol, and attending the Turumba Festival are just some of the activities which visitors can enjoy. The province also boasts two theme parks: Enchanted Kingdom and Splash Island Waterpark. *Apocalypse Now* and *Platoon* were filmed on location in the province. The Enchanted Kingdom theme park right off the Santa Rosa exit of the South Superhighway offers entertainment for children and families.

Juan de Salcedo pacified the lakeside settlements after Manila's foundation in 1571. Franciscan friars then established missions in Bay, Caliraya, Majayjay, Nagcarlan, Liliw, Pila, Santa Cruz, Lumban, Pangil and Siniloan between 1578 and 1583. The first provincial capital was Bay. It was transferred to Pagsanjan in 1688 and to Santa Cruz in 1858. The friars wielded great power and this became a source of conflict between them and the local inhabitants in the 19th century. Laguna was among the first provinces to join the revolutionary movement against Spanish authority. Despite this, Spanish influence in the province remained strong.

■ PLACES OF INTEREST

Calamba, the birthplace of Jose Rizal, is a market town on the shore of Laguna de Bay, 54 kilometres (34 miles) from Manila. A giant jar (*calamba*) inscribed with the names of the town's *barangays* (villages) is the focal point of the town plaza. Rizal's house, a two-storey Spanish-style structure of wood and stone, is now a national shrine (open 8 am to 12 noon, 1 to 5 pm daily). The shrine was recently restored to receive an influx of visitors; 1996 was the 100th anniversary of Rizal's death. In the garden of the shrine is a sculpture showing the boy Rizal with a dog.

Los Baños (The Baths) is the Philippines' spa, fed by hot springs, mineral and freshwater springs from Mt Makiling. There are several establishments between Pansol and Los Baños, some 62 kilometres (39 miles) from Manila, where one can soak in the therapeutic waters. The Franciscans built the Hospital de Aguas Santas here in 1602 to take advantage of the thermal waters. At Los Baños, one can visit the International Rice Research Institute (IRRI), a non-profit organization established in 1961 by the Ford and Rockefeller foundations. Many specialists from rice-producing countries are trained here. To visit the institute, contact the IRRI information office in Los Baños for an appointment.

The University of the Philippines' College of Agriculture and Forestry is at the foot of Mt Makiling. Many trees and plants of botanical interest are on the campus. There's a picnic area on the slopes nearby. One is cautioned not to swim in the stream or waterfalls as there are leeches. Mt Makiling, 1,090 metres (3,575 feet) high, is a dormant volcano, said to be inhabited by a goddess, Mariang Makiling. Its upper slopes are a national park. Birds, butterflies, flying lizards, orchids and huge trees abound. The Boy Scouts of the Philippines (BSP) has a camp site on the mountain, but permission must be sought from the BSP administration to use the site and swimming pools. The government also runs a resort at Pook ni Maria Makiling. There are cottages and an Olympic-sized swimming pool. The viewing deck commands a panoramic view of Laguna de Bay and the towns. The Philippine High School for the Arts is also located here.

Alaminos is the gateway to Hidden Valley Springs, a hideaway resort in a jungle setting of giant plants and ancient trees. Locals call it "*Ilalim*" (under) because it is located in an ancient 90-metre (295-foot) crater on the south side of Mt Makiling, believed to have been formed by a sudden drop in the earth's crust. The resort has five spring pools (warm, cold and alkaline), picnic huts, dressing and shower rooms. Lake Caliraya (elevation 366 metres/1,200 feet) is a man-made lake in Lumban favoured by water-skiers, windsurfers and anglers. Kayaking and sailing are also popular. The lake was built by American engineers in the 1930s to provide hydroelectric power in the area. Because of its refreshing climate and sylvan setting, it is an idyllic getaway. There are a few resorts ringing the lake and some private residences but bulldozers are now churning the red earth and before long, the once pristine, wooded area will be dotted with condominiums and townhouses. Developers are talking about golf courses, a convention centre, spa hotel, and tennis camp.

Paete and Pakil are the home of expert woodcarvers. Paete's artisans produce delicate filigree-like carvings from wood shavings. They also make jigsaw puzzles and animal cutouts from wood. Pakil (104 kilometres/65 miles, from Manila) used to be part of Paete. Pakil, like Paete, also produces papier-mâché figures. The Turumba Festival is held in this lakeshore town (see also page 277). Other points of interest in the province are Majayjay, with its colonial baroque church built by forced labour; Liliw, known for its handmade footwear and arrowroot biscuits; and Nagcarlan with its narrow three-storey houses, "Laguna-baroque" church and underground cemetery.

■ PAGSANJAN

Pagsanjan, 102 kilometres (63 miles) from Manila, is visited by tourists who want the experience of shooting the rapids. The one-hour, seven-kilometre (four-mile) *banca* (canoe) ride up Pagsanjan River and gorge offers spectacular scenery. Protect yourself from the sun by wearing a hat and covering thighs and legs that may get sunburnt. There's a 20-minute stop at the falls for photos, a swim, or a raft ride to a cave behind the falls. The fun part is going down river and shooting a series of 14 small rapids. The agile boatmen (two to a *banca*) guide the craft around boulders and swift currents. Be prepared to get wet. The best time to shoot the rapids is during the rainy months when the water is high. It is best to join a tour arranged by licensed tour operators in Manila as boatmen are known to charge exorbitant prices for independent tourists who hire their boats on the spot. Pagsanjan has several hotels, among them the Pagsanjan Garden Resort and La Corona de Pagsanjan. The former, located along the river bank, has a guest house, cottages, air-conditioned rooms and dormitories.

For those looking for adventure, La Corona de Pagsanjan Resort has the answer: a ropes challenge course involving low and high element exercises. The latter involve a 60-metre (200-foot) slide starting from a height of 18-metres (60 feet), and high V and high Y balancing acts on cables strung 40 feet overhead. There is also a man-made

(top left) A religious procession on the Feast of San Isidro, patron saint of farmers; (lower left) mangoes and farm produce festoon a window during the Harvest Festival, Lucban, Quezon

Coloured rice wafers (kiping), moulded from cacao leaves, decorate home fronts in the Pahiyas Festival, Lucban, Quezon

American Graffiti

The Philippines is not just the site of the largest U.S. military installations in the world. It is also perhaps the world's largest slice of the American Empire, in its purest impurest form. The first time I landed in Hong Kong, I felt a thrill of recognition to see the pert red letterboxes, the blue-and-white road signs, the boxes of Smarties that had been the props of my boyhood in England; upon arriving in Manila, I felt a similar pang as my eye caught Open 24-Hour gas stations, green exit signs on the freeways, Florida-style license plates and chains of grocery stores called 'Mom and Pop'. The deejay patter bubbling from the radios, the Merle Haggard songs drifting out of jukeboxes, the Coke signs and fast-food joints and grease-smeared garages-all carried me instantly back home, or, if not home, at least to some secondhand, beat-up image of the Sam Shepard Southwest, to Amarillo, perhaps, or East L.A.

America's honorary fifty-second state had received much more, of course, from its former rulers than star-spangled love songs and hand-me-downs jeans. The commercial area of Manila, Makati, looked not at all like Bakersfield or Tucson, but more like some textbook upper-middle-class California suburban tract. Jaguars lurked in the driveways of white split-level homes, maids sprinklered the lawns along leafy residential streets. The shopping strips were neatly laid out with a mall-to-mall carpeting of coffee shops and department stores. And though the area's jungle of high-rise office blocks seemed hardly to merit its title of 'the Wall Street of Asia', it did resemble the kind of financial district you might find in the Sunbelt-the downtown area of Salt Lake City, say, or San Diego.

Baguio too, the hill station designed as a summer retreat for the American rulers-a kind of New World Simla—revealed the American Empire in a more pastoral mood. I could not easily discern the town's resemblance to Washington, D.C.—on which, many Filipinos proudly informed me, it had been modeled—save for the fact that both places had roads and trees, as well as a *quorum of American servicemen, scientists and missionaries ('Most people in the U.S., I think,' said a local cabbie, 'are Christians and Mormons'). But Baguio was still a glistening vision of silver and green, graced with its own distinctive charm—white villas set among the thickly forested slopes of pine, quiet parks verdant in the mist. In the mild drizzle of a dark afternoon, the place had a cozy market-town feel of hot cakes and light rain; on a calm Sunday morning, the peal of church bells through the mist took me back to an English village. In Baguio, I settled down with an Elizabeth Bowen novel in the teapot snugness of a small café, and went on a gray afternoon to a crowded kiddies' matinee.*

For all its silvered, foggy charm, though, Baguio did not seem to have the imperiousness of a British hill station, or its weighted dignity. And in much the same way, I did not sense in the Philippines anything comparable to the kind of stately legacy that the British, for example, had bequeathed to India. India seemed to have gained, as a colony, a sense of ritual solemnity, a feeling for the language of Shakespeare, a polished civil service, a belief in democracy and a sonorous faith in upstanding legal or educational institutions; it had, in some respects, been steadied by the chin-up British presence. By contrast, the most conspicuous institutions that America had bequeathed to the Philippines seemed to be the disco, the variety show and the beauty pageant. Perhaps the ideas and ideals of Amercia had proved too weighty to be shipped across the seas, or perhaps they were just too fragile. Whatever, the nobility of the world's youngest power and the great principles on which it had been founded were scarcely in evidence here, except in a democratic system that seemed to parody the chicanery of the Nixon years. In the Philippines I found no sign of Lincoln or Thoreau or Sojourner Truth; just Dick Clark, Ronald McDonald and Madonna.

Pico Iyer, Video Night in Kathmandu, *1988*

30-foot high rock wall built beside the river for those who love rock-climbing in full view of boat riders. Tamer adventures like river fishing and boating, as well as the more traditional are offered by the resort. La Corona de Pagsanjan has 36 cottages offering a range of accommodation. The resort has three swimming pools as well as a basketball court, a multi-purpose court for tennis, volleyball and badminton and recreational games. There is a camp site at the back of the hotel for those who wish to pitch their own tent, or rent one. In addition to shooting the rapids (the resort has its own boatmen so guests don't get ripped off), La Corona also offers motoring tours to nearby places of interest, such as Paete, Pakil, and Liliw with their Spanish-era churches and Nagcarlan with its underground cemetery. Pakil and Paete are also famous for their woodcarvers. And when in season, a visit to a *lanzones* orchard is interesting.

■ SAN PABLO CITY/VILLA ESCUDERO

San Pablo City, 80 kilometres (50 miles) from Manila, is an important commercial and transportation centre linking the province to Batangas, Quezon and Rizal. Founded in 1678, it is a major copra centre, but is more famous for its seven crater lakes. These are circular, extremely deep (some as deep as 50 metres/164 feet) freshwater lakes formed about 2,000 years ago by phreatic explosions (a result of the interaction of magma and water). The crater lakes of San Pablo are depressions created by a single explosion of small, low-lying volcanos.

Beyond San Pablo near the border with Quezon province is Villa Escudero. Twenty-five hectares (62 acres) of land in the vast Escudero estate have been opened up to tourism to allow visitors from overseas to sample Filipino hospitality in the countryside. The villa has a museum with an eclectic collection of curios, antiques, icons an with beauty queen costumes and stuffed animals. Overnight

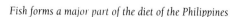

Fish forms a major part of the diet of the Philippines

accommodation is available in rustic cottages of bamboo and nipa palm. The Feast of the Ascension is celebrated on the plantation with feasting and merrymaking. The statue of the risen Christ is the focal point of the procession. Adding colour are the three-metre (ten-foot) *higantes*—giant papier-mâché figures dressed in rural costumes—marching to the accompaniment of a brass band.

RIZAL

Rizal province, named after the Philippines' national hero, is mostly flat terrain but becomes hilly and rugged as it joins the foothills of the Sierra Madre. Bounded on the west by Metro Manila, many of its western municipalities have been swallowed up by urban sprawl. The fish landing port of Navotas; the fishing town of Malabon; the duck-raising municipality of Pateros which produces *balut*—fertilized duck eggs; the shoemaking centre of Marikina; Las Piñas, home of Father Cera's bamboo organ; and Parañaque, Taguig and Mandaluyong which are now part of the National Capital Region were formerly municipalities belonging to the province. Makati was also part of Rizal at one time, but in the days when it was just swampland.

Rizal, however, has not been deprived of all its assets. There's still Angono, famous as an artists' colony, and Antipolo, scene of an annual May pilgrimage. The Carabao Festival of Angono and the Holy Week rites in Binangonan, Tanay and Taytay draw numerous spectators. Because of its proximity to Manila, Rizal was among the first provinces to be colonized by the Spaniards. Many missions were established in the late 16th century and early 17th century. Morong was made the capital of a politico-military district. Pasig, Cainta and Taytay were conquered by the British in 1762. When the British returned Manila to the Spaniards in 1764, the contingent of Sepoys from India who came with the British forces stayed behind in Cainta, and to this day you can spot their progeny among the populace.

■ ARTISTS' VILLAGE AT ANGONO

Angono, a town in the Rizal foothills and birthplace of the famous muralist and late National Artist Carlos "Botong" Francisco, is an artists' colony. It is not unusual to see whole families—the Miranda and Blanco families, for instance—painting and exhibiting their works in art galleries. Various facets of everyday Philippine life, customs and traditions, portraits and still life, landscapes and seascapes are depicted in their works. Jose 'Pitok' Blanco and all his seven children (the eldest was born in 1962, the youngest in 1980) paint. They have participated in family shows, the first held in 1978 at the National Museum. The family residence now has a wing that serves as the museum for their collections. Each artist has his own gallery to hang his paintings, and most are large. *Anak ng Magkakaingin* (The Hillside Farmer's Child) by

Glenn P Blanco (born 1962) measures 182.88 cm x 304.8 cm (72 inches x 120 inches). It was painted in 1980 when he was just 18. Nemesio Miranda's house and atelier, on the other hand, gives the impression that it just grew and grew; wherever space was needed it was added. The effect is like a patchwork quilt, quite interesting. One thing you can say for it—it has character. Like Blanco, all five children of Miranda (ranging in age from 19 to 5) paint. The youngest started at two and a half or thereabouts and at the ripe old age of five had her own money in the bank earned from her paintings. Her first painting was bought by a German tourist who wondered why there was no signature on the painting, only to learn that the artist could not yet write! Angono's visual artists have formed themselves into an art organization— The Angono Ateliers Association. Group and individual shows are mounted by members who are well regarded in Philippine art circles. The Angono Atelier holds its annual Art Festival in November. On the spot paintings are conducted. The artists give private art classes. Nemiranda conducts a summer workshop in visual arts in his atelier.

The discovery of Stone Age art inside an old cave located at the top right area of the East Ridge Golf and Country Club is considered to be a valuable find. The inscriptions on the rock walls depict humans and animals and reveal the lifestyle of the inhabitants thousands of years ago.

Angono is also well-known for its Carabao Festival celebrated in May on the feast of San Isidro de Labrador, patron saint of farmers. Pulilan, Bulacan has a similar festival (see Festivals, page 277). Angono's town fiesta on 22–23 November honours the patron saint, San Clemente. A parade of papier-mâché giants (*higantes*) on stilts dressed in Philippine costume is a highlight of the fiesta. There's a restaurant in the Doña Justa Subdivision of Angono which bills itself as the 'folk foods and folk arts restaurant'. This is the *Balaw Balaw*. It is decorated with papier-mâché horses and gigantic heads, wall hangings and easel paintings portraying Filipino folk ways. *Balaw balaw* is named after a special sauce or appetizer which the restaurant serves. The restaurant is part of Angono's culture and traditions, like the festivals they celebrate. It's worthwhile to stop here for a meal or snack (Filipino food is served) just for the ambience.

ANTIPOLO

The foothills of Antipolo, with their invigorating air, were a popular summer resort in Spanish times, when fashionable young men and women went to the waterfalls or Hinulugang Taktak to picnic under the trees. The image of Our Lady of Peace and Good Voyage (Nuestra Señora de la Paz y Buen Viaje) arrived by galleon from Mexico in 1626 and was given to the Jesuits. Believed miraculous, she was made the patron saint of the galleons, and between 1641 and 1748 sailed on eight return journeys between Manila and Acapulco. To celebrate her return in 1748, a serenade was held in Antipolo. The tradition has been revived, with dance performances on a stage close to the waterfalls. If you are in the Philippines in April or May, check the newspapers for announcements of concerts by the falls, or call the Cultural Centre of the Philippines. On the eve of 1 May, pilgrims assemble in Manila and set out on foot for Antipolo, arriving at dawn for the Mass at the shrine.

■ OTHER SIGHTS

The old municipalities of Morong, Baras and Tanay have noteworthy churches. Morong's Church, built by Chinese craftsmen from 1612–15, is a fine example of tropical baroque architecture. The stone lions guarding the entrance show an obvious Chinese influence. The stone altar in the Church of Baras is thought to be a sarcophagus which was dug up from beneath the church. The façade of Tanay's Church has columns topped by carved pineapples, and inside the church there are ornate altars and finely carved Stations of the Cross. Cardona is known for its *bangus* (milkfish) industry. Montalban has a dam and is a picnic area. Jalajala contains the ruins of the hacienda of Paul de la Gironier, a French doctor who lived in the Philippines from 1820 to 1840.

AURORA AND QUEZON

Down the eastern seaboard, facing the Pacific Ocean, is the long, thin province of Aurora and its twin, Quezon, extending down to the Bondoc Peninsula. Formerly called Tayabas, it was renamed Quezon by President Manuel Roxas to honour Manuel Quezon, President of the Philippine Commonwealth. The upper portion is now called Aurora, after President Quezon's wife. Aurora has reportedly good possibilities for surfing but has not been opened up to tourism. Quezon is coconut country and a major producer of copra. Quezon attracts visitors when it celebrates its Pahiyas Festival in mid-May in the towns of Sariaya and Lucban (see also Festivals, page 277). The Lucban Village Inn is a new 20-room hotel in Lucban. Travellers also go to Lucena City, the provincial capital, en route to Cotta where they board inter-island vessels to the Visayas.

Mt Banahaw, an extinct volcano rising 2,187 metres (7,175 feet) above Quezon and Laguna provinces, is held sacred by followers of some 17 religious sects. The natives were practicing divine worship in this 'mountain of many cathedrals' even before the Spanish conquest. Professing their belief in 'Three Persons One God' (the

Holy Spirit is also Jose Rizal, the national hero), the followers believe that Jesus Christ lived, died and was resurrected here. According to legend, seven angels transported Calvary to Mt Banahaw. Followers also believe that this is also the spot where the righteous will brave the last floods on earth. During Holy Week, worshippers gather at Kinabuhayan to begin the ascent to the mountain. They bathe in the holy springs and worship in the cathedral-like Kuweba ng Dios Ama, Cave of God the Father. The cave's 30-metre (98-foot)-high entrance is festooned with giant ferns, moss and orchids.

MINDORO

The rugged island of Mindoro (from the Spanish *mina de oro*, gold mine) is located off the coast of Batangas. Once a part of the former Bonbon province (see Batangas, page 180), Mindoro became a separate province at the beginning of the 17th century; in 1950 it was partitioned into Mindoro Oriental and Mindoro Occidental. Mindoro is the habitat of the Philippine crocodile and the *tamaraw*, a rare species of buffalo much smaller than a *carabao* and more ferocious. The *tamaraw* is protected in its home on Mounts Iglit and Baco, with their natural grasslands and dipterocarp forest. The island is also home to the music-loving, indigenous Mangyans, who possess a highly developed culture among the pre-Hispanic islanders. Mangyans are settled in the towns of Bulalacao and Mansalay.

PUERTO GALERA

Mindoro has a coastline indented by bays and coves. Puerto Galera, on the north-eastern tip of Mindoro Oriental, is one of the Philippines' most popular tourist destinations, especially for scuba divers (see page 289). Its outstanding natural and underwater beauty makes it an ideal holiday destination and scuba divers' Eden. Puerto Galera was Mindoro's old capital, and in Spanish times was a haven for Spanish galleons seeking shelter from heavy storms. Puerto Galera's port is probably the country's most picturesque and today it still provides a safe harbour for fishing boats, yachts and ships during typhoons. Within 10 kilometres (6.2 miles) of Puerto Galera are many little coves and larger bays, islands and islets. In addition to diving, other aquatic activities favoured are snorkelling, water-skiing, sea kayaking and deep-sea fishing. *Bancas* can be rented by the day at most resorts. Some resorts also rent out sailing boats, surfboards and snorkelling equipment.

■ ACCOMMODATION

Accommodation ranges from basic nipa huts to resorts which provide more amenities. Most have private shower and toilet. The better resorts have their own electric

Morong Church, Rizal Province

generators in case of power cuts. The most developed of the beaches is Sabang Beach on the easternmost side of the island. Most rooms here are basic. The beach is not good for swimming or snorkelling, though the area has a lively nightlife. A short walk away is Small La Laguna, less crowded than Sabang Beach and better suited for those who prefer peaceful surroundings. Big La Laguna, despite its name, is smaller than Small La Laguna. It is quiet and well developed and offers a variety of rooms and restaurants. A new condominium-hotel and resort has been built in the area. The town proper has several inns and pensions, as well as bars, restaurants and dive schools. One of the better resorts is the Coco Beach Resort with its own private beach. White Beach has a string of resorts and restaurants along a one-kilometre (0.6 mile) stretch of white sand beach. The Enceñada Beach Resort is on Enceñada Beach. Those who wish to be in quieter surroundings with more privacy can stay at the Tamaraw Beach Resort on Aninuan Beach or Talipanan Beach on the western side of the island.

Puerto Galera is not the only attraction on Mindoro Oriental. Located 20 kilometres (12.5 miles) from Calapan, the provincial capital, is Naujan National Park, one the country's protected areas. The freshwater Naujan Lake is a wildlife sanctuary. Here one finds various types of waterfowl—whistling duck, purple heron, swamp hen, cattle egret, common grebe and Philippine mallard duck. The lake is set amidst a dipterocarp forest.

MINDORO OCCIDENTAL

Mindoro Occidental occupies the western side of the island. It is bounded on the north by the Verde island passage and on the south by the Mindoro Strait. About 36 kilometres (22 miles) west of Mindoro Island is the Apo Reef National Marine Park, an atoll-like reef with two lagoon systems separated by a narrow channel with a sandy bottom and branching coral. The marine park includes the islands of Binangaan and Cayos del Bajo with their bird colonies, and the Apo Reef Island with a shallow lagoon in the middle of the island. Dive boats as well as motorized outrigger boats from Mamburao, the provincial capital, Sablayan and San Jose make the trip to the reef. There are daily flights from Manila to Mamburao and San Jose. Puerto Galera is accessible by bus or car and ferry from Batangas City.

The Bicol Region

Southeast Luzon is composed of the provinces of Camarines Norte, Camarines Sur, Albay, Sorsogon, plus the islands of Catanduanes, Masbate, Romblon and Tablas, collectively known as the Bicol region, or Bicolandia. The region is a bridge between the Tagalog and Visayan cultures. Some of the oldest Spanish churches, noted for their architecture, are found in Bicol. This is abaca country and handicrafts made of abaca and hemp are produced here. Bicol is also known for fiery cuisine which uses chillis and coconut milk. The presence of many volcanoes gives the region a fertile soil. The Bicol Volcanic Chain stretches from Camarines Norte in the north to Sorsogon in the south. The chain is composed of active and geologically young volcanoes, thought to be related to the Philippine Trench. There are also numerous hot springs, lakes, caves and forests. Many of these nature areas are protected by law as conservation areas.

ALBAY

Bicol's major tourist attraction is Mt Mayon, noted for its graceful form and symmetry. A stratovolcano rising to 2,462 metres (8,077.8 feet) above sea level in the province of Albay, Mt Mayon is considered the most active volcano in the archipelago (it has erupted 45 times since 1616) and continues to be closely monitored by volcanologists. Its most violent eruption was on 1 February 1814, severely damaging surrounding towns; 1,200 died. The ruins of the church of Cagsawa stand as a reminder of that eruption. Mt Mayon continues to challenge mountaineering clubs. The summer months are favoured by trekkers (see also Mountaineering, page 310). Other attractions of the province are the Tiwi Hot Springs and Hoyop-hoyopan Caves. Albay's capital, Legaspi, is the hub of transport in the region. Trains of the Philippine National Railways run from Manila to Albay. Flights from Manila to Legaspi take 45 minutes and from Cebu 50 minutes. Accommodation in Legaspi is available at the first-class Mayon International Hotel (Taysan Hills), the standard Hotel La Trinidad (Rizal Street) and the economy Tanchuling Hotel (Imperial Subdivision) among others. Perched on the northern slopes of Mayon Volcano, at an elevation of 762 metres (2,500 feet) is the Mayon Skyline. In Daraga, there is the economy Villa Amada Hotel (Rizal Street).

CAMARINES NORTE AND SUR

Camarines Norte (capital: Daet) is one of the country's richest mining areas, producing iron and gold. It also has a fishing port in Mercedes. The province had the distinction of being the first in the country to erect a monument in honor of the national hero, Dr Jose Rizal. The monument, completed in 1899, is in front of the Daet municipal hall. Daet is being promoted as a wave-surfing destination in the Philippines through cultural exchange with other countries. The town hosted the 1998 Philippine-USA Centennial Junior Surfing Cultural Exchange between a high

Rice Harvest, Bicol

school in California and local surfers of Daet. Camarines Sur (capital: Pili) is well-known for its festival in honour of the Virgin of Peñafrancia celebrated in Naga City every September (see Festivals, page 277). The Franciscans built many churches here, among them the San Francisco Church, one of the oldest in Bicol, constructed in 1578. The Bicol National Park bordered by Basud and Daet in Camarines Norte and Sipocot and Lupi in Camarines Sur is known for its scenic spots and recreational areas. It is a dipterocarp forest with natural swimming pools. Camarines Sur has many protected areas. There's Libmanan with its cataracts and series of crystal caverns with stalactites and stalagmites; Caramoan with its caves, panoramic hills, a superb shoreline and recreational areas. East of Naga are Mts Isarog (an inactive volcano) and Iriga. Mt Isarog National Park covers an area of 10,112 hectares (24,977 acres) touching Naga, Calabanga, Tinambac, Goa, Tigaon and Pili. Negritos live in the dipterocarp forest with its endemic wildlife. The scenery is superb and the climate invigorating. There are gorges and canyons, deep ravines and 40-metre high waterfalls dropping to a depth of 15 metres. Lake Buhi, 16 kilometres (10 miles) from Iriga, is another attraction. The lake used to have quantities of those tiny, three-millimetre fish called "*tabios*", a Bicol delicacy, but overfishing has greatly depleted their stock and these are now rare.

Where to stay in Naga City: Hotel Mirabella (Magsaysay Avenue), New Crown Hotel (E Angeles and P Burgos Streets) and Royal An (Concepcion Grande), all standard hotels; and the economy Grand Imperial Plaza (P Burgos Street and J Hernandez Avenue). Lucky Fortune Hotel is the city's newest, located on Abella Street. In Iriga City is the economy Emerald Resort Hotel (San Francisco).

CATANDUANES AND SORSOGON

Off the beaten track is the island province of Catanduanes, a windswept island in the path of typhoons which has earned it the nickname of "Land of the Howling Winds". Tabaco in Albay is the starting point for ferries going to the island. Another national park, Bulusan Volcano is found in Sorsogon province. The park extends over Casiguran, Barcelona, Irosin and Juban, covering an area of 3,673.29 hectares (9,072 acres). Bulusan, towering to about 1,559 metres (5,114 feet) above sea level, is a composite volcano flanked by several cones. It is one of the country's active volcanoes, with 12 recorded eruptions. The area is noted for its mineral hot springs, peculiar rock formations, verdant vegetation, and mountain lake of approximately 16 hectares (40 acres). It is a scenic spot and health resort. Sorsogon is linked by ferry to Masbate and the Visayan island of Samar. Bulan, 63 kilometres (39 miles) from the capital Sorsogon, is its ferry port for the province of Masbate. Ferries from Matnog, a fishing town 671 kilometres (417 miles) from Manila, 126 kilometres (78 miles) from Legaspi and 67 kilometres (42 miles) from Sorsogon, link the tip of southern Luzon with the Visayan chain. Luzon with the Visayas chain. A DOT-accredited hotel in Sorsogon, Sorsogon is the economy Fernando's Hotel (Pareja Street).

Mt Mayon rises to 3,500 metres (11,500 feet)

The Visayas

Located in the middle of the archipelago between the big islands of Luzon in the north and Mindanao in the south, are the islands of Panay, Guimaras, Negros, Cebu, Bohol, Siquijor, Leyte, Samar and Biliran. These, together with smaller islands, are collectively known as the Visayan Islands, a name believed to be derived from the Shri-Vijayan Empire that was in power in much of Southeast Asia from the 7th to the 12th centuries. The inhabitants of these islands had been trading with neighbouring Asian countries even before the arrival of the Spaniards, as evidenced by archaeological findings of Chinese and Southeast Asian porcelainware in pre-Hispanic burial sites. Ilonggos, Cebuanos and Warays make up the distinct cultural-linguistic groups. Spanish colonization started in the Visayas and moved northwards before it swept down to Mindanao. Most of the major islands have mountainous interiors with limited arable coastal lands. Administratively, the Visayas are divided into Western Visayas, Central Visayas and Eastern Visayas.

Western Visayas

Western Visayas is composed of the provinces of Iloilo, Capiz, Aklan and Antique on the island of Panay, Guimaras and the western half of the island of Negros— Negros Occidental. This is the home of the Ilonggos, distinguished by their lilting accents and fine cuisine. Iloilo and Bacolod are the leading cities. Panay is known for its rambunctious festivals and the holiday island of Boracay.

The triangular-shaped island of Panay is believed to have been inhabited by an ancient people, based on the discovery of stone implements found near a fossilised elephant in Cabatuan. The story that ten Bornean *datus* arrived in Panay in the early 13th century has no historical basis, according to the Ilonggo archaeologist Felipe Landa Jocano. According to the story, the *datus*, their families and followers landed on the bank of the Siwaragan River near the present town of San Joaquin in Iloilo in 1212 and were welcomed by the Atis, the dark-skinned, kinky-haired inhabitants of the island. Deciding to make the island their home, they arranged to purchase the lowlands from the Atis, in exchange for a golden *saduk* (a wide-brimmed helmet) for the Ati king Marikudo, a golden necklace for his wife Maniwangtiwang, and some gifts of coloured cloth, decorated weapons and trinkets for the Ati people. The exchange prompted festivities that later became the basis for the festivals celebrated on the island (see Festivals, page 277). After the purchase, Marikudo and his people moved to the mountains where their descendants still live today, while the *datus* divided the island into three *sakups* (districts)—Irong-Irong, Hamtik and Aklan. The *sakups* formed the Confederation of Madyaas to defend themselves against invaders. The *datus* passed the first laws of the land, namely the legal code of Maragtas promulgated in 1225 by Datu Sumakwel, the wisest of the 10 datus, and much later, the Code of Kalantiaw, written in Aklan in 1433.

Spanish conquest of the island came about in 1569 when the conquistador of Cebu, Miguel Lopez de Legaspi, driven by chronic food shortages in Cebu, was forced to seek food elsewhere. The name Panay is believed to be derived from the Spanish *pan hay* ('there is bread here'). Panay was divided into provinces in the 18th century. The old Hamtik became Antique; Irong-Irong, Iloilo. Aklan was later to be further divided into the provinces of Capiz and Aklan.

ILOILO

Iloilo province occupies the southeastern part of Panay and is the largest province on the island. High mountain ranges separate it from Antique on the west and Capiz on the north. The rest of the province is mostly plain with some upland portions. When the Spaniards arrived in Panay they established a settlement in Ogtong, now Oton. The seat of power was later transferred to La Villa de Arevalo, an old cultural centre. Attacked by the English led by Sir Thomas Cavendish, raided several times by the Dutch and constantly besieged by Muslims, the Spaniards finally transferred the seat of power to Iloilo which had a good harbour. They built Fort San Pedro and Iloilo City became the capital. The Augustinians built many fine churches on the island, but some were destroyed by earthquake or war.

Iloilo was one of the earliest ports opened to foreign trade, and was Cebu's rival until the 1930s. It was an important centre for the shipment of sugar from nearby Negros Island until declining world markets caused the industry to collapse. It still retains a genteel charm and continues to be an educational, cultural, religious, manufacturing and transportation hub in the Western Visayas. Iloilo City has several districts: La Paz and Jaro, north of the central business district; Arevalo and Molo, west of the city centre; Mandurriao and the city proper. Each district has its own plaza, church and market. Arevalo, the old capital, has many fine Spanish-style ancestral homes and is noted for its flower gardens and nurseries, Villa Beach and *sinamay* weavers. Molo is the home of the famous *pancit molo*, a soup dish similar to Chinese wonton soup. Molo was the former Chinese district of Parian. It was the Chinese who introduced the soup dish. The Gothic Renaissance Molo church made of coral rock is three kilometres (two miles) from the city proper. Jaro is another residential district with old colonial houses; the mansions of former sugar barons are

located here. Jaro is the seat of the Archbishopric of Western Visayas. The belfry of
the church in Jaro is one of the few in the country that stands apart from the church.
Other such bell towers are found in the Ilocos provinces. The belfry, ruined by
earthquake in 1948, has been restored.. There's also a statue of native son Graciano
Lopez Jaena who founded the revolutionary newspaper *La Solidaridad*. La Paz is
where the *batchoy*, a popular Ilonggo dish of noodle soup and meat with garnishings, originated. The airport is in Mandurriao.

■ HISTORIC AND NATURAL ATTRACTIONS

One of Iloilo's visitor attractions is the church in Miag-ao, 40 kilometres (25 miles)
southwest of Iloilo City. The fortress-like Church of Santo Tomas de Villanueva was
built by the Augustinians in the 18th century to withstand Muslim attack. Con-

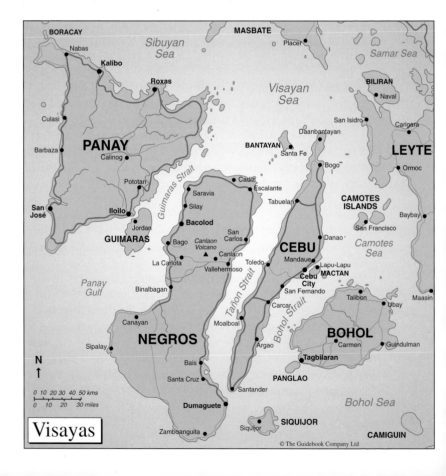

structed of yellow-orange sandstone with an elaborately embellished façade, it is cited as an outstanding example of baroque-style architecture blended with folk motifs. It was declared a World Heritage Site by UNESCO. The façade features carvings of St Christopher with rolled up trousers carrying the Christ Child on his back, a coconut tree, a papaya plant full of fruit and guava trees. The towers are dissimilar because the priest-foreman in charge of building the church died and his successor did not follow the original design. Another church of note is San Joaquin, 53 kilometres (33 miles) southwest of Iloilo City, which features in bas-relief the battle of Tetuan between Christians and Moors. The San Joaquin cemetery, built of coral rock, has a hexagonal chapel with rose windows at the main entrance. A balustraded stone staircase leads to the chapel. The Tigbauan Church with a baroque façade, 22 kilometres (14 miles) southwest of Iloilo City is another historic sight. Behind the rectory was the first Jesuit school for boys in the Philippines.

The Guimbal watchtowers, built to warn the people of pirates, are located 29 kilometres (18 miles) southwest of Iloilo City. The Church of Guimbal, made of yellow sandstone, is another attraction.

Thirteen kilometres (eight miles) northwest of the city is Pavia with its red brick Byzantine-style church that was used as a Japanese garrison.

There are enough waterfalls, lakes, and beaches to interest the nature-lover. For the golfer, one of the oldest golf courses in the country is a par-70 course set in 37 hectares (91 acres) of land in Santa Barbara. It was built by British engineers of the Panay Railways in 1907. It later became the Iloilo Golf and Country Club.

■ ACCOMMODATION

There is a choice of accommodation in the city and environs. Iloilo City's first-class hotels are Sarabia Manor and the new Days Hotel. The Amigo Terrace, Hotel del Rio, Four Seasons and La Fiesta are standard hotels. Among the economy hotels are River Queen, The Castle, Chito's Iloilo Hotel, Fine Rock Hotel, Jaro Bellevue Pensionne, Hotel Madia-as, and Iloilo Midtown. There are several pensions and inns in the city and beach resorts farther afield.

■ GETTING THERE

Iloilo is served by many inter-island vessels and is a crossroads of land transport and air traffic to other parts of the Visayas. There is a fast ferry to and from Bacolod, and a bus to Kalibo and Caticlan, for those wishing to go to Boracay. Domestic airlines fly daily to Iloilo from Manila (45 minutes) and Cebu (35 minutes). There are also flights, but less frequent, to and from General Santos and Puerto Princesa.

GUIMARAS

Once a sleepy sub-province in the backwaters of Iloilo, Guimaras— known for its succulent and sweet mangoes—is now a fully fledged province. Located southwest of Panay Island and northwest of Negros Island, rice, coconut, mangoes, vegetables, livestock, poultry are its major products while tourism, fruit processing, coconut processing, handicrafts, mining, quarrying and lime production are its main industries. There are five towns—Buenavista, Nueva Valencia, Jordan, San Lorenzo and Sibunag. Jordan is the capital. Hiligaynon is the province's spoken dialect. The island has several natural attractions.

What to do in Guimaras? Go swimming, snorkelling, boating, fishing, scuba diving, mountain biking, trekking, wind surfing, jet skiing or island-hopping. Visit a mango plantation. The island has more than 50,000 fruit-bearing mango trees. The major plantations are open to visitors. Oro Verde, located 10-12 kilometres (about 7 miles) from Sto Rosario Wharf in Buenavista, is reportedly the second largest mango plantation in the world. Southern Orchard in Jordan, 10-15 minutes by jeep from Jordan Wharf, with 22 hectares (54 acres) and 14,000 trees, is the second largest mango plantation in Guimaras. A Mango Festival is held during the third week in May. Tourists can also visit the Trappist Monastery which has a gift shop selling souvenir items, preserved fruits, religious articles, native bags, products made of coconut shells and other handicrafts of the cultural minorities assisted by the monks.

There are a number of beach and mountain resorts with cottages as well as resorts in offshore islets. Among these are Nagarao Island Resort, Costa Aguada Island Resort, Puerto del Mar.

Guimaras is accessible by ferry boat from Iloilo and Bacolod.

ANTIQUE

The elongated province of Antique lies along the west coast of Panay. The towns are ranged on a narrow coastal strip. At the southern end is the capital San Jose de Buenavista, 97 kilometres (60 miles) from Iloilo City. This is the embarkation point for those going by boat to Palawan and the Cuyo Islands. The old settlement of Hamtik (now Malandog), 17 kilometres (10.5 miles) south of San Jose, is the scene of the Binirayan Festival, held from 27 to 30 December, re-enacting with traditional costumes and decorated boats the landing of the Bornean *datus* on the shores of Panay. A marker in Hamtik shows the site of the 1212 landing.

CAPIZ

Capiz, in Panay's northeast, is a rice, corn, sugarcane and coconut producer with rich offshore fishing grounds. Prawn and *bangus* (milkfish) culture supplement the people's livelihood. As in other parts of Panay, weaving is a cottage industry. Roxas City is the capital, named in honour of a native son, Manuel A Roxas, who was Philippine president from 1946–48. The house where he was born is a national shrine. Some five kilometres (three miles) southeast of Roxas is the town of Pan-ay, settled by the Spaniards in 1569. The town has a church with thick walls made of white coral, and a massive bell weighing 10,400 kilos (22,880 pounds), housed in a five-storey belfry. It is said that 76 sacks of coins were collected from townspeople in the 18th century to make the bell. Another former Spanish settlement, Dumalag, is also noted for its church with yellow sandstone walls and a five-storey belfry.

The province celebrates in October the Halaran Festival (halad is a Hiligaynon word meaning to offer) commemorating the giving of gifts by the *datus* to the Atis for the purchase of the Panay lowlands. The festival is also held in thanksgiving for the harvest. Feasting and street parades feature in the celebration. Capiz has good beaches found in the coves of Ivisan and the offshore islands. There are also numerous caves, some of which, like the Pilar Caves, were pre-Hispanic burial sites. A minority tribe descended from the early Indonesian settlers, live in the remote forests. These are the Mundos, who still reproduce ancient Indonesian designs on their sword handles and sheaths, and whose traditional dance, the Sinulog, imitating the mating movements of a rooster and hen, has been adapted in Cebu and other parts of the Visayas. Roxas City is about 50 minutes by air from Manila and its port is served by many inter-island vessels.

AKLAN

Aklan occupies the northern part of Panay and was a part of Capiz until it became an independent province in 1956. Quiet for most of the year, it bursts into frenzied life in January when the province celebrates the Ati-Atihan Festival, commemorating the feasting that followed the purchase of Panay by the Bornean *datus* in the 13th century (see Festivals, page 277). The streets resound with the beat of drums and the hotels and lodging houses are full to capacity. Aklan is also well-known for the holiday island of Boracay.

Aklanons are proud of their roots, and have their own dialect, customs and traditions. A copy of the original Code of Kalantiaw is displayed in the Museo it Akean in Kalibo, the provincial capital. The Kalantiaw shrine is located in Batan. The province's natural attractions include beaches, waterfalls and caves. Afga Beach in Tangalan has powder-fine white sand. Twenty kilometres (13 miles) from Kalibo is Tinagong Dagat (hidden sea), so-called because it is obscured from view by two islands in Batan Bay. The area is rich in marine life and is ideal for snorkelling, scuba

diving and swimming. The seven-tiered Jawili Falls, 45 minutes from Kalibo by tricycle, has good swimming basins. Small resthouses have been built for visitors. Agnaga Falls in Malay is a good spot for private picnics. Tulingon Caves in Nabas, 55 kilometres (34 miles) from Kalibo, is believed to be the longest cave in the country. It extends for about 20 kilometres (13 miles) and has rich deposits of bat guano. Another cave that spelunkers can explore is Basang Cave, which has a swimming basin filled with clear spring water.

Kalibo is served by domestic air services while several ships call at Kalibo, Malay and New Washington/Dumaguit. Summer cruises are organized by tour operators and travel agents in Manila.

BORACAY

Boracay is a bone-shaped island of coralline limestone, 68 kilometres (42 miles) from Kalibo at the tip of Panay's northwestern coast. With its clear warm seas, white-sand beaches, coconut palms and balmy breezes, it is a popular tourist destination. Boracay has one of the world's best beaches, with soft, shimmering sand created over thousands of years by waves pounding on shells and coral, pulverizing them into extra fine particles. The whiteness comes from the absence of quartz, feldspar or magnetite.

In prehistoric times, Boracay was just a reef platform attached to Panay Island. The sea thrust up the reef and two islets were born. Sand built up between the two islets eventually joining them into one land mass. Boracay is about seven kilometres (four miles) long and not quite one kilometre (0.6 miles) wide at its narrowest point. It is divided into three barrios: Manoc-Manoc in the south, Balabag in the centre and Yapac in the north. The northern and southern sections are hilly, the central part fairly flat. A ribbon of road runs from north to south in the middle of the island and is the main thoroughfare for tricycles—motorized bikes with sidecars which are the main transport on the island.

It was the craze for *puka*-shell necklaces, bracelets and bangles in the 1960s that brought the early overseas visitors to Boracay. The Philippines, Bali and Hawaii are the world's major sources of *puka* shells and the Philippine variety is reportedly the finest in terms of whiteness and lustre. Digging for the small, round shells was a major source of income for the inhabitants. The shells have long since disappeared, but there is a privately-run Shell Museum.

■ ACCOMMODATION
Boracay's reputation as a holiday beach paradise grew over the years. From a few thatched-roof huts, cottages and bungalows started mushrooming along the beach as

(preceding pages) White sand and blue sky, Boracay Island

more and more visitors started arriving. The opening of upmarket resorts, like the Fairways & Bluewater Resort Golf and Country Club and other tourist developments is changing both the face and the pace of Boracay.

White Beach (the residents call it Long Beach), stretches from Balabag to Angol on the western side of the island. On this strip are hundreds of cottages, beach huts, hotels and resorts. This is the beach favoured by tourists. Those seeking solitude and quiet should look for accommodation on the north and south sides of the island. The eastern side of the island, with its steep rocky coastline, sand beaches and quiet bays has relatively little tourist infrastructure.

The top resorts are Club Panoly and Lorenzo Grand Villa, classified AAA by the Department of Tourism. Class AA resorts include: Paradise Garden, Lorenzo Main Beach and South Beach, Pink Patio, Laguna de Boracay, Sand Castles and Sea Wind. Titay South Beach Resort, Friday's Beach Resort, Alice in Wonderland, Milflores de Boracay, Pearl of the Pacific, Crystal Sand, Boracay Rain Forest, La Isla Bonita, Palm Beach Lanai, Nigi-Nigi Nu Noos, Jony's Place, Alyssa, Boracay Terraces and Queen's Beach Resort are all Class A resorts. Those at the top end of the market have swimming pools, tennis courts, and other amenities such as television.

Practically all the large resorts have their own restaurants serving Filipino and international dishes. There are also numerous small snack bars and fast-food shops. A Frenchman Roger Deparis and his Filipina wife, Lanie, run the French restaurant, Chez Deparis. A British deep-sea diver gave up his former career to open an English Bakery in Boracay. There is also a Swiss bakery on the island.

The high season from November to May necessitates reservations in the better resorts but during the low season, visitors can have a choice of accommodation without prior reservation.

■ ACTIVITIES

For the holidaymaker who likes crowds and informality, Boracay is a fun place to be. Snorkelling, scuba-diving, wind surfing, horseback riding, tennis, bowling and golf are the sports on the island. Diving and wind surfing lessons are available from accredited wind surfing schools and dive shops. The Greenyard Seasports offers wind surfing lessons and rents out surfboards. Accredited dive establishments on the island include Far East Scuba Diving, Lapu-lapu Diving School, Ocean Deep Diver Training Centre, Red Coral Diving School, Scuba World and Victory Scuba Diving School. These offer dive tours and instructions. Boracay has hosted international diving festivals. Local and foreign wind-surfing enthusiasts flock to Boracay for the International Funboard Cup held every January. In addition to this, there is an international beach volleyball competition every summer and an annual Paraw Regatta—

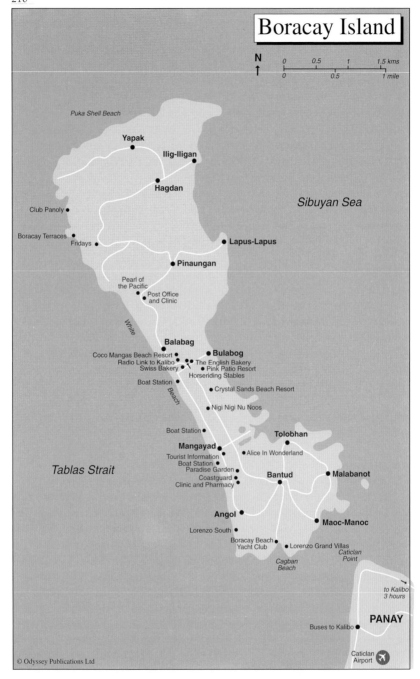

Boracay Island

N

| 0 | 0.5 | 1 | 1.5 kms |
| 0 | | 0.5 | 1 mile |

Puka Shell Beach

Yapak

Ilig-Iligan

Hagdan

Club Panoly ●

Boracay Terraces ●
Fridays ●

Sibuyan Sea

● **Lapus-Lapus**

● **Pinaungan**

Pearl of
the Pacific ●
● Post Office
and Clinic

White

Balabag

Coco Mangas Beach Resort ●
Radio Link to Kalibo ● ● **Bulabog**
Swiss Bakery ● ● The English Bakery
● Pink Patio Resort
Horseriding Stables
Boat Station ●

Beach

● Crystal Sands Beach Resort

● Nigi Nigi Nu Noos

Boat Station ●

Tolobhan ●

Mangayad ●
Tourist Information ●
Boat Station ● ● Alice In Wonderland
Paradise Garden ●
Coastguard ●
Clinic and Pharmacy ●

Bantud ●

● **Malabanot**

Tablas Strait

Angol ●

Lorenzo South ●

● **Maoc-Manoc**

Boracay Beach ●
Yacht Club ● Lorenzo Grand Villas
*Caticlan
Point*

*Cagban
Beach*

*to Kalibo
3 hours*

PANAY

Buses to Kalibo ●

Caticlan
Airport ✈

a race for outriggers. Since the inauguration of the par 72 golf course designed by Graham Marsh, a number of golf tournaments have taken place here.

For the visitor who wants to explore the island, there is a preserved dead forest in an inland water on the eastern side. Take Road 6 from the main road and hike all the way to the forest. Bat caves are located on the northern end of the island. Take Road 3. You can hike or bike there, or hire a motorcycle.

■ FACILITIES

The island has a small post office, a bank where foreign currency can be changed, a tourist office, and a police outpost. Communication facilities (long-distance telephone calls, fax, telex and telegraph) are provided by several operators. Medical services are available at the Boracay Island Municipal Hospital, and a small pharmacy stocks generic medicines. The island's flea market sells souvenirs, local handicrafts, and beach wear. There are also small shops selling shell necklaces and T-shirts. The better resorts have their own gift shops.

■ GETTING THERE

Boracay is accessible by air or sea. Flights land at Kalibo (50 minutes) and from there, visitors take an air-conditioned bus to Caticlan (90 minutes to two hours) for the sea crossing to Boracay. Other flights land directly at Caticlan (75 minutes). Check the domestic airlines to see what's on offer. Some airlines offer a package (airfare and hotel accommodation) or special promotional fares. It is also possible to get to Boracay by taking a WGA, Moreta Shipping Lines or Negros Navigation ship from Manila to Dumaguit/New Washington on the north coast of Panay, thence by bus or jeepney to Caticlan.

From Caticlan, motorized outrigger boats ferry passengers to their destination on the island, a trip that takes from 15 to 30 minutes, depending on their point of disembarkation. It is advisable to wear casual clothes. In the absence of ferry piers, disembarking visitors wade from the boat to the shore, a distance of a few metres, so be prepared with flip flops or the like. There are three boat stations on the island.

NEGROS OCCIDENTAL

The elongated island of Negros is situated between Panay and Cebu islands and is divided into the provinces of Negros Occidental (Western Negros) and Negros Oriental (Eastern Negros). Residents of the western province speak Ilonggo and are culturally closer to Panay than their neighbours to the east who are closely linked with Cebu. Negros Occidental's coastline is more irregular than that of Negros Oriental. The northern and western parts of the island are largely level plains and gently rolling slopes while the rest are sierras of varying elevations. A chain of volcanic mountain ranges runs from north to south. All are dormant except for Mt Kanlaon, at 8,100 feet the highest peak in the province and Central Visayas. Mt Mandalagan and Mt Silay are other prominent mountains. A largely agricultural province, Negros Occidental's rich volcanic soil is well suited to the cultivation of sugarcane as well as rice and corn. In the heyday of the sugar industry, the province enjoyed a thriving economy. It suffered a reversal of fortune when the world sugar market fell but it has come out of the doldrums. Today it continues to celebrate its victory over adversity in the yearly Masskara Festival celebrated in October (see page 286).

With the development of new industries and diversification of crops, there is an air of prosperity in the province. Ceramics and hand-painted porcelain have become money-spinners. In addition to decorative ceramics, the enterprising and creative people are producing papercraft, crocheted dolls, wrought iron and rattan furniture, placemats, tapestries, table runners, window blinds and upholstery fabrics made from raffia fibre and cotton thread, flowers made from wood shavings, coconut and corn husks. They have also started planting coffee, cacao, black pepper, fruit and ramie crops.

Negros Occidental has eight cities and 24 municipalities. In addition to Bacolod, the capital, the other cities are Bago, Cadiz, La Carlota, San Carlos, Silay, Talisay and Victorias.

BACOLOD

Bacolod, just over an hour's flight from Manila and 30 minutes away from Cebu, is one of the most progressive cities in the Visayas. The face of the city has been changing in the past ten years with the construction of new subdivisions, commercial and industrial centres. Shopping malls, the trademark of progress in an area, are much in evidence. There's an SM Megamall and a Robinson's Galleria. Gaisano is another shopping centre. The Association of Negros Producers has a showroom in Bacolod which displays Negrense products.

Antique collections in the city are found in various locations and are open to visitors, some by appointment. Wooden and ivory saints or *santos*, excavated Chinese and Indo-Chinese pottery, bowls and vases, furniture and orientalia are on view. Paintings and works of Bacolod artists are exhibited at the Art Association of Bacolod Gallery. Out of town collections are in Talisay and Silay City.

■ ACCOMMODATION

The Bacolod Convention Plaza Hotel (Magsaysay Ave) and L'Fisher (Lacson St) are the top hotels in Bacolod. The Goldenfield Garden Hotel (Goldenfield Commercial

Complex), and Sugarland Hotel (Singcang) are standard hotels, while Seabreeze Hotel (San Juan St) and Bascon Hotel (Gonzaga St) and Business Inn (South Lacson St) are economy hotels. There are several inns and pension houses. Food is fairly inexpensive. Ang Sinugba is a well-known restaurant serving broiled blue marlin, shrimp *binakol* (cooked in young coconut), crabs and *laing*. Bar 21 serves good seafood and is also favoured by Bacolod's yuppies as a night spot. Check the Goldenfield Commercial Complex which has several restaurants. Sweet mangoes come from nearby Guimaras island.

Bacolod is well served by air and sea. Domestic airlines operate several flights from Manila and Cebu. Ferries ply the route between Bacolod and Iloilo and inter-island vessels also call from Manila and other Philippine ports.

■ **PROVINCIAL ATTRACTIONS**

The province has much to offer the visitor with specialized interests. For railway buffs, many old steam engines are still in operation in the various sugar centres. These antiques, running on narrow-gauge tracks, can be seen in the sugar centres of Bacolod-Murcia, Binalbagan, La Carlota, Ma-ao, Sagay, San Carlos, Silay, Talisay, Tolosa and Victorias. Golfers can enjoy several rounds of golf at the Negros Occidental Golf and Country Club, popularly known as Marapara, a championship course right in the heart of the city. The clubhouse has fine facilities with a main restaurant serving good seafood for which Bacolod is famous. There's also a swimming pool and two tennis courts. Some 15 kilometres (nine miles) from Bacolod City is the 18-hole Bacolod Golf and Country Club in Hacienda Binitin, Murcia, 183 metres (600 feet) above sea level. Visitors are welcome to play when accompanied by members. There is a driving range and a clubhouse with a restaurant, bar and swimming pool. There are also new beach resorts for those who want to soak up sun by the sea.

■ **MARINE AND WILDLIFE SANCTUARY**

For ecologists and conservationists there is a marine and wildlife sanctuary some 175 kilometres (109 miles) from Bacolod. Danjugan, a 20-minute boat ride from Cauayan, is a 42-hectare island with lagoons lined by mangrove swamps and surrounded by a fringing reef of coral in the Sulu Sea. Danjugan shelters a rich biodiversity. Its forest cover is home to the endangered white-breasted sea eagle, as well as several species of bird, four of these endemic to the island—white-eared brown fruit doves, Philippine coucals, pygmy swiftlets and Philippine bulbuls. Migrating swallows and kingfishers flock to the island in summer. Bat colonies inhabit caves. Sea turtles lay their eggs on the seashore. Its marine population includes clown

Old steam train at Vicmico sugar plantation, Bacolod

triggerfish, clown anemone fish, blue-spotted rays, green moray eels, emperor angels and starfish, brain corals, gorgonian seafans and sea urchins. Thanks to the effort of concerned conservationists spearheaded by Gerry Ledesma, and with the assistance of the World Wide Land Conservation Trust, a UK-based charity, Danjugan has been saved from destruction by the combined effects of dynamite fishing, extensive trawling and silting. Today, the island is under the care of the Philippine Reef and Rainforest Conservation Foundation, Inc. (PRRCFI). Marine camps are held regularly to educate villagers and high school students on the importance of nature conservation and ecology. Arrangements for visits have to be made through the PRRCFI in Bacolod.

Central Visayas

Central Visayas consists of Negros Oriental, Cebu, Bohol and Siquijor—the eastern half of Negros Island. The waters around these islands are prime diving areas, rich in coral and marine life.

NEGROS ORIENTAL

Occupying the eastern portion of the island of Negros, facing Cebu, is the province of Negros Oriental. The province is characterized by low and serrated volcanic mountain ranges. The 2,435-metre (7,989 feet) Mount Kanlaon is the highest peak in the province. Located near the town of Vallehermoso, it is a popular trekking destination (see Mountaineering, page 310). West of Dumaguete City, the provincial capital, is the *Cuernos de Negros* (Horns of Negros, so-called because it has twin peaks), rising to a height of almost 2,000 metres (6,560 feet).

Because of its orientation to Cebu, the majority of the inhabitants of the coastal plains and valleys speak the Cebuano dialect, in contrast to its sister province to the west, whose inhabitants speak Ilonggo. Like the Cebuanos, corn is also their staple. Coconut, abaca and kapok are the cash crops. Sugar is grown around Bais City.

■ NATURAL ATTRACTIONS

The twin crater lakes of Balinsasayaw and Danao in Sibutan, Mabinay Spring and Subterranean River, the Manjuyod salt beds, Palinpinon hot springs, Calungan Twin Falls, the white-sand Tambubo Beach and Bonbonan Bay where tourists can wind-surf, sail and scuba dive are some of the province's natural attractions. Mountain climbers will be challenged by scaling the volcanic peak of Kanlaon, or climbing up Mt Talinis with its rare wildlife and flora, lakes, waterfalls and old forests. High up in Siaton is Lake Balanan. Spelunkers can explore the depths of Odioman Cave, or Pandalihan, Panligawan, Cayaso, Kopie and 17 other caves in the Mabinay area. Scuba divers and snorkellers will find the coral gardens of Apo Island off Dauin town and the Negros Oriental Marine Conservation Park an underwater world of spectacular beauty. Apart from these, the province has also historic landmarks and sights, such as the ancient watchtowers used as lookouts for Muslim pirates, the most popular being the dome-shaped tower on Dauin Beach. The province holds a harvest festival of thanksgiving—Buglasan Festival—highlighted by horse fights and a parade of costumed tribal groups.

Dumaguete City is the gateway to the province. The Protestant Silliman University, founded by American missionaries in 1901, is located here. The university maintains a private anthropology museum which contains, among other things, voodoo paraphernalia from the nearby island province of Siquijor which is known for the practice of witchcraft. The university's Marine Laboratory is outside the city. The Sumilon Island Marine Laboratory, nearer Cebu island, is administered from Dumaguete.

The province is involved in reforestation and environmental conservation. The Central Visayas Regional Projects has developed an established forest in Banban, Ayungon town. And Silliman University's Centre for Tropical Conservation Studies has a wooded area planted with indigenous species with enclosures for endemic and endangered birds and wildlife such as the rare Spotted Deer. This is now open to the public.

■ BEACH RESORTS

With 1,377.6 kilometres (860 miles) of coastline, Negros Oriental has many beach resorts to cater for sun-seekers and water sports buffs. Around the capital Dumaguete, you have a choice of the following: El Oriente Beach Resort in Mangnao, Sta Monica Beach Resort in Banilad and South Sea Resort hotel in Piapi. In the south are Salawaki Beach Resort in Zamboanguita, Eric's Yacht Club and Mark's Beach in the Tambubo and Antulang bays of Siaton. The north has Panoramahaus in Cangmating and San Moritz in Agan-an, Sibulan town, Pacific Reef in Amlan, Lag-it and Mapao in Bais City and Wuthering Heights in San Jose.

■ OTHER VISITOR ATTRACTIONS

Tanjay celebrates the Sinulog festival in July in honour of its patron saint and in December lanterns light up the houses and tall trees lining the streets. Bais City's Christmas display at the plaza is a picture of light and colour while its Hudyaka festival is held in September. Canlaon City holds a harvest festival in March featuring a parade of costumes fashioned from fruits and vegetables.

Every Wednesday the quiet seaside barangay of Malatapay in Zamboanguita bursts into life. This is Market Day and all sorts of people converge on this one spot to buy and sell. There is a picnic atmosphere as stalls spring up under the coconut trees. Fresh catch from the sea is cooked to your specification. There's meat barbecuing on spits; sellers of bread and cakes, fruit and vegetables, housewares, handicrafts, clothes, mats and baskets, livestock. The crowd is enormous and the event draws people from far and near. It's worth going to for local colour if you are ever in the province.

Dumaguete is accessible by air and sea. There are daily flights to and from Manila and Cebu. The airport is 3.5 kilometres (2 miles) outside the city. Inter-island vessels also stop over.

CEBU

Cebu, 587 kilometres (365 miles) south of Manila, is a progressive province with first-class hotels and beach resorts, restaurants, a lively nightlife, money-spinning export industries and quality handicrafts. The excellent dive areas around Cebu and the offshore islands make it a prime destination for scuba divers. Tourists from neighbouring Asian countries fly in to enjoy the sea and sun.

Cebu's central location makes it the hub for air and sea traffic in the Visayas and Mindanao. The Mactan International Airport is the second gateway to the Philippines. International flights land in Cebu-from Hong Kong, Japan, Malaysia, Singapore, South Korea, and Australia. There are several flights a day from Manila which is only 55 minutes away by jet. From Cebu it is a short hop to other destinations in the Visayas and Mindanao. An important inter-island and international seaport, Cebu is served by more than a dozen shipping lines. Many of the Philippine shipping line operators are based in Cebu.

As the kingdom of Sugbo (or Zubu) it was a thriving entrepôt before the coming of the white men. When Magellan entered the harbour in April 1521, he observed traders from China, Siam and Arabia. The kingdom was ruled by Rajah Humabon, who was lord over eight other chieftains. Magellan's chronicler, Antonio Pigafetta, noted that the people wore jewellery and gold ornaments; that they had music, laws, industries and commerce.

Trading and manufacturing are the people's lifeline, along with shipping and tourism. Cebu is the most populous province in the country, and has the greatest growth rate. The province, made up of 167 islands and islets, is flanked by Bohol to the east and Negros to the west. The main island is long and narrow, with a mountainous spine and flat coastal strips along which the towns and cities have grown. There are five cities—Cebu, Danao, Lapu-Lapu, Mandaue and Toledo—and 48 municipalities. The fastest rate of urban development and industrialization is in the metropolitan area made up of Cebu, Mandaue and Lapu-Lapu. Cebu City, the provincial capital, contains the Capitol building, hotels, entertainment and shopping districts, commercial areas and Old Town. Mandaue on the coast is the manufacturing centre, with the San Miguel brewery, Coca Cola plant, glass factory, agri-industrial complex and factories turning out stonework, shellwork, rattan furniture, handicrafts and tableware. The international airport is located in Lapu-Lapu City on Mactan Island, linked by bridge to Mandaue. The island boasts many fine beach resorts, the Mactan Export Processing Zone, and cottage industries devoted to the manufacture of guitars, shell lamps and jewellery. In addition to growing corn, which is the staple in Cebu, the province also grows mangoes which are most sought after for their succulence and sweetness.

Cebu is one of the most progressive provinces in the country today. The Mactan Export Processing Zone contributes a large amount to the country's export receipts. Exports as varied as furniture, shrimp, ignition wire and jewellery were top-selling

THE PHILIPPINE FLAG

A sun with eight rays and three yellow stars in a triangular field of white; an upper blue stripe and a lower red stripe. This is the Philippine flag today. It was designed by General Emilio Aguinaldo, in consultation with other revolutionary leaders, while he was in exile in Hong Kong. The white triangle signifies equality. The eight rays of the sunburst symbolize the first eight provinces that revolted against Spain: Manila, Laguna, Pampanga, Cavite, Bulacan, Nueva Ecija, Batangas and Tarlac. The three stars in each corner of the triangle stand for the main islands of Luzon, the Visayas and Mindanao. The blue upper stripe symbolizes peace, truth, and justice; the red stripe, valour and patriotism. In times of peace, the blue stripe is uppermost, but when the nation is at war, the red stripe is on top.

It was in a house at 535 Morrison Hill Road that the first flag, made of silk, was hand-sewn. It took five days for Marcella Agoncillo, the 38-year-old wife of Felipe Agoncillo, head of the Central Revolutionary Committee in Hong Kong, assisted by her seven-year-old daughter

Participants in a parade carry a giant Philippine flag

Lorenza and Delfina Rizal Herbosa, a 19-year-old niece of Dr Jose Rizal, to finish the flag. General Aguinaldo returned to the Philippines on 17 May 1898 with the flag on board the *McCulloch* and on 28 May 1898 it was unfurled for the first time to signal the victory of Filipinos over Spanish forces after a five-hour battle at barrio Alapan in Imus, Cavite.

The flag was officially hoisted as the national emblem in Kawit, Cavite on 12 June 1898 when General Aguinaldo proclaimed independence from Spain. While the colours were being raised, the San Francisco de Malabon band played a rousing hymn composed by a young pianist-composer named Julian Felipe which was adopted as the official hymn of the new republic. The hymn had no lyrics until Jose Palma, a young soldier-poet wrote a Spanish poem to the music. English lyrics were used later and today the national anthem is sung in Pilipino.

A reenactment of the sewing of the first flag was carried out in Hong Kong as part of the centennial celebrations. The flag, measuring 30 feet by 60 feet was later brought to Manila and hoisted at ceremonies on 28 May 1998 to commemorate the 100th anniversary of the Battle of Alapan. Another reenactment was held at the Malacañang Palace grounds when then First Lady Amelita 'Ming' Ramos led 100 ladies, among them the secretaries and undersecretaries of President Ramos' Cabinet, in the sewing of a 100-foot-long flag which was raised at the Rizal Park flagpole on 28 May. The period from 28 May to 12 June every year has been declared as Flag Days. One hundred flags were on parade at Rizal Park during the start of the National Flag Days. At the same time, thousands of flags were paraded or hoisted in towns and cities across the country. Flags also draped the façades of homes and commercial establishments and government offices and fluttered from flagpoles throughout the land in a show of nationalism.

Celebrity families, sports personalities and Filipinos from various walks of life participated in building a giant Philippine flag consisting of 275,013 Lego bricks. The 'Building a Nation' event was part of the Centennial celebration at Glorietta in Makati City. A 100-metre-long flag was also raised at the Expo Pilipino site at Clark.

items in the past. Cebu is engaged in infrastructure projects, massive construction and reclamation and real estate development. The face and pace of Cebu is rapidly changing.

CEBU CITY

Founded in 1565, Cebu City is the Philippines' oldest city. It is the country's third most densely populated city, after Manila and Davao. The shrines and monuments, churches and colonial houses in the city and throughout the province reflect Cebu's historic past. Its attractions include:

Magellan's Cross, the oldest historic relic of the Spanish era in Cebu, planted by Ferdinand Magellan in 1521. Fragments of the original cross are encased in a wooden cross of later make housed in a tile-roofed kiosk close to the City Hall. It marks the spot where the mass baptism of Rajah Humabon, his wife Juana, and some 400 of his followers was held. People throw coins inside the kiosk for good luck. Women sell candles outside the kiosk. They offer prayers for anyone who buys their candles by waving lighted tapers. A few metres away is the church, now a minor basilica, dedicated to the Santo Niño or Child Jesus, Cebu's patron saint. A new open shrine to the Santo Niño was constructed in 1994 outside the church and is open Fridays and Sundays for masses. There is a museum within the shrine.

The Santo Niño statue was Magellan's baptismal gift to Queen Juana. Forty-four years later, when Miguel Lopez de Legaspi landed in Cebu, the statue was discovered, undamaged by a fire that swept the city in 1565. The Augustinians built a church on the spot where the relic was found. The church was burnt in 1568 and rebuilt in 1602. The Santo Niño, dressed in sumptuous robes encrusted with precious stones, is encased in glass and stands to the right of the altar. It is an object of veneration and its feast in January is celebrated in various parts of the country with pilgrimages, religious processions, feasting and merrymaking. Cebu's principal festival is the joyous Sinulog Festival (see Festivals, page 277).

FORT SAN PEDRO

Fort San Pedro, located at Plaza Independencia, is the oldest and smallest fort in the country, was the nucleus of the first Spanish settlement in the Philippines. Legaspi ordered its construction shortly after the colonizers landed in Cebu to protect themselves from possible sea and land attacks. Two sides of the triangular-shaped fort fronted the sea and the third faced inland. The earlier structure, a wooden palisade, was later replaced by one of stone. There were three bastions: La Concepcion in the southwest, Ignacio de Loyola in the southeast and San Miguel in the northwest. The main gate faced the city. It was named San Pedro after Legaspi's flagship.

Fort San Pedro has a chequered history. First a Spanish fort, it became in turn a prison cell for Cebuano revolutionary soldiers who fought against the Spaniards, an American barracks, a prewar schoolhouse, a World War II Japanese redoubt, a post-liberation emergency hospital, a post-war garden, then a zoo, until finally in 1968 the authorities restored it to its original state. At that time, only two towers were recognizable; the rest had been destroyed. To restore the fort, coral was hauled in from the sea near the coast. The façade, main building, top walk and observatory roof garden were restored. The fort now houses the National Museum Regional Office (open 8.30 am to 5 pm Wednesdays to Sundays; closed on Mondays and Tuesdays and national holidays). You pay a small entrance fee to the fort; admission to the museum is free. The inner court has an open-air theatre and visitors can take refreshments in the walled gardens. Parts of the fort are also available for private functions such as weddings. Festive events in the city are also held here.

About a hundred metres from Fort San Pedro is Colon Street, the oldest street in the Philippines. Today it is in the heart of downtown Cebu and is home to Chinese-owned department stores. Not far from Colon was the shoreline where coal was dumped from the mines in the surrounding hills. The dumping ground was known as Carbon, now the site of Carbon Market. Visitors come here to buy inexpensive souvenirs.

Casa Gorordo is a restored 19th-century Spanish house where four generations of Gorordos lived, the most famous being Juan Gorordo (1862–1934), the first Filipino Bishop of Cebu. The house is located in what was once the main street of the Parian district. Like the district of the same name outside Intramuros in Manila, Parian was a Chinese quarter in the 16th century and later became a residential area for Cebu's professionals, landowners and merchants. The house itself was acquired by the Gorordos in 1863, shortly after Cebu was opened to world trade. The Aboitiz Foundation acquired the house in 1980 and after extensive research, it was restored to its original form. On the ground floor are paintings by Cebu artists and fine arts students. Upstairs there is a small chapel, a dining room, *sala* (living room), master bedroom, library and office with original period furniture. Yellowing copies of Rizal's novels, *Noli Me Tangere* and *El Filibusterismo*, old books and photographs are in the library. A balcony runs the length of the house with a trellis overhead while a spreading talisay tree provides cool shade. For those who want to know more about life in the old house and the district in which it is located, Resil Mojares' book on the house includes a historical description of Philippine domestic architecture, urban history, and a portrait of the turn-of-the-century Filipino urban family. Hours: 9 to 12 noon, 2 to 6 pm Monday to Saturday; closed Sundays and holidays. There is a small admission fee for adults and children.

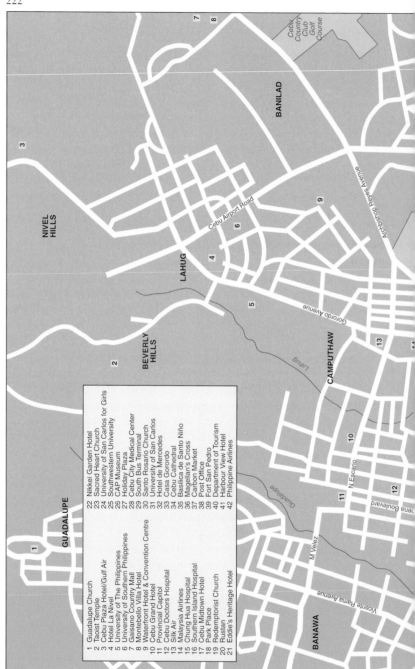

GUADALUPE

NIVEL
HILLS

BEVERLY
HILLS

LAHUG

BANILAD

CAMPUTHAW

BANAWA

Cebu
Country
Club
Golf
Course

Cebu Airport Road

Gorordo Avenue

Archbishop Reyes Avenue

Lahug

Guadalupe

N Escario

M Velez

Vicente Rama Avenue

lena Boulevard

1 Guadalupe Church
2 Taoist Temple
3 Cebu Plaza Hotel/Gulf Air
4 Hotel La Nivel
5 University of The Philippines
6 University of Southern Philippines
7 Gaisano Country Mall
8 Montebello Villa Hotel
9 Waterfront Hotel & Convention Centre
10 Cebu Grand Hotel
11 Provincial Capitol
12 Cebu Doctors Hospital
13 Silk Air
14 Malaysia Airlines
15 Chung Hua Hospital
16 Southern Island Hospital
17 Cebu Midtown Hotel
18 Park Place
19 Redemptorist Church
20 Rustan
21 Eddie's Heritage Hotel
22 Nikkei Garden Hotel
23 Sacred Heart Church
24 University of San Carlos for Girls
25 Southwestern University
26 CAP Museum
27 Holiday Plaza
28 Cebu City Medical Center
29 South Bus Terminal
30 Santo Rosario Church
31 University of San Carlos
32 Hotel de Mercedes
33 Casa Gorordo
34 Cebu Cathedral
35 Basilica de Santo Niño
36 Magellan's Cross
37 Carbon Market
38 Post Office
39 Fort San Pedro
40 Department of Tourism
41 Harbour View Hotel
42 Philippine Airlines

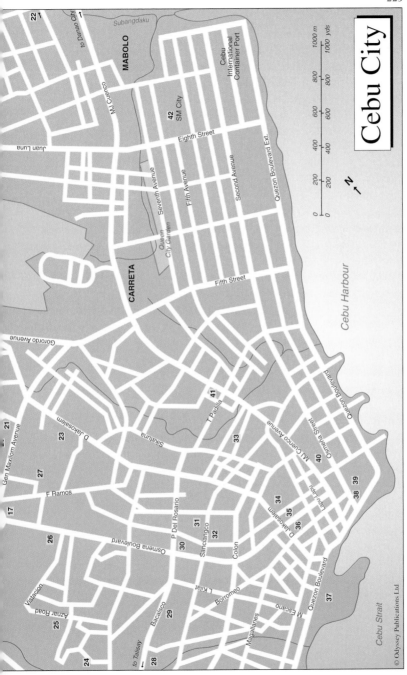

Cebu City

Subangdaku

to Danao City

MABOLO

M.J. Cuenco

Juan Luna

22

1

1

42 SM City

Eighth Street

Seventh Avenue

Fifth Avenue

Second Avenue

Cebu International Container Port

Quezon Boulevard Ext.

Queen City Garden

CARRETA

Fifth Street

Gorordo Avenue

D. Jakosalem

Sikatuna

Sanciangco

T. Padilla

41

33

40

M.J. Cuenco Avenue

Osmeña Street

Quezon Boulevard

Legaspi

38 39

21

23

27

17

26

25

24

28

F. Ramos

Gen Maxilom Avenue

Vistacion

Aznar Road

Osmeña Boulevard

Bacalso

29

30

31

32

P Del Rosario

Colon

L. Kiat

Borromeo

Magallanes

M. Escano

Quezon Boulevard

34

35

36

D. Jakosalem

37

to Talisay

Cebu Harbour

Cebu Strait

N

0   200   400   600   800   1000 m
0   200   400   600   800   1000 yds

© Odyssey Publications Ltd

Cebu has several museums, among them the University of San Carlos Museum, Southwestern University Museum and CAP Museum of President Osmeña's memorabilia. Also of interest to visitors is the Jumalon Art Gallery at the back of the Basak Elementary School housing Prof Julian Jumalon's collection of portraits using butterfly wings, unique in the Philippines. Another visitor attraction is the Taoist Temple in Beverly Hills which conducts regular ceremonies every Wednesday and Sunday. Visitors climb up 99 steps to the temple to light joss sticks and have their fortunes read.

■ **OTHER SIGHTS**

On Mactan Island, one can see a mural depicting the Battle of Mactan fought between Lapu-Lapu and Magellan and his men. Lapu-Lapu was the chieftain of the neighbouring island of Mactan who refused to accept Spanish sovereignty. Magellan engaged him in battle on 27 April 1521, but was slain on the shores of the island. Lapu-Lapu was the first Filipino to defend the cause of freedom against a foreign invader and in tribute to his bravery the Lapu-Lapu Monument was erected on the site of the battle. Nearby is Magellan's Marker built in 1886 by the Spanish authorities. It is said that Rajah Humabon offered a handsome ransom to retrieve Magellan's remains but these were never recovered. In Mandaue City the Chapel of the Last Supper features hand-carved, life-sized statues of Christ and His apostles. Maribago town is famous for its guitars. It also produces ukeleles, mandolins and banjos and visitors can observe the craftsmen at work.

■ **AROUND THE PROVINCE**

Travelling around the island, the visitor comes across centuries-old churches and cathedrals, ranging from simple stone chapels to baroque churches with ornate façades and richly decorated altars, detailed frescoes, ceiling paintings and well-preserved religious icons. The Augustinians, Jesuits and Recollects left their mark in these churches. The old municipalities and suburbs have retained their town plazas and Antillian houses. Along the east coast heading south from Cebu City, you pass Talisay, with its ancient church dedicated to St Teresa of Avila. The church in Naga, made of coral, has a façade featuring angels and gargoyle-like figures. Carcar, founded in 1599, has a well-preserved town plaza surrounded by the church, hospital and colonial houses with wrought-iron balconies. The town was once a crossroads of commerce but is now better known for its shoe industry. Hand-crocheted espadrilles, slippers and other footwear made here are sold locally and exported to Saudi Arabia and the USA. The town of Sibonga, with its 19th-century church dedicated to

Our Lady of Pilar, was inhabited by Spanish families. Grape farming was introduced here in the 1960s.

Argao has a baroque and rococo church with an unusual ceiling painted with religious motifs. It was constructed by the Augustinians and completed in 1788. The Chinese introduced cotton weaving in the 16th century and this is still an important industry today. The town produces handwoven blankets, towels and robes. Past Argao is Dalaguete, whose church, dedicated to San Guillermo, has crystal chandeliers and a baroque altar finished in gold leaf. Beyond Dalaguete is Boljoon with its 400-year-old church. Along the southwestern coast in Barili, the province's subcapital in 1614, old houses can still be found. A church and convent constructed of coral blocks dating back to 1854 can be found in Dumanjug, south of Barili.

The church in Danao City is the third largest in Cebu. Built in 1775, it was destroyed by fire in World War II and completely renovated in 1981. On the northeastern tip of the island, the junction town of Bogo has many old commercial houses. On Bantayan Island there is a town dating back to 1598 which also has many old houses.

The small islands and islets surrounding Mactan are popular destinations for island-hopping tours. These include Sta Rosa, Nalusuan, Hilutungan and Olango islands. Bird-watching is an activity on Olango island.

■ HOTELS AND RESORTS

Cebu boasts several hotels and beach resorts with accommodation ranging from basic to luxurious. In the de luxe class are the 359-room Mactan Shangri-La Island Resort and the 188-room Plantation Bay Mactan, both in Lapu-Lapu City. The Shangri-La sprawls across 13 hectares of landscaped grounds on Punta Engaño. Each of the rooms has a balcony with views of the ocean, the pool or gardens. The hotel boasts sports and recreational facilities and is adding more rooms to the property. New hotels located close to the airport are the 167-room Waterfront Mactan Island Hotel and Casino, rated first-class by the Department of Tourism and the 127-room Days Hotel. The 80-room Delta Philippine Dream Hotel is also on Mactan. Scattered along Mactan's east coast are several resorts. Among these are the popular Tambuli, which offers water sports, diving instruction and a lively disco; Coral Reef Hotel, separated from the rest of the island by a causeway (it has a putting green and driving range); the vacation membership club, Maribago Bluewaters; Mar y Cielo; Costabella and Hadsan.

Other beach resorts require a long drive from Cebu City. On the southwest coast is Moalboal, a scuba divers' heaven. The Badian Island Beach Hotel and Cebu Green Island Club are in Badian, also on the southwest. There are good beaches north of

Cebu City on the east coast at Consolacion, Liloan, Compostela, Danao, Carmen and Sogod. The Cebu Club Pacific and Alegre Beach Resort, a sister company of Cebu Plaza Hotel, are in Sogod. The Alegre was the recipient of the 1996 Kalakbay Resort of the Year award. (National tourism awards are presented yearly to deserving corporate entities and individuals in the field of travel and tourism.) Special interest resorts, catering for scuba divers, are Santa Fe Beach Resort and the Kota Beach Resort on Bantayan Island. These resorts have swimming pools and various recreational and sporting facilities and offer accommodation in cottages and rooms built of traditional native materials. All have lovely natural settings, with a profusion of coconut palms, shore plants and flowering shrubs.

Among the city's hotels are the Cebu Plaza on Nivel Hills in Lahug, with a pool, tennis courts and golf course; the Cebu Midtown Hotel in Fuente Osmeña; the Spanish-type Montebello Villa Hotel in Banilad, and Centrepoint Hotels International (corner Osmeña Blvd and Plaridel St. Standard hotels include the Acropolis (Guadalupe), Cebu Grand Hotel (Capitol Commercial Complex, Escario Street), Harbour View (M J Cuenco Ave), the Park Place Hotel (Fuente Osmeña), Hotel de Mercedes (Pelaez St) and Vacation Hotel (Juana Osmeña and Don Jose Avila Sts). Hotel Esperanza (Manalili St) and Kan-Irag (F Ramos St) are economy hotels. There are also pensions and tourist inns. One of the latest additions to the city's hotels is the Nikkei Garden Hotel on Hernan Cortes St, with 60 rooms that open to a small landscaped garden. A small conference and meeting room can seat 50 persons.

Marriott International's first hotel in the Philippines opened recently in Cebu. Strategically located in Cebu's Business Park, the 303-room hotel, with its meeting rooms and business centre, work stations with fax and modem connections on its executive floors, is geared for business travellers. Also opened in 1998 was the 560-room Waterfront Hotel and International Convention Centre in Lahug City, site of the 1998 ASEAN Tourism Forum. Other hotels that will start operations soon are the Sheraton SM Cebu Hotel and Armada's Suite Hotel and Resort.

■ FOOD AND DRINK

Cebu has many restaurants serving a variety of cuisines: Filipino, Chinese, Japanese, continental and others. Fresh prawns, lobsters, crab and fish are served in seafood restaurants such as Seafood City (Salinas Drive); Golden Cowrie (Salinas Drive, Lahug); Lighthouse (Gen Maxilom Ave); Alavar's (Gorordo Ave); Chika-an sa Cebu (Century Plaza complex). These restaurants also serve Filipino cuisine. For Chinese food, there's Great Han Palace (Osmeña Blvd); Grand Majestic Restaurant (Gorordo Ave); Family Choice (Lahug); or White Gold House (Reclamation area). American and European food is available at Eddie's Log Cabin (Briones St); Swiss Restaurant

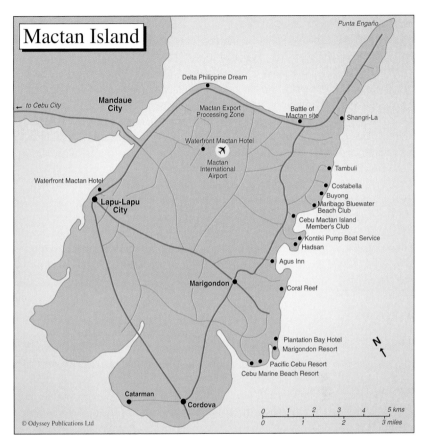

Mactan Island

Punta Engaño

Delta Philippine Dream

← to Cebu City

Mandaue City

Mactan Export Processing Zone

Battle of Mactan site

Shangri-La

Waterfront Mactan Hotel

Mactan International Airport

Waterfront Mactan Hotel

Lapu-Lapu City

Tambuli

Costabella

Buyong

Maribago Bluewater Beach Club

Cebu Mactan Island Member's Club

Kontiki Pump Boat Service

Hadsan

Agus Inn

Marigondon

Coral Reef

Plantation Bay Hotel

Marigondon Resort

Pacific Cebu Resort

Cebu Marine Beach Resort

N

Catarman

Cordova

0   1   2   3   4   5 kms
0   1   2   3 miles

© Odyssey Publications Ltd

(Maxilom St); Vienna Kaffeehaus (Gen Maxilom St); and Lantau Plaza (Cebu Plaza Hotel). Royal Concourse, with a dining room in the lower level and a café on the upper level, serves Japanese food and American-style steaks. Japanese food is found at Bari-Bari (Banilad); Fujiyama (Gorordo Ave); Ginza (Old Banilad Rd); Kyoto (Gen Maxilom St) and Mikado (SM City and Mango Plaza). Patio Isabel beside Ginza Restaurant, serves Philippine dishes but specializes in Pampango preparations. Mai Thai (Gorordo Ave) serves Thai food.

At the Shangri-La, you have a choice of dining in various outlets. Malaysian, Thai and Indian delicacies are served at the Asiatica Restaurant; Cantonese cuisine and dim sum at the Shang Palace, while fresh seafood buffet and grill can be enjoyed at the Cowrie Cove restaurant by the sea.

■ ENTERTAINMENT AND NIGHTLIFE

Visitors to Cebu who want to have a flutter at the gaming tables are well served by the province's casinos, recently upgraded by the Philippine Amusement and Gaming Corporation (Pagcor), operators of casinos nationwide. Asia's high-rollers are beating a path to Cebu's casinos. Japanese, Korean and Taiwanese, as well as Singaporeans, Europeans and Americans are frequent visitors to the Cebu Casino Filipino on Mactan Island, located just minutes away from Cebu's international airport. Pagcor also inaugurated its new casino in Lahug, close to Cebu's financial district and shopping malls. Casino Filipino Cebu, which used to be in Nivel Hills close to the Cebu Plaza Hotel, now occupies the second and third floors of the Waterfront Hotel and Convention Centre. It has a playing area of 11,000 square metres (118,360 square feet) with four VIP rooms. Entertainers are flown in from Manila.

For nightowls on the prowl, check out the entertainment offered by the city's new hotels, as well as what's on in the music lounges and supper clubs. The CoCo LoCo Entertainment Centre at the Shangri-La features top bands alternating with a disc jockey. City Lights (Nivel Hills), Cities Music Lounge and Ball's Disco on General Maxilom Street are Cebus oldest nightspots.

■ SHOPPING

In addition to guitars, ukeleles and mandolins that Cebu craftsmen are famous for, Cebu also produces beautiful pieces of jewellery, fashion accessories, home furnishings and tableware made from shells, corals, and other natural materials. Hand-crocheted and handmade espadrilles, light shoes, sell in Carcar for a fraction of the price they fetch in Cebu City and Manila. These are also exported to the Middle East and the USA. Cebu is a centre for the manufacture of furniture. Many factories turn out not only traditional rattan and wicker furniture but more *avant garde* pieces made of stone, coral and Philippine marble which are gaining a wider export market.

Cebu has its own Ayala Centre and SM City—huge shopping malls—as well as Gaisano, Robinson's, Rustan's, White Gold, Rosita's. These are the main shopping centres and department stores. For handicrafts, there's still Artevalmann Handicraft Market (Baklid, Mandaue), Narda's Handicrafts (Nivel Hills), the guitar factories in Lapu-Lapu City and several gift and souvenir shops. Carbon Market (Briones and Calderon Sts) is a well-known public market.

BOHOL

Lying southeast of Cebu and southwest of Southern Leyte is the oval-shaped province of Bohol, noted for its Spanish churches, the Punta Cruz watchtower in Maribojoc that served as a lookout for Muslim pirates, centuries-old houses, natural scenic attractions such as the Chocolate Hills, fine beaches and excellent dive sites. Whale-watching is a new sport here. Bohol is the birthplace of Carlos P Garcia, the fourth President of the Philippine Republic, as well as the site of the blood compact between Rajah Sikatuna and Miguel Lopez de Legaspi in 1565. It is also the home of the tarsier, a tiny primate with huge eyes and squat body measuring just 7.7 to 15.2 cm (3 to 6 inches) long and weighing between 113 and 142 grammes (4 to 5 oz).

Much of Bohol still retains a rural unsophisticated charm. Visitors come to this island mainly for diving. But those who take time out to travel around the province will be rewarded with a wealth of history and natural beauty. Tagbilaran, the capital, made a chartered city in 1968, is the gateway to the province. Philippine Airlines flies daily from Manila and Cebu. Boats based in Tagbilaran also journey to Cebu, Cagayan de Oro and Manila. There is a fast ferry that travels from Cebu to Tagbilaran, cutting down on journey time.

TAGBILARAN

Tagbilaran has a charming tree-lined plaza surrounded by old stone buildings, the restored capitol building and the cathedral dedicated to St Joseph the Worker. The original church built of coral slabs by the Jesuits in 1767 was burned in 1798. It was reconstructed and enlarged from 1839–1855 but between 1952 and 1970 the façade and choir loft were totally changed. It is considered one of the seven 'magnificent' churches in Bohol. Ancestral homes, one of them a 300-year-old house belonging to a former mayor, are built on the steep rise from the picturesque causeway. Other visitor attractions in the city are the Governor's Mansion, official residence of the provincial governor, and the former residence of President Garcia converted into the Bohol Provincial Museum. The family apartment on the upper floor remains intact; it houses in addition the former President's memorabilia and mementoes (medals and ribbons, plaques and awards, gifts and souvenirs) received while in office. The ground floor displays relics, antiques and artefacts from Bohol's early settlers. It includes a 500-year-old skeleton of a Boholano recovered from a pre-Spanish burial site and a 500-year-old remnant of a house, part of a settlement discovered in Guiwanon, Baclayon. Bohol's early contact with travellers from China and other Southeast Asian civilizations is proven by the presence of T'ang Dynasty porcelain, Sung and Ming vases and other artefacts excavated from ancient burial grounds on the island. Entrance fee is P10 for adults and visitors. The Agora Public Market, the Torralba Market selling the native products of Bohol and the Dynasty Antique Shop are included in the standard city tour.

*'Sketch of new volcano on Camiguin Island' from HMS
Challenger, London Illustrated News, 15 May, 1875*

■ **BLOOD COMPACT**

Some three kilometres (two miles) from the city centre is the site of the first treaty of friendship between a representative of the Spanish crown and a Filipino chieftain, sealed by a blood compact. Boholanos re-enact this event on the last week of July during the annual celebration of Sandugo (one blood) Festival. Protagonists draw blood from a cut in their arm. The drops of blood are mixed with wine in a common cup and drunk. Another historic site in the province is the Dagohoy Marker in Danao which honours the deeds of Francisco Dagohoy who led a rebellion in 1774 against Spanish rule; for 80 years Bohol ran its own government.

Among the churches of note in the province is the one in Baclayon, built in 1595 of sea coral, and dedicated to Our Lady of the Immaculate Conception. The original statue is said to be a donation of Queen Isabela of Spain. The church has a museum with a rich collection of Boholanos religious art, church vestments embroidered in gold thread and librettos of church music printed in Latin on animal skins. The Jesuit-built church in Loboc, second oldest in Bohol, is also interesting. Some of the original relief carvings can still be seen, as well as the blue and white Mexican tiles. The ceiling is painted with scenes of the Crucifixion, Ascension, Jesus as the Good Shepherd, Mary Queen of Heaven and Earth, God the Father, etc. The church in Dauis on the island of Panglao is another of Bohol's noteworthy churches. The Virgin of the Assumption is its patroness and is said to have wrought miracles. One story says that the townsfolk locked themselves inside the church when pirates invaded the town, and when their provisions and water ran out, there suddenly appeared a well at the foot of the altar. The well is still there to this day and is said to have curative powers.

■ **CHOCOLATE HILLS**

A not-to-be-missed sight for visitors to Bohol are the Chocolate Hills, Bohol's most famous landmark. Consisting of 1,268 mounds scattered over the municipalities of Carmen, Sagbayan and Batuan, they are named Chocolate Hills because they are shaped like chocolate drops and are brown during the dry summer months. Believed to be formed by metamorphic process of rainwater and erosion acting on thin, soluble limestone formation over thousands of years, these mounds were declared a National Geological Monument in 1988 by the Philippines' National Commission on Geological Science. They are best seen from Carmen which has a viewing deck reached by climbing 214 steps. There is a hostel and restaurant, swimming pool and tennis court nearby. Most standard tours include this in their itinerary. However, you may also hire a car from your hotel if you do not wish to join a tour group. On the way to Carmen you pass through a man-made mahogany forest, the habitat of rare and endangered flora and fauna.

Some tour itineraries also include a river safari on the Loboc River, cruising along the towns of Loboc and Loay, with a barbecue lunch or brunch on board a native floating restaurant. This may include a stop at Busay Falls, located inland of the Loboc River past the town of Sevilla. Two little islets in the middle of the river make this a favourite bathing area. The river ride may also end near the Tontonan Waterfalls with several smaller cascades. The falls power the Tontonan hydroelectric plant in the town of Loboc.

If you are in Bohol on a Sunday, a visit to Antequera town, a short drive from Tagbilaran Airport, gives you a glimpse of local life. Sunday is a Market Day and the people from neighbouring towns bring their products (baskets, mats, and other handicrafts) made from rattan, coconut midribs, bamboo, *nito* and the like. It's a lively scene and you can buy some very inexpensive baskets and other local products. A few kilometres from the town is Mag-aso Falls for picnics and swimming.

Other visitor attractions in the countryside are the Badian Spring, Hinagdanan Cave in Dauis on the island of Panglao with its underground bathing pool illuminated by a pair of natural skylights, beaches (Caingit in Tagbilaran, Laya in Baclayon, Santa Fe in Albuquerque, Clarian in Loay, and Momo in Panglao).

■ OUTLYING ISLANDS

Bohol's outlying islands, Cabilao, Panglao, and Balicasag are prime, year-round diving sites (see page 289). On Panglao, the Bohol Beach Club is the most developed resort and has the best facilities. The Alona Kew White Beach in Tawala, Panglao is another place favoured by divers. A new resort that opened up in 1994 is the Blue Sky Sea Resort occupying 35 hectares (86 acres) of land perched on a rocky promontory. Accommodation is in duplex cottages. At present the place can only accommodate 50 persons. The best vantage point for whale-watching is from the resort's wide-angle dining room. Humpback whales and pilot whales are regularly seen in the waters bounded by Cebu, Negros Oriental, Bohol and Siquijor. There are whale-watching expeditions in Pamilacan island and Bais City, Negros Oriental.

Panglao is one of the sites targeted by the government for development into a tourism estate. Some 120 hectares (296 acres) are set aside for an airport capable of landing 737 aircraft. The project is seen to be environmentally friendly.

For now, Bohol is still a place to enjoy the wonders of nature undisturbed by hordes of tourists.

Eastern Visayas

The first islands sighted by Ferdinand Magellan in 1521 were the islands off Samar and Leyte. From Homonhon Island, off Samar, Magellan sailed to Limasawa, off Leyte, where he celebrated Easter Sunday Mass. The name Las Islas Felipinas given by Villalobos originally referred to Samar and Leyte. The two islands are separated by the narrow San Juanico Strait but joined by the long San Juanico bridge. Waray-waray and Cebuano are spoken. The Sohoton National Park and Underground Caves are the main attractions in Samar, while Leyte is famous as the landing place of General Douglas MacArthur and his liberation forces in 1944. Frequent typhoons from the Pacific lash these two islands, hindering their economic development.

SAMAR ISLAND
Samar Island is subdivided into three provinces: Northern Samar, Western Samar and Eastern Samar. Northern Samar grows rice and abaca and has good beaches, offshore islands, waterfalls and hot springs. Its capital is Catarman, an old Spanish port, a university town and commercial centre for the island's northern plains. Western Samar is the largest of the three provinces, with Catbalogan, its provincial capital, and Calbayog City as its two most important centres. Fishing, the growing of abaca and mat-making are the main activities. The Sohoton Natural Bridge National Park, which entails a trip upriver and features limestone cliffs and a series of caves, is a well-known tourist attraction near Basey. Eastern Samar (capital: Borongan, a former Spanish military outpost and trading base) has mineral resources. The golden cowrie and other rare shells are found in the province.

LEYTE
The irregularly shaped island of Leyte is composed of two provinces: Leyte and Southern Leyte. A rugged mountain range of volcanic peaks bisects the island from north to south. One third of the island is heavily forested. This natural barrier is

responsible for the different cultural orientation of the islanders. The inhabitants of
Leyte province, the bigger of the two provinces, speak Waray on the east coast and
Cebuano on the west coast.

Leyte played a decisive role in World War II history. Japanese forces landed on
the island in May 1942. Two years later, in October 1944, US liberation forces under General Douglas MacArthur landed on Red Beach. Battle markers and monuments attest to the bloody fighting on the island. The 50th anniversary of the Leyte
Landing was marked by a re-enactment of the landing participated in by American
and Filipino forces. Televised and telecast by satellite, it drew the attendance of
several hundred war veterans and their families from the Philippines, headed by
President Fidel Ramos, and overseas.

Tacloban City, the provincial capital, and Ormoc, the main port, are the two
most important cities. Ormoc is an old fishing village founded in 1597. Palo, the
first town to be liberated by the American landing forces, and Red Beach can be
visited as a day trip from Tacloban. Palo is an old town. Jesuits founded a mission
here in 1596. Among the natural attractions are the Tongonan Hot Spring National
Park and Lake Danao National Park near Ormoc, the Mahagnao Volcano National
Park, 68 kilometres (42 miles) from Tacloban. Ormoc has the new, deluxe Ormoc

Bailing water from a banca

Days Hotel, a Mediterranean-style villa with 49 guestrooms and suites located on the boardwalk in Ormoc's business district. It has a swimming pool with waterfalls, health club with sauna, steam bath and exercise equipment.

Southern Leyte province (capital: Maasin) is a gateway to Mindanao. Across the strait is Surigao. The small port of Padre Burgos is the embarkation point for the 45-minute *banca* ride to the island of Limasawa, now a national shrine. Magellan's Cross and a marker on the site where the first Catholic Mass was celebrated in the Philippines are found on the island. Here is also the grave of Rajah Kolambu who welcomed Magellan and helped to pilot him to Cebu.

BILIRAN

Biliran, a sub-province of Leyte until it was elevated to the status of a province in 1992, is a small and compact island with a mountainous interior and narrow coastal lowlands. Mangrove swamps, hot springs, streams and waterfalls abound. On the south side of the island is the 80-metre (262-foot) high Casyawan Falls, thundering down a steep rock face to a crystal pool below. The majority of the inhabitants live in the lowlands, making their living from fishing and farming. Rice is cultivated on the terraced hillsides fed by mountain streams. From Tacloban, it's a three-hour journey through northern Leyte by bus to the island's capital, Naval. The gateway to the island is the Biliran Bridge, spanning the narrow channel of the Samar Sea.

Palawan—The Call of the Wild

Jutting out like a spur on the western flank of the Philippine Archipelago is Palawan, consisting of 1,768 islands and islets, making it the largest province in the country. Northern Palawan is a place of breathtaking beauty with towering black limestone and marble cliffs surrounded by waters of incredible clarity, rich with marine life. The area is one of ecological and anthropological value.

Described in tourist literature as the Last Frontier, much of the province is still virgin territory, with rainforests, wilderness and jungle. Unexplored caves and coves, pristine beaches and spectacular underwater gardens, wild orchids, butterflies, birds, shells, primitive tribes, paleolithic caves, rare animals—all are to be found in this remarkable province.

Palawan is located nearer the Visayan Islands and Mindanao but administratively is considered part of Luzon. The main island is 425 kilometres (264 miles) long, varying in width from 8.5 kilometres (5.3 miles) to 40 kilometres (25 miles). Puerto Princesa is the provincial capital and the main entry point to the province. The major island groupings are the Calamian group in the north, including Busuanga, Coron and Culion; the Dumaran-Cuyo group in the northeast; and the Balabac Bugsuc group in the southwest.

It was in the Tabon Caves in western Palawan, facing the South China Sea, that the fossilized skullcap of Tabon Man, carbon dated to 22,000 years ago, was discovered in 1962 by Dr Robert Fox. The archaeological site also unearthed prehistoric relics of tools, human bones and utensils. The skullcap is now on display at the National Museum in Manila.

Palawan's original inhabitants can still be seen today but they live in remote areas. The Bataks, a tribe related to those in Sumatra, subsist on fishing, hunting, growing coffee and collecting honey. Descendants of the ancient peoples who came to Palawan via the land bridges, they are the smallest ethno-linguistic group on the island. To visit them entails hiring a guide and undertaking a rigorous trek through the jungles. The Bataks are traditionally nomadic people and used to relocate as frequently as three times a year. Their traditional clothing is made of bark cloth. The nomadic seafaring Tagbanuas live in northern Palawan and are the largest of the minority groups in the province. They practise a thanksgiving ritual called *Pagdiwata* which is popularised by folk dance troupes such as the Bayanihan Dance Company. The Pala'wan are another large group living in the southern highlands. They weave bamboo and rattan baskets and have a syllabic script consisting of 13 consonants and three vowels. The Tau't Batu (People of the Rock) live much as they did 20,000 years ago. They hunt with blowguns and gather fruit, roots, frogs, and insects. Other minorities include the Ken-uy who inhabit the mountains between Quezon and Brooke's Point, the Kalamians living in the Calamianes and Tagabato on Coron Island. The population is also made up of Muslims, ethnic Chinese, Tagalogs and Western Visayans. Majority of the non-tribes live in the plains and valleys and along the coast.

FLORA AND FAUNA

Palawan is noted for its biodiversity. Many species of hardwood trees, ornamental plants, orchids and ferns abound. Aeons ago, Palawan was linked by a land bridge to Borneo and on this submerged isthmus animals now long extinct such as the stegodon and elephas, once travelled. Plants also spread via this bridge. Much of Palawan's flora and fauna is related to that of Borneo.

Rare and endangered species exist in the wild or are protected in national parks, marine and wildlife sanctuaries. Most of Palawan's forests have been declared national parks or wilderness areas. The Calauit Game Preserve and Wildlife Sanctuary in Northern Palawan, St Paul Subterranean River National Park and Tubbataha Reef National Marine Park in the Sulu Sea fall under the National Integrated Protected Areas System. Special permits are required to visit the game preserve and underground river park.

Palawan is an ideal holiday destination for lovers of aquatic sports, particularly diving and fishing. Spelunking, trekking, adventure tours and nature study are also favoured. For mountain climbers, peaks to scale include Mt Capoas and Cleopatra's Needle in Northern Palawan; Thumb Peak and Mt Stavely in Central Palawan, Bulajao Range, Mt Matalingahan, Mt Landargan, End Peak, Victoria Peak, The Teeth, and Anapahan Peak in Southern Palawan.

The best time to visit Palawan is during the dry season, between December and May. January is the coolest month and May the hottest. June to October are generally wet months. Visitors should note that there is some risk of contracting malaria when going into the jungle; necessary precautions should be taken.

■ TRANSPORT

Palawan can be reached by air or sea and is served by regular air services and chartered aircraft to the resort areas. Boats call in from Luzon and Visayan ports. Cruises from Manila to the Calamianes islands are also conducted on a non-regular basis during the summer. A twin-hulled catamaran with 10 air-conditioned cabins cruises the northern islands, exploring the remote bays and rarely visited coves between El Nido and Coron.

Nipa hut village by the sea, Palawan

Independent travellers can hire jeepneys, pumpboats and motorized outrigger *bancas* for long-haul travel. It's a bumpy, dusty ride by public bus and jeepney which can be tiring and time-consuming. Prices for hiring pumpboats are displayed in the local hotels and inns in Puerto Princesa and the wharf at Tagburos. Tricycle hire to the wharf costs more than P200. For those who have the means, chartering a small aircraft is the fastest way to get about. Visitors who want a hassle-free holiday should look into the offerings of tour operators in Manila. Scuba divers may want to make advance arrangements in Manila for a boat-based diving holiday around the more remote islands, and sportfishermen can contact the Philippine Game Fishing Association to arrange fishing near the Tubbataha Reefs. Trekking and spelunking can be fun with members of mountain-climbing clubs. Accommodation ranges from hotels, tourist inns and modest guest houses to deluxe resorts.

Central Palawan

Most commercial flights land in Puerto Princesa. The city proper is about 1.5 kilometres (one mile) from the airport. Tricycles are the most common mode of transport for short distances. The Asiaworld Hotel, with a swimming pool set in landscaped grounds, is favoured for conventions and large groups. Casa Linda or Bahay Natin Tourist Inn owned by Mrs Linda Mendoza is a charming, rustic inn set in a small side street off the main road. It has only 11 guest rooms and because it is so popular with overseas visitors, it is a good idea to reserve a room in advance; telephone (63 48) 433-2606 . Accommodation is also provided by the Badjao Inn located on the main highway from the airport. A 48-room boutique hotel, the Hotel Fleuris Palawan, located in the middle of Puerto Princesa's business and commercial district, is being added to the town's accommodation.

In addition to the dining rooms in the hotels and inns, there are several restaurants in the city serving Chinese (Edwin's), Spanish (Café Puerto), and Filipino food (Kalui, Kamayan). This last is a charming native house decorated with rattanwork. The city itself has little to detain the tourist but is the springboard for excursions to the rest of the island and the province.

EXCURSIONS FROM PUERTO PRINCESA

Excursions to Iwahig Penal Colony and Honda Bay can be undertaken from Puerto Princesa. Iwahig is an open prison where the colonists (as the inmates are called) are

St Paul's Bay, Palawan

free to move about and work. Some colonists are allowed to live with their families. Iwahig has some old colonial buildings and a store selling items made by the prisoners.

Honda Bay is dotted with many small islands and islets of fine white sand which disappear at high tide. It's a 30-minute tricycle ride from the city centre to the wharf where you hire a motorized outrigger *banca* to visit any of the islands; the price depends on how far the island is. Señorita is the farthest and most expensive to visit. Snake Island, Pandan Island (site of the Coco Loco Resort) and Starfish Island are less expensive. You can stay put in one island for the day or visit three islands. Some places charge entrance fee. At Lu-li, so-called because it is submerged (*lubog*) at high tide and afloat (*litao*) at low tide, there are a few huts on stilts where you can stop for a picnic lunch and a swim. Meara Marina is one of the better developed resorts, popular with divers and expatriates from Manila. Managed by an Austrian, Franz Urbanek, and his Filipino wife, Jane, Meara Marina occupies three hectares of the big island which has two lagoon systems inland. The place has modest, comfortable bungalows and diving facilities. For those who don't dive, sightseeing, shell-hunting and snorkelling are favourite activities. A retired captain of merchant ships, Franz is doing his bit to produce environmentally-friendly boats and claims to save ten trees out of every boat.

Bat Island is inhabited by thousands of bats. As regular as clockwork, the bats fly out at 6.15 pm every day, their departure signalled by bird calls, and return home around 4 am.

TABON CAVES

Forty two kilometres (26 miles) southwest of Puerto Princesa, in Lipoon Point on the island's western side, are the Tabon Caves. Evidence of human life in this part of the archipelago thousands of years ago was unearthed by Dr Robert Fox. Of the more than 200 caves in this area, only a few have been excavated. Paleolithic tools and animal bones were also found in the caves, along with the skullcap of Tabon Man. The Palawan State College Museum in Tinuguiban showcases archaeological finds, tribal art, native handicrafts, a butterfly and shell collection and artifacts.

Northern Palawan

Here in this Eden, where the beauty and grandeur of nature takes one's breath away, man is made aware that he is only an infinitesimal part of the cosmos. St Paul Subterranean River National Park, Port Barton, Cleopatra's Needle and El Nido are

Northern Palawan's greatest attractions. Cleopatra's Needle is a rock formation rising to a height of 1,584 metres (5,199 feet) north of Honda Bay. It is one of the peaks to challenge mountain climbers. The best view of the rock is from the sea.

St Paul Subterranean River National Park

Honda Bay is linked to Ulugan Bay on the western side by a narrow lowland that crosses the island. At the head of Ulugan Bay is the village of Baheli or Bahile, the gateway to St Paul Subterranean River National Park. It is about 48 kilometres (30 miles) from Puerto Princesa. From Baheli one travels by *banca* to Tagnipa or Sabang, or by road to Cabayugan and Sabang. The park covers 5,390 hectares (13,373 acres) of lush forest, limestone mountains, towering cliffs, caves and silica beaches. The underground river snakes for more then eight kilometres (five miles) under the limestone mountains and is navigable for about four kilometres (2.5 miles) emerging at St Paul's Bay on the South China Sea. The river can be explored by a small boat provided by the park authorities and equipped with a kerosene lamp. An official guide accompanies visitors. The cave has many interesting stalactites. In addition to spelunking, visitors can swim, sunbathe, snorkel, scuba dive or trek in the park. Some 60 species of birds have been identified, such as the white-bellied sea eagle, Philippine cockatoo, Pacific reef egret and Tabon bird. Troops of chattering monkeys are sometimes seen along the trails. The trip to the Underground River entails an overnight stay as it is impractical to attempt a return trip to Puerto Princesa on the same day. A possibility is to stay at Casa Linda at Marufinas, some 15 minutes from the park. Be sure to make advance arrangements with the manager at Casa Linda in Puerto Princesa before leaving the city.

Port Barton

Port Barton is a quaint fishing town with a long stretch of white sandy beach and offshore islands rich in marine life. Wood, bamboo and nipa houses line the beachfront where tourists can be accommodated. At the end of the main street is an old logging road which leads to a 21-metre (70-foot) waterfall. The journey to Port Barton from the capital is long and tiring, best undertaken by those with patience and stamina. An alternative is to hire a jeepney for the 1.5-hour ride to Baheli on the coast, and then take a motorized outrigger *banca* to Port Barton. The Manta Ray Resort at Capsalay Island is worth a visit for those in Port Barton. The Swissipini Lodge Resort is in San Vicente, Port Barton.

Also in Northern Palawan is the small fishing port of Taytay, founded in 1622 by the Spaniards. It was the old provincial capital and functioned as a military base. The ruins of a fort and the church still stand today.

Palawan

South China Sea

Cuyo Islands
Cuyo

Cagayan
Islands

Cavili Island

Arena Island

Linapacan
Island

Dumaran
Island

Pagdanan
Range

Roxas

El Nido

Port Barton

Saint Paul
Subterranean
National Park

Honda Bay

Puerto Princesa

Mt Aborian

Victoria
Peak

Quezon

Mt Gantung

Batarasa

Brooke's Point

Island Bay

Palawan Passage

Tubbataha
Reefs

Sulu Sea

Calauit Island

Busuanga
Island

Coron
Island

Bulalacao
Island

Culion Island

Linapacan
Island

Palawan Island

Pandanan Island
Bancalan Island
Matangulin Island
Canabungan Island
Candaraman Island
Balabac Island

Bugsuk Island

N

0   25   50   75   100 kms

0   25   50 miles

© The Guidebook Company Ltd

EL NIDO

El Nido in Northern Palawan is an area of incredible natural beauty with towering black limestone and marble cliffs, lush forests, caves, coves, lagoons and clear seas teeming with marine life. Thousands of swifts make their home in the cliffs. The birds' nests (*nido*) are edible and are the principal ingredient in nido soup, an expensive Chinese delicacy much prized by gourmets. The offshore islands of Miniloc and Pangulasian are the setting for two first class resorts: El Nido on Miniloc Island and El Nido on Pangulasian Island. From Manila, it's an hour and 15 minutes' flight by private aircraft to El Nido municipality, followed by a 30- to 45-minute boat ride to the resorts. Accommodation is in air-conditioned cottages or guest houses. The waters around the resorts are a paradise for divers, with at least 26 different dive sites ranging from rock formation, slope reef and submerged reef to drop-off and tunnel dives. In addition to diving, windsurfing, canoeing, snorkelling and water-skiing, island-hopping, spelunking and trekking, more conventional sports are available for visitors. Enquire about holiday package rates.

CALAMIAN ISLANDS

Busuanga, Culion and Coron are the three big islands in this group comprised of 95 other smaller islands. Busuanga and Coron towns are the two main settlements on Busuanga Island. The Mindoro Strait separates these islands from Mindoro. Commercial flights land at Busuanga while boats from Manila and Batangas dock at Coron. Accommodation on the island is available at Club Paradise, Bayside Divers Lodge, Dy Tulay Lodge and Sea Breeze Lodge.

CALAUIT GAME PRESERVE

The game preserve and wildlife sanctuary on Calauit Island off Busuanga Island's northwestern coast is like something out of Africa. Zebra, giraffe, eland, impala and gazelle graze in the grasslands. These refugees from Kenya were given a permanent home here in 1977 when the Philippines responded to an appeal by the International Union of Conservation of Nature (IUCN) to save endangered African animals. The African animals have thrived in their adopted home. The forests, grasslands and mangrove swamps of this conservation area are also the breeding ground for some of the Philippines' rarest and most endangered species such as the Philippine mouse deer, Calamian deer, Palawan bearcat, leopard cat, tarsier, Palawan pheasant peacock, scaly anteater and monitor lizard. The swamp is also the domain of the man-eating Philippine crocodile. Offshore are marine reservation sites. There is a rearing station for sea turtles (*pawikan*) at Ilultuk Bay and an egg-laying area on Tanobon Island. The seas around the island are the abode of the giant clam, measuring 1.25

metres (4.1 feet) wide and weighing 300 kilos, (660 pounds), sea cows (dugong), and a wide variety of fish. The island of Tanobon is also a bird sanctuary and a station for birds migrating south.

Permission to visit the game preserve may be obtained by writing or contacting the Conservation and Resource Management Foundation, Ground Floor, IRC Bldg, 82 EDSA, Metro Manila.

To get there: fly to Busuanga. From the airport, board a jeep to Decalatiao, then go by *banca* to Maricaban Bay where you transfer to a larger boat which will take you to Calauit.

THE CUYO GROUP

North of the Sulu Sea and east of Northern Palawan is the Cuyo Islands, consisting of Cuyo, Agutaya and about 45 islets. These are rich fishing grounds and underwater visibility is excellent, making it a superb place for snorkelling. The islands have been known since early times because they were along the trade route of sailing ships between China and Borneo. People in these islands, hardly touched by tourism, earn their living from fishing and seaweed production. The volcanic Cuyo Island has a Spanish fort with massive stone walls two metres thick and ten metres high built in 1677 to withstand pirate attacks. The upscale Amanpulo Resort is located on Pamalican Island in the Quiniluban group. The rich and famous, the high and mighty have come to this hideaway island. Accommodation is in air-conditioned *'casitas'*—the modern version of a Filipino nipa hut with all the luxuries and amenities of a first-class hotel. Forty of these *casitas* are along the beachfront, on a hilltop or between trees. There's a clubhouse, dining room, swimming pool, tennis courts, picnic grove, library, gift shop. All types of water activities are offered such as swimming, sailing, rowing, fishing, snorkelling and scuba diving; in addition there's jogging, mountain biking, hiking and picnics. Guests are ferried by chartered aircraft from Manila directly to the island which has its own private airstrip.

A Corrupting Influence

The chief amusement of the Filipinos is cock-fighting, which is carried on with a passionate eagerness that must strike every stranger. Nearly every man keeps a fighting cock. Many are never seen out of doors without their favorite in their arms; they pay as much as $50 and upwards for these pets, and heap the tenderest caresses on them. The passion for cock-fighting can well be termed a national vice; but the practice may have been introduced by the Spaniards, or the Mexicans who accompanied them, as, in a like manner, the habit of smoking opium among the Chinese, which has become a national curse, was first introduced by the English. It is, however, more probable that the Malays brought the custom into the country. In the eastern portion of the Philippines, cock-fighting was unknown in the days of Pigafetta. The first cock-fight he met with was at Palawan, where they keep large cocks, which from a species of superstition, they never eat, but keep for fighting purposes. Heavy bets are made on the upshot of the contest, which are paid to the owner of the winning bird. The sight is one extremely repulsive to Europeans. The ring around the cockpit is crowded with men, perspiring at every pore, while their countenances bear the imprint of the ugliest passions. Each bird is armed with a sharp curved spur, three inches long, capable of making deep wounds, and which always causes the death of one or both birds by the serious injuries it inflicts. If a cock shows symptoms of fear and declines the encounter, it is plucked alive. Incredibly large sums, in proportion to the means of the gamblers, are wagered on the result. It is very evident that these cock-fights must have a most demoralising effect upon a people so addicted to idleness and dissipation, and so accustomed to give way to the impulse of the moment. Their effect is to make them little able to resist the temptation of procuring money without working for it.

Fedor Jagor, Travels in the Philippines

Mindanao

Mindanao, the second largest island in the Philippines, forms the southern part of the Philippine archipelago, lying close to the Equator between the latitudes of 5° and 10°N. Its area of 102,074 square kilometres (39,410 square miles) accounts for one-third of the national territory. The Mindanao Sea on the north separates it from the Visayas. It is bounded on the east by the Pacific Ocean, on the south by the Celebes Sea and on the west by the Sulu Sea. Its topography is varied and irregular, characterized by high and rugged mountain ranges, dormant volcanoes, rolling plateaus, extensive plains, major rivers and lakes. The Philippines' highest mountain, Mt Apo (3,143 metres /10,311 feet) is in Mindanao. The peak and pristine part of Mt Apo is located in Kidapawan, Cotabato, but the 72,796 hectares of rainforest that surround the volcanic peak loop around the territories of Davao del Sur, Davao City and Bukidnon. The forested slopes of Mt Apo are the breeding grounds of the endangered Philippine eagle and the habitat of wild orchids and endemic fauna. Mindanao has two great river systems—the Agusan in the east and the Cotabato (or Rio Grande de Mindanao)/Pulangi River in the south and centre. The Agusan is the third largest river in the country, flowing for 300 kilometres (186 miles) from the highlands of Davao del Norte down to Butuan Bay. Mindanao experiences extremes of rainfall. The driest province in the country is South Cotabato and the wettest is Surigao del Norte. However, most parts of Mindanao have a generally moderate climate; very few typhoons hit the island, making it agriculturally productive.

Twenty-two provinces (18 on the main island and four on the outer islands), 17 chartered cities and 312 municipalities make up Mindanao. Administratively, it is divided into Western Mindanao, Northern Mindanao, Southern Mindanao, Central Mindanao, The Administrative Region of Muslim Mindanao, and the newly created Caraga Region composed of Agusan del Norte, Agusan del Sur, Surigao del Norte and Surigao del Sur. The entry point into Mindanao from the Visayas is Surigao del Norte in the northeast.

PEOPLE

Archaeological findings suggest that Mindanao and Sulu were inhabited as early as 4,000 years ago, probably by the same type of people that inhabited other islands of Southeast Asia. Today, the inhabitants of Mindanao belong to three main cultural groups: Muslims who were converted to Islam and regard Mindanao as their homeland; Christians who migrated from Luzon and the Visayas and settled in various parts of Mindanao; and the indigenous tribes, or "cultural communities" who live in the highlands and peripheral areas.

The Islamic groups can·be further divided into the Maranao who live near Lake Lanao, the Maguindanao of Cotabato; the Sanggil in Cotabato's far south; the Yakan of Basilan Island; the Taosug of Jolo; the Samal of Tawi-Tawi and nearby islands; and the Jama Mapun of Cagayan de Sulu. The cultural communities consist of 13 groups—the Ata, Bagobo, Bilaan, Bukidnon, Higaonon, Ismal, Mandaya, Manobo, Subanon, Tagakaolo, Tasaday, T'boli, and Tiruray. The Muslims and the cultural communities are distinguished by their colourful clothing, headdress and elaborate ornaments. Men and women wear embroidered or appliquéd costumes embellished with tassels, shells, beads and metal discs, which give an indication of the tribe and status of the wearer. However, not all wear tribal costumes nowadays, except perhaps on special occasion. The Badjaos or sea gypsies have been known for centuries as expert pearl divers. The tropical waters around Mindanao are the habitat of a rare breed of oysters which yield superb specimens of South Sea pearls. In fact, traders have been coming to the Philippines since as early as the Sung Dynasty for these pearls. The Pinctada Maxima pearl oyster yields white and golden pearls while the Pinctada Margaritifera produces the black pearl. The South Sea Pearl, also known as the Philippine pearl, has been declared the country's national gem by presidential proclamation.

NATURAL RESOURCES

Mindanao's climate, rich volcanic soil and abundant water supply combine to make it an agriculturally productive region. Twenty-three per cent of the country's rice, 67 per cent of its corn, 62 per cent of its coconut are supplied by Mindanao. There are vast pineapple plantations in South Cotabato, banana plantations in Davao, citrus orchards in Bukidnon. All the Cavendish bananas for export to Japan, Korea, the Middle East and other countries are grown in Mindanao. The provinces in the northern and eastern coastlines have vast timberlands and there are large deposits of high-grade copper, silver and gold. Three-fourths of the Philippines' iron reserves and a third of its coal resources are found in Mindanao. The island has also one of the richest nickel deposits in the world. Geothermal energy is tapped from volcanic sources.

Lured by the economic opportunities offered by this 'Land of Promise', thousands of migrants from Luzon and the Visayas settled here. From a population of 933,000 in 1913, numbers rose to 1.8 million in 1939, 7.9 million in 1970 and 14.2 million in 1990. The Christian migrants in the 1960s and 1970s settled in the sparsely populated provinces of Bukidnon, Cotabato and Davao. Today, they are spread throughout Mindanao and, except for Lanao del Sur and the Sulu archipelago where Muslims predominate, Christians account for more than 80 per cent of the population in every province. The influx of lowland and Christian settlers into lands which the Muslims consider their domain has given rise to conflicts. The creation of the Administrative Region of Muslim Mindanao ensures that Muslims can run their own affairs on the basis of Islamic principles, beliefs and customs, yet within the framework of the Philippine constitution and Philippine laws.

Once considered the Philippines' backwater, Mindanao today is fast-tracked for development to catapult it to the 21st century. The formation of the East ASEAN Growth Area (EAGA) linking Mindanao and Palawan with North Sulawesi, East and West Kalimantan, Sabah and Sarawak and Brunei Darussalam is contributing greatly to this change. The regional economic cooperation forged by the governments of Brunei Darussalam, Indonesia, Malaysia and the Philippines (BIMP) focuses initially on trade, joint tourism ventures, expansion of air linkages, sea transport and shipping services, and fisheries development within the growth polygon. Eventually this will be expanded to include environmental protection and management, energy development, construction, telecommunications, human resources development, agri-industry, capital formation, forestry and financial services. As a vital part of the BIMP-EAGA project, Mindanao is set to change dramatically in the next several years.

Much of Mindanao, however, still remains unexplored by tourists. While scenic attractions abound, it is the juxtaposition of tribal, Islamic and Christian cultures that makes the area so fascinating to visitors. Shopping for ethnic handicrafts, brassware, woven clothes, mats and food covers; and sampling exotic fruit such as durian and rambutan are some of the delights for visitors. For those who are interested in Muslim culture, a visit to the provinces of Lanao del Sur and Maguindanao affords a peek into their lifestyle. Lanao del Sur with its majestic Lanao Lake, is the centre of Islam in the south. The Mindanao State University, the King Faisal Centre for Arabic Studies and the Aga Khan Museum are repositories of Muslim culture. In remote areas, visitors may chance upon festivals that transcend time. Lovers of nature also will find plenty to interest them here. Trekking on Mt Apo, the country's highest peak, is a popular activity of mountaineering clubs.

The Zamboanga Peninsula

The Zamboanga peninsula lies at the western end of Mindanao. It has a total land area of 1,403 square kilometres (242 square miles), much of it still dense forests, swamps, plains and beaches. It consists of the provinces of Zamboanga del Norte (capital: Dipolog) and Zamboanga del Sur (capital: Pagadian) with Zamboanga City at the southern tip. Zamboanga del Norte occupies the northern coast of the peninsula facing the Sulu Sea. Most of the inhabitants are migrants from the Visayas and the Sulu archipelago. Indigenous Subanons inhabit the interior. Dipolog, the provincial capital and centre of commerce, and Dapitan, the place of exile of the Philippines' national hero Dr Jose Rizal, are the important towns. Dipolog is the jump-off point for Dakak-bound tourists.

DAKAK

Dakak Park and Beach Resort is a popular tourist destination in Zamboanga del Norte. From Dipolog airport, it's a 25-minute bus ride through the rural country-side—a green landscape dotted with coconut groves, banana plantations and mango orchards brightened by splashes of colour from flowering bougainvillaea. At Dapitan River, which flows out to sea, visitors board a motorized outrigger boat for the 20-minute ride to Dakak. The resort is situated in one of the coves facing the Sulu Sea. Limestone cliffs tower above the headland and vegetation covers the hillside. The rustic cottages of thatched nipa and bamboo in the 15-hectare resort blend with the tropical setting of mango trees and coconut palms, banana and papaya plants, or-chids and frangipani growing in the wild. Duplex-style cottages come in standard, deluxe and super-deluxe rooms, all with a small verandah and modern amenities. The resort has two swimming pools fed by natural spring water: one for adults and another—with waterfalls, water chutes and a mini island—for children. A private open-air jacuzzi and sauna cater for guests. There are three tennis courts with flood lighting; a three-hole, par 4 practice golf course; four lanes of ten pin bowling, and billiards. The Aqua Sports Centre offers a pro dive shop, scuba diving, masks and fins, jet skis and waterbikes, power boats, windsurfers and hobie cats. Dive cruises for up to 10 days on Dakak's private yacht, tours and excursions, cruises and visits to Dapitan and Dipolog markets and Rizal Shrine are offered guests. Horseback riding is available on 30-minute notice. There is a chapel, a large dining room and an open terrace where a seafood buffet is served al fresco in the evenings. The resort has trained its staff to entertain guests with folk dances in the evening, and the dis-cotheque is open from 10 pm until the wee hours.

DIPOLOG AND DAPITAN

Dakak organizes day trips to Dipolog City, which has a bustling market. On Market Day, villagers from neighbouring places converge there to sell their produce and wares. Dipolog itself does not have much to interest the tourist, but one can browse among the stores along Rizal Avenue, and stop for a chicken lunch, if you wish. A night tour is also available. Dipolog, made a Spanish settlement in 1834 and a char-tered city in 1970, boasts karaoke bars, pubs and discos.

(above) T'boli women from South Cotabato are identified by their wide-brimmed hats; (below) T'boli girls in their traditional dress

Another side trip for tourists is Dapitan City, 14 kilometres (nine miles) away. An old Spanish settlement and trading town, Dapitan shares a good harbour with Dipolog. The Jesuits founded a mission here in 1629 and the Spanish authorities built a fort. Dapitan is a heritage town, selected as one of the 22 historic sites of the Centennial Freedom Trail by the National Centennial Commission to commemorate the Philippines' 100 anniversary of nationhood.

The Philippines' national hero, Dr Jose Rizal, was exiled in Dapitan in 1892 by the Spanish colonial government who found his writings inflammatory and likely to incite nationalistic feelings among his countrymen. A marker on Santa Cruz beach shows the spot where Rizal landed. Casa Real, the official residence of the politico-military governor, was where Rizal stayed for a month before moving to nearby Talisay. It still stands at the edge of the plaza, near the church of St James where he used to attend Mass. He also used to work in the hospital treating patients. Dr Rizal was an ophthalmologist, among other things. Rizal also made a grassy relief map of Mindanao in the plaza.

The Casa Real was reconstructed to serve as the new museum while the old convent building nearby was restored to provide accommodation for visitors. The waterworks system which Rizal designed and built for the town, starting from the dam at the top of Linao Hill and ending at the fountain on the riverbank, was also restored.

Talisay, about four kilometres (under three miles) from the city centre, is where the Rizal shrine is located. It is easy to hire a tricycle from the town centre to visit the shrine. Talisay is a tranquil place, with many trees spreading their cool shade. A promenade faces the sea. Rizal lived here from 1893 to 1896. It was here where he wrote his poem *Mi Retiro* (My Retreat). There is a small museum at the entrance to the shrine containing Rizaliana memorabilia. The existing wooden replicas of his house, the clinic where he saw patients, the amphitheatre and the aqueduct he built were renovated to conform as closely as possible to the original wooden structures both in their exterior and interior. The surrounding landscape was also restored to its original form. The Centennial Commission, in planning the development of the Talisay estate and the Dapitan town plaza, hoped to give visitors a better understanding of Rizal's selfless activities and service to community and country while in exile.

Zamboanga City

Zamboanga is one of those places popularized in song: *Faraway places with strange sounding names* and *Don't you go, don't you go to far Zamboanga*, an old Philippine folk song. Strategically located by the sea, Zamboanga from days of old was an important port and the gateway to the Sulu Archipelago and Basilan. "Jambangan" was how the

T'boli Tribal Festival

The weekend began with the delicate, hollow sound of a wooden flute announcing the coming of dawn. It was 15 September, the first day of the two-day T'boli Tribal Festival on Lake Sebu, South Cotabato. Several mountain tribes converged to celebrate Mass and display their ancient traditions. We were at the Santa Cruz Mission, a wooden school built by an American priest who introduced Christianity to the tribes. The Mass itself was a peculiar mix of Sunday tradition and T'boli mystique in which Roman Catholicism supplanted the T'boli animist beliefs. Today, most of them are converts.

Tribal chants and drumbeats awaited the arrival of datus on horseback, symbolizing wealth and power; women and children resplendent in traditional costumes and intricate native jewellery; lines of people wrapped in tubaws and malongs decorated with belts of bronze bells. The Mass ended with a vibrant show of male war dances, female graces and horse fights lasting until dusk.

The same flute woke us up before dawn the next day, the same melodic chants and hypnotic gongs. It was dark. From a hilltop we viewed the festival grounds where the High Mass would be celebrated once more. Firecrackers signalled the beginning of the procession, and out of the dark came bright, flickering torches that snaked their way to the festival grounds. The flow of lights continued until dawn, punctuated by drums, gongs, chants and bells.

We left the Mission with memories of the exuberance of the rich tribal ceremony the T'bolis had performed, not for us who had come to visit, but for themselves, who live to preserve it. For two days we had immersed ourselves in the drama, the excitement and the beauty of a world totally different from ours, less complicated and a lot calmer. All told, we learned the secrets to happiness, unity, love, family, an ardent faith, and perhaps even simplicity, taught to us by the soft, melting notes of a wooden flute.

Troy Bernardo, Trail Notes

early Malay settlers called the place because flowers grew profusely. It was later called 'Samboangan', meaning anchorage, from which the present name is derived. Zamboanga became a Spanish city on 23 June 1635, when the cornerstone of Fort Pilar was laid by the Spanish Jesuit priest-engineer Melchor de Vera. 'Real Fuerza de Nuestra Señora del Pilar de Zaragoza', to give the fort's full name, was built of coral, with one-metre (3.28 feet) thick walls to withstand Muslim raids and foreign attack. The original fort was destroyed in 1663. Reconstructed in 1718, the fort had for its patroness the Nuestra Señora del Pilar de Zaragoza. The fort still stands today and is one of the city's historic sites. A branch of the National Museum is located within the fort. It is said that in past centuries, while the image was borne in procession in the village, the alert came that the Muslims were about to attack. In the confusion that followed people rushed inside the fort, leaving the Image of Our Lady outside the entrance. Unaccountably, the fort's entrance was sealed with lime and stone. After the attack a frantic search was made for the missing image which was found atop the entrance that had been miraculously sealed. Today, above the old entrance is the carved and painted image of the Virgin and Child with seven stars and two cherubim. The image is surmounted by a huge crown and a diadem of seven stars. Every October, Zamboanga celebrates the Feast of Our Lady of Pilar with religious fervour. It is a time for homecomings and feasting. The city's Hispanic heritage is also seen in the descendants of the Spaniards, in the Spanish-sounding Chabacano dialect spoken by many Zamboangueños today, and in the colonial-style town plaza, buildings and houses along acacia-lined streets.

The Muslim character of the city provides a colourful contrast. Taosugs, Samals and Badjaos are clustered along the Rio Hondo in their houses standing on stilts over the water. This village is some 200 metres (656 feet) from Fort Pilar. Taluksan-gay Village, a Samal colony dominated by a mosque with red minarets, is situated 19 kilometres (12 miles) east of the city. This, too, has a floating village.

Seven kilometres (four miles) north of the city is Pasonanca Park, a cool forest reserve 150 metres (500 feet) above sea level. At the park is a children's pool with concrete slides, a natural pool, regular swimming pool and a treehouse. Located some 7.5 kilometres (4.6 miles) from the city is the Zamboanga Golf and Beach Park.

The Santa Cruz Islands, about 25-minutes' ride by pumpboat from the Zamboanga wharf, are popular for picnics, sunbathing, snorkelling and scuba-diving. The beach has pinkish sands, the effect of pulverized coral washed ashore. The islands have been declared a national park. There is a Samal burial ground on the larger island as well as a Samal fishing village.

■ HOTELS AND RESORTS

The city has some 700 hotel rooms ranging from first class to budget inns and pensions. The best rated are the Lantaka Hotel by the Sea and the Garden Orchid Hotel. The Grand Astoria is a standard hotel while Argamel, GC Hotel, Marcian Garden and Viva Pension House are economy hotels. In the afternoons, Samal and Badjao sea gypsies tie up along the wharf by the hotel, selling their wares of coral and shell. The city also has several restaurants serving Filipino, Chinese, and European food. The *curacha*, a cross between a crab and a lobster, is a local delicacy.

■ SHOPPING

Indigenous handicrafts such as brassware, pottery, ceramics, mats, and tribal costumes, as well as shell craft are readily available in the shopping areas. The Public Market is a good place to see what's on offer. Aside from locally produced products and handicrafts, you get a selection of batiks from neighbouring countries. The fruit market has all the exotic fruit like durian, mangosteen, marang, and rambutan.

■ GETTING THERE

Zamboanga is served by a number of flights from Manila and the Visayas. Travelling time by air from Manila is 90 minutes. There are ferry boats to other islands in the Sulu Sea. Inter island vessels also dock in Zamboanga and call at other ports in Mindanao such as Cotabato, Iligan, Cagayan de Oro and Davao.

Northern Mindanao

MISAMIS PROVINCES

The Misamis provinces (Oriental and Occidental) lie along the northern coast of Mindanao, separated by Lanao del Norte. Misamis Occidental (capital: Oroquieta

Young fisherman with his catch, Camiguin Island

Sea gypsies in the early morning, Bongao Bay, Tawi-Tawi

City) lies to the east of Zamboanga del Norte and north of Zamboanga del Sur. Misamis Oriental (capital: Cagayan de Oro) has beaches stretching from Medina in the east to the Costa Brava Resort in Lugait in the west, waterfalls, caves and good diving around Gingoog City, and the Gardens of Malasag, the country's first eco-tourism village.

Cagayan de Oro

Misamis Oriental's gateway city is Cagayan de Oro, linked by air, sea and land with other destinations in Luzon, the Visayas and Mindanao. The city is noted for its parks. Xavier University is located here and its Folk Museum is worth a visit. The Museo de Oro houses one of the Philippines' best collections of pre-Christian folk artefacts. A short drive from the city is Macahambus Cave, where Filipino forces were victorious in a battle fought during the Philippine-American War at the turn of the century.

Cagayan de Oro offers a variety of accommodation. Pryce Plaza is the city's first-class hotel. The Dynasty Court Hotel and Lauremar Hotel are other places to stay. Other standard hotels accredited by the Department of Tourism are Discovery Hotel, Excelsior Hotel, Grand City, Harbor Lights, Philtown, Southwinds and VIP Hotel. Cagayan Riverview Inn, Casa Crystalla, Estrella Hotel and Hotel Ramon are economy hotels. There are also pensions and inns.

GARDENS OF MALASAG

Twelve kilometres (7.5 miles) from the city is a new tourist attraction—The Gardens of Malasag. Opened in August 1997, it serves as a learning centre for eco-tourism and environmental protection, and a cultural showcase of northern Mindanao's ethnic communities. The eco-tourism village occupies 7.2 hectares (17.8 acres) of land but the forest reserve that surrounds the village covers 195 hectares (482 acres). A flower garden and orchidarium and wildlife sanctuaries are features of Malasag. A five-metre-long hanging bridge, known as 'Canopy Walk', observation decks and view decks enable visitors to appreciate the various wonders of the place. To introduce visitors to the culture of the ethnic minorities in Mindanao, authentic tribal houses have been constructed on the site and programmes are presented regularly by the different cultural communities. Malasag has picnic groves and food kiosks for day trippers. Visitors who wish to stay overnight can also rent cottages. There are restaurants and shower rooms, an area for camping and a swimming pool. A museum, amphitheatre, and conference hall are other features.

BUKIDNON

South of Misamis Oriental is the province of Bukidnon. The drive to the provincial capital of Malaybalay is via a scenic route through canyons and valleys. Bukidnon is known for its vast orchards and plantations and the Benedictine Monastery of Transfiguration high on a hill. The monks produce their own brand of coffee called Monk's Blend, which they roast and grind. In September the province holds its Kaamulan Festival in Malaybalay, a spectacle of tribal dances, sports and games.

CAMIGUIN

Off the mainland of northern Mindanao is a cluster of seven volcanic islands belonging to Camiguin province. The biggest and most active is Mt Hibok-Hibok, a challenge for mountain climbers. The volcano last erupted in 1951. It takes five and a half hours by boat from Cagayan de Oro City to Binone wharf on the main island (capital: Mambajao). Travel by jeepney to Katibawasan Falls, a 20-metre (66-foot) cascade five kilometres (three miles) southeast of Mambajao town, and on to Ardent Hot Spring in Esperanza for a dip in the warm water. Three kilometres (two miles) off Agoho is White Island, a sand bar in the middle of a coral reef which is submerged during high tide. Sagay Beach and the Sto Niño Spring in Catarma are other attractions. In October, Mambajao celebrates the harvest of its lanzones fruit with a Lanzones Festival characterized by street dancing, pageants and sports activities.

Places to stay: Ardent Hot Spring Resort, Camiguin Beach Club and Camiguin Island Resort. Restaurants on the island include J&A Fishpan, Lab-As Restaurant, Paradiso Bar and Restaurant.

Central Mindanao

The two Lanao provinces (Norte and Sur) and the old empire of Cotabato, which has been carved up into four provinces (Maguindanao, Sultan Kudarat, North Cotabato and South Cotabato), occupy central and southwestern Mindanao. In this vast region, tribal, Islamic and Christian cultures and traditions converge, making it a fascinating area to visit. Like other parts of the Philippines, it boasts serene lakes, rivers and waterfalls, caves and mountains, distinctive handicrafts, colourful festivals, music and dances.

LANAO DEL NORTE
Its location along the northwestern coast of Mindanao (Iligan Bay is on the north, Panguil Bay on the west) makes Lanao del Norte one of the gateways to Mindanao. Because of its proximity to the Central Visayan islands, the province was an ideal migration destination for Cebuano-speaking people. Most of its present-day inhabitants are Cebuano-speaking Christians. Maranao is the second dialect spoken in the province.

ILIGAN CITY
Iligan is the province's industrial city. The 98-metre (320-foot) high Maria Cristina Falls, a major source of hydroelectric power in Mindanao, is the most famous of the province's more than 20 waterfalls. Mimbalut Falls, Tinago Falls, Dodiongan Falls are all less than 15 kilometres (nine miles) from Iligan City. Farther away is Limunsudan Falls, claimed to be the country's highest, falling a total of 265 metres (870 feet) in two tiers. This is in Barangay Rongongon, close to the eastern boundary of the province with Bukidnon and Lanao del Sur.

LANAO DEL SUR
Lanao del Sur is the centre of Islam in the south. For those interested in Muslim culture, a visit to Marawi City and the interior towns of Lanao del Sur and

Maguindanao affords a glimpse of their lifestyle. The Mindanao State University, the King Faisal Centre for Arabic Studies and the Aga Khan Museum are repositories of Muslim culture.

MARAWI CITY

Marawi City is a showcase of Maranao culture. At least 95 per cent of the inhabitants are Maranao or 'People of the Lake'. The buildings, musical instruments, personal ornaments and household implements of the Maranaos show a distinctive carving design and motifs known as *okir*. The finest examples of Maranao architecture are found in Marawi City and the municipalities of Taraka, Ramain, Molundo, Maciu, Bacolod-Calawi, Tugaya, Bayang and Ganassi. In these places, one finds the traditional *torogan*—the ancestral house of a *datu* or a sultan which serves not only as a royal residence but also as a venue for important ceremonies in the community such as weddings, funerals, religious gatherings and community meetings. The *torogan* is a symbol of rank, status and power. The front part of the house has protruding beams (*panolong*) which flare upward. The beams are elaborately carved with fern-like (*pako rabong*) or serpent (*naga*) motifs. The panelings and posts also are beautifully decorated with *okir* designs.

Also of architectural interest are the mosques or *masjids*, usually built by the lake, and patterned after western Asian designs. There is a niche in the wall which points to the direction of Mecca. The stairs leading to the pulpits are also made of *okir*-carved wood. The three-tiered mosque in Taraka is laid out as proscribed in Islamic prayer. Other interesting structures are the *mala-a-walai* or large Marano houses decorated with *okir* designs, the *lamin*—a tower-like structure which serves as a hideaway for a royal princess, old bridges and old forts.

Of the natural attractions, there is Lake Lanao in Marawi City. It is one of the major tropical lakes in Southeast Asia, the second largest lake in the Philippines and the deepest (maximum depth is 112 metres/367 feet).

Southwestern Mindanao

The old Cotabato Empire was the stronghold of Islam. Sharif Kabunsuwan from Johore introduced Islam here and when he married the daughter of a sultan, he set up the Maguindanao Sultanate whose influence extended from the Zamboanga peninsula in the west to Sarangani Bay and Davao in the east. The province of Sultan Kudarat is named after Mindanao's greatest ruler in the 17th century who united Mindanao and Sulu in resisting Hispanization. Maguindanao province is named after the Maguindanao people who inhabit the place. Cotabato City is in Maguindanao. It is Region XII's administrative centre. Cotabato and Sultan Kudarat are part of the rice granary of the Philippines. Kidapawan, the capital of North Cotabato, now simply known as Cotabato, is the starting point for the ascent to Mt Apo. It is two hours (107 kilometres/66 miles) from Davao City. The Flortam Hot Springs in Makilala is visited especially by the elderly with arthritis and rheumatism, hence it is refered to as the 'Fountain of Youth'. Also in Makilala is Le Reve Swimming Resort, a popular getaway place. The rare Philippine crocodile may still be found in the vicinity of Midsayap. In Pikit there is an old Spanish fort.

Southeastern Mindanao

This part of Mindanao, composed of the provinces of Davao (Norte, Sur, Oriental and Compostela Valley), South Cotabato, Sarangani and the cities of Davao and General Santos, is Region XI.

SOUTH COTABATO

South Cotabato (capital: Koronadal) is known for Lake Sebu, a 365-hectare (900-acre) lake in the mountains. Giant *tilapia* are cultured here in fish pens. Market day on Saturdays is ablaze with colour as the T'boli men and women in their traditional costumes come to buy and sell. There is a T'boli festival in March and the Helobung festival at Lake Sebu in November. Another lake in South Cotabato is Lake Maugham which abounds in flora and fauna, including a rare species of butterfly. General Santos is known as Mindanao's Tuna City. General Santos now boasts a fishing port complex with state-of-the-art facilities at Makar Wharf. The opening of the port is part of a five-year assistance programme for South Cotabato, Sarangani province and General Santos City which includes the development of roads, airport, sea port and telecommunications. The city also has white sand beaches. General Santos is accessible by air, sea, and land from Manila and other parts of the Visayas and Mindanao.

Places to stay in General Santos City: Anchor Hotel, East Asia Royale Hotel and Phela Grande Hotel.

Sarangani (capital: Alabel) offers a vista of mountain ranges and flat fertile plains. The surrounding seas teem with marine life.

COTABATO

Cotabato, occupying Mindanao's southwest region, was the biggest province in the whole country before it was carved up into four parts. Today it is made up of Maguindanao, Sultan Kudarat, North Cotabato and South Cotabato. The second

longest river in the country, the Rio Grande de Mindanao, also known as the Mindanao River and its tributary the Pulangi, is in Cotabato. Cotabato was the stronghold
of Islam. Sharif Kabungsuwan from Johore introduced Islam here and, when he
married the daughter of a sultan, he set up the Maguindanao Sultanate whose influence extended from the Zamboanga peninsula in the west to Sarangani Bay and
Davao in the east. The province of Sultan Kudarat is named after Mindanao's greatest ruler in the 17th century who united Mindanao and Sulu in resisting Hispanici-
zation. Maguindanao province is named after the Maguindanao people who inhabit
the place. Cotabato City is in Maguindanao. Kidapawan, the provincial capital of
North Cotabato, two hours (107 kilometres/66 miles) from Davao City, is the starting point for the ascent to Mt Apo. The main attraction in South Cotabato is Lake
Sebu. Market Day on Saturdays is a blaze of colour as T'boli men and women in
traditional costume come to buy and sell. There is a T'boli festival in March and a
festival at Lake Sebu in November.

Davao

Davao is a vast region dominating Mindanao's southeast. Although Spanish missionaries established churches along the Davao Gulf area—Caraga in 1591, Cateel in
1597 and Banganga—the region remained under the jurisdiction of the Sultanate of
Maguindanao until it was ceded by the Sultan to Spain in 1844. Davao was one big
province until 1967 when it was divided into three provinces, namely: Davao del
Norte with Tagum as its capital, Davao del Sur (capital: Digos), Davao Oriental
(capital: Mati) and the sprawling city of Davao. Davao del Norte was divided into
two separate provinces in 1998 and Tagum was made a city. The new province is
Compostela Valley or Comval, with Nabunturan as its capital. Tagum remains the
capital of Davao del Norte. Various cultural minorities inhabit the hinterlands of this
region. The Mandayas, Mansakas, Lamlingans, Dibabaons and Atas, Talaingods,
Talaandigs are found in Davao del Norte and Comval provinces; the Mangguangans
and other Mandayas in Davao Oriental; Manobos, Kalagans, Tagakaolos, and B'laans
on Davao Gulf's western shores, and Bagobos on the central plains. Muslims, Chinese descendants of early migrants and Christian settlers from the Visayas and elsewhere, add to the ethnic mix. The Japanese started arriving in the early 1900s. They
established abaca plantations around Davao Gulf as well as other industries which
spurred the region's economic development.

    Bananas, corn, rice, abaca, ramie, coconuts for copra, and coffee are grown in
the fertile plains. Davao also grows the foul-smelling durian, regarded by aficionados

as the 'fruit of the gods'. This is sold in the fruit markets or is made into candies and preserves. Davao province has huge banana plantations which cater for the export market. The manufacture of rattan furniture for export and mining are other income-earners. Small-scale miners operate in the seven gold mines in the province which has rich deposits of metallic and nonmetallic mineral especially gold, silver, copper, silica and guano. Davao del Sur is dominated on the north by Mt Apo. San Miguel Corporation inaugurated in 1995 its brewery in Barangay Darong, Sta Cruz. In the southeast corner of Mindanao is Davao Oriental. Mati was the site of the former Menzi Plantation. The Menzi Mansion which stands in the middle of the old plantation overlooking Mayo Bay has been converted by the Provincial Tourism Office into a hotel. Cape San Agustin is the southeasternmost tip of the Philippines.

Pristine beaches, waterfalls, Mt Apo National Park, wildlife, orchid gardens and fruit orchards, golf, diving, trekking, holiday resorts, festivals are among the attractions for the visitor.

DAVAO CITY

Davao City sprawls across an area covering 2,440 square kilometres (942 square miles). It is one of the biggest cities in the world in land size. Within its borders are plantations, orchards and orchid farms, wildlife sanctuaries, an isolated forest which is the habitat of rare plant and animal species. Progressive and forward-looking, Davao is the third-ranking city in the Philippines, next to Metro Manila and Cebu. New hotels, low- and medium-cost housing units and residential subdivisions are mushrooming in various parts of the city. Not to be left behind, Davao also boasts a huge commercial complex—the Victoria Plaza—with an ice skating rink, six cinemas, fast food centre, various shops, and a bank; the 2,000 seat Central Bank Convention Hall; a Duty Free shop, a casino, and championship golf courses. There are agri-industrial estates and ongoing infrastructure projects. Davao is attracting a growing number of investors eager to tap into its potential, particularly in agribusiness and tourism. Many companies in Metro Manila are setting up factories in Davao.

■ GARDENS, FARMS AND ORCHARDS

Davao is the Garden City of the Philippines. Orchids, anthuriums, and roses grow in abundance here. Different varieties of ornamental plants are cultivated by cooperatives to meet the demands of landscapers and the cutflower industry. Orchids, especially, thrive here. The *waling-waling* (*Vanda Sanderiana*) is the pride of Davao, named after Frederick Sander who discovered it on the foothills of Mt Apo. Today, the *waling-waling* and hybrids are propagated in the many orchid farms scattered around the city. About ten kilometres (six miles) from the city centre in Greenhills,

Catalunan Pequeño is the Yuhico farm. Five hectares (12 acres) of rolling terrain are planted to various types of orchids: *vandas*, *dendrobiums*, *cattleyas*, *arandas*, *kagawaras*. The farm has produced an award-winning *waling-waling*. The Puentespina Orchid Garden along J P Cabaguio Avenue and Derling Worldwide Orchid Corporation in Dumoy are also well-known. A nominal fee is charged for entrance to the orchid gardens. Aside from orchids, Davao is also well-known for its exotic fruits—mangosteen, rambutan, *marang*, *lanzones*, pomelo and durian—sold in such fruit markets as the Madrazo Fruit Centre (Bangoy St), Claveria Fruit Centre (C M Recto St) and Anda Rizal Fruit Centre. They are plentiful and cheap when in season from August to December. During this time the fruit farms are heady with the scent of ripe fruit.

At Mintal, some 14 kilometres (nine miles) from the city, is the Bago Oshiro Experimental Station, an abaca plantation where ornamental plants are cultivated and Philippine fruits and flowers are cross-bred. Not too far from downtown Davao (15 minutes by car) in Green Valley, Ma-a is a ten-hectare pomelo, rambutan and

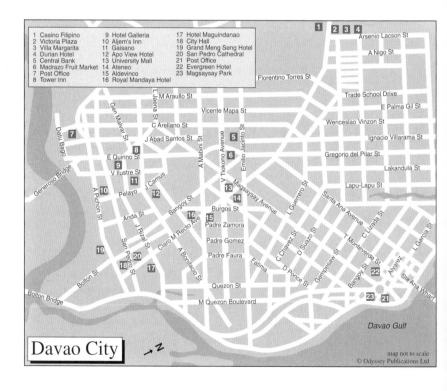

1 Casino Filipino
2 Victoria Plaza
3 Villa Margarita
4 Durian Hotel
5 Central Bank
6 Madrazo Fruit Market
7 Post Office
8 Tower Inn
9 Hotel Galleria
10 Aljem's Inn
11 Gaisano
12 Apo View Hotel
13 University Mall
14 Ateneo
15 Aldevinco
16 Royal Mandaya Hotel
17 Hotel Maguindanao
18 City Hall
19 Grand Meng Seng Hotel
20 San Pedro Cathedral
21 Post Office
22 Evergreen Hotel
23 Magsaysay Park

Davao City

map not to scale
© Odyssey Publications Ltd

sweet tamarind orchard. This is the Gap Farming Resort, with a swimming pool, a cave, cottages, a chapel dedicated to the Santo Niño and our Mother of Perpetual Help. Eighteen kilometres (11 miles) south of Davao City in Marapangi, Toril District, is the Nenita Stock Farm, or Pork's Park. It has a Muslim-designed resthouse overlooking ramie and sorghum plantations, affording a panoramic view of the city.

A good time to visit Davao is in August when the city celebrates its Kadayawan sa Dabaw, a Thanksgiving festival. Then the orchids are in full bloom and exotic fruit are in season. Contests are held among orchid-growers to select the best *waling-waling* hybrids. The 1995 festival featured for the first time a parade of flowers, fruits and vegetables as well as a floricultural convention. There are horsefights, street dancing, art exhibitions and agri-industrial fairs. The Festival is also an occasion for the gathering of tribes dressed in their traditional costumes. A better understanding of the ethnic diversity of Mindanao can be gleaned from the displays of tribal arte-facts, ethnic costumes and dioramas at the Davao Museum in Lanang.

Of interest to nature conservationists is the ongoing conservation programme at Malagos, Calinan, to save the endangered Philippine Eagle (*Pithecophaga jefferyi*).

The rare, endangered Philippine Eagle, second largest in the world, is now being bred in captivity near Mt Apo, Davao

Madder Music, Stronger Wine

About nightfall, as we were strolling through the town, we were attracted by the sounds of music in an adjoining street. We altered our course accordingly, and on arrival at a large thatched house, perceived through the open windows that it was filled with musicians and dancers. We were immediately observed, and the owner of the house, in the most courteous manner, and in tolerable English, requested us to enter, which request we immediately complied with. We imagined that it was a ball, perhaps a wedding; but what was our surprise on entering to see a table in the middle of the room, on which was placed a dead child! It was neatly dressed, and ornamented with flowers, looking more like a wax doll than a corpse. The ball, we were informed, was given in honour of its funeral. The dancing had not yet commenced, so we were in excellent time. The master of the house was extremely polite, and requested that we would consider ourselves at home. We took his advice, and immediately separated, and paid our addresses to the ladies which most interested us by their appearance. A great many of them were exceedingly pretty, and they were dressed enchantingly. Their hair was drawn back, and collected in a knot behind, their bosoms covered by a light muslin jacket with short sleeves. A petticoat of many colours was sufficiently short to disclose their naked feet, on which was a slipper of velvet, embroidered with gold or silver lace. Two or three great gold ornaments completed their costume. Add to this their sparkling eyes, regular features, and an air of naiveté—inseparable from Spanish girls—and you have some idea of the witchery of the belles of Samboanga.

We were very soon on excellent terms, and the table with the dead child being removed to a corner, the father and mother of the deceased opened the ball with a slow waltz. This being concluded, we selected our partners, and a livelier air being struck up, off we all went at a splendid pace. The women waltzed well. The music was excellent. In the first round all the ladies lost their slippers, which were without heels; and in the second the pace became fearful, and the old house shook under the active bounds and springs of some twenty or thirty couples. Spanish quadrilles succeeded the waltz, and then we had the country dance. This latter is complicated, but very pretty, and, with the assistance of our partners, in a short time we were quite au fait to its mysteries.

The music, which consisted of violins and guitars, bore up indefatigably. About twelve o'clock we ceased dancing, and preparations were made for supper. This was laid on the floor, clean grass mats serving as table cloths. The contents of the dishes were of the most novel description, and rice was the only article which I could recognize as unmixed. The repast spread, the host requested us to place ourselves. I followed my pretty partner's example, and came to an anchor on the floor alongside of her. I was most assiduous in helping her to whatever she pointed out; and, as nearly as I can recollect, the plate contained a curious medley of rice, prawns, fowls' legs, apples, besides other articles unknown, at least to me. I had observed a total want of knives, forks, and spoons, but this was explained when I saw that all ate with their fingers. Seeing no objection to this primitive plan, I was about getting a plate for myself, when I was informed by my partner, in the most insinuating way, that I was to consider her plate as my own. I fully appreciated the compliment, and at once commenced, assisting her to demolish the pile that I had collected, as I thought, for her use alone. On looking round I found that we were not singular, and that every couple were, like us, dipping into one dish. Never was there a more merry and delightful supper. As soon as it was over, which was not very soon, for I could have gone on eating a long while for the very pleasure of meeting the pretty little fingers in the plate, we rose, the mats and dishes were cleared away, and we resumed the dancing, and it was at a late hour that we made our buenas noches to the fair girls of Samboanga.

Frank S Marryat, Borneo and the Archipelago, 1843

Here, at the foothills of Mt Apo, some 32 kilometres (20 miles) from the city centre is the Philippine Eagle Nature and Research Centre, managed by the Philippine Eagle Foundation Inc. After 14 years of experimentation, the breakthrough came when two eagles were bred and hatched in captivity. Visitors are shown a film on the captive breeding programme and field operations and get to see the eagles. There are 19 now in captivity. The Centre is located in an isolated forest. Within the 235-hectare (580-acre) area are 200-year-old trees, a natural stream, wild palms and a diversity of plant life. There is also a mini zoo and aviary. Several birds confiscated from poachers or donated are now in residence at the Centre. These include the serpent eagle, grey-headed fish eagle, white-breasted sea eagle, and Philippine hawk eagle. There is an entrance fee.

Just five kilometres (three miles) from the Eagle Centre is the Malagos Garden Resort. Here in 18 hectares (45 acres) of cultivated gardens and wilderness grow hundreds of orchids of different varieties and other exotic flowers and plants. A butterfly sanctuary is another attraction. The place can be visited as a day trip or visitors can stay overnight. There are cottages with air-conditioned rooms, hot and cold water, TV and refrigerator. Activities include swimming (there's a swimming pool), mountain biking, horseback riding and fishing. The place can be reached by car or public bus. The bus terminal is at CM Recto to the right of Aldevinco in Davao City.

■ **HOTELS AND RESORTS**

Davao City has more than 2,000 hotel rooms ranging from modest inns and pension houses to first class. The city's premier resort hotel is the 219-room Insular Century Hotel Davao, winner of the 1996 Kalakbay Award for First Class Hotel of the Year. Set in landscaped tropical gardens and coconut groves right on the Gulf of Davao, it's just minutes away from the airport and next door to Lanang Country Club and Golf Course. The hotel, redecorated and refurbished, has a swimming pool, tennis court, pitch and putt golf greens and a jetty to the offshore islands. In the heart of the city, the best known hotel is the family-owned Apo View, expanded and redecorated. A new ballroom was added in 1995. With the completion of the annexe, the hotel now has 205 rooms, with two swimming pools, a music lounge and one of the most popular discos in town. Standard city hotels accredited by the Department of Tourism are Villa Margarita, recipient of the 1997 Hotel of the Year in the annual Kalakbay Awards of the DOT, the Maguindanao and Evergreen hotels (without swimming pools), Ramona Plaza and Tierra Verde. Among the inns are Galleria Inn, Tower Inn, The Manor Inn and Aljem's Inn. On the outskirts of the city, some ten to 15 minutes from the city centre are Marina Azul Resort Hotel in Matina overlooking Samal Island, and the Villa Victoria Beach Resort in Bago Aplaya which has convention

(preceding pages) Houses on stilts, Tawi-Tawi

halls and cottages by the sea, as well as pools and playgrounds. The first-class Royal Mandaya Hotel in Davao City started a multi-million-peso expansion which was expected to be completed at the end of 1998. New hotels are also planned; among these is the Marco Polo Davao.

Davao has several restaurants catering to a range of palates. New restaurants include Fiesta Dabaw, Kanaway sa Magsaysay, Karenderia, Calzada and Patio Valencia. There's also Bistro Rosario (steak and seafood), Harana (Filipino), Kristin's, Tsuru (Japanese), Mongolian Garden, Majestic (Chinese), Zugba at Apo View Hotel (seafood), the fast-food court at Victoria Plaza featuring Korean, Japanese, Chinese, European, American and Filipino food; Annie's Grill, Luz Kinilaw Place (seafood) at Santa Ana wharf. These are some of the places visitors can go to, aside from the food and beverage outlets of the hotels.

■ SHOPPING

Check out the Victoria Plaza which houses many shops. The new Aldevinco shopping centre is a good source for handicrafts, brassware, shells, handwoven ethnic cloth, bags and accessories featuring *t'nalak* and *dagmay* weaves, wooden crafts, dusters, robes, blouses, shirts, scarves and bags made of batik. Nieva's Arts and Crafts, located along the road to the airport, sells Philippine items. Hand-painted ceramics, woodcraft and fashion accessories and kitchenware are found in the shop's exclusive *Lumad* (native of) range. If you are looking for something unique to buy from Davao, browse at the Gilded Expressions boutique in the Apo View Hotel arcade. The boutique features exquisite pieces of jewellery and sculpture in 24K gold, silver and other alloys, all individually designed by Ann Tiukinhoy Pamintuan. This talented young woman has found a permanent way of preserving the beauty of nature found in the lush environment of Mindanao by selecting flowers, leaves, ferns and roots in their perfect state and gilding them into permanent expressions of beauty and form. She likes working with bougainvilleae, fern and orchid root for their shapes and textures. Her products are marketed under the name AnnTiu. Ann has exhibited her works in trade fairs and exhibitions in Manila, Brunei and Washington, DC. The United States, France, Japan and Spain are her export markets.

SAMAL ISLANDS

The Samal Islands is a group of nine islands bounded by the Gulf of Davao and within easy reach by motorized outrigger boats from the Davao Insular jetty or the Santa Ana wharf. The biggest island—Samal—and smaller Talikud Island and Malipano Islet with their string of resorts are popular for day excursions as well as weekend stays. Mountainous, with isolated hills and scattered lowlands, Samal island has three municipalities: Babak, Peñaplata and Kaputian. Villagers make their living from growing mangoes and orchids to meet the demand for cut flowers. Mount Puting Bato (White Rock) is the island's highest peak (410 metres/1,346 feet high) and is used by mountaineering clubs to initiate first-time climbers before they scale Mount Apo. The trek to the summit from the jump-off point at Peñaplata takes six hours. Waterfalls and caves also are found on the island, making it a good destination for adventure tours. Paradise Island, Coral Reef, Costa Marina, Palm Hill and Samal Beach Park resorts are in Babak, the municipality nearest Davao City. These can accommodate overnight guests in native-style cottages. Paradise Island and Samal Beach Park resorts have air-conditioned rooms. The Samal Beach Club in Peñaplata has thatched cottages which are used for local conferences.

SMALL PEARL FARM RESORT

Some 40 to 45 minutes by boat from the city is the upscale Samal Pearl Farm Resort, one of the top holiday resorts in the country. It started operations in 1992 on the site of the former Aguinaldo Pearl Farm. The whole resort has been designed so that the natural beauty of the area was not only preserved but enhanced. Nineteen hous-

es patterned after the houses of seafaring Samals, stand on stilts over the water. These serve as the reception area, Front Desk, Executive offices and guestrooms. The longhouse on the hilltop with verandas on all sides has conference rooms, a games room and piano bar, and 44 guest rooms capable of accommodating 80 persons; these will be expanded to 100 rooms. The resort has six sea-front, two-storey deluxe suites with glassed-in veranda and furnished with king-sized beds; a dining pavilion, hexagonal bar accessible from the sea, and a boutique. The Mandaya Weaving Centre has relocated to the

Tribal women in Bukidnon, Northern Mindanao

The head man of a Muslim village on the Zamboanga peninsula, Mindanao

Pearl Farm Resort. Two tribeswomen demonstrate ancient weaving techniques on looms, using abaca fibre which has been dyed with tree bark and roots as well as river mud to produce the ethnic colours of black, red or maroon and yellow. The finished products, made into wall hangings, are for sale.

There are two tennis courts for day and night play and a swimming pool overlooking the sea. For guests keen on water sports, there's windsurfing, jet skiing, sailing, diving. Aqua Ventures provides diving instructors and divemasters. Courses for open water diving, advance, up to divemaster level are available. Beginning divers are brought to Talikud Island while advance divers are brought to Marissa Reef. Diving here is year-round.

Across the waters on the small island of Malipano, Pearl Farm resort has seven private luxury villas each with its own butler. The management plans to construct a swimming pool on this island.

Talikud Island resorts include the Isla Reta, Dayang Beach, Babu Santa and Isla Cristina.

Four thousand hectares on (9,880 acres) Kaputian and 2,000 hectares on Talikud Island are to be developed by private enterprise with the help of the government into resort complexes. The plan calls for the construction of bungalows, condominiums, a hotel, villas and pension houses totalling 3,835 rooms as well as shopping malls and boutiques, speciality markets, a hospital and clinic, a church, plus facilities for sports and recreation such as a swimming pool, tennis courts, basketball and volleyball courts, squash courts, jogging and hiking trails, and a 36-hole golf course.

■ GETTING THERE

Davao is accessible by air, sea and land. Davao City is an international gateway to Southern Philippines with domestic and international flights landing at the Davao International Airport. Chartered light planes and helicopters also touch down at the Davao Airport.

Passenger ships call in regularly at the port of Davao which services not only local but foreign vessels. It takes about three days and two nights for the sea voyage from Manila to Davao.

Overland, Philtranco buses travel the Manila-Davao route via the Pan-Philippine Highway with ferry connections between Surigao (Mindanao) and Leyte/Samar (Visayas) and Sorsogon (Luzon). The journey takes 48 hours. Several bus companies (Bachelor Express Line, Surigao Bus Co, Mindanao Transport Co, Ceres Line, Yellow Bus Line) connect Davao City to other provinces and cities in Southern Mindanao. Hire cars are also available. Avis is based at the Davao Insular, Marconi at the Apo View.

As part of the East ASEAN growth polygon, the Philippines has expanded its air and sea linkages. The Mindanao Economic Development Council Secretariat reported increases in passenger traffic within the Brunei Darussalam, Indonesia, Malaysia, Philippines-East ASEAN growth area. Bouraq Airlines now services the Davao-Manado (Indonesia) route twice a week while SilkAir operates the Davao-Singapore route. The M/V Tilongkabila and M/V Ellyana are passenger ships servicing the region. To promote travel within the BIMP-EAGA and Singapore, airline and shipping companies now offer great value fares and promotional packages. Sampaguita Shipping and Aleson Shipping are among those offering reduced fares.

Caraga

The country's 13th administrative region, popularly known as Caraga, is located in Northeastern Mindanao. It is composed of the provinces of Surigao del Norte (capital: Surigao City), Surigao del Sur (Tandag), Agusan del Norte (Butuan City), Agusan del Sur (Prosperidad) and several offshore islands, among them the holiday island of Siargao, known as the Surfing Capital of the Philippines. The region is rich in natural attractions, making it an ideal destination for eco-tourism. The Agusan Wildlife Sanctuary and Siargao Wildlife Sanctuary are among the ten priority sites identified by the Department of Environment and Natural Resources (DENR) as protected areas covered by the NIPAS Act which works for the conservation of wildlife resources. Bird-watching, river safaris, boating, snorkelling, and surfing are favoured activities in the region. Rich deposits of nickel and cobalt, forest reserves and the best rattan in the country are found in this region.

SURIGAO (NORTE AND SUR)
Surigao del Norte on the northeastern tip of the mainland, is the entry point to Mindanao, for those travelling overland from Luzon and the Visayas through Samar and Leyte. A ferry crossing from Maasin in Southern Leyte brings you to Surigao. The provincial capital and trade centre is Surigao City, already a thriving settlement when the Spaniards arrived. The city has a bustling waterfront market. Missionaries visited Surigao in 1597 but without much success. Spanish authority was established only in 1609. Early settlements were in Tandag and Bislig which became a large mission centre.

SIARGAO AND BUCAS GRANDE
Off Surigao, served by *bancas* and launches, are several islets and islands facing the Pacific Ocean, with powdery beaches, crystal-clear waters and abundant marine life.

The larger islands are Dinagat and Siargao, the latter known for its big waves and good surf. General Luna is the main destination of travellers to Siargao. The First International Surfing Cup was held here in 1996. Surfing season is between July and November, when the waves are high. For non-surfers, the island invites exploration. There are caves with magnificent rock formations, mountain lakes and large areas of mangroves. The wildlife sanctuary on the island is a protected site. The resorts on Siargao are the Blue Room, Cloud Nine and Pansukian. The fastest way to get there is to fly to Cebu, stay overnight and catch the 7 am Mindanao Express flight (every Tuesday, Thursday and Saturday) to Surigao. There are regular and charter boats from Surigao to Dapa on the island with jeepney transfers to those going on to General Luna. Another island worth visiting is Bucas Grande. Its main attraction is the Sohoton Cave, accessible by *bancas* only at low tide. It is approached through a series of rocky islets. You glide through a dark chamber and emerge into an enchanting, islet-strewn lagoon ringed by hills clad in thick foliage. Kayaking and snorkelling are some of the activities here.

Other places of interest in Surigao are Cagwait Beach Resort and Pig-ot Hideaway Resort, a cluster of islets interlinked by wooden bridges where one can peer into the clear waters to see the aquatic life among the coral reefs. Some 43 kilometres (27 miles) south of Surigao City is Lake Mainit. It is astride the boundary between Surigao del Norte and Agusan del Norte, surrounded by mountains and lush vegetation. Herons and exotic fowl abound in the lakeshore. One can go fishing and boating here.

Surigao del Sur is heavily forested with a coastline indented by bays—Lianga Bay, Lanuza Bay, Bislig Bay. The province is a major source of hardwood and forest by-products. Bislig was an important timber port in the heyday of the logging industry and the site of a major pulp and paper and industrial wood complex. Tandag, the provincial capital, was the site of an old Spanish fort.

AGUSAN (NORTE AND SUR)

The Agusan provinces are located in the valley where the Agusan River flows from the highlands of Davao del Norte down to Butuan Bay. Both provinces are mountainous along the eastern and western boundaries, with the Diwata Mountains separating Agusan from Surigao del Sur. Agusan provinces were once heavily forested, but because of logging, extensive areas have been deforested. The soil is generally fertile. Copper and manganese are mined in the interior. Agusan is settled by migrants from the Visayas and other places. The indigenous cultural communities living here are the Mamanwa, Higaonon and Manobo. The Manobos have been called the 'lords of the marsh'. They live in clusters of wood and bamboo houses built on rafts of floating logs. They move freely from one lake to the other, over silt and mud, and through stretches of floating water hyacinths.

Central Agusan Valley is a region of marshes and lakes but gives way to uplands in the south, near the border with Davao del Norte. During the rainy season, several hundred square kilometres become swamp land. The Agusan Marsh is the largest wetland in the Philippines, covering an area of more than 19,000 hectares (47,000 acres). Forty-nine per cent is swamp forest; the rest lothic and riverine ecosystem. The marshlands are a sanctuary of purple herons, storks, sea eagles, wild ducks and many endangered bird species. This is protected wildlife area. Bird-watching is best here from November to January.

The province's history is closely connected with the river, for a long time the only means of access to the interior. Foreign merchants were trading with the riverine settlements when the Spaniards arrived. It is not known whether Magellan touched down in Agusan. There is controversy over whether the first Mass in the Philippines was celebrated in Masao, at the mouth of the Agusan River, or Limasawa in Southern Leyte. At any rate, a marker in the town of Magallanes commemorates the event.

BUTUAN CITY

Sprawling over a flat marshy area on both sides of the Agusan River is the city of Butuan, the provincial capital, a sea and river port, an important market centre in the region, and hub of transportation. It is linked by road to Surigao City, Prosperidad, the capital of Agusan del Sur, and Davao City. It was in the marshy terrain near Butuan City that the remains of three *balanghais*, the boats used by early migrants for travel throughout Southeast Asia, were unearthed. Subsequent diggings uncovered several more *balanghais*. Carbon-dating of the wood identified one boat as 4th century and another as 13th century. Fifteenth-century wooden coffins were also found in the vicinity, along with tradeware and skulls. The unique find was the result of excavations initially made to unearth more pottery in the area, after the discovery in 1976 of Chinese ceramic ware dating back to the Tang and succeeding dynasties. The National Museum in Manila now displays some of the *balanghais*.

The history and culture of the province can be appreciated by visiting the Regional Museum in Doongan. Displayed in the museum's Archaeological Hall are specimens of stonecraft, metalcraft, pottery, gold work, burial coffins and other objects from archaeological excavations, proving Butuan's prehistoric existence. The Ethnological Hall on the other hand exhibits the rich cultural heritage of the city.

Butuan celebrates the Santacruzan and Balanghai festivals in May. In July the Kahimonan Festival takes place, and a fluvial procession in honour of Santa Ana is held on the Agusan River.

Almont Hotel (San Jose St), Balanghai Hotel in Doongan, Butuan Royal Plaza Hotel (Calo) and Gardenville Hotel (Km 3, Baan) are Butuan City's standard hotels.

PROSPERIDAD

Located about 56 kilometres (35 miles) south of Butuan City is Prosperidad, capital of Agusan del Sur. It is a small agricultural town in an area of rolling mountains. Binaba Falls, said to be connected with an underground stream, and San Lorenzo Falls, are in the vicinity. Prosperidad celebrates its town fiesta on 29 September.

Many cultural communities live in Agusan del Sur. Large concentrations of them are found in the hills and riverbanks of Bayugan, Salug, Esperanza, San Luis, and Talacogon. The Higaonon live in tree houses in the forested foothills. Oratory is an artform among these people, who are known to conduct arguments in metred verse. The province is traversed by a single highway running east of the river, connecting Butuan City to Davao City. Buses run regularly between Davao City and Butuan City and other parts of the region.

Fiestas

Fiestas are the bright flecks in the fabric of Philippine life. They are religious and folk celebrations rolled into one and provide the perfect occasion for feasting, fellowship and family get-togethers. They are the glue that hold together far-flung members of the family who come home for reunions on just such occasions. Fiestas reflect the Philippines' diverse cultural heritage and provide marvellous opportunities for visitors to experience Filipino warmth, hospitality and *joie de vivre*.

Among the noteworthy festivals that attract large numbers of local and foreign visitors are the Ati-Atihan in Aklan, Sinulog in Cebu and Dinagyang in Iloilo in January; the Holy Week rites around March or April; the Moriones Festival in Marinduque at Easter; the May-time Flores de Mayo and Santacruzan in various parts of the country; the Carabao and Harvest Festivals in Bulacan and Quezon provinces, also in May; the fluvial festivals in Bulacan, Pampanga and Camarines Sur between June and September; the moveable series of Turumba rites in Pakil, Laguna; the Masskara Festival of Bacolod City, Negros Occidental and the Zamboanga Hermosa Festival on Zamboanga City in October; the big Cañao Festivals of the mountain provinces; Paskuhan—Christmas festivities which extend from mid-December until 6 January throughout the country; and the Giant Lantern Festival in San Fernando, Pampanga in December.

Some present-day festivals began as pagan or animist rites of thanksgiving, fertility or prayers for rain. But with the introduction of Christianity by the Spanish friars, elements of Christian belief and ceremony were added. Eventually such secular features as beauty pageants, cockfights, cultural presentations and exhibitions turned festivals into a combination of rambunctious hilarity, pageantry that sometimes borders on the bizarre, and religious piety.

Filipino-Chinese celebrate the Lunar New Year and Mid-Autumn Festivals while Filipino Muslims mark the New Year, Ramadan, Hari Raya Puasa, and Hari Raya Hadji. Cultural minorities in the mountain provinces hold cañaos—great tribal gatherings and feasts.

Anyone contemplating attending any of the festivals should plan well ahead of time and book airline or boat tickets early and secure accommodation. All available hotel rooms, pensions and inns are booked sometimes months before a major festival. Some festival sites have Homestay Associations whose members offer family accommodation. Again advance reservations are necessary. You can also join package tours offered by local travel agents. If you anticipate travelling immediately after a festival, make sure you have a confirmed flight or seat. Always reconfirm your flight as soon as you arrive at your destination to avoid being delayed indefinitely. Avoid having an open-dated ticket when travelling to or from popular destinations.

ATI-ATIHAN

This festival, held on the third weekend of January in the Visayan province of Aklan, principally in Kalibo and Ibajay, commemorates the purchase of the lowlands of Panay Island around the 13th century by the Bornean *datus* from the aboriginal inhabitants, the black Atis or Aetas. In exchange for the land, the *datus* gave Marikudo, the king of the Atis, a golden *salakot* (a conical-shaped hat) and his queen, a golden necklace and other trinkets. To seal the purchase, a feast was held with the *datus* blackening themselves with soot to resemble the Atis (Ati-Atihan means to make like the Atis). After the introduction of Christianity to the islands, the feast of the Holy Child Jesus, traditionally celebrated in January, was merged with the pagan festival. The week-long Mardi Gras-like celebration reaches a climax at the weekend, when the whole town dances in the streets dressed as tribespeople, their faces blackened by soot, or wearing all manner of unusual costumes. On Sunday evening, the festival concludes with a candlelit religious procession bearing the image of the Santo Niño, or Holy Child, to the church. All visitors to Kalibo are given a sooty welcome by the townspeople. This serves as an icebreaker, and before long, visitors join the shuffling crowds and are dancing to the insistent rhythm of the drums.

As this is a major festival, package tours are sold by travel agents and tour operators in Manila. Philippine Airlines schedules additional flights and accommodation is tight. To ensure a place to stay, it is recommended that you make arrangements well in advance. The Aklan Homestay Association has a list of member families which offer accommodation for visitors. Contact the Department of Tourism for this. Most visitors make a side trip to nearby Boracay Island, popular for its fine beaches, swimming and snorkelling. Ships call at Aklan from Manila so if you want to try inter-island travel, contact the shipping lines in Manila.

SINULOG

Held on the third weekend of January in Cebu City, on the Visayan island of Cebu, Sinulog honours the Santo Niño, the city's patron saint. It is said that the image of the Holy Child was Magellan's baptismal gift to Queen Juana, wife of the reigning Rajah Humabon, who was baptized as Carlos. When Miguel Lopez de Legazpi colonized Cebu 44 years later, the image was discovered to have survived a fire that swept through the city. The friars subsequently erected a church on the spot where the image was found and the Santo Niño is now enshrined in the Basilica Minore of San Agustin. "Sinulog" refers to the supplications of women holding lighted candles who wave their arms in a gesture of entreaty. A petitioner whispers his or her petition to a woman, who then lights one or several candles and prays for the plea to be granted. Colourful street parades and joyous processions are also features of the

Moriones Festival, Mogpog town, Marinduque

festival. It is Cebu's most popular and celebrated annual event and marks the emotional homecoming of the province's sons and daughters who have emigrated to distant lands.

Package tours are available and transport to Cebu City is heavily booked. It is therefore wise to make travel arrangements and hotel reservations in advance.

DINAGYANG

Dinagyang is the Ilonggo term for the revelry that accompanies the festival of the same name held in Iloilo City on the island of Panay on the fourth weekend in January. Like Sinulog and Ati-Atihan, the feast honours the Child Jesus. Prayers and offerings, a religious procession and street dancing highlight the celebration. Dance groups engage in friendly competition to pick the best-looking costumes and choreography. Those attending the Ati-Atihan in Kalibo can stay on for Dinagyang, and take the opportunity to explore the island of Panay and the historic sites around Iloilo. The province has a number of interesting old churches, and is also well known for its cuisine.

HOLY WEEK

On Good Friday, Christ's Seven Last Words are read from pulpits across the land. A funeral procession with the figure of the dead Christ inside a glass case is held in some churches. In the provinces of Bataan, Bulacan, Pampanga, Cavite and Rizal, flagellants wearing a crown of thorns walk barefoot through the streets scourging themselves. Penitents carry wooden crosses in fulfilment of vows, and some even submit to the ritual of being nailed to a cross. On Easter Sunday a dawn procession of the Risen Christ takes place outside the church. As Jesus and Mary meet beneath an especially constructed arch, a little girl dressed as an angel is lowered in a cage-like contraption to snatch the black veil from the Mother of Sorrows while a choir of children dressed as angels sings *Alleluia*. Joyous Masses are celebrated to the pealing of church bells.

As part of the Lenten observance, dramatizations of the Passion of Christ known as senaculos are presented in such communities as Malabon in Metro Manila, Cainta and Talim Island in Rizal, and other parishes in Bulacan, Pampanga and Nueva Ecija. Verses are read in the vernacular and may depict the Last Supper and Judas' betrayal of Jesus, the Crucifixion, and the meeting of the Risen Lord and His mother.

MORIONES FESTIVAL

This is a unique street pageant held during Holy Week, sometime in March or April, on the island province of Marinduque, 580 kilometres (363 miles) south of Manila. It re-enacts the drama of Longinus, the one-eyed Roman centurion whose sight is

Various styles of masks at the Ati-Atihan festival

miraculously restored when a drop of blood from Jesus' side touches his blind eye after he pierces the crucified Christ with his spear. Proclaiming the divinity of Jesus, Longinus incurs the ire of the authorities who order his arrest.

For this spectacle, the whole town becomes a stage and the townsmen players. Dressed up as Roman centurions, with vivid tunics and capes and fierce-looking, outsized painted masks carved out of a soft wood called *dapdap*, they roam the streets beginning on Holy Wednesday. On Good Friday, the drama of *Kalbaryuhan*, depicting Christ carrying the cross to Calvary, takes place. A mournful procession of onlookers and flagellants, whipping their backs raw, wends its way from the church of Boac up a hill for the crucifixion with Longinus in attendance. The climax is on Easter Sunday when the dramatic chase and beheading (*pugutan*) take place along the riverbank. Longinus gives the spectators a grand show as he flees his would-be captors. Twice he is caught and twice he escapes, until he is caught once again and beheaded. The head is presented to the authorities on a platter and the festival ends. Similar pageants on a smaller scale take place in the municipalities of Gasan and Mogpog. This is another well-attended festival, so those contemplating on going to Marinduque should plan early and make advance arrangements for travel and accommodation.

SANTACRUZAN

This Maytime procession of obscure origins is based on the search for the Holy Cross (Santa Cruz) by Queen Helena (Reina Elena) whose son, King Constantine had been converted to Christianity. The present-day Santacruzan bears little resemblance to the Cross and is actually a parade of the loveliest girls, usually daughters of prominent citizens of the city or town and village, or movie stars and a fashion show of creations by local designers. The girls participate as Reina Elena, the princesses of Faith, Hope and Charity (Fe, Esperanza and Caridad) and *sagalas* (female participants) representing biblical and mythological characters. Escorted by handsome young men, they march under floral arches in a candlelit evening procession which winds its way along the main streets to the church. The procession's route is flanked by a crowd of onlookers. A *pabitin* is held in the churchyard afterwards. The *bitin* is a trellis hung with wrapped favours and gifts. This is lowered briefly from a height, and young boys and girls jump up to grab the gifts.

MARIAN FESTIVALS

Filipinos have a special devotion to the Blessed Virgin Mary, the Mother of God. She is the patroness of many towns and cities from the north to the south. May is the

Blackened with soot, participants in the Ati-Atihan Festival don bizarre and unusual costumes

traditional month of Mary and in various parts of the country the offering of flowers by young girls dressed in white at the altar of the Blessed Mother is held. This is called the *Flores de Mayo*. While May is the traditional month honouring Mary, there are many feasts in the country held in her honour at other times of the year. In addition to the specific Marian festivals detailed here, there are towns and cities that hold special celebrations. The La Naval de Manila held in honour of Our Lady of the Rosary every October at the Santo Domingo Church in Quezon City, Metro Manila, commemorates the naval victory of a vastly outnumbered Spanish fleet over a superior Dutch fleet in the 1600s. Zamboanga City also celebrates the Feast of Our Lady of Pilar in October. Our Lady of Piat's feast in July is an occasion to draw Cagayanos to her shrine in Cagayan province. Our Lady of Peace and Good Voyage attracts pilgrims to her shrine in Antipolo, Rizal on the first of May. There are many Marian shrines throughout the country which are the object of special pilgrimage and devotion as Our Lady continues to manifest her special care over those who implore her help.

HARVEST FESTIVALS

The *carabao* (water buffalo)—the farmer's best friend—is king for the day in towns like Pulilan in Bulacan province, on 15 May. Scrubbed of its daily coat

of mud and bedecked with flowers, the *carabao* participates in a grand parade where its minder makes it kneel in front of the church to be blessed. The grey mass of garlanded *carabaos* going down on their front knees is a sight to behold.

San Isidro Labrador, the farmer's patron saint, is honoured on 15 May by exuberant harvest festivals and prayers for another bountiful harvest. The towns of Sariaya and Lucban in Quezon province are well-known for their elaborate street displays of fruit and vegetables. Known as *pahiyas*, the decorations of bananas, sugarcane, pineapples and coconuts festoon windows and doorways. Along with these are traditional, varicoloured leaf-shaped decorations called *kiping* strung together or gathered in sheaves. *Kiping* are made from rice flour and water and tinted with food colouring. The dough is moulded on cacao leaves, and then steamed until it separates from its leaf mould. It dries and hardens to a brittle transparency. The residents of the decorated houses along the processional route often give away their decorations by hanging goodies (such as sticky rice wrapped in banana or *pandan* leaves and *pinipig* or new rice similar to rice crispies) from a bamboo trellis. When the procession passes by, the bamboo is lowered and there's a scramble for the goodies as well as the decorations. It's open house in the towns the whole day and anyone is welcome to partake of the fiesta fare set on the table, a wonderful example of Filipino hospitality.

FERTILITY RITES

In the fishing town of Obando in Bulacan province, a three-day religious festival, each day honouring a different saint, is held every May. In a ritual based on ancient fertility rites, childless couples journey to Obando to dance the *pandango* in the hope of being blessed with offspring. Others go there to pray for a mate, to be cured of an ailment, or simply to pray for a good harvest. Those whose prayers have been answered also dance in thanksgiving. The first day is dedicated to San Pascual Baylon, the second to Santa Clara (also known as Clarang Pinongpino) and the third day to the Virgin of Salambao. According to legend, a fisherman found the image of the Virgin in his *salambao* (fish trap). The dancing, to the music of brass bands, takes place before the church altar.

TURUMBA

This was originally a gathering of the sick, the invalid and the dying who came from afar and danced before Our Lady of Sorrows of Turumba (Nuestra Señora de los Dolores de Turumba) in Pakil, Laguna to seek a cure. Claimed miraculous, the Image of the Virgin was found floating in the choppy waters of Laguna de Bay by fishermen. They hauled the image in their net but could not land anywhere except

Pakil. Townspeople found the image on a rock on 15 September 1788, so celebrations centre on this date. Seven novenas, known as 'lupi' are held each year in Pakil to commemorate the Virgin's seven sorrows. Prayers start on the Friday before Palm Sunday and end on Pentecost Sunday; the days for 'lupi' are movable.

The word *turumba* is likely to have come from *turo*, "to point" and *umbay*, a dirge sung by invalids. Today's *turumba* dancers hobble and crouch in the manner of invalids as they sing and chant praises to the Virgin. The bicentennial of the discovery of the image was celebrated in grand style by the town with choral and folkloric dance performances, a Sunday Mass celebrated by Ricardo Cardinal Vidal, and a tumultuous procession.

FLUVIAL PROCESSIONS

River towns celebrate the feast of St John the Baptist in June with mass baptisms and parades. The baptism is a feature of the celebration; everybody, visitor or not, is fair game for the pranksters who go around with pails of water dousing people, all in the spirit of fun. In Balayan, Batangas, a unique parade of fancily dressed roast pigs—*paradang lechon*—takes place. The roast pigs sport wigs, sunglasses, raincoats and bikinis—depending on the whim of their owner. A *lechon* "queen" (a non-porcine female) reigns over the festivities. The dousing starts after Mass and the parade, and the roast pigs are fair game too, hence the raincoats. The *lechon's* moment of glory is short-lived; it is consumed in no time at all.

Fluvial processions are staged in Pampanga, Bulacan and Camarines Sur. On the first Sunday of July, Bulakeños hold their grand *Pagoda sa Wawa* (Pagoda in the River) in which a replica of the Cross is mounted on a pagoda in a procession escorted by gaily decorated *bancas* and barges. Said to be miraculous, the Holy Cross of Wawa was found floating on the river more than 100 years ago. A novena is held prior to the procession.

The town of Apalit in Pampanga, some 55 kilometres (34.17 miles) north of Manila, holds a three-day fluvial festival in honour of their patron—St Peter, affectionately called *Apung Iro*. The life-size image is brought from the caretaker's house to the church during the festival and then to the river for the festival. Decorated boats participate in the festival while bands play music on the river.

Another grand fluvial procession is the Peñafrancia festival in honour of the Virgin of Peña de Francia. This is held every September in Naga, Camarines Sur. It is said that a secular priest of Spanish ancestry, cured of many chronic illnesses through his devotion to the Blessed Virgin, vowed to build a shrine in her honour. When he became Vicar General of the diocese of Caceres, he commissioned a local artist to carve a replica from the picture of the original Virgin in Spain. The sculptor needed blood to paint the Madonna a reddish shade, so a dog was killed. When the dead dog was thrown in the river, it sprang to life and swam back to its master. The miracle was attributed to the Virgin and devotion to her started. Other miracles were also said to have happened through her intercession. The feast starts with an afternoon procession in which the image of Our Lady is taken from her shrine in the basilica to the Naga Cathedral for the novena prayers and Masses. On the ninth day, the image is returned to the basilica via a fluvial parade. A pagoda is constructed on a barge and the image is installed inside for the trip back to the basilica, accompanied by hundreds of decorated boats while thousands of people lining the river banks wave handkerchiefs in greeting.

MASSKARA FESTIVAL
The festival celebrates man's indomitable courage in the face of economic disaster. When the bottom fell from the sugar industry in the 1980s, the sugar-growing province of Negros Occidental suffered serious economic dislocation. However, the people refused to be fazed by it and adopted a smiling papier mâché mask as their symbol. Thus began the Masskara Festival (from *mascara*, mask). The festival is held in Bacolod City on 19 October. People wear smiling masks and the city holds band contests and sports events. During the festival, handicrafts of the province are displayed and sold. The province has recovered and turned defeat into success by harnessing their skills to other money-spinning industries and cottage crafts. The Association of Negros Producers now has a showroom in Bacolod City displaying products made from paper, beads, shells, wood shavings, coconut and corn husks, ceramics and terracotta.

ALL SOUL'S DAY
On the second day of November the living honour the dead, as people flock to the cemeteries to clean the graves of departed relatives, lay flowers, light candles and make food offerings. There is a carnival air as the living bring food and drink and play music. A good place to watch this celebration is the La Loma Cemetery in the northern part of Manila. Next door is the Chinese Cemetery where the mausoleums resemble the mansions of the living. All Souls Day is the Western equivalent of the Qingming and Chung Yeung festivals when Chinese people perform the traditional grave-sweeping ceremonies in honour of their dead.

PASKUHAN (CHRISTMAS FESTIVITIES)
For the Christian Philippines, Christmas is the biggest festival of the year, celebrated by rich and poor alike with Masses and feasting. It is said that the Philippines has the

longest Christmas celebration—from the 16th of December to the 6th of January. Long before that, radio stations are already playing Christmas tunes and carols and shops are selling Christmas decor and items. Streets are festively decorated with lights; homes and buildings display coloured lights and there are contests for the Best Nativity Scene or the Best Christmas decor. The star lantern is the traditional symbol of Christmas in the Philippines. Christmas is a time for family gatherings and homecomings from members who live abroad. From 16 to 24 December, the cock's crow is the signal for the faithful to get up and attend the Misa de Gallo or Mass at Cock's Crow. Christmas Eve is a day for the family. After Midnight Mass, they partake of the *Noche Buena*, a spread of traditional Christmas fare, and open presents. The following day, godchildren flock to their godparents' homes for the time-honoured *Mano*, kissing the hand as a sign of filial respect. Christmas officially ends on 6 January. Some families still practise the tradition of giving gifts to their children on the Feast of the Three Kings.

LANTERN FESTIVAL

The most important symbol of Christmas for the Filipinos is the star-shaped lantern or *parol*, signifying the star that shone over Bethlehem. Star lanterns traditionally

The Moriones Festival in Marinduque, with its carved painted masks of softwood

hang from the windows of houses and families display Nativity scenes or Belen at home. A Giant Lantern Festival and Parade is held before Christmas at the Paskuhan (Christmas) Village in San Fernando Pampanga. In this theme park, it is Christmas every day of the year. The lanterns are masterful pieces of artistry and craftsmanship and lantern makers vie for prizes on the best lantern. The giant lanterns, some measuring as much as 40 feet in diameter, are constructed of coloured crepe paper, Japanese paper and *capiz* shells and are illuminated by as many as 1,600 bulbs. The most common shape is the five-pointed star but over the past decades, this design has evolved into geometric shapes to produce a kaleidoscope of whirling lights and vivid colours in designs featuring a rose, snowflakes, sea urchin, etc. The towns of San Jose, Dolores, Del Pilar, San Pedro, Sto Niño, Sta Lucia and San Nicolas in Pampanga enter their lanterns in a competition. The entries are a closely guarded secret. Winners are judged on colour, design, originality, craftsmanship and interplay of lights. So huge are the entries that they have to be mounted on flatbed trucks. People from all over the region and farther afield flock to the Paskuhan Village in San Fernando, Pampanga, to watch the parade and marvel at the ingenuity and creativity of the lantern-makers. Aside from the Giant Lantern Festival, the 'Pamaagsadya Quing Pascu' or Preparation for Christmas is held on the 15th of December. The people of San Fernando parade with their homemade lanterns to Paskuhan Village, attend mass, have their lanterns blessed and bring them home so that their light may shine for all. The village also re-enacts the search of Joseph and Mary for a place for their child to be born. This is called "Panunuluyan" and the folk drama is also held in other parts of the country.

Public holidays in the Philippines:

1	January	New Year's Day
	March/April	Maundy Thursday, Good Friday (moveable)
9	April	Day of Valour
1	May	Labour Day
12	June	Philippine National Day
29	August	National Heroes Day
1	November	All Saints' Day
30	November	Bonifacio Day
25	December	Christmas Day
30	December	Rizal Day

The Sporting Life

Scuba Diving

The Philippines' underwater world is one of spectacular beauty. For the scuba diver, snorkeller, underwater photographer or marine biologist, exploring what lies beneath the warm tropical waters can be full of excitement and discovery. The archipelago has 27,000 square kilometres (10,400 square miles) of coral reef which supports an incredibly rich marine ecosystem. Underwater visibility is excellent. The archipelago is reputed to have more dive sites than any other country in the world, and with more than two million square kilometres (750,000 square miles) of surrounding waters, there are plenty of pristine areas offering a wide variety of diving experiences. Many dive sites are still the preserve of local divers who may keep their existence a secret. Some others may as yet be uncharted.

The best dive areas in the country, based on their location, accessibility by public transport and the availability of accommodation, dive facilities, and services by dive boats, are around Batangas and Mindoro, Cebu, Bohol, Siquijor, Negros Oriental, Leyte, Palawan and the Sulu Sea. These areas have been identified by the Philippine Commission on Sports and Scuba Diving (PCSSD), the body that takes charge of developing and promoting scuba diving in the Philippines. The PCSSD formulates rules and regulations, safety standards and operating procedures for scuba diving and licences and regulates diving-related establishments and dive masters. They are located at DOT Bldg, T M Kalaw St, Ermita, Manila; tel 524-3735 / 525-4413.

DIVING SEASON

The time of year to visit will determine the available dive areas. The Philippines has two monsoon seasons—the southwest monsoon (*habagat*) from June to October, and the northeast monsoon (*amihan*) from November to March. Late March to June is a slack period. April and May are usually calm. Some places like Palawan and Cebu-Bohol have year-round diving.

■ **MAKING ADVANCE ARRANGEMENTS**

If you are considering a diving holiday in the Philippines, bring along your C-card and logbook. Philippine law requires these from anyone who rents equipment or hires guides. Decide beforehand what kind of diving arrangements you wish to make, shore-based or boat-based. Accessibility and refilling tanks are other major considerations. If you intend to dive in remote, exotic sites such as Apo Reef or

Tubbataha Reefs, going with a specialized dive boat is the best arrangement. The accommodation is good, the food fine, and there is unlimited air supply and experienced dive masters aboard. Shore-based arrangements range from basic and modest to deluxe. First-class dive resorts have air-conditioned bedrooms, with private shower and bath, restaurants, bars, and other recreational facilities, in addition to full scuba services. Modest resorts and dive camps may just have simple accommodation but offer complete scuba services. The best areas for shore-based diving are around Batangas, Puerto Galera, Cebu and Bohol, and Northern Palawan. Small, on-site dive shops rent all the necessary equipment and provide boats and dive masters at reasonable prices by international standards. All arrangements can be made by dive shops in Manila, Cebu, Puerto Galera or the resorts themselves. To reduce costs, individual divers can join larger groups, and share the expenses for a boat and dive master with the rest of the group. For a current list of licensed dive resorts, dive shops, dive boat operators and packagers, contact the Philippine Commission on Sports Scuba Diving. Those interested in obtaining nautical charts may write to or visit the Bureau of Coast and Geodetic Survey, 421 Barraca St, San Nicolas, Binondo, Manila.

In case of emergencies, recompression chamber facilities are available at the following places: Manila: AFP Medical Centre, V Luna Road, Quezon City, tel (02) 920-7183; contact Jojo R Bernardo, MD, or Fred C Martinez; Subic: Subic Bay Freeport Zone, SMBA, Olongapo City, Zambales, contact

(top) Pink sea anemone; (above) Moray eel circling a papaya reef

Lito Roque or Rogelio de la Cruz; Cebu: Viscom Station Hospital, Camp Lapu-lapu, Lahug, Cebu City, contact Macario Mercado or Mamerto Ortega, c/o PTA/PCSSD (032) 255 7748. For evacuation assistance, call the Search and Rescue Facilities, GHQ Philippine Air Force, Villamor Air Base, Pasay City, Metro Manila, tel (02) 911-7996 / 911-6385.

BATANGAS

Batangas is a short drive from Manila and because of its proximity and the presence of a number of dive resorts and shops it is a popular destination for divers. Jumping-off points are Anilao, Nasugbu and Batangas City. The diving season in Nasugbu is from November to June, but in Balayan Bay and Verde Island it is possible to dive all year round. Some of these spots, however, have moderate to strong currents, which

can be treacherous at times, and therefore only experienced divers should attempt them. Morning dives are favoured in some cases, as the winds in the afternoon can make for a choppy ride and underwater visibility can be poor. Soft and hard coral abound in many of the sites and there are plenty of reef and pelagic fish. Rays, grunts, jacks, snappers, tuna, barracuda, and white-tip sharks can also be found. Many first-time divers head for Anilao which has an abundance of corals and invertebrate life. Well-known dive sites include The Cathedral, with a good reef population. Moorish idols, parrot fish and other types of fish swim close to divers waiting for morsels of food. A good choice for a shallow dive is Caban Cove with exotic coral formations and plenty of small tropical fish. It is fairly sheltered but watch out for currents near the outer edges of the cave. Sepok is a very good dive site with many varieties of marine life, while Batalan Rock, with its abundant and varied coral formations and fish life, is ideal for wide-angle and macro-photography, best done in the morning. Mainit is considered an exciting dive site, with its nine metre (30-foot) deep coral cave where sharks sometimes rest.

A nudibranch searches for supper

The Verde Island passage separating Batangas from Mindoro Island is protected by Verde Island. There are drop-off walls on the southern point of the island, with a wealth of coral and fish.

Aquaventure Reef Club, Anilao Seasports Centre, Dive South Marina Resort, Philpan Diving Resort, all in Anilao are accredited by the PCSS, as well as the Maya-Maya Reef Club in Natipuan Bay, Nasugbu and Bonito Resort on Baranggay Tisa, Tingloy.

Buses serve Batangas from Manila. Resorts provide transport for guests.

MINDORO

The waters around Mindoro Island attract divers and Puerto Galera on the north-eastern tip of the island is a scuba diver's haven. Located 130 kilometres (80.7 miles) from Manila, Puerto Galera is a 90-minute ferry ride from Batangas City pier. From Manila, the trip takes around four hours. Coral gardens, a rich marine population of morays, stingrays, scorpion and stonefish, white-tip sharks, turtles, sweet-lips, barracuda, tuna, octopus, and small tropical fish, as well as sandy beaches, picturesque coves, islands and islets make Puerto Galera a paradise for scuba-divers, snorkellers, beach lovers, and marine biologists. Several diving schools and dive camps operate in Puerto Galera. Diving courses organized according to the PADI system are conducted in various languages for Open Water Diver, Advanced Open Water Diver, Rescue Diver, Dive Master, and Assistant Dive Master. Discounts are usually given if two or more people enrol together.

Popular dive sites are the Canyons and Shark Caves. Other sites include The Boulders, Ernie's Cave, Sabong Point, the reef between Sabang and Small La Laguna, Coral Gardens, Monkey Beach, Manila Channel, Batangas Channel and Balatero Reef. Many of the dive sites around Puerto Galera lend themselves to underwater photography. Night dives are popular in places like Big La Laguna (also used as a training area), Monkey Beach and The Boulders. The wreck of a 17th-century trading vessel which carried Ming pottery lies in the Manila Channel while a Japanese ship sunk by an American plane in 1944 rests on the sea bottom close to The Boulders. Diving here is extremely hazardous and should only be attempted by experienced divers accompanied by local experts.

Licensed dive resorts and establishments in Puerto Galera include Action Divers, Atlantis Beach Club, Captain Gregg's Dive Centre, Cocktail Divers, La Laguna Beach Club and Dive Centre, Philippine Divers Corporation, and Seoul Beach Club. These offer air refills, food and accommodation, dive tours, instructions and rentals. Accommodation ranges from basic to air-conditioned rooms with hot water, cable TV and communications.

The peak season is between November and February but bookings are also heavy over the Christmas and Easter holidays. It is best to secure accommodation before going to Puerto Galera to avoid disappointment.

Getting there: a private, air-conditioned bus operated by Sicat Ferries Inc leaves at 9 am daily from the Sundowner Hotel, 1430 A Mabini St, Ermita, Manila. This connects with the Sicat ferry which departs from Batangas pier at 11.45 am, arriving at Puerto Galera at 1 pm. For reservations, ring 521-3344 or 521-5955. It is best to book a day or so in advance, particularly during the busy season. The return ferry departs from Puerto Galera at 9.30 am. Arrival in Manila is around 1 pm. This is the most convenient way of getting to Puerto Galera. Alternatively, you could catch the 9 am Batangas City-bound BLT bus from Plaza Lawton or the bus terminal at EDSA, Pasay City, which arrives just in time to connect with the public ferry leaving Batangas pier at 12.30 pm. There is no service after 12.30 pm which means you'll have to overnight in Batangas if you miss the boat. Jeepneys wait at the ferry pier near Puerto Galera town to transport visitors to Sabang, White Beach and Tapilanan.

The main diving sites on the western side of Mindoro Island are Ambulong Island, Ilin Island, White Island and Apo Reef. There are also rich fishing grounds around Lubang Island. The Apo Reef Marine Nature Park is one of the 10 priority protected areas of the Philippines under the Integrated Protected Areas System. Located about 36 kilometres (22 miles) west of Mindoro Occidental, it is an atoll-like reef with two lagoon systems separated by a narrow channel with a sandy bottom and branching coral. Some 385 species of marine fish thrive in this area, including families of sharks, stingrays, mantas, schools of jackfish and snappers, swarms of tropical aquarium fish and morays, biennies and gobies; 400 to 500 species of soft and hard coral; and varied invertebrates. This site is only for experienced divers. The marine park includes the islands of Binangaan and Cayos del Bajo with their bird colonies, and the Apo Reef Island.

Dive boats operating from San Jose, the industrial centre and largest town in Mindoro Occidental, Anilao in Batangas, and Manila usually include Apo Reef in their itineraries, weather permitting. Motorized outrigger boats from the provincial capital Mamburao, as well as Sablayan and San Jose can also make the trip to the reef. There are daily flights from Manila to Mamburao and San Jose.

CEBU

The Visayan islands of Cebu, Bohol, Negros Oriental and Western Leyte are also popular diving destinations. These islands are accessible by plane or by boat. Cebu offers the widest variety of dive resorts and facilities. The main diving areas are on the southeastern side of Mactan Island off Buyong Beach and Maribago. Visibility is good to excellent. Diving is best from March to October. Opposite Mactan Island, across the Hilutangan Channel is the Olango island group. Diving here is recommended only for experienced divers because of strong currents.

Mactan is the jumping-off point for Danajon Banks, a double barrier reef complex off northern Bohol. Caubian Island, located on the outer barrier reef, has a diverse coral reef habitat and a great variety of fish. Diving is possible year-round except during strong northeastern monsoon rains. Moalboal, on the southwestern side of Cebu, is one of the most popular diving areas in the country. Diving here is best from October to May. Dive sites include Pescador Island, with spectacular reef cliffs pockmarked by caves and overhangs; Pinagsama Beach; Saavedra/Bas Diot, a haunt of large snakes and big fish (two caves in the vicinity of the Moalboal Reef Club are the hiding places of big groupers); and Tapanan/Tongo Point, which offer some of the finest diving in Moalboal. October to March are the best times to dive here. South of Moalboal Island is Badian Island, a good site for beginners who are not afraid of the sight of large sea snakes. Northeast of Sogod Beach is Capitancillo Islet, a flat coralline islet in the middle of a coral reef, some two to three hours away by motorized outrigger boat. Diving here is from March to November. Also notable are the reefs and shoals off Bantayan Island northeast of Cebu, and Gato Islet off the northern part of Cebu island (jumping-off point is Barrio Tapilon, 5 kilometres/3

miles, from Daan Bantayan) where sea snakes breed in the caves and lagoons from March to September. The snakes are caught barehanded by "catchmen" but exploitation has caused their numbers to dwindle. Where in years past a night's catch would yield 100 snakes, only a dozen or less are caught now.

Dive establishments approved by the PCSSD are Aqua World, Escort Marine Inc, Fun & Sun Development, Hanuri Marine Sports Centre, Island Message Corporation, Makiko Dive Shop, Marine Village Enterprises, Marina's Dive Services, Scotty's Dive Centre, Scuba world, Seven Seas Aquanaut, Sunrise Diving Centre, Santa Cruz Marine Club Resort, and Visaya Divers.

Scuba diving, Club Paradise, Palawan

BOHOL

Bohol, the island southwest of Cebu, is one of the Philippines' top destinations for scuba divers. The warm waters surrounding the outlying islands of Panglao, Cabilao and Balicasag are prime year-round diving sites. There is a great variety of dive sites and several drop-offs whose bottoms range from 24 to 37 metres (80 to 120 feet). Visibility is very good from 18 to 37 metres (60 to 120 feet). Panglao and Balicasag are especially favoured for shore-based dives because of the presence of resorts and dive shops. Panglao Island on the southwestern tip of the mainland has crystal-clear waters, cliffs and reefs, schools of tuna, mackerel, surgeonfish and, at lower depths, large snappers, groupers and an occasional black-tip shark. Dolphins and pilot whales are found farther out. The island's top resort is the Bohol Beach Club, a sprawling complex with beachfront cottages offering accommodation ranging from standard rooms to deluxe suites, with a swimming pool and jacuzzi, game room, a restaurant offering international and Philippine dishes, a beachside bar and facilities for water sports. A string of small resorts and dive shops (Atlantic Dive Centre and Sharky's Divers) are located on Alona Beach, Barangay Tawala.

Bohol's most popular dive area is around Balicasag, a low flat island about 4 kilometres (2.4 miles) southwest of Doljo Point and 35 minutes by boat from Panglao, or two hours from Tagbilaran port. Virtually any spot around the island is a good dive site as Balicasag is totally ringed by fringed reefs and drop-offs. Not far from shore is a 400-metre fish sanctuary. Experts describe the visibility as incredible, the coral cover excellent, and fish abundant. You have large fish here including barracuda, jacks, parrotfish and garoupa. The popular dive spots here are Cathedral, Royal Garden and Black Forest. South Sea Dive conducts dive safaris as well as Open Water I, Advanced and Speciality certificate courses. One can hire diving equipment, glass bottom boats and paddle boats.

Accommodation is available in 10 naturally ventilated, native-style duplex cottages (20 rooms) at the Balicasag Island Dive Resort. Facilities include a restaurant for 40 persons. The resort offers diving packages around the island and night dives.

Cabilao is a small island lying at the junction of Cebu Strait and Bohol Sea. The surrounding waters are frequented by hammerhead sharks, tuna, dolphins, groupers and mackerel. Cervera Shoal, with its caverns inhabited by various sizes, colours and variety of sea snakes, is a thrilling and challenging dive site. Groupers, barracudas and sharks may sometimes be spotted here.

Getting there: There are daily flights from Manila and Cebu to Tagbilaran, the capital of Bohol. Airport pickup is provided by the Bohol Beach Club. Ships also make the Cebu-Bohol crossing and there are now fast ferries which make the trip in one and a half hours.

COCKFIGHTING

Cockfighting is deeply ingrained in Filipino culture. *Sabong*, as it is known in Tagalog, is a national pastime that knows no social distinctions. Not a sport for the faint-hearted, it pits two roosters of comparable weight that fight each other until one is killed or turns tail and flees. The bout is usually brief and bloody. Razor-sharp spurs called *tadi* are attached to the birds' legs. With neck feathers ruffled, the birds dance around each other, testing each other's strength. There's a swish of blades and swirl of feathers, roars rise from the gallery, and in a few minutes it's all over. If both birds are still alive after ten minutes of skirmishing, the bout is declared a draw. Sometimes special matches called *carambolas* are also held, where five or more birds are placed in the arena at the same time to fight it out until only one remains.

Every cockfighter has his own method of training his birds, some claiming to use secret formulas and special diets. It is even said that gamecocks eat better than most people (sometimes including their owners' children). Gamecocks are imported or bought from local breeders in Cavite, Negros and Iloilo.

There are various cockfighting associations, the most exclusive of which is the Philippine Cockers Club and over one thousand cockpits, or *galleras* in the country. They vary in size and sophistication, but the basic design is the same, consisting of the pit proper surrounded by a grill or fence where the game cocks fight, and around that the tiers of benches. Ringside seats are the most expensive.

In former days in the rural areas, you could always tell a cockfight was on when a small red flag was hoisted from a slim bamboo pole outside the *sabungan* or *gallera*. If this escaped you, the high decibel count in the direction of the cockpit certainly would not. A writer once described the roar of the fans as that of 'a baseball stadium when a player clouts a home run'.

Cockfighting, like horse racing, has specialist bookies and touts. Bets can run into hundreds of thousands of pesos and are paid immediately after each fight. It is said that houses, land titles, and car registrations have been wagered at cockfights and gaming tables.

Cockfights are a popular feature of town fiestas. Special fights, called derbies, are staged regularly in various venues. The biggest and most prestigious derbies are held in Metro Manila. These usually feature huge cash prizes. Some of these derbies are international championships participated in by game-fowl raisers from other parts of the world. These stag derbies offer aficionados of the sport thrilling entertainment from fierce fighting birds. Among the popular venues are the Araneta Coliseum in Quezon City, the San Juan Coliseum, the Roligon Mega Cockpit and the new Elorde Sports Stadium in Sucat, Parañaque City.

Tourists who wish to see a cockfight should check the newspapers for the stag derbies. It is advisable to go with a guide or someone knowledgeable about the game who can explain the intricacies of betting. Bets are indicated by a series of hand signals, such as the wiggling of a thumb or the wagging of a hand. The position of the palm—whether up, vertical, or down, means that bets are in the tens, hundreds or thousands of pesos. The man who calls the bets, without the use of a computer or written slips, is the *kristo* so-called because his posture of extended arms resembles Christ nailed to the cross. You can either bet on the cock that is favoured to win (*llamado*) or the less popular one (*dejado*). You get more if the *dejado* wins, depending on the odds, which start at ten per cent and go up to 50 per cent, or even as high as 100 per cent if the favourite is pitted against a lesser-known rooster. You normally tip the *kristo* ten per cent of your winnings; nothing if you lose.

NEGROS ORIENTAL

Dumaguete City, the capital and gateway to the province, is the jump-off point for the diving areas of Siquijor, Apo Island and Sumilon Marine Park. The marine sanctuary, approximately 12 kilometres (7.5 miles) northeast of Dumaguete City and near Cebu's southern tip, has black coral gardens teeming with marine life.

Beach resorts in the province offering a range of accommodation include South Sea Island, El Oriente, and Sta Monica.

Other dive sites in the Visayas are found near Panaon and Limasawa islands, off Southern Leyte, and Calanggaman Island, midway between Cebu and Leyte.

PALAWAN

The waters around Palawan provide excellent shore-based and boat-based diving. The best sites are around Northern Palawan, the Calamianes Islands (jumping-off point is Coron, and diving is year-round) and Cuyo Islands, good from March to June and October (jumping-off point is Cuyo town). Dive boats operate from San Jose, Mindoro and regular as well as charter aircraft fly to Busuanga, Coron and Cuyo. The islets have white sand beaches ringed by fringing reefs. Santa Filomena Shoal at the group's southern extremity, has an extinct underwater volcano with a "blue hole" crater and a large underwater cave. Northern Palawan has many excellent dive sites. Wreck diving is a speciality here. The area around El Nido is a marine sanctuary. The top-rated El Nido Miniloc and El Nido Pangulasian resorts make excellent shore bases for diving enthusiasts. Twenty-six dive sites of different formations have been identified around El Nido's offshore islets. These are rock formation, slope reef, submerged reef, drop-off and tunnel dive. The waters around Pamalican Island in the Cuyo Group also have good dive sites readily accessible from the deluxe Amanpulo Resort. The House Reef, on the southern side of the island is considered good for beginners as it starts at around 10 feet and ends in a slightly sloping area approximately 50 feet down. Numerous species of fish can be found here. The Fan Coral Wall, so-called because of the abundance of fan coral growing out of the wall, starts at 40 feet and drops to 100 feet. Sightings of pelagic fish have been reported. Another dive site called the Windmill going down to a depth of 120 feet is noted for the Napoleon Wrasse growing to the size of a round table for six. There is a resident stingray in the area. The Sharks Playground is a dive site only for experienced divers not just because of the presence of White Tip Sharks and Grey Reef Sharks but because of the changing water conditions. Big pelagics also frequent the area, such as tuna, wahoo, jack and sturgeon fish. Amanpulo has resident dive masters and diving instructors. Courses are offered and diving equipment are available for rent. Non-certified divers are advised to bring a medical certificate.

El Nido, Palawan, is a divers' paradise

An introductory scuba non certificate tuition is available. PADI certification courses are also offered.

Other dive areas in Palawan are found in Honda Bay such as Panglima Reef, West Pasig and the shoals off Rasa and Fortune Islands. Outriggers reach these shoals from Puerto Princesa. The relatively shallow waters off Western Palawan, particularly on the southern end, are pristine dive sites. These include Pagoda Reef, Collingwood and Antelope Shoals, and Paragua Ridge, and across the Palawan Passage there are atolls and shoal reefs that may match or surpass Tubbataha and Apo Reefs.

One of the most spectacular diving areas in the country is the Tubbataha Reef National Marine Park occupying an area of 33,200 hectares (82,000 acres). Located 98 nautical miles southeast of Puerto Princesa City in the Central Sulu Sea, Tubbataha has two atolls—north and south—with a narrow shallow platform enclosing a lagoon and a precipice. The reef harbours a diverse coral assemblage with about 46 *coral genera*, and a very high diversity of reef fish with at least 40 families and 379 species. These include cat sharks, manta rays, banded sea snakes, surgeon, batfish, butterfly fish, etc. The sandy beach in both reefs are nesting and roosting sites of marine turtles (*Chelonia mydas*) and five species of water birds. Tubbataha is under the National Integrated Protected Areas System and has been declared a UNESCO World Heritage Site. It is best explored by joining a dive boat. Cauayan Island off Calandagan, and Cambari Islands off the big island at Dumaran, are also visited by dive boats.

OTHER DIVING AREAS

There are many other dive areas in the Philippines, from the tip of Northern Luzon to the bottom of Mindanao. The dive areas and dive sites in Luzon are: Batanes—Fuga Island (diving season: April and May); La Union—Lingayen Gulf (jumping-off point: San Fernando; season: November to June); Pangasinan—Santiago Island (jumping-off point: Bolinao; season: November to June); Zambales—Hermana Mayor (jumping-off point: Iba/Botolan; season: November to June); Subic Bay (jumping-off point: Olongapo; diving all year); Quezon—Polillo Islands (jumping-off points: Infanta/Jomalig/Balesin; season: April to October); Marinduque—Tres Reyes Islands (jumping-off point: Gasan; season: October to April).

In the Visayas: Romblon—Dos Hermanos Island (jumping-off point: Gasan; season: October to April); Aklan—Boracay Island (jumping-off points: Kalibo/Caticlan/Roxas City; season: November to May); Iloilo—Balbalan Island (jumping-off point: San Jose; season: April to June); Cresta de Gallo Ridge and Nagas Island (jumping-off-point: San Joaquin; year-round).

In Mindanao: Davao—Samal Island (jumping-off point: Davao City; year-round); Zamboanga—Santa Cruz, Limpapa, Manalipa and Coco islands (jumping-off point: Zamboanga City; year-round); Camiguin—Mambajao (jumping-off point: Balingoan; all year).

Game Fishing

The waters of the Philippines offer international sport fishermen not only excitement but a good chance of landing a world-record catch. In May 1990, a 93.75-kilogram (206-pound), 3.4-metre (11-foot) Pacific sailfish was caught by Noel Jones of Hong Kong on 30-lb line off Tubbataha Reef in Palawan, breaking the previous 33-year record of 89.81 kilograms (198 pounds) set in August 1957 in La Paz, Baja California, Mexico. The occasion was the 12th Asian Fishing Championships hosted by the Philippine Game Fishing Association. His teammate, Alan Curtis, also broke a Philippine record by landing a 70.4 kilogram (155-pound) sailfish in the same class. Anglers from the Philippines, Hong Kong, Japan, Taiwan, Thailand, Switzerland and the United States competed. In 1991, Jessie Cordova set a new world record for all-tackle by landing a 38.5 kilo Great Barracuda off Scarborough Shoals.

If you want to make a world-record catch, fish in the Pacific Ocean off Quezon province, says Dr Bart Lapus, a marine biologist, who holds many records in Philippine game fishing. Facilities, however, are limited here and you must fish at the right time.

There are over two million square kilometres (800,000 square miles) of fishing grounds in the Philippines, from the northern waters off Cagayan province to the southern seas off Mindanao. The warm, tropical seas abound with king mackerel, great barracuda, snapper, sea bass, wahoo, swordfish, sailfish, yellowfin and bluefin tuna, marlin, dolphin, shark, manta ray and jackfish while the freshwater lakes yield largemouth and Florida bass. Fishing is by drift-netting or trolling with rod and reels using natural or artificial bait.

■ **FISHING FOR JACKS**
The coral reefs along the eastern coast of the Calatagan peninsula in the province of Batangas, are fair fishing grounds for jacks. The jumping-off point is in Barrio Talisay, Calatagan. From Manila, it is approximately 115 kilometres (72 miles), a two-hour drive south along Cavite's coastal road, the General Emilio Aguinaldo Highway, towards Tagaytay City, thence to Lian Town and Calatagan. Boats, equipped with rod holders for spinning rods and scooping nets, can be hired in

Our Policy and Work

In the Philippines, there was an insurrectionary party claiming to represent the people of the islands and putting forth their claim with a certain speciousness which deceived no small number of excellent men here at home, and which afforded to yet others a chance to arouse a factious party spirit against the President. Of course, looking back, it is now easy to see that it would have been both absurd and wicked to abandon the Philippine Archipelago and let the scores of different tribes—Christian, Mohammedan, and pagan, in every stage of semi-civilization and Asiatic barbarism—turn the islands into a welter of bloody savagery, with the absolute certainty that some strong Power would have to step in and take possession. But though now it is easy enough to see that our duty was to stay in the islands, to put down the insurrection by force of arms, and then to establish freedom-giving civil government, it needed genuine statesmanship to see this and to act accordingly at the time of the first revolt. A weaker and less far-sighted man than President McKinley would have shrunk from a task very difficult in itself, and certain to furnish occasion for attack and misrepresentation no less than for honest misunderstanding. But President McKinley never flinched. He refused to consider the thought of abandoning our duty in our new possessions. While sedulously endeavouring to act with the utmost humanity toward the insurrectionists, he never faltered in the determination to put them down by force of arms, alike for the sake of our own interest and honour, and for the sake of the interest of the islanders, and particularly of the great numbers of friendly natives, including those most highly civilised, for whom abandonment by us would have meant ruin and death. Again his policy was most amply vindicated. Peace has come to the islands, together with a greater measure of individual liberty and self-government than they have ever before known. All the tasks set us as a result of the war with Spain have so far been well and honourably accomplished, and as a result this nation stands higher than ever before among the nations of mankind. . .

Theodore Roosevelt, Our Policy and Work

Barrio Talisay (enquire at Lilia's store on the left side of the road). Those wishing to stay overnight can look for accommodation in any of the small inns at Matabungkay Beach, some seven kilometres (four miles) away, or make advance reservations in Manila. You can arrange for the boatman to pick you up at the resort of your choice the following day.

■ EMBARKATION POINTS

The most convenient embarkation points for the sport fishing grounds in the archipelago are San Jose in Mindoro, Naic in Cavite, Puerto Princesa in Palawan, Bagac in Bataan, Port San Vicente in Cagayan Valley, and Surigao in Mindanao. Ordinary boats, usually the three-to-four-metre (12-to-14-foot) *banca* with outriggers, powered by ten- or 16-horsepower inboard motors are used for fishing. Fishing from this type of boat, which is only centimetres above water level, and with limited space and an unsteady platform, is a test of endurance and skill. Imagine going after tuna in Surigao during tuna season. The proven method is driftfishing, according to Vic-Vic Villavicencio, one of the avid promoters of sport fishing in the Philippines. But try grappling to land a 120-kilo (265-lb) yellowfin on a 23-kilo (50-lb) line in an outrigger canoe just big enough to hold you and your boatmen... "Ernest Hemingway would have loved every minute of that," he said. Bigger boats called *basnigs* are also used.

Outrigger boats especially designed by anglers for sportfishing have been built with funds from the Philippine Department of Tourism and the Philippine Game Fishing Association. They have sleeping quarters for four anglers, a toilet, cooking facilities, rod holders and line spreaders. These boats can be chartered from the PGFA. Some of the smaller boats are used by sport fishermen going after sailfish, marlin and dorado in the northeastern waters off San Vicente, Santa Ana, Cagayan. Others are deployed in the Palawan area. It takes eight hours' sailing in calm weather from Puerto Princesa to Tubbataha Reefs. A four-day trip allows for two complete days of fishing while a five-day trip gives you three. There are daily flights to and from Puerto Princesa, usually around noon.

■ FISHING CLUBS

There are several fishing clubs in the Philippines. The umbrella organization is the Philippine Game Fishing Association (PGFA), founded in 1940 to promote sport fishing and marine conservation in the archipelago. PGFA is affiliated with the International Game Fish Association and is a member of the Asian Game Fishing Federation. It holds eight to ten tournaments a year with light- and heavy-tackle fishing, fishing clinics for its members, and monthly get-togethers. A 60-page guide to sport fishing in the Philippines produced by the Department of Tourism in cooperation with the PGFA gives valuable information on rules for fishing in fresh and salt water. It also gives details on boats and equipment, safety procedures, the most productive fishing areas, how to get there, accommodation, fishing seasons and coastal maps. For further information, contact the Philippine Game Fishing Association at 1055 Ongpin St, Sta Cruz, 1003 Manila.

Golf

The Philippines is one of Asia's top destinations for golfers. Golf can be enjoyed year-round in a number of locations. There are at least 20 championship courses designed by well-known names in the golfing world. Most of these courses are in spectacular settings with resort facilities. Golf is growing in popularity and more Filipinos are taking to the game. As a result, international-standard golf courses are now being integrated into the design of masterplanned communities in prime locations, along with recreational and entertainment centres. The Philippines is part of the Asian golf circuit and such events as the Philippine Open, Philippine Masters and World Cup add lustre to the scene.

Many of the world's top golfers have played in the Philippines. In December 1997, the Fairways and Bluewater championship course on the holiday island of Boracay was the venue for the third round of the Johnnie Walker Super Tour. In November 1996 the World Amateur Golf Team Championship for men and women was held at the Manila Southwoods and Santa Elena courses. And in 1995, the Johnnie Walker Classic was held at the Orchards course in Dasmariñas, Cavite.

Golf was introduced to the Philippines at the turn of the century. Baguio, Iloilo, Manila and Zamboanga were the first to have golf clubs. Today there are more than 70 golf courses and more are under construction. These are complemented by five-star facilities and pro shops. Most of the golf clubs are private membership clubs, and come at a price. Public golf courses are rare. Some clubs have reciprocal arrangements with other major clubs overseas. Guest privileges and tour packages can be arranged with advance notice of at least a week. The advantage of playing golf in the Philippines is that caddies speak English and know how to play the game. They are helpful in giving tips, correcting swings or selecting clubs for amateur players. Golfers also have the luxury of having 'umbrella girls' who shade them from the sun.

CHAMPIONSHIP COURSES

Within driving distance of Metro Manila, notably in the provinces of Cavite, Batangas and Laguna, are several championship courses. These include:

The Manila Southwoods Golf and Country Club in Carmona, Cavite, composed of two 18-hole courses designed by Jack Nicklaus with championship-sized greens and wide fairways. The 'Legends' is a 6,778-yard, par-72 course characterized by high mounds; it was the venue for the 1993 Philippine Open. The 6,881-yard, par 72 'Masters' is accentuated by traps and water hazards. Southwoods is the first in the country to bear Nicklaus' signature. Facilities include a driving range, two golfers' verandas and a clubhouse with a formal dining room and banquet hall. Southwoods is about 25 minutes' drive from Makati through the South Luzon tollway.

The Orchards Golf and Country Club in Dasmariñas, Cavite with two 18-hole courses: 'The Legacy' designed by Arnold Palmer and 'The Tradition' designed by Gary Player. It is set amidst fruit trees, lakes, lagoons and hills covering 131 hectares (324 aces). Special Tifton 419 grass covers the fairways and Tifdwarf the greens. When the 1995 Johnnie Walker Classic was held here, Arnold Palmer partnered then President Ramos, an avid golfer, for a round in the pro-celebrity event. Facilities include a large clubhouse with restaurant, bar, coffee shop, a pro shop, basketball court, gym, tennis courts, bowling centre, swimming pool, sauna and whirlpool baths. It's a 20- to 30-minute drive from the international airport along the Aguinaldo Highway.

The Tagaytay Highlands International Golf Club, located 500 metres above sea level in Tagaytay, is a par 72, 6,820-yard championship course affording views of Mounts Makiling and Banahaw, Laguna de Bay and Manila Bay. A cable car system ferries golfers from the 9th and 18th holes to the 1st and 10th holes, so great is the difference in elevation. Facilities include a driving range for practice and a clubhouse with two main dining areas and a bar. It is an hour and 45 minutes away by car from Metro Manila on the South Luzon Tollway or the Coastal Road. Helicopter service is also available.

The Santa Elena Golf Club is a 27-hole, all-weather golf course set in 120 hectares (296 acres) of rolling terrain in Santa Rosa, Laguna. Robert Trent Jones Jr designed the course combining modern technology with the natural features of the place. Facilities include a driving range and putting greens, a clubhouse with a restaurant, dining room, cocktail lounge, game room and function rooms. The club is located about 30 to 40 minutes from Makati. Travelling along the South Superhighway it is about two kilometres from the Cabuyao interchange.

The Evercrest Golf Club and Resort in Batulao, Nasugbu, Batangas, is a par 72 championship course. Designed by Arnold Palmer as an all-weather course, it has

greens planted to Tifdwarf grass laid over a bed of fine beach sand and uses the latest methods of drainage and irrigation. Facilities include a clubhouse with restaurant and bar, pro shop, sauna bath, jacuzzi; a swimming pool and a driving range.

Eastridge Golf Club in Angono, Rizal is set in 80 hectares (198 acres) of land. It is a par 72 all-weather course. A driving range, modern clubhouse with dining room, cocktail lounge and function rooms are among its facilities.

METRO MANILA

The avid golfer has a choice of excellent courses in the city. The Wack Wack Golf and Country Club on Shaw Boulevard, Mandaluyong, is one of the oldest and most revered clubs in the Philippines, and the traditional home of the Philippine Open. It has two 18-hole courses: the East course (7,009 yards, par 72) and the West course (6,418 yards, par 71/73). The East course, designed by American architect and golf pro Jim Black, has been renovated by Ron Kirby-Gary Player Associates using Tifton 328 grass. Sand traps have been added and the finishing greens redesigned so that they require more delicate putting. The 13th, noted for Severiano Ballesteros' eagle which helped Spain win the 1977 World Cup, has been narrowed into a rolling, bunkered hole. Facilities include a driving range, pitching green, swimming pool, tennis courts and clubhouse with first-class restaurants and bars.

One of the most exclusive clubs, founded in 1901, is the Manila Golf and Country Club in Forbes Park, Makati. A rolling terrain characterizes the 6,313-yard par 71 course. The fairways are surrounded by trees and flowering shrubs and the greens are planted to Zoysia Japonica grass. The club has hosted the US LPGA mixed pro-am. Facilities include a well-maintained driving range and a modern clubhouse with all the amenities. It's close to the Makati Commercial Centre.

The Villamor Golf Club (7,010 yards, par 72) inside the Philippine Air Force base in Pasay City is just ten minutes from Makati. It is one of the longest championship courses in the country, ideal for big hitters. *Agoho* trees, *ipil-ipil, narra* and some mango trees line the fairways of this well-tended course. Villamor hosted two Philippine Opens and Philippine Masters and the Epson Classic. It has a driving range, restaurant and bar.

The Capitol Hills Golf and Country Club (6,925 yards, par 72) in Old Balara, Quezon City overlooking the water filtration plant, is a championship course on rolling terrain with deep ravines and water hazards. The back nine is challenging; the 10th and 13th greens are on a plateau, and the 18th includes a double dogleg. Facilities include a restaurant, bar, function rooms, game room, swimming pool, tennis court. Golf clubs and shoes are available for rent.

Also in Quezon City is the Veterans Golf Course (5,718 yards, par 70), located

Tagaytay Highlands International Golf Club

within the Veterans Memorial Medical Centre compound on Mindanao Avenue. It has tight fairways and well-placed bunkers. There is a driving range and a clubhouse with restaurant, function rooms and other amenities.

The El Club Intramuros de Manila (3,352 yards, par 60) outside historic Intramuros and near Rizal Park, is the oldest in the city—built around 1907 by Gen John J Pershing who also constructed the Zamboanga golf course. It is characterized by narrow fairways. Lagoons, sand traps, and other obstacles make a game here exciting. It is only a golf swing away from Manila Hotel. The course is illuminated for nighttime play. Club Intramuros is open to the public but it is necessary to reserve two or three days before play date.

The 18-hole, par 72 Alabang Country Club Golf Course in Ayala Alabang Village, Muntinglupa is set on 58 hectares (143 acres) of land with lakes, a creek and mango trees. Facilities include a driving range, restaurants, bar, swimming pools, bowling alleys, billiards, tennis courts and gym. It's about 18 kilometres (11 miles) south of Makati on the South superhighway.

OUT OF TOWN

Thirty minutes away from Manila, in the rolling hills of Antipolo, is the Valley Golf and Country Club (7,097 yards, par 72). The course was designed by Englishman Fred Smith, and includes lakes, brooks and trees. The course is well-bunkered with narrow fairways. Wild shots are severely penalized. Valley Golf was the venue for two Philippine Opens, and it is maintained in championship condition. Facilities include a driving range, restaurants, bars, and function rooms. The main clubhouse will be renovated and the 36 holes upgraded into an international, all-weather golf course.

A 55-minute drive from Manila on the South Superhighway brings you to Canlubang Golf and Country Club at the foot of Mt Makiling in Laguna. Designed by Robert Trent Jones Jr, it is the first 36-hole course of an international standard in Southeast Asia. The championship North course (6,929 yards, par 72) has ravines, man-made lakes, waterfalls and coconut palm trees. A number of holes have water hazards. The elevated South course (6,785 yards, par 72) also features ravines and water hazards. There's a driving range, putting green, clubhouse with restaurants and bar, swimming pool, and tennis and squash courts.

Another course designed by Robert Trent Jones Jr is that of Calatagan Golf Club occupying 64 hectares on the headlands of Batangas affording spectacular views. The 18-hole par 71 course built on undulating terrain with lakes and plenty of trees, offers many challenges. It's about two-and-a-half hours' drive from Metro Manila.

The Puerto Azul Beach and Country Club in Ternate, Cavite, less than two hours by car from Manila, is one of the earliest resort courses. The 18-hole, par-72 championship course designed by Ron Kirby-Gary Player Associates makes full use of the natural features of the forested setting. The seventh and eighth holes are on a plateau which is reached by cable car or golf cart. Some of the greens are known for their steepness and have challenged the pros. The sea is the backdrop for the second nine and some memorable golf is played here: the 12th hole is breathtaking and the 17th has been described as the "monster hole". Normally a par 4, it becomes a par 3 during big tournaments. There's a driving range, clubhouse with restaurant and bar. The par 68 golf course at Club John Hay in Baguio is being redeveloped and upgraded.

The Baguio Country Club also has an 18-hole, par 61 course. The club is one of the oldest in the country and has a good sports complex. Restaurants, bar, tennis, bowling, pool, table tennis, golf pro shop are among its facilities. The Luisita Golf and Country Club at Hacienda Luisita, San Miguel, Tarlac is a 6,908-yard, par 72 course.

The Lake Paoay Golf Course in Laoag, Ilocos Norte, designed by Gary Player, and built at the time of President Ferdinand Marcos, a keen golfer, is another championship course. The Subic golf course was redesigned and completed in time for the APEC meeting last November 1996.

THE VISAYAS AND MINDANAO

The Cebu Country Club (6,288 yards, par 71), relatively flat, but interesting is located in Banilad, Cebu City. It is the regular venue of the PAL tournament.

The Negros Occidental Golf and Country Club, located some six kilometres from downtown Bacolod City is a 6,300-yard, par 72 championship course. Popularly known as Marapara, it is fairly flat with winding fairways. Players have to beware of unpredictable gusts of wind which can drive balls into bunkers. The 18th hole poses a challenge to average golfers because of its length—635 yards. Facilities include a clubhouse with restaurant, bar and pro shop, swimming pool and two tennis courts.

The oldest golf course in the Visayas is in Santa Barbara, a former railroad town some 16 kilometres (10 miles) outside Iloilo City. British engineers who ran the railway are said to have constructed the course which later became the Iloilo Golf and Country Club. From an abbreviated nine-hole layout, it expanded to an 18-hole par 36-34-70 course set in hilly terrain.

On the island of Mindanao, the popular courses are in Davao and Zamboanga. The Lanang Country Club and Golf Course (6,326 yards, par 71), six kilometres (about four miles) from the centre of Davao City along the national highway, is a picturesque course laid out amidst orchids and flowering shrubs. Doglegs abound. It has a fine clubhouse, restaurant and bar. The Apo Golf and Country Club is a

7,200-yard, par 72 course laid out on a former coconut plantation with Mt Apo as the backdrop. Several improvements have been made to the course, the clubhouse and related facilities. Fairways and greenside bunkers have been added and the back nine is full of hazards. The 80th Philippine Open, the first to be held outside Luzon, took place at the Apo Golf and Country Club in February 1995.

The Zamboanga Golf and Beach Park is an 18-hole championship course set on sprawling greenery surrounded by mango and giant acacia trees in Upper Calarian, 7.5 kilometres (almost five miles) from the city proper. The par 72, 6,404-yard course is considered one of the most beautiful in the Philippines. It has a driving range. Facilities include dressing and shower rooms, locker rooms, a restaurant, grills and barbecue pits, food stalls, a kiosk and pavilion, picnic sheds and tables. This is the oldest course in Mindanao, built in 1911 by Gen John J Pershing, commander of all American forces in Mindanao.

NEW COURSES

Golf courses are springing up all over the country. Greg Norman, Nick Faldo, Isao Aoki and Andy Dye are lending their names to some of the new projects. Inaugurated in May 1998 was the Riviera Golf and Country Club, located 1,000 feet above sea level in Silang, Cavite, just eight kilometres from Tagaytay Rotunda. The 18-hole championship course designed by Bernhard Langer made full use of the hilly countryside and affords golfers breathtaking views of the picturesque Ilang-Ilang River. Under construction is the Splendido Taal, a 7,000-yard, par 72, all-weather championship course designed by Greg Norman. It will be a spectacular course with its setting along Tagaytay Ridge overlooking Taal Volcano and lake. The Mount Malarayat Golf and Country Club in Lipa City, Batangas is a 27-hole golf course. The country club also has a children's pavilion, sports centre and sports lounge and equestrian facilities. The Graham Marsh-designed, par 72, Fairways & Bluewater championship golf course on the holiday island of Boracay opened just in time for the third round of the four-country Johnnie Walker Super Tour in December 1997.

Mountaineering, Trekking and Spelunking

The Philippines is an exciting destination for those seeking adventure in the great outdoors. From Batanes in the north to Sulu in the south there's enough wilderness, mountain ranges and caves to keep Philippine mountaineering and spelunking clubs busy all year round. Philippine mountains are rugged, and trekking through them is recommended only for those who seek real adventure. Pitons, carabiners and pick-axes are unnecessary. What you need is plenty of stamina; and you must be physically fit.

Most trail heads in the Philippines can be reached by a combination of bus, jeep, tricycle and/or motorized *banca* (pumpboat). Some trail heads are two to three hours' drive from Manila. Others involve travel by air (45 to 90 minutes) or sea (14 to 20 hours). Mt Apo in Davao, Mt Pulog in Benguet, Mt Halcon in Mindoro, Mt Mayon in Albay, Mt Giting-giting in Romblon, Mt Kanlaon in Negros Occidental, Mt Hibok-hibok in Camiguin and Mt Kitanlad in Bukidnon are some of the peaks that challenge mountain climbers. Other popular destinations are Mt Makiling, Mt Banahaw, Mt Arayat, Pico de Loro and Taal Volcano. It is advisable to check with the field stations of the Philippine Institute of Volcanology and Seismology (PHIVOLCS) if you plan to undertake an expedition to one of the active volcanoes such as Mayon, Taal, Bulusan, Kanlaon, Hibok-hibok, Mt Pinatubo, Mt Parker or Camiguin. If you are in Manila, talk to Mr Warner Andrada or Mr Travis Allan at the fourth floor of the Department of Tourism (T M Kalaw Street). The Ascent Mountaineering Club is based there. They can advise you on trekking and spelunking in the Philippines. You might also drop by the ground floor to have a chat with a Tourist Information Officer who will give you practical and up-to-date information on transport and accommodation in the places you wish to visit.

■ **WHAT TO TAKE**

On half- or full-day excursions, wear T-shirts and shorts (long trousers are preferable if you are climbing up volcanic slopes or hiking through tall grasses) and a pair of comfortable but sturdy rubber-soled shoes with good traction. You will also need a waterproof windbreaker with hood, sun hat, gloves to protect your hands from hot volcanic rocks and, when scaling volcanic peaks, a mask to prevent inhaling sulphurous fumes and a hard hat or similar headgear to protect you from falling stones.

Consider bringing sunblock or sunscreen lotion, moist towelettes, tissue paper, a canteen for water, sweets or biscuits, a first-aid kid, insect repellent, Swiss Army knife/pocket knife, matches/lighter, and a flashlight with extra batteries. For longer expeditions, pack extra clothes, socks, sandals, spoon, fork, plastic lunch box and cup, toilet paper, essential personal toiletries, towel, sleeping bag or thick blanket, plastic sheet, tent, and food and drink to last you for the duration of the trek. In the nearest town or city, buy your provisions (bread, canned food such baked beans or corn beef, instant soups and instant noodles, sachets of coffee, sugar, milk, tea; dried and fresh fruit, fruit juice concentrates. It's good to save the salt and pepper packets, cream and sugar sachets that you get with your meals in the aircraft. Water in a large plastic container is a must. Miscellaneous extras: string or fine nylon rope, empty sack for porter's use, plastic bags for garbage and to protect articles from rain or mist, camera, pen, writing pad, whistle, pocket mirror, sewing needles and thread, ID card. Mountain tops can be very cold at night so be sure to have ample warm clothing.

■ **TIPS FOR MOUNTAIN CLIMBERS**
—Before undertaking an expedition check with the local Tourism Office, the local mountaineering clubs, as well as the Phivolcs and Philippine Atmospheric, Geophysical and Astronomical Services Administration (PAGASA) regarding safety, weather and other conditions prevailing in your destination.
—Mountain trails in the Philippines are not well defined so trekkers need a guide. Fees vary; inquire from local clubs for the going rate.
—A sturdy tent is a must for climbers as there are neither shelters nor huts along trails or on mountain tops. Except in Mayon, local guides rely on climbers to provide them with tents.
—Good rain gear is imperative. Weather conditions in the mountains can change rapidly, so you should be prepared at all times.
—If you plan to cook, bring a portable camping stove rather than using wood.
—Non-biodegradable rubbish such as plastic bags should not be buried or thrown away. These should be carried down to the lowlands for proper disposal.
—Insect repellent and water-purifying tablets or devices are essential.

MT APO

Mt Apo, the 'Lord' of Philippine mountains, soars 3,143 metres (10,311 feet) above sea level, the highest peak in the country. An inactive volcano with a series of three peaks, Mt Apo is the largest national park in the Philippines, covering an area of 72,796 hectares (179,806 acres) straddling the provinces of Davao and North Cotabato in Mindanao. It takes three to four days to reach the summit (more if you linger to study the flora and fauna, take photographs or visit tribes). The trek is strenuous but well worth the effort. Along the way you see giant candle-trees, bearded moss, carnivorous pitcher plants, rare orchids and butterflies. Interesting features are rock formations, sulphur craters, waterfalls, crystal clear and boiling mountain lakes, medicinal hot and cold springs, and a dipterocarp forest. Mt Apo is also the habitat of the endangered Philippine eagle, the national bird of the Philippines. At the Eagle Centre in the foothills of Mt Apo, there is an ongoing programme to breed the eagle in captivity. Two female eaglets were successfully hatched in January and October 1992.

The most popular route to Mt Apo's summit is via the Kidapawan Trail (jump-off at Ilomavis and Lake Agko). The Magpet Trail or the Bongolan Trail are other alternatives. Davao City or Cotabato City are the two entry points to Kidapawan, North Cotabato. It's a two-hour ride from Davao City's Ecoland Bus Terminal; three hours from Cotabato City's Magallanes Street terminal. Mintranco, NCTC, Weena Express and E.V. Liner buses depart every 30 minutes from both cities. For big groups, it is better to charter your own transport. Climbers register, pick up guides and porters at Ilomavis or Magpet.

Depending on the trek schedule, climbers may camp overnight at Lake Agko, otherwise if you arrive there before noon, you can proceed to Marbel campsite. From Lake Agko the trail leads down to Marbel River then goes up a ridge, passing through dense forests. After clambering up a nearly vertical wall you reach Lake Venado, an area of marshland which resembles a golf course during the dry summer months and a big lake during the rainy season. From Marbel to Lake Venado is a six to eight-hour trek. You take your lunch along the way. You camp on the lake's southwest shore near the forest, among centuries-old trees. From Lake Venado, it takes another three or four hours of trekking over tall cogon grass to reach the summit. The higher you go the sparser the vegetation and the more stunted the trees. The summit has several good camp sites. The trail leads directly to the most popular camp, well sheltered against the wind. Dwarf trees and wild berries grow on the summit and there's a water source nearby. There are several peaks to explore from here. It is best to stay one whole day at the summit exploring the area and enjoying the view. On the eastern side of the summit, facing Davao City, is an old crater the size of a track-and-field oval. Farther down are the famous 'rockies' and sulphur vents. This is the white rock face of Mt Apo visible from Davao City on a clear day. Trekking to the sulphur area and back to the camp site takes about three hours.

The other route to the peak via the Magpet Trail entails a five-day trek. From Kidapawan you travel by jeepney to Magpet then to Magcaalam, then hike to Manobo Tico where you camp overnight. Day Two is an eight-hour hike to Mab-bu Falls campsite. Day 3 is another eight-hour hike to Lake Venado campsite. The following day is the climb to the peak. Enjoy lunch at the peak, then start the descent to Lake Venado and Dal-lag, overnighting at Dal-lag for the trip back to Magcaalam, Magpet, and Kidapawan. Should you wish to stay overnight in Kidapawan, accommodation is available at the Kidapawan Vista Lodge or the AJ Hi-Time or in private homes under the Department of Tourism's Homestay Programme. Contact the Kidapawan Tourism Council, J P Laurel St., Kidapawan, North Cotabato, for further information.

The best months to ascend Mt Apo are October, November, December, April and May. Temperatures range from 15°C (60°F) during the day and may drop to a chilly 5°C (40°F) or less at night, especially around the crater. Warm clothing is essential.

The Department of Tourism in Davao City as well as the Kidapawan Tourism Council in North Cotabato organize treks to Mt Apo. Check also with the local mountaineering clubs based in Davao City.

MT MAYON

Mt Mayon is a tourist attraction in Southeastern Luzon. Rising 2,462 meters (8,078 feet) above sea level in the eastern part of Albay province, it is the most active volcano in the archipelago with at least 43 eruptions since 1616. The most violent and destructive was on 1 February 1914 when it severely damaged the towns of Camalig, Cagsawa and Budiao, killing at least 1,200 people.

From afar, the near-perfect cone with its smoothly sloping sides looks deceptively easy to climb, but actually it is one of the most difficult. To reach the summit you have to negotiate a precarious 40-degree slope amidst loose boulders and cinders. One false move and you start an avalanche.

The trail head is at Barangay Buyuan on the Legaspi City side. The climb goes through varied terrain, from tropical rainforest to grassland. There are magnificent vistas of sea and sky, plains and neighbouring mountains. It takes two days for the ascent and descent, with an overnight stop some 1,921 metres (6,300 feet) above sea level. During the dry months, you will have to haul water from Camp One to Camp Two. The climb starts at 762 metres (2,500 feet) above sea level on a ledge where the Volcanology (Phivolcs) station is located. The trail snakes upwards through a tropical secondary forest with a wide variety of flora and fauna, and cuts across razor-sharp *talahib* grass. Lava flows from the last eruption and the discharge of volcanic debris have eroded the gullies and changed the known paths. You encounter rocks and boulders, loose volcanic cinders and lava sand on the way to the summit. Here you must be careful as the surface on the peak is hollow and there is a danger of falling. Tying a rope to a big boulder is a great help.

March, April and May are the best months to make the ascent. Avoid climbing when there is heavy rainfall, particularly from November to January. To get there: Fly to Legaspi City (one hour from Manila). Overland, it takes from eight to ten hours. For guides, contact the Tourism Office in Legaspi. The Department of Tourism organizes an annual climb to Mayon in April or May. Certificates are given to successful registered climbers.

Mt Pulog

Rising to a height of 2,930 metres (9,613 feet), Mt Pulog in Benguet province is the second-highest peak in the Philippines. Located between Baguio and Ambuklao in the Central Cordilleras, it is considered an essential destination by local mountaineers. Covering an area of 11,550 hectares (28,529 acres), it is classified as a national park, and is noted for its pine forests, mountain lakes, dwarf bamboos, deep ravines, and temperate climate. From October to December, the landscape is dotted with tiny white flowers.

Pulog in the Ibaloi dialect means 'bald'. A veteran climber describes its summit 'like a grassy cap, there is nothing like it in other Philippine mountains'. At the top, you are afforded panoramic views of the Cagayan River Valley, Sierra Madre mountains, Cordillera mountain range, the Pacific Ocean and the China Sea. Mountain climbing expeditions, usually a four-day hike, take place in February, March and April. Avoid climbing during the rainy season, particularly in July and August as the trails become slippery. January is the coldest month, and if you attempt the climb during this time, guard against the cold with warm woollens and thick blankets.

There are three routes to the summit: via Kabayan (Ellet River); via Kabayan town proper and Lusod; and via Ambangeg through Palansa. The most popular is the Ambangeg route. Jump-off at the Trade school (contact Mr Cosme). There is a road leading all the way up to Lebang Lake accessible by four-wheel drive vehicles during the dry months. However, check whether the roads leading to the trail heads are passable as landslides occasionally block highways.

Mt Kanlaon

Mt Kanlaon on the island of Negros in the Visayan chain, is one of the 22 active volcanoes in the Philippines. Its first recorded eruption was in 1866. A large strato-volcano with a maximum elevation of 2,435 meters (7,989 feet), Mt Kanlaon consists of several craters and parasitic cones aligned linearly, with an older *caldera* in its central portion. Most of the older craters have formed lakes or lagoons. Classified as a national park spread across 24,557 hectares (60,656 acres), Kanlaon has a wide variety of flora and fauna. The ground orchid *Calanthe-elmeri* was discovered here. There is a lot of endemic wildlife here such as the Negros fruit dove, although this is now believed to be extinct. Along the top ridges of the mountain range, however, one still encounters pristine wilderness and tropical rainforest. Waterfalls, hot springs, gorges, rock formations, and caves containing columns of stalagmites and stalactites are found here.

The park has more than 40 kilometres (25 miles) of foot trails, and walks can last from a few hours to several days. A pleasant one-day hike to the old crater is possible by following the Ara-al and Mago Trails. The Masulog Trail is the shortest route to the old crater (7.5 kilometres/14.7 miles) but it is a steady uphill climb. The Wasay Trail is a two-day trek through still unspoilt rainforest. Mt Kanlaon's summit is an active crater about 300 metres (984 feet) in diameter with a straight drop to a depth of about 265 metres (869 feet). Rumbling sounds can be heard and sulphurous vapours and steam are constantly emitted. No vegetation grows on the slopes below the crater for about 300-500 metres (985-1,640 feet). North of the active crater lies an oval-shaped crater 200 metres (656 feet) in diameter with a flattened sandy area inside known as the Margaha Valley. When it rains, water collects in the three-hectare (seven-acre) valley transforming it into a small lake. But during the summer it is dry and campers use it as a camp site. There are no trails to the volcano's active crater. To reach the summit from the old crater you must climb on all fours along eroded gulleys and steep, bare slopes.

Mt Kanlaon is part of the volcanic arc related to subduction along the Negros Trench. There are other volcanic mountains on the island which are part of the volcanic arc. In the south about 16 kilometres (10 miles) northwest of Dumaguete City is Mt Talinis, the second-highest mountain in Negros. Early settlers called it *Cuernos de Negros* (Horns of Negros) because it has two peaks. The 2,100-metre (6,888-foot) inactive volcano is heavily forested. Mt Silay to the north is another inactive volcano but its appeal is confined to jungle trekking.

The best time to climb Mt Kanlaon is from March to May. The temperature near the summit is about 8° C (46°F), but subzero temperatures can also be experienced. Remain alert for adverse weather conditions. Annual rainfall is evenly distributed. Check with the montaineering clubs in Negros regarding security in the area and which trails to take. The Negros Mountaineering Club in Bacolod City can be contacted through the local tourist office and the San Agustin Mountaineering Club can be reached through the Colegio de San Agustin in Bacolod.

Bacolod City is an hour's flight from Manila or 30 minutes from Cebu. The journey by sea takes a day from Manila and several hours from Iloilo City.

TAAL VOLCANO

Located in the middle of a lake, Mt Taal is one of the world's lowest and most active volcanoes. It is said to have at least 35 cones and 47 craters, and more than 30 submerged volcanic landforms. From a high vantage point such as Tagaytay Ridge, you can see a crater within a lake enclosed by another crater in a larger lake. To get there, take a BLTB bus or jeepney (1.5 hours) to Talisay, a lakeside town in Batangas. Coordinate with the Municipal Hall personnel or Natalia's Guesthouse for trekking this area. Permits are required. Hire a motorized *banca* to take you across the lake to the Commission on Volcanology station. Trek towards the old crater and then to the other side of Volcano Island. During the summer the trek is very hot and dusty. Take a motorized *banca* back to Talisay. It is advisable to stay overnight in Talisay or in one of the beach resorts in Batangas.

■ MOUNTAINEERING CLUBS

The National Mountaineering Federation of the Philippines (NMPP) is the umbrella organization for about 27 mountaineering clubs throughout the country. It was organized in 1980 to promote backpacking and mountaineering in the Philippines and to encourage environmental consciousness among its members. The federation holds an annual congress and climb in the summer with member clubs taking turns organizing and hosting the event. The founding members are: Antique Mountaineering Society, Baguio-Benguet Mountaineering Society (BBMS), Cebu Assailants of Mountain Peaks (CAMP), Iloilo Mountaineering Club (IMC), Mountaineering Association of the Philippines (MAP), Mt Apo Climbers Association of Davao City (MACADAC), Philippine Airlines Mountaineering Club (PALMC), Negros Mountaineering Club, Philippine Mountaineering Society and San Agustin Mountaineering Club (SAMOC) of Bacolod City, and the University of the Philippines Mountaineers (UPM). These groups organize outings that range from easy one-day walks to overnights beside a waterfall in the depths of a forest, to advanced spelunking and treks traversing vast expanses of tropical forests. The PALMC is a well-travelled club which has pioneered a variety of outdoor activities. The group has a year-round schedule of treks with at least two activities each month. Its members have trekked around the entire islands of Batan, Sabtang and Itbaya in Batanes. They have reached the highest summits in the country—Mt Apo, Pulog, Halcon and Kanlaon, and scaled some of the most difficult peaks—Mt Mayon, Hibok-hibok and Giting-giting.

If you plan to go trekking in the Philippines get in touch with PALMC at Philippine Airlines, Mr Libosado at the Department of Tourism, or any of the above-mentioned mountaineering clubs. They can package an expedition for you or assist you in arranging your itinerary and obtaining guides and camping equipment (tents, backpacks, sleeping bags, camping stoves and cooking utensils). If there is no scheduled club activity for the month, some members may be willing to go on an expedition with you.

Spelunkers are discovering the wonders of Philippine caves. Many are still undocumented and unexplored. The Callao Cave system in Cagayan Province is one of the most extensive and well-known, although only a very small portion of the system has been explored. Other spelunking areas are in Palawan and Sagada in the Mountain Province. There are many others scattered throughout the country. Spelunking clubs exist. Obtain a list and contacts from the Department of Tourism.

Practical Information

Basic Filipino Vocabulary

GREETINGS

Welcome / Long live!	*Mabuhay*
Good morning	*Magandang umaga (po)*
Good afternoon	*Magandang hapon (po)*
Good evening	*Magandang gabi (po)*
Good morning to all	*Magandang umaga sa inyong lahat*
Goodbye	*Paalam na*
How are you?	*Kumusta ka*
Fine	*Mabuti naman*
Thank you	*Salamat (po)*
You are welcome	*Walang anuman*
Yes	*Oo (ho or po)*
No	*Hindi (po or ho)*

Filipinos use the word *po* or *ho* at the end of phrases in polite speech. *Ho* is generally used when you speak with strangers. *Po* is more deferential and respectful. *Ka* (you) is the familiar form of address; the plural form (*kayo*) is more formal or polite. Example: *Kumusta ka (kayo)?*

PRONOUNS

I	*Ako*
My	*Ang aking*
Mine	*Sa akin* or *akin*
You	*Ikaw*
Your	*Ang iyong*
Yours	*Sa iyo* or *iyo*
He-she	*Siya*
His-her	*Ang kaniyang*
His-hers	*Sa kaniya*
We	*Kami*
Our	*Ang ami ng*
Ours	*Sa amin* or *amin*
You (plural)	*Kayo*
Your (plural)	*Ang inyong*
Yours (plural)	*Sa inyo* or *inyo*
They	*Sila*
Their	*Ang kani lang*
Theirs	*Sa kanila*

DIRECTIONS

Here	*Dito*
There (nearby)	*Diyan*
There (distant)	*Doon*
Stop here	*Para dito*
Can I ask your help?	*Maari ba pong magtanong?*
Where is ... ?	*Saan naroon ang...?*
Hotel	*Otel*
Store	*Tindahan*
Church	*Simbahan*
Drugstore	*Botika*
Restaurant	*Restauran*
Eating place	*Kainan*
Office	*Opisina*
Train station	*Himpilan ng tren*

House	*Bahay*	Flimsy	*Marupok*
Road	*Daan*	Colour	*Kulay*
		Red	*Pula*
Is it far from here?	*Malayo ba?*	White	*Puti*
Turn left	*Kumalia ka*	Black	*Itim*
Turn right	*Kumanan ka*	Blue	*Bughaw*
Straight ahead	*Tuloy-tuloy lang*	Green	*Berde*
		Yellow	*Dilaw*

SHOPPING

OTHER ADJECTIVES AND NOUNS

This	*Ito*		
That	*Iyan*		
Like this	*Ganito*	Good	*Mabuti*
Like that	*Ganyan*	Bad	*Masama*
Many	*Marami*	Clean	*Malinis*
Few	*Kaunte (konti)*	Dirty	*Madumi*
How much is this?	*Magkano ito?*	Easy	*Madali*
How many?	*Ilan?*	Difficult	*Mahirap*
Big	*Malake*	Salty	*Maalat*
Small	*Maliit*	Bitter	*Mapait*
Wide	*Malapad*	Delicious	*Masarap*
Narrow	*Mak itid*	Strong	*Malakas*
Thick	*Makapal*	Weak	*Mahina*
Thin	*Manipis*	Fast	*Mabilis*
Loose	*Maluwag*	Slow	*Mabagal*
Tight	*Masikip*	Fat (person)	*Mataba*
Long	*Mahaba*	Thin (person)	*Payat*
Short	*Maiksi*	Rich	*Mayaman*
Sweet	*Matamis*	Poor	*Mahirap*
Sour	*Maasim*	Male	*Lalake*
Hard	*Matigas*	Female	*Babae*
Soft	*Malambot*	Old	*Matanda*
Heavy	*Mabigat*	Young	*Bata*
Light	*Magaan*	Father	*Ama*
Beautiful	*Maganda*	Mother	*Ina*
Ugly	*Pangit*	Child	*Anak*
Fragrant	*Mabango*	Sibling	*Kapatid*
Foul-smelling	*Mabaho*		
Durable	*Matibay*		

QUESTIONS

Who?	Sino?
What?	Ano?
Where?	Saan?
When?	Kailan?
Why?	Bakit?

EXPRESSIONS OF TIME

One moment	Saglit lang
Minute	Minuto
Hour	Oras
Year	Taon
Month	Buwan
Day	Araw

What time is it?	Anong oras na ba?

Two o'clock...	Alas dos...
in the morning	ng umaga
in the afternoon	ng hapon

NUMBERS

One	Isa
Two	Dalawa
Three	Tatlo
Four	Apat
Five	Lima
Six	Anim
Seven	Pito
Eight	Walo
Nine	Siyam
Ten	Sampu
11-19	add labing + number
11	Labing isa
19	Labing siyam
20	Dalawang pu

30	Tatlong pu
40	Apat na pu
50	Limang pu
60	Anim na pu
80	Walong pu
90	Siyam na pu

add *at* meaning 'and' in its abbreviated form

21 etc	Dalawang pu at isa
100	Isang daan
200	Dalawang daan
400	Apat na daan
1,000	Isang libo
1,000,000	Isang milyon

When referring to money, add the word *piso* for pesos, ie, *limang piso* (five pesos). Spanish-derived words are still in use for numbers. For example:

5	Singco
10	Diyes (pronounced gees)
20	Beinte
30	Trenta / trienta
40	Kuwarenta
50	Sinkwenta
60	Sesenta
70	Setenta
80	Otsenta
90	Nobenta

DAYS OF THE WEEK

Monday	*Lunes*
Tuesday	*Martes*
Wednesday	*Miyerkoles*
Thursday	*Huwebes*
Friday	*Biyernes*
Saturday	*Sabado*
Sunday	*Linggo*

MONTHS OF THE YEAR

January	*Enero*
February	*Pebrero*
March	*Marso*
April	*Abril*
May	*Mayo*
June	*Hunyo*
July	*Hulyo*
August	*Agosto*
September	*Septiyembre*
October	*Oktubre*
November	*Nobiyembre*
December	*Disiyembre*

Information Directory

Directory Assistance	114
Direct Dialing Assistance	112
Overseas long distance	108
Domestic long distance	109
Police	166

Government Offices

Department of Foreign Affairs
2330 2330 Roxas Blvd
Pasay City, Metro Manila
tel (632) 834-4444 / 831-4783

Department of Finance
DOF Bldg
BSP Complex
Roxas Blvd, Manila
tel (632) 524-7011 / 524-4287

Bureau of Export Trade and Promotion
Solidbank 5/F–8/F New Solid Bldg
357 Sen. Gil Puyat Ave
Makati, Metro Manila
tel (632) 890-5203
fax (632) 890-4711

Bangko Sentral ng Pilipinas
Central Bank Complex
A Mabini St, Manila
tel (632) 524-7011

National Economic and Development
Authority
NEDA Bldg
Amber Ave, Pasig City, MM
tel (632) 631-0945 to 56
631-0957 to 68

Securities and Exchange Commission
SEC Bldg
EDSA near Ortigas Ave.
San Juan, Metro Manila
fax (632) 722-0090

Development Bank of the Philippines
Sen Gil Puyat corner Makati Ave
Makati, Metro Manila
tel 818-9511 to 20
fax (632) 817-2097

Board of Investments
385 Sen. Gil Puyat Ave
Makati, Metro Manila
tel 897-6682
896-7342 (Investments Assistance)
895-3638 (BOI Managing Head)
fax (632) 895-8322 /895-3512
e-mail: boimis@mnl.sequel.net

Department of Tourism
DOT Bldg
TM Kalaw St, Ermita, Manila
tel   (632) 523-8411
fax (632) 521-7374

Overseas Tourist Offices

North America
NEW YORK
Ms Emma Ruth Yulo Kitiyakara
Philippine Tourism Centre
556 Fifth Ave, New York
New York 10036
tel (212) 575-7915
fax (212) 302-6759

LOS ANGELES
Atty Orestes Ricaforte
Philippine Consulate General
3660 Wilshire Blvd 900
Suite 825, Los Angeles
California 90010
tel (213) 487-4527
fax (213) 386-4063

SAN FRANCISCO
Ms Elena Pelaez Villanueva
Philippine Consulate General
447 Sutter St, 5/F, Suite 507
San Francisco, California 94108
tel (415) 956-4060
fax (415) 956-2093

CHICAGO
Ms Marina V Velmin
Suite 913
30 N Michigan Ave
Chicago 60602
tel (312) 782-2475
fax (312) 782 2476

Europe

FRANCE
Ms Jasmin Esguerra
Service de Tourisme
Ambassade des Philippines
3 Faubourg Saint Honore
75008 Paris
tel (331) 4265-0234 to 35
fax (331) 4265-0238

GERMANY
Mr Domingo Ramon C. Enerio
Philippine Department of Tourism
Kaisser Strasse 15
60311 Frankfurt am Main 1
tel (069) 20893/20894
fax (069) 285-127

ITALY
Mr Gastone Nardoni
G S Air s.r.l. Rome
Via Cassia 901/A00187
tel (396) 474-4062/474-3780
fax (396) 474-3780

SPAIN
Mr Pedro Oviedo
Torre de Madrid, Planta Oficina 7
Plaza de España, 28008 Madrid
tel (341) 541-2359/542-3711 to 13
tel/fax (341) 217-7268

UNITED KINGDOM
Mr Eduardo A Jarque Jr
Philippine Department of Tourism
17 Albemarle St, London WIY 7HA
United Kingdom
tel (44 171) 499-5652/499-5443
fax (44 171) 499-5772

Asia-Pacific

AUSTRALIA
Ms Consuelo Jones
Consulate General of the Philippines
Wynyard House Suite 703, Level 7
301 George St
Sydney, NSW 2000
tel (612) 9299-6815/9299-6506
fax (612) 9299-6817

HONG KONG
Ms Rowena Severino
Philippine Consulate General
Room 602, 6/F, United Centre
95 Queensway, Hong Kong
tel (852) 2866-6471/2866-7665
fax (852) 2866-6521

JAPAN
Ms Araceli Soriano
Embassy of the Philippines
11-24 Nampeidi Machi
Shibuya-ku, Tokyo
tel (813) 3464-3630/35
         3396-2209
fax (813) 3464-3690

Ms Marite Sison
Philippine Tourism Centre
2/F Dainan Bldg
2-19-23 Sinmachi
Nishi-ku, Osaka 550
tel (816) 535-5071 to 72
fax (816) 535-1235

KOREA
Mr Cho Myung Ho
DOT/PCVC Marketing Representative
1107 Renaissance Bldg.
1598-3 Socho-dong
Socho-ku, Seoul
tel (822) 598-2292
fax (822) 598-2293

SINGAPORE
Mr Phineas Alburo
Philippine Tourism Office
06-24 Orchard Towers
400 Orchard Road
tel (65) 737-3977
fax (65) 733-4591

TAIWAN
Mr Jemy Sy
Manila Economic and Cultural Office
4/F Metrobank Plaza
107 Chung Hsiao E Road
Section 4, Taipei
Taiwan
tel/fax (886 2) 2741-5994/
2773-5724

Tourist Offices in The Philippines

DOT REGIONAL OFFICES
*REGIONAL DIRECTOR
**OFFICER-IN-CHARGE

NATIONAL CAPITAL REGION
* Mr Robert Lyndon Barbers
Room 207, Department of Tourism
T M Kalaw Strret
Ermita, Manila
tel (632) 524-2345/ 25-6114/524-
6566/523-8411, local 197
fax (632) 524-8321/521-1088
e-mail: dotncr@mnl.sequel.net

Airport
tel (632) 832-2964
Tourist Security
tel (632) 524-1660/524-1728

CORDILLERA ADMINISTRATIVE REGION
* Mr Edgar Jullanbal
Department of Tourism
DOT Complex, Gov Pack Rd
Baguio City
tel (074) 442-6708/442-7014
fax (074) 442-8848

REGION 1. NORTHERN LUZON
* Ms Rowena Calica
DOT, Mabanag Justice Hall
San Fernando, La Union
tel (072) 312-2699/412-411
fax (072) 412-098

LAOAG CITY SUB-OFFICE
** Ms Milagros Gonzales
DOT, Ilocano Heroes Hall
Laoag City
tel (077) 772-0467

REGION II: CAGAYAN VALLEY
* Ms Blesida G Diwa
DOT, 2/F Tuguegarao Supermarket
Tuguegarao, Cagayan
tel (078) 844-1621/5364
fax (078) 844-1621

REGION III: CENTRAL LUZON
* Mr Ronaldo Tiotuico
DOT, Phil Christmas Village
San Fernando, Pampanga
tel (045) 921-2665/961-2612
fax (045) 961-2612
e-mail: dotr3@sfp.irnet.net.ph
web site: www.irnet.net.ph/dotr3

Clark Field Sub-Office
DOT, Terminal Bldg
Clark Intl Airport
Aviation Complex
Clark Field, Pampanga
tel (045) 599-2843/599-2897, loc 805

REGION IV: SOUTHERN TAGALOG
* Ms Louella C Jurilla
Rm 208 Department of Tourism
T M Kalaw St
Ermita, Manila
tel (632) 524-1528/524-1969/523-8411, loc 183
fax (632) 526-7656
e-mail: dot@mnl.sequel.net

REGION V. BICOL REGION
*Mrs Pilar Hilario
3/F Meliton Dy Bldg
Rizal St, Legaspi City
tel (052) 214-3215/480-6439
fax (052) 214-3286

REGION VI. WESTERN VISAYAS
* Mr Edwin Trompeta
DOT, Western Visayas Tourism Centre
Capitol Ground
Bonifacio Drive, Iloilo City
tel (033) 337-5411/337-8874
fax (033) 335-0245
e-mail: deptour6@iloilo.net

BACOLOD FIELD OFFICE
** Mr Edwin V Gatia
DOT, Bacolod Plaza
Bacolod City
tel/fax (034) 29021

BORACAY FIELD OFFICE
**Ms Judith Icotanim
DOT, Balabag, Boracay
Malay, Aklan
tel/fax (036) 288-3689

REGION VII. CENTRAL VISAYAS
* Ms Patria Aurora B Roa
DOT, 3/F GMC Plaza Bldg
Legaspi Ext, Cebu City
tel (032) 254-2811/254-6077/254-6650
fax (032) 254-2711
e-mail: dotr7@skyiert.net

REGION VIII. EASTERN VISAYAS
*Ms Norma Morantte
DOT, Children's Park
Sen Enage St, Tacloban City
tel (053) 321-4333/321-2048
fax (053) 325-5279
e-mail: dotr8@mozcom.com

IX. WESTERN MINDANAO
* Mr Ricardo A San Juan
DOT, Lantaka Hotel by the Sea
Valderrosa St, Zamboanga City
tel (062) 991-0218/993-0029 to 30
fax (062) 991-0217

REGION X. NORTHERN MINDANAO
* Ms Dorothy Jean Pabayo
DOT, A Velez St,
Cagayan de Oro City
tel (08822) 723-696/726-394
fax (08822) 723-696/727-432 c/o PTA

REGION XI. SOUTHERN MINDANAO
* Ms Catalina S Dakudao
DOT, Door 7, Magsaysay Park Complex
Santa Ana District, Davao City
tel (082) 221-6955
tel/fax (082) 221-0070/221-6798

REGION XII. CENTRAL MINDANAO
* Ms Sohura Dimaampao
DOT, Elizabeth Tan Bldg.
De Mazenod Ave., Cotabato City
tel (064) 421-1110
tel/ fax (064) 421-7868

REGION XIII. CARAGA REGION
** Mr Rafael V Flores
DOT, DNV Plaza II Bldg
J C Aquino Ave
Butuan City
tel (085) 225-5712
    416-371 (Piltel)
tel/fax (085) 225-6201
24-hour Tourist Assistance hotlines
tel 524-1728/524-1660

PHILIPPINE CONVENTION & VISITORS CORPORATION
4/F, Suite 10–17, Legaspi Towers
Roxas Blvd, Manila
tel (632) 525-9318 to 32
fax (632) 521-6165
e-mail: pcvcnet@mnl.sequel.net

HOTEL AND RESTAURANT ASSOCIATION OF THE PHILIPPINES
Room 205 Regina Bldg
Aguirre St, Legaspi Village
Makati, Metro Manila
tel 815-4659/815-4661

NATIONAL COMMISSION FOR CULTURE AND THE ARTS
633 Gen Luna St
Intramuros, Manila
tel 527-2197/527-2217
fax (632) 527 2194

Embassies and Consulates

ARGENTINA (E)
6/F ACT Tower
135 Sen Gil J Puyat Ave,
Salcedo Village, Makati
tel 810-8301/893-6091

AUSTRALIA (E)
Doña Salustiana Ty Tower
104 Paseo de Roxas
Legaspi Village, Makati
tel 750-2850

AUSTRIA (E)
4/F Prince Bldg
117 Rada St
Legaspi Village, Makati
tel 817-9191/817-4992

BANGLADESH (E)
2/F Universal Re Bldg
106 Paseo de Roxas, Makati
tel 817-5010/817-5001

BELGIUM (E)
9/F Multinational Bancorporation
Centre
6805 Ayala Ave
Makati City
tel 845-1869/845 1874

BOLIVIA (C)
47 Juan Luna St
San Lorenzo Village
Makati City
tel 817-1128

BRAZIL (E)
6/F RCI Bldg
105 Rada St
Legaspi Village, Makati
tel 892-8181 to 82

BRUNEI DARUSSALAM (E)
11/F Ayala Wing, BPI Bldg
Ayala Ave, Makati
tel 816-2836 to 38

CANADA (E)
9/F Allied Bank Center
6754 Ayala Ave, Makati
tel 867-0001

CHILE (E)
6/F Doña Salustiana Ty Tower
104 Paseo de Roxas
Legaspi Village, Makati
tel 816-0395/810-3194

CHINA, PEOPLE'S REPUBLIC OF (E)
4896 Pasay Road
Dasmariñas Village, Makati
tel 844-3148/843-7715

COLOMBIA (E)
18/F Aurora Tower
Araneta Center
Cubao, Quezon City
tel 911-3101, ext 3294

CUBA (E)
11/F Heart Tower Condominium
Valero St, Salcedo Village
Makati City
tel 817-1192/817-1284

CZECH, REPUBLIC OF (E)
1267 Acacia Road
Dasmariñas Village, Makati
tel 812-9254

DENMARK (E)
6/F Doña Salustiana Ty Tower
104 Paseo de Roxas
Legaspi Village, Makati
tel 894-0086

DOMINICAN REPUBLIC (CG)
312 Shaw Blvd
Mandaluyong City, MM
tel 532-3215/532-2890

ECUADOR (CG)
7/F Phinma Bldg
166 Salcedo St
Legaspi Village, Makati
tel 810-9526, ext 349

EGYPT (E)
2229 Paraiso St
Dasmariñas Village
Makati
tel 843-9220/843-9232

FINLAND (E)
21/F Far East Bank Center
Sen Gil Puyat Ave
Makati City
tel 891-5011 to 15

FRANCE
16/F Pacific Star Bldg
Makati Ave corner
Sen Gil J Puyat Ext, Makati
tel 810-1981 to 86

GERMANY (E)
6/F Solidbank Bldg
777 Paseo de Roxas, Makati
tel 892-4906

GREECE (CG)
11/F Sage House
110 Herrera St
Legaspi Village, Makati
tel 816-2316

HOLY SEE (E)
Apostolic Nunciature
2140 Taft Ave
Manila
tel 521-0306 to 07

HONDURAS (C)
5/F Cacho Gonzales Bldg
Trasierra cor Aguirre St
Legaspi Village, Makati
tel 750-0425 to 27

ICELAND (CG)
c/o Magsaysay Lines Inc
520 T M Kalaw St
Ermita, Manila
tel 521-0635

INDIA (E)
2190 Paraiso St
Dasmariñas Village, Makati
tel 843-0101 to 02

INDONESIA (E)
Indonesian Embassy Bldg
185 Salcedo St
Legaspi Village, Makati
tel 892-5061 to 68

IRAN (E)
4/F Don Jacinto Bldg
Salcedo and de la Rosa Sts
Legaspi Village, Makati
tel 892-1561 to 63

IRAQ (E)
2261 Avocado St
Dasmariñas Village
Makati
tel 843-9835/843-9838

IRELAND (C)
3/F Port Royal Place
118 Rada St
Legaspi Village
Makati
tel 819-1581 to 87

ISRAEL (E)
23/F Trafalgar Plaza
H V de la Costa St
Salcedo Village, Makati
tel 892-5329 to 32

ITALY (E)
6/F Zeta II Bldg
191 Salcedo St
Legaspi Village, Makati
tel 892-4531 to 34

JAPAN (E)
2627 Roxas Blvd
Pasay City
tel 551-5710

KOREA (E)
10/F Pacific Star Bldg
Makati Ave, Makati
tel 811-6139 to 46

KUWAIT (E)
6/F Morning Star Bldg
347 Sen Gil Puyat Ave
Makati City
tel 892-6680

LAOS (E)
34 Lapu-Lapu St
Magallanes Village
Makati City
tel 833-5759

LIBYA (E)
2416 Bougainvilla St
Dasmarinas Village, Makati
tel 844-2045 to 46

MALAYSIA (E)
107 Tordesillas St
Salcedo Village, Makati
tel 817-4581 to 85

MALTA (E)
6/F Cattleya Condominium
235 Salcedo St
Legaspi Village, Makati
tel 817-1095

MEXICO (E)
18/F Magsaysay Center
1680 Roxas Blvd
Pasay City
tel 526-7461

MYANMAR (BURMA) (E)
4/F Dao II Bldg
Basic Petroleum Condominium
104 Carlos Palanca St
Legaspi Village, Makati
tel 817-2373

NETHERLANDS (E)
9/F King's Court Bldg
2129 Pasong Tamo St
Salcedo Village, Makati
tel 812-5981 to 83

NEW ZEALAND (E)
23/F Far East Bank Center
Sen Gil Puyat Ave
Makati City
tel 891-5358 to 67

NICARAGUA (C)
c/o Meridian Assurance Corp
Unit 711 West Tower
Philippine Stock Exchange Center
Exchange Road, Ortigas Center
Pasig City, MM
tel 631-3004

NIGERIA (E)
2211 Paraiso St
Dasmariñas Village, Makati
tel 843-9866/817-8836

NORWAY (E)
69 Paseo de Roxas
Urdaneta Village, Makati
tel 893-9866 to 72

PAKISTAN (E)
6/F Alexander House
132 Amorsolo St
Legaspi Village, Makati
tel 817-2772/817-2776

PALESTINE (C)
Penthouse, LPL Towers
112 Legaspi St
Legaspi Village, Makati
tel 818-1083/817-6723

PANAMA (E)
Rm 501 Victoria Bldg
429 UN Ave, Manila
tel 521-2790/521-1233

PAPUA NEW GUINEA (E)
2280 Magnolia St
Dasmariñas Village, Makati
tel 844-2060/844-2051

PERU (E)
7/F Unit 7-B Country Space One Bldg
Sen Gil Puyat Ave
Makati City
tel 813-8731

PORTUGAL (E)
14/F, Unit D Trafalgar Plaza
105 HV de la Costa St
Salcedo Village, Makati
tel 848-3789 to 90

QATAR (E)
1346 Palm Ave
Dasmariñas Village, Makati
tel 812-8144

ROMANIA (E)
1216 Acacia Road
Dasmariñas Village, Makati
tel 843-9014

RUSSIA (E)
1245 Acacia Road
Dasmariñas Village, Makati
tel 817-5406/893-0190

SAUDI ARABIA (E AND C)
Saudi Embassy Bldg
389 Sen Gil J Puyat Ave Ext
Makati City
tel 890-9735

SENEGAL (C)
21 Lincoln St
Greenhills West
San Juan, MM
tel 721-2273

SEYCHELLES (C)
Tektite Tower I
Suite 1904-B
Philippine Stock Exchange Centre
Exchange Road
Ortigas Centre, Pasig, MM
tel 635-3047

SINGAPORE (E)
6/F ODC International Plaza
219 Salcedo St
Legaspi Village, Makati
tel 816-1764 to 65

SOUTH AFRICA (CG)
Tektite Tower I
Suite 3103-B
Philippine Stock Exchange Bldg
Exchange Road
Ortigas Centre, Pasig, MM
tel 635-5023/25/29

SPAIN (E)
5/F ACT Tower
135 Sen Gil J Puyat Ave
Makati
tel 818-3561/818-5526

SRI LANKA (C)
1143 Pasong Tamo
Makati
tel 812-0175

SWEDEN (E)
16/F PCI Bank Tower II
Makati Ave cor De la Costa St
Makati City
tel 819-1951

SWITZERLAND (E)
18/F Solidbank Bldg
777 Paseo de Roxas
Makati City
tel 892-2051

TAIPEI
(Economic and Cultural Office)
28/F Pacific Star Bldg
Sen Gil J Puyat Ave
Makati
tel 892-1381

THAILAND (E)
Royal Thai Embassy Bldg
107 Rada St
Legaspi Village
Makati City
tel 815-4220/816-0697

TONGA (C)
Rm 326 Makati Stock Exchange Bldg
Ayala Ave, Makati
tel 810-0993

TURKEY (E)
2268 Paraiso St
Dasmariñas Village
Makati
tel 843-9705

UNITED ARAB EMIRATES (E)
2/F Renaissance Bldg
215 Salcedo St, Legaspi Village
Makati City
tel 817-3906

UNITED KINGDOM (BRITAIN) (E)
15 to17/F LV Locsin Bldg
6752 Ayala corner Makati Ave
Makati City
tel 816-7116/816-7271 to 72

UNITED STATES OF AMERICA (E)
1201 Roxas Blvd
Ermita, Manila
tel 523-1001

URUGUAY (C)
7/F PCCI Bldg
118 Alfaro St
Salcedo Village, Makati
tel 815-0625/31

VENEZUELA (E)
6/F Majalco Bldg
Benavidez cor Trasierra St
Legaspi Village, Makati
tel 817-9137

VIETNAM (E)
554 P Ocampo St
Malate, Manila
tel 524-0364/521-6843

EUROPEAN UNION
7/ F Salustiana D Ty Bldg
104 Paseo de Roxas
Legaspi Village
Makati City
tel 812-6421

Foreign Language and Cultural Centres

ALLIANCE FRANÇAISE
2/F Keystone Bldg,
220 Sen Gil J Puyat Ave
Makati City, Metro Manila
tel 893-1974/892-1768

BRITISH COUNCIL
10/F Taipan Place
Emerald Ave near cor J Vargas
Ortigas Complex
Pasig City, Metro Manila
914-1011 to 14

GOETHE-INSTITUT
687 Aurora Blvd
Quezon City, Metro Manila
tel 722-4671-73

THOMAS JEFFERSON CULTURAL CENTER
395 Sen Gil Puyat Ave, Makati
tel 897-1994

AUSTRALIA CENTRE
G/F, Salustiana Ty Tower
104 Paseo de Roxas cor Perea St
Legaspi Village, Makati City
1229 Metro Manila
tel 754-6135

INSTITUTO CERVANTES
Spanish Cultural Centre
2515 Leon Guinto corner Estra Streets
Malate, Manila
tel. 526-1482 to 85

Airlines

AIR CANADA
Multi-national Bancorporation
6805 Ayala Ave, Makati
tel 845-2619 to 23, local 111

AIR FRANCE
Century Towers
100 Tordesillas St
Salcedo Village, Makati
tel 813-1160/894-1830

AIR INDIA
Philam Life Centre
126 Alfaro St
Salcedo Village, Makati
tel 815-1280/815-2441

AIR NAURU
G/F Pacific Star Bldg
Makati Ave cor Sen Gil Puyat Ave
Makati
tel 819-7241/818-3580

AIR NEW ZEALAND
Multi-national Bancorporation
6805 Ayala Ave, Makati
tel 845-2619 to 23, local 108

AIR NIUGINI
G/F Fortune Office Bldg
160 Legaspi St
Legaspi Village, Makati
tel 891-3342

ALITALIA
M-3 Gallery Bldg
Amorsolo St
Legaspi Village
Makati
tel 844-1051/844-4071 to 75

ASIANA AIRLINES
G/F Care Bldg
De la Rosa cor Legaspi St
Makati
tel 892-5688

BRITISH AIRWAYS
Filipino Merchants Bldg,
Legaspi cor de la Rosa St,
Legaspi Village, Makati
tel 817-0361

CANADIAN AIRLINES
G/F Saville Bldg
Paseo de Roxas, Makati
tel 895-5591 to 93

CATHAY PACIFIC AIRWAYS
24/F Trafalgar Plaza Bldg
105 H V de la Costa St
Salcedo Village, Makati
tel 848-2747/848-2701
    525-9367 to 70

CHINA AIRLINES
G/F Manila Midtown Arcade
Adriatico St
Ermita, Manila
tel 521-5287

CONTINENTAL MICRONESIA
G/F SGV Bldg
6760 Ayala Ave
Makati
tel 818-8701

DELTA AIRLINES
4/F Universal Re Bldg
Paseo de Roxas
Legaspi Village, Makati
tel 810-1167/892-9215

EGYPTAIR
Windsor Tower Bldg
163 Legaspi St
Legaspi Village, Makati
tel 815-8476

EL AL ISRAEL AIRLINES
3/F Rajah Sulayman Bldg
108 Benavidez St
Legaspi Village, Makati
tel 816-2387

EMIRATES AIRLINES
Country Space 1 Bldg
Sen Gil Puyat Ave
Makati
tel 816-0744

EVA AIR
5438 Don Tim Bldg
South Superhighway
Makati
tel 894-5671

FINNAIR
Cityland 10, Tower II
Makati
tel 892-2701

GARUDA INDONESIAN AIRLINES
G/F Pacific Star Bldg
Makati Ave cor Sen Gil Puyat Ave
Makati
tel 811-5611 to 12/811-5502

GULF AIR
G/F Don Chua Lam Co Bldg
Alfaro St cor De la Costa
Salcedo Village, Makati
tel 817-8383/526-0450

JAPAN AIRLINES
Dusit Hotel Nikko
Makati
tel 812-1591 to 99
    810-9352 to 55

KLM ROYAL DUTCH AIRLINES
Athenaeum Bldg
160 Alfaro St
Salcedo Village, Makati
tel 815-4790

KOREAN AIR
G/F LPL Plaza
124 Alfaro St
Salcedo Village, Makati
tel 815-8911 to 13
    815-9261 to 62

KUWAIT AIRWAYS
G/F Jaka II Bldg
150 Legaspi St
Legaspi Village, Makati
tel 817-2778

LUFTHANSA GERMAN AIRLINES
Legaspi Park View Condominium
134 Legaspi St
Legaspi Village, Makati
tel 810-4596

MALAYSIA AIRLINES
G/F Legaspi Towers 300
Roxas Blvd cor P Ocampo St
Manila
tel 525-99404 to 08

NORTHWEST AIRLINES
G/F Athenaeum Bldg
160 Alfaro St
Salcedo Village, Makati
tel 819-7341

PAKISTAN INTERNATIONAL AIRWAYS
G/F Colonnade Bldg
Carlos Palanca St
Legaspi Village, Makati
tel 818-0502

PHILIPPINE AIRLINES
PAL Bldg II
Legaspi Street, Makati
tel 816-6691/819-1771
    817-1479

QANTAS AIRWAYS
Filipino Merchants Bldg
De La Rosa & Legaspi Sts
Legaspi Village, Makati
tel 812-0607

ROYAL BRUNEI AIRLINES
Saville Bldg, Paseo de Roxas
cor Sen Gil Puyat Ave
Makati
tel 897-3309

ROYAL JORDANIAN AIRLINES
L/G, Unit 1 Cityland X, Tower II
De La Costa St
Salcedo Village, Makati
tel 893-0018/893-7736

SAUDI ARABIAN AIRLINES
Cougar Bldg
114 Valero St
Salcedo Village, Makati
tel 818-7866/818-4722

SCANDINAVIAN AIRLINES SYSTEM
Gr/F F & M Bldg
144 Legaspi St
Legaspi Village, Makati
tel 810-5050

SINGAPORE AIRLINES
138 H V de la Costa St
Salcedo Village, Makati
tel 810-4951 to 59
    810-4960 to 69

SOUTH AFRICAN AIRWAYS
Multi-national Bancorporation
6805 Ayala Ave, Makati
tel 845-2619 to 23, local 112

SWISSAIR
G/F Zuellig Bldg
Malugay St, Makati
tel (R/T) 818-8351 to 54

THAI AIRWAYS INTERNATIONAL
G/F Country Space I Bldg
H V de la Costa St
Salcedo Village, Makati
tel 815-8421 to 27
    815-8431 to 37

TRANS WORLD AIRLINES
Saville Bldg
Sen Gil Puyat Ave
cor Paseo de Roxas
Makati
tel 895-4751 to 55

UNITED AIRLINES
G/F Pacific Star Bldg
Makati Ave, Makati
tel 818-5421

US AIR
402 Alexander House
132 Amorsolo St
Legaspi Village, Makati
tel 815-4381
    815-4329

DOMESTIC AIRLINES
R: reservations
T: ticketing
F: flight information

PHILIPPINE AIRLINES
Greenbelt Centre
Legaspi St, Makati City
tel R: 816-6691/819-1771/815-0054
    T: 817-1509 (domestic)
        817-1470 (international)
    F: 818-6757

S & L Bldg
1515 Roxas Blvd,
Ermita, Manila
tel T: 521-8821 to 30

AEROLIFT PHILIPPINES CORPORATION
The Gallery, G-VIII A
Amorsolo St, Makati City
tel 843-4605
fax 819-0385

ASIAN SPIRIT
G/F, LPL Towers
112 Legaspi St, Legaspi Village
Makati City
tel R: 840-3811 to 16
    T: 750-4193

CEBU PACIFIC AIR
Robinson's Galleria
Level 1, Ortigas Ave side
Pasig City
tel R: 636-4938 to 45

Midtown Hotel
Adriatico St
Ermita, Manila
tel T: 526-9988

GRAND INTERNATIONAL AIRWAYS
Mercure Philippine Village
Airport Hotel
MIA Road, Pasay City
tel 831-3035

G/F, APMC Bldg
Amorsolo St
Legaspi Village, Makati City
tel 893-9770 to 74

AIR PHILIPPINES
7/F Ramon Magsaysay Bldg
Roxas Blvd, Manila
tel 526-4741 to 50

STAR ASIA AIRWAYS
G-4 Sedeño Manor
Valero cor Sedeño Sts
Salcedo Village, Makati City
tel 892-2150

SUBIC AIR
Columbia Motors Bldg
Andrews Ave cor Aurora Blvd
Pasay City
tel 833-3511 to 19/831 8257

Road and Rail Transport

PHILIPPINE NATIONAL RAILWAYS
Pasay Road Station
tel 844-7755

BALIWAG TRANSIT
99 Rizal Avenue Extension
Caloocan City
tel 364-0778

**BATANGAS LAGUNA TAYABAS BUS CO
(BLTB CO)**
3 EDSA Malibay
Pasay City
tel 833-5501 to 08

PHILIPPINE RABBIT BUS LINES, INC
819 Oroquieta St, Sta Cruz, Manila
tel 711-5819

PHILTRANCO
EDSA, corner Apelo Cruz St
Pasay City
tel 833-5061

VICTORY LINES
561 E de los Santos Ave, Pasay City
tel 833-0293
713 Rizal Ave Ext, Caloocan City
tel 361-1506

Shipping Lines

ASUNCION SHIPPING LINES
Pier 2, North Harbour
tel 711-3743

ESCAÑO LINES
Pier 16, North Harbour
tel 263-871

MAGSAYSAY LINES
520 T M Kalaw St
Ermita, Manila
tel 521-0635

NEGROS NAVIGATION CO INC
Loyola Bldg
849 Pasay Road, Makati
tel 816-3481 to 82
818-3804 (Passage information)

SULPICIO LINES
415 San Fernando, Binondo
tel 241-9701 to 04
Pier 12, Manila
tel 245-0616

WG&A
Piers 4,8,10, 14
Central Booking Office
2/F, 110 Legaspi Street
Legaspi Village, Makati
tel 894-3211

Hotels in Metro Manila

Hotels are classified by the Department of Tourism. An indication of price is given by the following, based on one person/one night occupation, plus ten per cent service charge and government tax (12–13.7 per cent): Deluxe Hotels–US$200 and above. First Class Hotels–US$200. Standard Hotels–below US$100. Enquire from your travel agent regarding package rates, corporate rates and executive rates. Major credit cards are accepted.

DELUXE HOTELS

All have swimming pools, meeting and banqueting facilities, business centres, fitness/health centres or gym, beauty salon and barber shop, shopping arcade, and room amenities such as refrigerator and mini-bar. Computerised door locks, in-room safety deposit boxes, coffee and tea-making facilities are features in most of these hotels.

CENTURY PARK (500 ROOMS)
P Ocampo and M Adriatico Sts, Malate, Manila; tel 522-1011/522-8888; fax (632) 521-3413; Located next to Harrison Plaza shopping centre and Rizal sports complex; close to the Philippine International Convention Centre and Central Bank. Lobby.

DUSIT HOTEL NIKKO (549 ROOMS)
Ayala Centre, Makati; tel 810 4101-/
867-3333; fax (632) 817-1862; Rooms
and restaurants totally renovated. Japanese, Thai, Chinese, Italian restaurants,
German pub. Close to shops.

HERITAGE HOTEL, THE (447 ROOMS)
Roxas Blvd corner EDSA, Pasay City,
MM; tel 891-8888; fax (632) 891-8833;
A Bay area hotel, member of CDL Hotels of Singapore. FB outlets include a
Cantonese restaurant.

**HOLIDAY INN MANILA PAVILION (590
ROOMS)**
UN Ave, Ermita, Manila; tel 522-2911;
fax (632) 522-3144; Walking distance
to Rizal Park, WHO Bldg. Casino Filipino is located within the hotel.

**HOTEL INTER-CONTINENTAL MANILA
(338 ROOMS)**
One Ayala Ave, Makati; tel 815-9711;
fax (632) 817-1330; Within Makati
business centre; close to shops. Has a
popular discotheque, Euphoria.

**HOTEL SOFITEL GRAND BOULEVARD
MANILA (500 ROOMS)**
1990 Roxas Blvd, Manila 1057; tel 526-
8588; fax (632) 526-0112; The former
Silahis Hotel, it has been refurbished
and boasts a 24-carat gold-plated revolving
door. The hotel is near Malate Church;
has spectacular views of Manila Bay.

HYATT REGENCY MANILA (260 ROOMS)
2702 Roxas Blvd, Pasay City; tel 833-
1234; fax (632) 833-5913; A Bay area
hotel located between the Cultural
Centre Complex and airport. Completely
refurbished. Has popular Japanese restaurant and music lounge, Calesa Bar.

**MANDARIN ORIENTAL MANILA (464
ROOMS)**
Makati Ave, Makati 1226; tel 893 3601;
fax (632) 817-2472; One of the hotels
favoured by business travellers. Close to
shops and restaurants in the Makati
business district.

MANILA DIAMOND HOTEL (500 ROOMS)
Roxas Blvd corner J Quintos St, Ermita,
Manila; tel 526-2211; fax (632) 526 -
2255; Elegant hotel in Tourist Belt with
tennis court, health club, gym, indoor/
outdoor jacuzzi.

**MANILA GALLERIA SUITES (289
ROOMS)**
One Asian Development Bank Ave,
Pasig City; tel 633-7111; fax (632) 633-
2824; Located in the financial and business district of Ortigas Centre, close to
Philippine Stock Exchange and Asian
Development Bank. Shopping complex
directly accessible from hotel.

MANILA HOTEL, THE (570 ROOMS)
One Rizal Park, Manila; tel 527-0011;
fax (632) 527-0022 to 23; Historic and
elegant, a landmark, close to Intramuros
and Rizal Park. General Douglas
MacArthur was a longtime resident.

NEW WORLD HOTEL, THE (600 ROOMS)
Esperanza St corner Makati Ave, Makati;
tel 811-6888; fax (632) 811-6777; A 25-
storey hotel located within the Makati
business and commercial district, close to
the Greenbelt Park, restaurants and
shops.

PENINSULA MANILA, THE (500 ROOMS)
Corner Ayala Ave & Makati Ave, Makati;
tel 819-3456; fax (632) 815-4825, Located in the heart of Makati's business district, close to shops. Fully renovated. The
lobby is a popular meeting place of business people and the social set.

SHANGRI-LA EDSA PLAZA (440 ROOMS)
1 Garden Way, Ortigas Center, Mandaluyong City 1650, Metro Manila; tel 633-
8888; fax (632) 631-1067; Hotel has
additional rooms in Tower Wing. Close
to shopping centre, Asian Development
Bank and Philippine Stock Exchange.

**SHANGRI-LA HOTEL MANILA (703
ROOMS)**
Ayala corner Makati Ave, Makati City
1200; tel 813-8888; fax (632) 813-5499;
Plush sister hotel of Shangri-La EDSA
Plaza in Makati's business district. Night-
spot, Zu, is the in-place for Manilans.

WESTIN PHILIPPINE PLAZA (670 ROOMS)
Cultural Center Complex, Roxas Blvd,
Pasay City 1300; tel 551-5555; fax (632)
551-5610; Convenient to Cultural Centre
and Convention Centre. Has a driving
range and 18-hole putting green. Hotel
completely renovated.

FIRST CLASS HOTELS
AMBASSADOR HOTEL (250 ROOMS)
2021 A Mabini St, Malate, tel 506-011
to 19/521-5554; fax (632) 521-5557;
Swimming pool, Chinese restaurant, 24-
hr coffee shop, disco on 16th floor.

BAYVIEW PARK HOTEL (275 ROOMS)
1118 Roxas Blvd corner U N Ave.,
Ermita, Manila; tel 526-1555; fax (632)
521-2674. Completely renovated hotel
in front of US Embassy in tourist district. Rooftop swimming pool, fitness
centre, International restaurant.

MANILA MIDTOWN HOTEL (576 ROOMS)
Pedro Gil corner M Adriatico St, Ermita,
Manila; tel 526-7001; fax (632) 522-
2629 Swimming pool, gym, sauna,
tennis courts. Next door to shopping
complex and close to nightlife district.

**MERCURE HOTEL PHILIPPINE VILLAGE
AIRPORT MANILA (400 ROOMS)**
Nayong Pilipino Park, Pasay City; tel
833-8080; fax (632) 833-8248; Convenient to the international and domestic
airports. Next to Nayong Pilipino.
GrandAir terminal is in a wing of the
hotel. Swimming pool, tennis court,
health club.

TRADERS HOTEL (305 ROOMS)
3001 Roxas Blvd, Pasay City; tel 523-
7011; fax (632) 522-3985; Fronting the
Cultural Centre complex, it was the
former site of the Holiday Inn. Now a
Shangri-La business hotel, it has been
fully renovated. Swimming pool, health
club, meeting rooms, Japanese restaurant.

STANDARD HOTELS

GARDEN PLAZA HOTEL (125 ROOMS)

1030 Belen St, Paco, Manila 1007; tel 522-4835 to 38/522-4841 to 46; fax (632) 522-4840; This is the old Hotel Swiss next to Paco Park. Completely refurbished with new rooms added. Still has Old Swiss Inn Restaurant, 24-hour coffee shop.

HOTEL LAS PALMAS (92 ROOMS)

1616 A Mabini cor Pedro Gil St, Malate, Manila; tel 524-5602; fax (632) 522 1699; Swimming pool, coffee shop, piano bar, 24-hr room service. Rooms with kitchenette on request.

MIDLAND PLAZA HOTEL (42 ROOMS)

M Adriatico, Ermita, Manila; tel 525-9033 to 38; fax (632) 521-8522; Rooms renovated. Kitchenette and TV in suites; top rooms have view of Manila Bay. Coffee shop, function rooms, secretarial services.

PALM PLAZA HOTEL (120 ROOMS)

524 Pedro Gil corner M Adriatico St, Malate, Manila; tel 521-3502/524-7127; fax (632) 525-8013. A business boutique hotel in the Tourist Belt, close to shopping mall. Swimming pool, banquet and meeting facilities, coffee shop.

ROTHMAN INN HOTEL (91 ROOMS)

1633 M Adriatico St, Malate, Manila; tel 521-9251; fax (632) 522-2606; Seven-storey hotel in Tourist Belt; restaurant, coffee shop. Sister hotel, the newly built Riviera Mansion (tel 521-2381 to 86) is adjacent to Rothman Inn.

Recommended Reading

HISTORY AND ETHNOHISTORY

Kasaysayan. *The Story of the Filipino People*, 10 vols (Asia Publishing Co, Ltd, Manila,1998). A readable narration of the history of the Philippines from earliest times to the EDSA Revolution, with photographs and rare illustrations gathered from archives. The series presents unique perspectives on a diverse range of topics and provides a variety of viewpoints and insights into Philippine history.

Lietz, Rudolf J.H. *The Philippines in the 19th Century* (Manila, 1998). A coffee-table book launched during the Philippines' centennial celebrations establishes the Philippines as one of the major destinations for foreign expeditions and focuses on Filipino life and culture in the 19th century. Includes rare prints and lithographs. Lietz is a fellow of the Royal Geographic Society in London.

Nakpil, Carmen Guerrero *Centennial Reader Selected Essays* (Nakpil Publishing, Manila, 1998) Fifty-two essays of varying length dealing with the background and aftermath of the Philippine Revolution of 1896 and the First Philippine Republic.

Corpus, O D *Roots of the Filipino* 2 vols (Aklahi Foundation, Quezon City, 1989). An authoritative, well-researched work on the origins and historical development of the Filipino people and their country.

Patanñe, E P *The Philippines in the 6th to the 16th Centuries* (LSA Press, Manila, 1996). Explores the genesis of Philippine statecraft and culture, drawing data from archaeology, paleography/epigraphy and linguistics.

Aluit, Alfonso J *By Sword and Fire* (National Commission for Culture and the Arts, Manila, 1994) Deals with the destruction of Manila in World War II, focusing on the period between the 3 February and the 3 March, 1945.

Berlow, Alan *Dead Season* (Pantheon Books, New York, 1996) The investigation of a seemingly senseless killing of a sugarcane worker, weaving a mixture of myth and politics, religion and superstition, rumour and history, and shedding light on the culture and history of the island of Negros in the Visayas.

LITERATURE, ART AND CULTURE

Roces, Alfredo *Hidalgo and the Generation of 1872* (Eugenio Lopez Foundation, Metro Manila, 1998). A coffee-table book on the life and times of Felix Resurreccion Hidalgo who, with other Filipino painters, triumphed in Europe in the late 19th century. The book is illustrated with over 300 full-colour photographs by Dick Baldovino of never-before published paintings, photographs and various Hidalgo memorabilia.

Cristobal, Adrian *The Tragedy of the Revolution* (National Centennial Commission, Metro Manila, 1998). The first-ever coffee-table book on Andres Bonifacio, founder of the Katipunan and Father of the Philippine Revolution, narrates in detail the events of the 1896 Revolution, the life and times of Bonifacio, his battles and his death. This is the second of a three-part project. The first, *In Excelsis: The Mission of Jose P Rizal* , was written by Felice Sta Maria.

Francis, Luis, ed *Brown River, White Ocean* (Rutgers University Press, New Jersey, USA, 1993) An anthology of 20th-century Philippine Literature in English featuring 31 short stories and 108 poems representing a spectrum of contemporary Philippine society.

Tiongson, Nick *Tuklas Sining* (Cultural Centre of the Philippines, Manila) An over-all view of arts in the Philippines.

Goquingco, Leonor Orosa *Dances of the Emerald Isles* (National Commission for Culture and the Arts, Manila) A book on Philippine dance.

Jose, Regalado *Trota Simbahan* (Ayala Museum, Manila, 1991). A survey of church art in colonial Philippines from 1565 to 1898.

Joaquin, Nick *A Question of Heroes* (Ayala Museum, Manila, 1977). Critical essays on ten key figures in Philippine history. The focus is on the last three decades of the 19th century which the author sees as the period of the 'flowering of the Filipino'.

LEGEND AND FOLKLORE

Gorospe, Vitaliano R, SJ *Banahaw* (Bookmark Inc, 1992). Conversations with a pilgrim to the Power Mountain.

Jocano, F Landa, *Myths and Legends of the Early Filipinos* (Quezon City, 1971)

BIOGRAPHY, GENERAL BOOKS

Guerrero, Leon Maria *The First Filipino* (Guerrero Publishing/Anvil Publishing, Manila, 1998). A new edition of Jose Rizal's biography issued to celebrate the national hero's 137th anniversary, and the centennial of the proclamation of Philippine Independence. The book takes a fresh look at Rizal's life, making extensive and sensitive use of Rizal's correspondence and writings to give a more human picture of Rizal.

Hamilton Paterson, James *Ghosts of Manila* (Jonathan Cape, London, 1994) Describes the personages who peopled the Manila of old.

Seagrave, Sterling *The Marcos Dynasty* (Harper & Row, New York, 1988)

Steinber, David Joel *The Philippines: A Singular and a Plural Place* (Westview Press, Boulder, Colorado, 1982)

Karnow, Stanley *In Our Image* (Random House)

Joaquin, Nick *The Aquinos of Tarlac* (Cacho Hermanos Inc, Manila)

Ellison, Katherine *Imelda* (McGraw Hill)

Index